INTERNATIONAL CONVENTION
FOR THE
SAFETY OF LIFE AT SEA

CONSOLIDATED TEXT OF

THE 1974 SOLAS CONVENTION
THE 1978 SOLAS PROTOCOL
THE 1981 AND 1983 SOLAS
AMENDMENTS

IMO
London, 1986

First published in 1986
by the INTERNATIONAL MARITIME ORGANIZATION
4 Albert Embankment, London SE1 7SR

Printed in Great Britain by The Bath Press, Bath

Reprinted 1986 (twice)
Reprinted 1987
Reprinted 1989

ISBN 92-801-1200-7

IMO PUBLICATION
Sales number: 110 86.02.E

CONTENTS

Page

Foreword v

Articles of the International Convention for the Safety of Life at Sea,
1974 1

Articles of the Protocol of 1978 relating to the International Convention
for the Safety of Life at Sea, 1974 9

Consolidated text of the Annex to the 1974 SOLAS Convention and
the 1978 Protocol relating thereto, incorporating the 1981 and 1983
amendments 15

    Chapter I – General provisions 15

    Chapter II–1 – Construction – Subdivision and stability, machinery
        and electrical installations 33

    Chapter II–2 – Construction – Fire protection, fire detection and
        fire extinction 107

    Chapter III – Life-saving appliances and arrangements 225

    Chapter IV – Radiotelegraphy and radiotelephony 301

    Chapter V – Safety of navigation 331

    Chapter VI – Carriage of grain 355

    Chapter VII – Carriage of dangerous goods 385

    Chapter VIII – Nuclear Ships 395

    Appendix – Certificates 399

    Annex 1 – Construction and equipment requirements relating to
        existing ships 422

    Annex 2 – Future amendments to the 1974 SOLAS Convention 426

    Annex 3 – Forms of Attachments to the Cargo Ship Safety Con-
        struction Certificate and Cargo Ship Safety Equipment
        Certificate 437

FOREWORD

1   The International Convention for the Safety of Life at Sea, 1974 (1974 SOLAS)[1] was adopted by the International Conference on Safety of Life at Sea on 1 November 1974 and its Protocol of 1978 (1978 Protocol)[2] by the International Conference on Tanker Safety and Pollution Prevention on 17 February 1978.

2   The 1974 SOLAS entered into force on 25 May 1980 and its 1978 Protocol entered into force on 1 May 1981.

3   The Maritime Safety Committee of the International Maritime Organization, on 20 November 1981, adopted amendments to the 1974 SOLAS (1981 SOLAS amendments)[3] and amendments to its 1978 Protocol (1981 Protocol amendments) in accordance with the procedure specified in article VIII. The 1981 SOLAS amendments and the 1981 Protocol amendments entered into force on 1 September 1984.

4   The Maritime Safety Committee, on 17 June 1983, adopted further amendments to the 1974 SOLAS (1983 SOLAS amendments)[4] in accordance with the procedures specified in article VIII and determined that these amendments shall enter into force on 1 July 1986 unless prior to 1 January 1986 more than one third of Contracting States to the Convention or Contracting States, the combined merchant fleets of which constitute not less than 50 per cent of the gross tonnage of the world's merchant fleet, have notified their objections.

5   On 17 June 1983 the Maritime Safety Committee adopted the International Code for the Construction and Equipment of Ships Carrying Dangerous Chemicals in Bulk (IBC Code)[5] and the International Code for the Construction and Equipment of Ships Carrying Liquefied Gases in Bulk (IGC Code)[6]. The 1983 SOLAS amendments (parts B and C of chapter VII) make these Codes mandatory under the Convention.

6   This publication contains a consolidated text of the 1974 SOLAS Convention, the 1978 SOLAS Protocol and the 1981 and 1983 SOLAS amendments. The text has been compiled by the Secretariat at the direction of the Maritime Safety Committee, and is intended to provide an easy reference to all SOLAS requirements applicable from 1 July 1986.

The texts of the instruments have been issued in the following publications:

[1] 080 75.01.E
[2] 088 78.09.E
[3] 092 82.01.E
[4] 096 83.10.E
[5] 100 83.11.E
[6] 104 83.12.E

7   Those provisions of chapter I of the 1974 SOLAS which have been modified by the 1978 Protocol are indicated by the letter $\boxed{P}$. No such letter is shown for provisions in other chapters of the 1974 SOLAS which were modified by the 1978 Protocol, since those provisions have been superseded by the 1981 SOLAS amendments. In chapters II–1 and II–2 letter $\boxed{F}$ makes reference to future amendments listed in Annex 2.

8   In general, the requirements for construction and equipment contained in the consolidated text are applicable to ships constructed on or after 1 July 1986. To identify requirements applicable to ships constructed before that date, previous texts of the SOLAS Conventions, the 1978 Protocol and the 1981 amendments to the 1974 SOLAS and the 1978 Protocol should be consulted, in addition to those provisions in this consolidated text specifically addressed to such ships. For instance, special requirements for existing passenger ships are contained only in part F of chapter II–2 of the 1974 SOLAS and neither in chapter II–2 of the 1981 amendments nor in this consolidated text. Annex 1 shows a list of construction and equipment requirements relating to existing ships constructed before the dates of entry into force of the 1978 Protocol, the 1981 and 1983 SOLAS amendments.

9   With the exception of the footnotes in chapter IV which were adopted with the text of the Convention, the footnotes given in this consolidated text refer to codes, guidelines and recommendations relating to a particular text which have been updated by the Secretariat. In addition, certain explanatory footnotes have been inserted based on relevant texts of codes, guidelines, recommendations or other decisions of the Maritime Safety Committee. The forms of attachments to the cargo ship safety construction and equipment certificates issued under the 1978 SOLAS Protocol are given in Annex 3.

10   In general, this publication reproduces the text of the 1974 SOLAS Convention including the modifications and amendments as given in the authentic text, but the regulations have been slightly edited to achieve a degree of consistency between the texts taken from the 1974 SOLAS Convention and the 1978 Protocol and the 1981 and 1983 SOLAS amendments. Such editing is limited to the following:

   .1   in chapter I, the expressions "the present Protocol", "the Convention and the present Protocol", "the present Convention" and "the present Convention and the present Regulations" are replaced by a simple term "the present regulations". Similarly, the expression "chapter I of the Convention and the present Protocol" is replaced by the term "this chapter"; and

   .2   the use of initial capitals and spelling follow the guidelines in the IMO Style Manual which conforms to the style adopted for the 1983 SOLAS amendments.

11   On the other hand, attention is drawn to the following matters which have not been regularized by editing:

.1 while the decimal numbering system is used for paragraphs and sub-paragraphs of regulations in chapters II–1, II–2, III and VII which were completely rewritten in the 1981 and 1983 amendments, the existing numbering system is retained in other chapters;

.2 the references to regulations, paragraphs and chapters in the texts adopted in the 1981 and 1983 amendments use an abbreviated form, e.g. regulation II–2/55.5, whereas the existing reference system is retained in unamended regulations, e.g. "regulation 8 of chapter IV", "paragraph (a) of this regulation";

.3 the term "tons gross tonnage" is retained, which encompasses the gross tonnage determined by the International Convention on Tonnage Measurement of Ships, 1969, and the tons gross tonnage determined by existing national tonnage measurement regulations (resolution A.493(XII));

.4 references to imperial units have been retained when they occur in texts that were not amended in 1981 or 1983, on the understanding that, when the relevant texts are amended, metric values of the SI system will be used to the exclusion of imperial units in accordance with resolution A.351(IX);

.5 the corrections of errors found in the texts which are in the process of rectification are not incorporated but appropriate errata will be issued upon completion of the rectification process.

Articles of the International Convention for the Safety of Life at Sea, 1974

THE CONTRACTING GOVERNMENTS,

BEING DESIROUS of promoting safety of life at sea by establishing in common agreement uniform principles and rules directed thereto,

CONSIDERING that this end may best be achieved by the conclusion of a Convention to replace the International Convention for the Safety of Life at Sea, 1960, taking account of developments since that Convention was concluded,

HAVE AGREED as follows:

ARTICLE I

General obligations under the Convention

(a)   The Contracting Governments undertake to give effect to the provisions of the present Convention and the Annex thereto, which shall constitute an integral part of the present Convention. Every reference to the present Convention constitutes at the same time a reference to the Annex.

(b)   The Contracting Governments undertake to promulgate all laws, decrees, orders and regulations and to take all other steps which may be necessary to give the present Convention full and complete effect, so as to ensure that, from the point of view of safety of life, a ship is fit for the service for which it is intended.

ARTICLE II

Application

The present Convention shall apply to ships entitled to fly the flag of States the Governments of which are Contracting Governments.

ARTICLE III

Laws, regulations

The Contracting Governments undertake to communicate to and deposit with the Secretary-General of the Inter-Governmental Maritime Consultative Organization* (hereinafter referred to as "the Organization"):

(a) a list of non-governmental agencies which are authorized to act in their behalf in the administration of measures for safety of life at sea for circulation to the Contracting Governments for the information of their officers;

(b) the text of laws, decrees, orders and regulations which shall have been promulgated on the various matters within the scope of the present Convention;

(c) a sufficient number of specimens of their Certificates issued under the provisions of the present Convention for circulation to the Contracting Governments for the information of their officers.

ARTICLE IV

Cases of force majeure

(a) A ship, which is not subject to the provisions of the present Convention at the time of its departure on any voyage, shall not become subject to the provisions of the present Convention on account of any deviation from its intended voyage due to stress of weather or any other case of *force majeure*.

(b) Persons who are on board a ship by reason of *force majeure* or in consequence of the obligation laid upon the master to carry shipwrecked or other persons shall not be taken into account for the purpose of ascertaining the application to a ship of any provisions of the present Convention.

ARTICLE V

Carriage of persons in emergency

(a) For the purpose of evacuating persons in order to avoid a threat to the security of their lives a Contracting Government may permit the carriage

---

* The name of the Organization was changed to the "International Maritime Organization" by virtue of amendments to the Organization's Convention which entered into force on 22 May 1982.

of a larger number of persons in its ships than is otherwise permissible under the present Convention.

(b)   Such permission shall not deprive other Contracting Governments of any right of control under the present Convention over such ships which come within their ports.

(c)   Notice of any such permission, together with a statement of the circumstances, shall be sent to the Secretary-General of the Organization by the Contracting Government granting such permission.

ARTICLE VI

Prior treaties and conventions

(a)   As between the Contracting Governments, the present Convention replaces and abrogates the International Convention for the Safety of Life at Sea which was signed in London on 17 June 1960.

(b)   All other treaties, conventions and arrangements relating to safety of life at sea, or matters appertaining thereto, at present in force between Governments parties to the present Convention shall continue to have full and complete effect during the terms thereof as regards:

   (i)   ships to which the present Convention does not apply;

   (ii) ships to which the present Convention applies, in respect of matters for which it has not expressly provided.

(c)   To the extent, however, that such treaties, conventions or arrangements conflict with the provisions of the present Convention, the provisions of the present Convention shall prevail.

(d)   All matters which are not expressly provided for in the present Convention remain subject to the legislation of the Contracting Governments.

ARTICLE VII

Special rules drawn up by agreement

When in accordance with the present Convention special rules are drawn up by agreement between all or some of the Contracting Governments, such rules shall be communicated to the Secretary-General of the Organization for circulation to all Contracting Governments.

ARTICLE VIII

Amendments

(a)   The present Convention may be amended by either of the procedures specified in the following paragraphs.

(b)   Amendments after consideration within the Organization:

    (i)   Any amendment proposed by a Contracting Government shall be submitted to the Secretary-General of the Organization, who shall then circulate it to all Members of the Organization and all Contracting Governments at least six months prior to its consideration.

    (ii)   Any amendment proposed and circulated as above shall be referred to the Maritime Safety Committee of the Organization for consideration.

    (iii)   Contracting Governments of States, whether or not Members of the Organization, shall be entitled to participate in the proceedings of the Maritime Safety Committee for the consideration and adoption of amendments.

    (iv)   Amendments shall be adopted by a two-thirds majority of the Contracting Governments present and voting in the Maritime Safety Committee expanded as provided for in sub-paragraph (iii) of this paragraph (hereinafter referred to as "the expanded Maritime Safety Committee") on condition that at least one-third of the Contracting Governments shall be present at the time of voting.

    (v)   Amendments adopted in accordance with sub-paragraph (iv) of this paragraph shall be communicated by the Secretary-General of the Organization to all Contracting Governments for acceptance.

    (vi)   (1)   An amendment to an Article of the Convention or to Chapter I of the Annex shall be deemed to have been accepted on the date on which it is accepted by two-thirds of the Contracting Governments.

        (2)   An amendment to the Annex other than Chapter I shall be deemed to have been accepted:

            (aa)   at the end of two years from the date on which it is communicated to Contracting Governments for acceptance; or

            (bb)   at the end of a different period, which shall not be less than one year, if so determined at the time of its adoption by a two-thirds majority of the Contracting Governments present and voting in the expanded Maritime Safety Committee.

However, if within the specified period either more than one-third of Contracting Governments, or Contracting Governments the combined merchant fleets of which constitute not less than fifty per cent of the gross tonnage of the world's merchant fleet, notify the Secretary-General of the Organization that they object to the amendment, it shall be deemed not to have been accepted.

(vii) (1) An amendment to an Article of the Convention or to Chapter I of the Annex shall enter into force with respect to those Contracting Governments which have accepted it, six months after the date on which it is deemed to have been accepted, and with respect to each Contracting Government which accepts it after that date, six months after the date of that Contracting Government's acceptance.

(2) An amendment to the Annex other than Chapter I shall enter into force with respect to all Contracting Governments, except those which have objected to the amendment under sub-paragraph (vi)(2) of this paragraph and which have not withdrawn such objections, six months after the date on which it is deemed to have been accepted. However, before the date set for entry into force, any Contracting Government may give notice to the Secretary-General of the Organization that it exempts itself from giving effect to that amendment for a period not longer than one year from the date of its entry into force, or for such longer period as may be determined by a two-thirds majority of the Contracting Governments present and voting in the expanded Maritime Safety Committee at the time of the adoption of the amendment.

(c) Amendment by a Conference:

(i) Upon the request of a Contracting Government concurred in by at least one-third of the Contracting Governments, the Organization shall convene a Conference of Contracting Governments to consider amendments to the present Convention.

(ii) Every amendment adopted by such a Conference by a two-thirds majority of the Contracting Governments present and voting shall be communicated by the Secretary-General of the Organization to all Contracting Governments for acceptance.

(iii) Unless the Conference decides otherwise, the amendment shall be deemed to have been accepted and shall enter into force in accordance with the procedures specified in sub-paragraphs (b)(vi) and (b)(vii) respectively of this Article, provided that references in these paragraphs to the expanded Maritime Safety Committee shall be taken to mean references to the Conference.

(d)   (i)   A Contracting Government which has accepted an amendment to the Annex which has entered into force shall not be obliged to extend the benefit of the present Convention in respect of the certificates issued to a ship entitled to fly the flag of a State the Government of which, pursuant to the provisions of sub-paragraph (b)(vi)(2) of this Article, has objected to the amendment and has not withdrawn such an objection, but only to the extent that such certificates relate to matters covered by the amendment in question.

        (ii)   A Contracting Government which has accepted an amendment to the Annex which has entered into force shall extend the benefit of the present Convention in respect of the certificates issued to a ship entitled to fly the flag of a State the Government of which, pursuant to the provisions of sub-paragraph (b)(vii)(2) of this Article, has notified the Secretary-General of the Organization that it exempts itself from giving effect to the amendment.

(e)   Unless expressly provided otherwise, any amendment to the present Convention made under this Article, which relates to the structure of a ship, shall apply only to ships the keels of which are laid or which are at a similar stage of construction, on or after the date on which the amendment enters into force.

(f)   Any declaration of acceptance of, or objection to, an amendment or any notice given under sub-paragraph (b)(vii)(2) of this Article shall be submitted in writing to the Secretary-General of the Organization, who shall inform all Contracting Governments of any such submission and the date of its receipt.

(g)   The Secretary-General of the Organization shall inform all Contracting Governments of any amendments which enter into force under this Article, together with the date on which each such amendment enters into force.

ARTICLE IX

Signature, ratification, acceptance, approval and accession

(a)   The present Convention shall remain open for signature at the Headquarters of the Organization from 1 November 1974 until 1 July 1975 and shall thereafter remain open for accession. States may become parties to the present Convention by:

(i)   signature without reservation as to ratification, acceptance or approval; or

(ii) signature subject to ratification, acceptance or approval, followed by ratification, acceptance or approval; or

(iii) accession.

(b)   Ratification, acceptance, approval or accession shall be effected by the deposit of an instrument to that effect with the Secretary-General of the Organization.

(c)   The Secretary-General of the Organization shall inform the Governments of all States which have signed the present Convention or acceded to it of any signature or of the deposit of any instrument of ratification, acceptance, approval or accession and the date of its deposit.

ARTICLE X

Entry into force

(a)   The present Convention shall enter into force twelve months after the date on which not less than twenty-five States, the combined merchant fleets of which constitute not less than fifty per cent of the gross tonnage of the world's merchant shipping, have become parties to it in accordance with Article IX.

(b)   Any instrument of ratification, acceptance, approval or accession deposited after the date on which the present Convention enters into force shall take effect three months after the date of deposit.

(c)   After the date on which an amendment to the present Convention is deemed to have been accepted under Article VIII, any instrument of ratification, acceptance, approval or accession deposited shall apply to the Convention as amended.

ARTICLE XI

Denunciation

(a)   The present Convention may be denounced by any Contracting Government at any time after the expiry of five years from the date on which the Convention enters into force for that Government.

(b)   Denunciation shall be effected by the deposit of an instrument of denunciation with the Secretary-General of the Organization who shall notify all the other Contracting Governments of any instrument of denunciation received and of the date of its receipt as well as the date on which such denunciation takes effect.

(c)   A denunciation shall take effect one year, or such longer period as may be specified in the instrument of denunciation, after its receipt by the Secretary-General of the Organization.

ARTICLE XII

Deposit and registration

(a)   The present Convention shall be deposited with the Secretary-General of the Organization who shall transmit certified true copies thereof to the Governments of all States which have signed the present Convention or acceded to it.

(b)   As soon as the present Convention enters into force, the text shall be transmitted by the Secretary-General of the Organization to the Secretary-General of the United Nations for registration and publication, in accordance with Article 102 of the Charter of the United Nations.

ARTICLE XIII

Languages

The present Convention is established in a single copy in the Chinese, English, French, Russian and Spanish languages, each text being equally authentic. Official translations in the Arabic, German and Italian languages shall be prepared and deposited with the signed original.

IN WITNESS WHEREOF the undersigned,* being duly authorized by their respective Governments for that purpose, have signed the present Convention.

DONE AT LONDON this first day of November one thousand nine hundred and seventy-four.

----

* Signatures omitted.

Articles of the Protocol of 1978 relating to the International Convention for the Safety of Life at Sea, 1974

THE PARTIES TO THE PRESENT PROTOCOL,

BEING PARTIES to the International Convention for the Safety of Life at Sea, 1974, done at London on 1 November 1974,

RECOGNIZING the significant contribution which can be made by the above-mentioned Convention to the promotion of the safety of ships and property at sea and the lives of persons on board,

RECOGNIZING ALSO the need to improve further the safety of ships, particularly tankers,

CONSIDERING that this objective may best be achieved by the conclusion of a Protocol Relating to the International Convention for the Safety of Life at Sea, 1974,

HAVE AGREED as follows:

ARTICLE I

General obligations

The Parties to the present Protocol undertake to give effect to the provisions of the present Protocol and the Annex hereto which shall constitute an integral part of the present Protocol. Every reference to the present Protocol constitutes at the same time a reference to the Annex hereto.

ARTICLE II

Application

1.   The provisions of Articles II, III (other than paragraph (a)), IV, VI(b), (c) and (d), VII and VIII of the International Convention for the Safety

of Life at Sea, 1974 (hereinafter referred to as "the Convention") are incorporated in the present Protocol, provided that references in those Articles to the Convention and to Contracting Governments shall be taken to mean references to the present Protocol and to the Parties to the present Protocol, respectively.

2.   Any ship to which the present Protocol applies shall comply with the provisions of the Convention, subject to the modifications and additions set out in the present Protocol.

3.   With respect to the ships of non-parties to the Convention and the present Protocol, the Parties to the present Protocol shall apply the requirements of the Convention and the present Protocol as may be necessary to ensure that no more favourable treatment is given to such ships.

ARTICLE III

Communication of information

The Parties to the present Protocol undertake to communicate to, and deposit with, the Secretary-General of the Inter-Governmental Maritime Consultative Organization* (hereinafter referred to as "the Organization"), a list of nominated surveyors or recognized organizations which are authorized to act on their behalf in the administration of measures for safety of life at sea for circulation to the Parties for information of their officers. The Administration shall therefore notify the Organization of the specific responsibilities and conditions of the authority delegated to the nominated surveyors or recognized organizations.

ARTICLE IV

Signature, ratification, acceptance, approval and accession

1.   The present Protocol shall be open for signature at the Headquarters of the Organization from 1 June 1978 to 1 March 1979 and shall thereafter remain open for accession. Subject to the provisions of paragraph 3 of this Article, States may become Parties to the present Protocol by:

---

* The name of the Organization was changed to the "International Maritime Organization" by virtue of amendments to the Organization's Convention which entered into force on 22 May 1982.

(a) signature without reservation as to ratification, acceptance or approval; or

(b) signature subject to ratification, acceptance or approval, followed by ratification, acceptance or approval; or

(c) accession.

2. Ratification, acceptance, approval or accession shall be effected by the deposit of an instrument to that effect with the Secretary-General of the Organization.

3. The present Protocol may be signed without reservation, ratified, accepted, approved or acceded to only by States which have signed without reservation, ratified, accepted, approved or acceded to the Convention.

ARTICLE V

Entry into force

1. The present Protocol shall enter into force six months after the date on which not less than fifteen States, the combined merchant fleets of which constitute not less than fifty per cent of the gross tonnage of the world's merchant shipping, have become Parties to it in accordance with Article IV of the present Protocol, provided however that the present Protocol shall not enter into force before the Convention has entered into force.

2. Any instrument of ratification, acceptance, approval or accession deposited after the date on which the present Protocol enters into force shall take effect three months after the date of deposit.

3. After the date on which an amendment to the present Protocol is deemed to have been accepted under Article VIII of the Convention, any instrument of ratification, acceptance, approval or accession deposited shall apply to the present Protocol as amended.

ARTICLE VI

Denunciation

1. The present Protocol may be denounced by any Party at any time after the expiry of five years from the date on which the present Protocol enters into force for that Party.

2.	Denunciation shall be effected by the deposit of an instrument of denunciation with the Secretary-General of the Organization.

3.	A denunciation shall take effect one year, or such longer period as may be specified in the instrument of denunciation, after its receipt by the Secretary-General of the Organization.

4.	A denunciation of the Convention by a Party shall be deemed to be a denunciation of the present Protocol by that Party.

ARTICLE VII

Depositary

1.	The present Protocol shall be deposited with the Secretary-General of the Organization (hereinafter referred to as "the Depositary").

2.	The Depositary shall:

(a)	inform all States which have signed the present Protocol or acceded thereto of:

(i)	each new signature or deposit of an instrument of ratification, acceptance, approval or accession, together with the date thereof;

(ii)	the date of entry into force of the present Protocol;

(iii)	the deposit of any instrument of denunciation of the present Protocol together with the date on which it was received and the date on which the denunciation takes effect;

(b)	transmit certified true copies of the present Protocol to all States which have signed the present Protocol or acceded thereto.

3.	As soon as the present Protocol enters into force, a certified true copy thereof shall be transmitted by the Depositary to the Secretariat of the United Nations for registration and publication in accordance with Article 102 of the Charter of the United Nations.

ARTICLE VIII

Languages

The present Protocol is established in a single original in the Chinese, English, French, Russian and Spanish languages, each text being equally authentic. Official translations in the Arabic, German and Italian languages shall be prepared and deposited with the signed original.

IN WITNESS WHEREOF the undersigned* being duly authorized by their respective Governments for that purpose have signed the present Protocol.

DONE AT LONDON this seventeenth day of February one thousand nine hundred and seventy-eight.

---

* Signatures omitted.

Consolidated text of the
Annex to the 1974 SOLAS Convention

Chapter I

GENERAL PROVISIONS

Page

PART A – APPLICATION, DEFINITIONS, ETC.

1 Application 17
2 Definitions 17
3 Exceptions 18
4 Exemptions 19
5 Equivalents 19

PART B – SURVEYS AND CERTIFICATES

6 Inspection and survey 20
7 Surveys of passenger ships 21
8 Surveys of life-saving appliances
   and other equipment of cargo ships 23
9 Surveys of radio and radar installations
   of cargo ships 23
10 Surveys of hull, machinery and equipment
    of cargo ships 24
11 Maintenance of conditions after survey 25
12 Issue of certificates 25
13 Issue of certificate by another Government 27
14 Duration and validity of certificates 27
15 Form of certificates 28
16 Posting up of certificates 29
17 Acceptance of certificates 29
18 Qualification of certificates 29

15

19 Control 29
20 Privileges 30

PART C – CASUALTIES

21 Casualties 31

PART A – APPLICATION, DEFINITIONS, ETC.

Regulation 1

Application

(a)   Unless expressly provided otherwise, the present regulations apply only to ships engaged on international voyages.

(b)   The classes of ships to which each chapter applies are more precisely defined, and the extent of the application is shown, in each chapter.

Regulation 2

Definitions

For the purpose of the present regulations, unless expressly provided otherwise:

(a)   *Regulations* means the regulations contained in the Annex to the present Convention.

(b)   *Administration* means the Government of the State whose flag the ship is entitled to fly.

(c)   *Approved* means approved by the Administration.

(d)   *International voyage* means a voyage from a country to which the present Convention applies to a port outside such country, or conversely.

(e)   A passenger is every person other than:

(i)   the master and the members of the crew or other persons employed or engaged in any capacity on board a ship on the business of that ship; and

(ii)   a child under one year of age.

(f)   A passenger ship is a ship which carries more than twelve passengers.

(g)   A cargo ship is any ship which is not a passenger ship.

17

(h)   A tanker is a cargo ship constructed or adapted for the carriage in bulk of liquid cargoes of an inflammable* nature.

(i)   A fishing vessel is a vessel used for catching fish, whales, seals, walrus or other living resources of the sea.

(j)   A nuclear ship is a ship provided with a nuclear power plant.

(k)   *New ship* means a ship the keel of which is laid or which is at a similar stage of construction on or after the date of coming into force of the present Convention.

(l)   *Existing ship* means a ship which is not a new ship.

(m)   A mile is 1,852 metres or 6,080 feet.

(n)   *Age of a ship* means the elapsed period of time determined from the year of build as indicated on the ship's registry papers. ⟦P⟧

Regulation 3

Exceptions

(a)   The present regulations, unless expressly provided otherwise, do not apply to:

  (i)   Ships of war and troopships.

  (ii)   Cargo ships of less than 500 tons gross tonnage.

  (iii)   Ships not propelled by mechanical means.

  (iv)   Wooden ships of primitive build.

  (v)   Pleasure yachts not engaged in trade.

  (vi)   Fishing vessels.

(b)   Except as expressly provided in chapter V, nothing herein shall apply to ships solely navigating the Great Lakes of North America and the River St. Lawrence as far east as a straight line drawn from Cap des Rosiers to West Point, Anticosti Island and, on the north side of Anticosti Island, the 63rd meridian.

---

* "Inflammable" has the same meaning as "flammable".

Regulation 4

Exemptions

(a)   A ship which is not normally engaged on international voyages but which, in exceptional circumstances, is required to undertake a single international voyage may be exempted by the Administration from any of the requirements of the present regulations provided that it complies with safety requirements which are adequate in the opinion of the Administration for the voyage which is to be undertaken by the ship.

(b)   The Administration may exempt any ship which embodies features of a novel kind from any of the provisions of chapters II–1, II–2, III and IV of these regulations the application of which might seriously impede research into the development of such features and their incorporation in ships engaged on international voyages. Any such ship shall, however, comply with safety requirements which, in the opinion of that Administration, are adequate for the service for which it is intended and are such as to ensure the overall safety of the ship and which are acceptable to the Governments of the States to be visited by the ship. The Administration which allows any such exemption shall communicate to the Organization particulars of same and the reasons therefor which the Organization shall circulate to the Contracting Governments for their information.

Regulation 5

Equivalents

(a)   Where the present regulations require that a particular fitting, material, appliance or apparatus, or type thereof, shall be fitted or carried in a ship, or that any particular provision shall be made, the Administration may allow any other fitting, material, appliance or apparatus, or type thereof, to be fitted or carried, or any other provision to be made in that ship, if it is satisfied by trial thereof or otherwise that such fitting, material, appliance or apparatus, or type thereof, or provision, is at least as effective as that required by the present regulations.

(b)   Any Administration which so allows, in substitution, a fitting, material, appliance or apparatus, or type thereof, or provision, shall communicate to the Organization particulars thereof together with a report on any trials made and the Organization shall circulate such particulars to other Contracting Governments for the information of their officers.

PART B – SURVEYS AND CERTIFICATES

Regulation 6 $\boxed{\text{P}}$

Inspection and survey*

(a)   The inspection and survey of ships, so far as regards the enforcement of the provisions of the present regulations and the granting of exemptions therefrom, shall be carried out by officers of the Administration. The Administration may, however, entrust the inspections and surveys either to surveyors nominated for the purpose or to organizations recognized by it.

(b)   The Administration shall institute arrangements for unscheduled inspections to be carried out during the period of validity of the certificate. Such inspections shall ensure that the ship and its equipment remain in all respects satisfactory for the service for which the ship is intended. These inspections may be carried out by the Administration's own inspection services, or by nominated surveyors, or by recognized organizations, or by other Parties upon request of the Administration. Where the Administration, under the provisions of regulations 8 and 10 of this chapter, establishes mandatory annual surveys, the above unscheduled inspections shall not be obligatory.

(c)   An Administration nominating surveyors or recognizing organizations to conduct inspections and surveys as set forth in paragraphs (a) and (b) shall as a minimum empower any nominated surveyor or recognized organization to:

   (i)   require repairs to a ship, and

   (ii)   carry out inspections and surveys if requested by the appropriate authorities of a port State.

The Administration shall notify the Organization of the specific responsibilities and conditions of the authority delegated to nominated surveyors or recognized organizations.

(d)   When a nominated surveyor or recognized organization determines that the condition of the ship or its equipment does not correspond substantially with the particulars of the certificate or is such that the ship is not fit to proceed to sea without danger to the ship, or persons on board, such surveyor or organization shall immediately ensure that corrective action is taken and

---

* Reference is made to the Guidelines on Mandatory Annual Surveys, Unscheduled Inspections of all Cargo Ships as well as Intermediate Surveys on Tankers of Ten Years of Age and Over, under the Protocol of 1978 relating to the International Convention for the Safety of Life at Sea, 1974 (resolution A.413(XI) as amended by resolution A.465(XII)).

The Maritime Safety Committee urged Governments to institute mandatory annual surveys and not unscheduled inspections (circular letter No. 817).

shall in due course notify the Administration. If such corrective action is not taken the relevant certificate should be withdrawn and the Administration shall be notified immediately; and, if the ship is in the port of another Party, the appropriate authorities of the port State shall also be notified immediately. When an officer of the Administration, a nominated surveyor or recognized organization has notified the appropriate authorities of the port State, the Government of the port State concerned shall give such officer, surveyor or organization any necessary assistance to carry out their obligations under this regulation. When applicable, the Government of the port State concerned shall ensure that the ship shall not sail until it can proceed to sea, or leave port for the purpose of proceeding to the appropriate repair yard, without danger to the ship or persons on board.

(e)   In every case, the Administration shall fully guarantee the completeness and efficiency of the inspection and survey, and shall undertake to ensure the necessary arrangements to satisfy this obligation.

Regulation 7

Surveys of passenger ships

(a)   A passenger ship shall be subjected to the surveys specified below:

(i)   A survey before the ship is put in service.

(ii)   A periodical survey once every twelve months.

(iii)   Additional surveys, as occasion arises.

(b)   The surveys referred to above shall be carried out as follows:

(i)   The survey before the ship is put in service shall include a complete inspection of its structure, machinery and equipment, including the outside of the ship's bottom and the inside and outside of the boilers. This survey shall be such as to ensure that the arrangements, material, and scantlings of the structure, boilers and other pressure vessels and their appurtenances, main and auxiliary machinery, electrical installation, radio installation, radiotelegraph installations in motor lifeboats, portable radio apparatus for survival craft, life-saving appliances, fire-protection, fire-detecting and extinguishing appliances, radar, echo-sounding device, gyro-compass, pilot ladders, mechanical pilot hoists and other equipment, fully comply with the requirements of the present regulations, and of the laws, decrees, orders and regulations promulgated as a result thereof by the Administration for ships of the service for which it is intended. The survey shall also be such as to ensure that the workmanship of all parts of the ship and its equipment is in all respects satisfactory, and that the ship is

21

provided with the lights, shapes, means of making sound signals and distress signals as required by the provisions of the present regulations and the International Regulations for Preventing Collisions at Sea in force.

(ii) The periodical survey shall include an inspection of the structure, boilers and other pressure vessels, machinery and equipment, including the outside of the ship's bottom. The survey shall be such as to ensure that the ship, as regards the structure, boilers and other pressure vessels and their appurtenances, main and auxiliary machinery, electrical installation, radio installation, radiotelegraph installations in motor lifeboats, portable radio apparatus for survival craft, life-saving appliances, fire-protection, fire-detecting and extinguishing appliances, radar, echo-sounding device, gyro-compass, pilot ladders, mechanical pilot hoists and other equipment, is in satisfactory condition and fit for the service for which it is intended, and that it complies with the requirements of the present regulations, and of the laws, decrees, orders and regulations promulgated as a result thereof by the Administration. The lights, shapes and means of making sound signals and the distress signals carried by the ship shall also be subject to the above-mentioned survey for the purpose of ensuring that they comply with the requirements of the present regulations and of the International Regulations for Preventing Collisions at Sea in force.

(iii) A survey either general or partial, according to the circumstances, shall be made after a repair resulting from investigations prescribed in regulation 11 of this chapter, or whenever any important repairs or renewals are made. The survey shall be such as to ensure that the necessary repairs or renewals have been effectively made, that the material and workmanship of such repairs or renewals are in all respects satisfactory, and that the ship complies in all respects with the provisions of the present regulations and of the International Regulations for Preventing Collisions at Sea in force, and of the laws, decrees, orders and regulations promulgated as a result thereof by the Administration. $\boxed{P}$

(c) (i) The laws, decrees, orders and regulations referred to in paragraph (b) of this regulation shall be in all respects such as to ensure that, from the point of view of safety of life, the ship is fit for the service for which it is intended.

(ii) They shall among other things prescribe the requirements to be observed as to the initial and subsequent hydraulic or other acceptable alternative tests to which the main and auxiliary boilers, connections, steam pipes, high pressure receivers, and fuel tanks for internal combustion engines are to be submitted including the test procedures to be followed and the intervals between two consecutive tests.

Regulation 8 $\boxed{P}$

*Surveys of life-saving appliances and
other equipment of cargo ships*

(a)   The life-saving appliances, except a radiotelegraph installation in a motor lifeboat or a portable radio apparatus for survival craft, the echo-sounding device, the gyro-compass, the fire-extinguishing appliances and the inert gas system of cargo ships to which chapters II–1, II–2, III and V apply, shall be subject to initial and subsequent surveys as prescribed for passenger ships in regulation 7 of this chapter with the substitution of 24 months for 12 months in subparagraph (a)(II) of that regulation. The fire control plans in new ships and the pilot ladders, mechanical pilot hoists, lights, shapes and means of making sound signals carried by new and existing ships shall be included in the surveys for the purpose of ensuring that they comply fully with the requirements of the present regulations and, where applicable, the International Regulations for Preventing Collisions at Sea in force.*

(b)   Intermediate surveys shall be made for tankers of ten years of age and over, within three months before or after the anniversary date of the Cargo Ship Safety Equipment Certificate, to ensure that equipment specified in paragraph (a) of this regulation has been maintained in accordance with regulation 11 of this chapter and that it is in good working condition. Such intermediate surveys shall be endorsed on the Cargo Ship Safety Equipment Certificate issued in accordance with regulation 12(a)(iii) of this chapter.**

Regulation 9

Surveys of radio and radar installations of cargo ships

The radio and radar installations of cargo ships to which chapters IV and V apply and any radiotelegraph installation in a motor lifeboat or portable radio apparatus for survival craft which is carried in compliance with the requirements of chapter III shall be subject to initial and subsequent surveys as provided for passengers ships in regulation 7 of this chapter.

---

* Reference is made to the Record of approved cargo ship safety equipment (SLS.14/Circ.1).
** Reference is made to the Guidelines on Mandatory Annual Surveys, Unscheduled Inspections of all Cargo Ships as well as Intermediate Surveys on Tankers of Ten Years of Age and Over, under the Protocol of 1978 relating to the International Convention for the Safety of Life at Sea, 1974 (resolution A.413(XI) as amended by resolution A.465(XII)).

Regulation 10 $\boxed{\text{P}}$

Surveys of hull, machinery and equipment of cargo ships

(a)   The hull, machinery and equipment (other than items in respect of which Cargo Ship Safety Equipment Certificates, Cargo Ship Safety Radiotelegraphy Certificates or Cargo Ship Radiotelephony Certificates are issued) of a cargo ship shall be surveyed on completion and thereafter in such a manner as the Administration may consider necessary in order to ensure that their condition is in all respects satisfactory and at the following intervals:

(i)   at intervals specified by the Administration but not exceeding five years (periodical surveys);

(ii)   in addition to such periodical surveys a tanker of ten years of age and over shall undergo a minimum of one intermediate survey during the period of validity of its Cargo Ship Safety Construction Certificate.* In cases where only one such intermediate survey is carried out in any one certificate validity period, it shall be held not before six months prior to, nor later than six months after, the half-way date of the certificate's period of validity.

(b)   The initial and periodical survey shall be such as to ensure that the arrangements, material and scantlings of the structure, boilers and other pressure vessels, their appurtenances, main and auxiliary machinery including steering gear and associated control systems, electrical installation and other equipment are in all respects satisfactory for the service for which the ship is intended. Such surveys shall, in the case of tankers, also include inspection of the outside of the ship's bottom, pump-rooms, cargo and bunker piping systems, vent piping, pressure vacuum valves and flame screens.

(c)   The intermediate survey of tankers of ten years of age and over shall include inspection of steering gear equipment and associated control systems, pump-rooms, cargo and bunker piping systems on deck and in pump-rooms, vent piping, pressure vacuum valves and flame screens, the electrical installations in dangerous zones, and the outside of the ship's bottom.** In addition to the visual inspection of the electrical installation, the insulation resistance of the electrical equipment in dangerous zones is to be tested. If, upon examination, there should be any doubt as to the condition of the piping, extra measures, such as pressure tests and thickness determination, shall be taken as necessary. Such intermediate surveys shall be endorsed on the Cargo Ship

---

* Reference is made to the Guidelines on Mandatory Annual Surveys, Unscheduled Inspections of all Cargo Ships as well as Intermediate Surveys on Tankers of Ten Years of Age and Over, under the Protocol of 1978 relating to the International Convention for the Safety of Life at Sea, 1974 (resolution A.413(XI) as amended by resolution A.465(XII)).

** Reference is made to the circular concerning inspection of the outside of the ship's bottom (PSLS.2/Circ. 5).

Safety Construction Certificate issued in accordance with regulation 12(a)(ii) of this chapter.

(d)   A survey, either general or partial according to the circumstances, shall be made when required after an investigation prescribed in regulation 11 of this chapter, or whenever any important repairs or renewals are made. The survey shall be such as to ensure that the necessary repairs or renewals have been effectively made, that the material and workmanship of such repairs or renewals are in all respects satisfactory, and that the ship is fit to proceed to sea without danger to the ship or persons on board.

Regulation 11 $\boxed{P}$

Maintenance of conditions after survey

(a)   The condition of the ship and its equipment shall be maintained to conform with the provisions of the present regulations to ensure that the ship in all respects will remain fit to proceed to sea without danger to the ship or persons on board.

(b)   After any survey of the ship under regulations 6, 7, 8, 9 or 10 of this chapter has been completed, no change shall be made in the structural arrangement, machinery, equipment and other items covered by the survey, without the sanction of the Administration.

(c)   Whenever an accident occurs to a ship or a defect is discovered, either of which affects the safety of the ship or the efficiency or completeness of its life-saving appliances or other equipment, the master or owner of the ship shall report at the earliest opportunity to the Administration, the nominated surveyor or recognized organization responsible for issuing the relevant certificate, who shall cause investigations to be initiated to determine whether a survey, as required by regulations 6, 7, 8, 9 or 10 of this chapter, is necessary. If the ship is in a port of another Party, the master or owner shall also report immediately to the appropriate authorities of the port State and the nominated surveyor or recognized organization shall ascertain that such a report has been made.

Regulation 12

Issue of certificates

(a)   (i)   A certificate called a Passenger Ship Safety Certificate shall be issued after inspection and survey to a passenger ship which complies with the requirements of chapters II–1, II–2, III and IV and any other relevant requirements of the present regulations.

(ii) A certificate called a Cargo Ship Safety Construction Certificate* shall be issued after survey to a cargo ship which satisfies the requirements for cargo ships on survey set out in regulation 10 of this chapter and complies with the applicable requirements of chapters II–1 and II–2 other than those relating to fire-extinguishing appliances and fire control plans.

(iii) A certificate called a Cargo Ship Safety Equipment Certificate* shall be issued after inspection to a cargo ship which complies with the relevant requirements of chapters II–1, II–2 and III and any other relevant requirements of the present regulations.

(iv) A certificate called a Cargo Ship Safety Radiotelegraphy Certificate shall be issued after inspection to a cargo ship, fitted with a radiotelegraph installation, which complies with the requirements of chapter IV and any other relevant requirements of the present regulations.

(v) A certificate called a Cargo Ship Safety Radiotelephony Certificate shall be issued after inspection to a cargo ship, fitted with a radiotelephone installation, which complies with the requirements of chapter IV and any other relevant requirements of the present regulations.

(vi) When an exemption is granted to a ship under and in accordance with the provisions of the present regulations, a certificate called an Exemption Certificate shall be issued in addition to the certificates prescribed in this paragraph.

(vii) Passenger Ship Safety Certificates, Cargo Ship Safety Construction Certificates, Cargo Ship Safety Equipment Certificates, Cargo Ship Safety Radiotelegraphy Certificates, Cargo Ship Safety Radiotelephony Certificates and Exemption Certificates shall be issued either by the Administration or by any person or organization duly authorized by it. In every case, that Administration assumes full responsibility for the certificate.

(b) Notwithstanding any other provision of the present Convention any certificate issued under, and in accordance with, the provisions of the International Convention for the Safety of Life at Sea, 1960, which is current when the present Convention comes into force in respect of the Administration by which the certificate is issued, shall remain valid until it expires under the terms of regulation 14 of chapter I of that Convention.

(c) A Contracting Government shall not issue certificates under, and in accordance with, the provisions of the International Convention for the Safety of Life at Sea, 1960, 1948 or 1929, after the date on which acceptance of the present Convention by the Government takes effect.

---

* Reference is made to the circular concerning issue of supplements and attachments (PSLS.2/Circ.1).

Regulation 13

Issue of certificate by another Government

A Contracting Government* may, at the request of the Administration, cause a ship to be surveyed and, if satisfied that the requirements of the present regulations are complied with, shall issue certificates to the ship in accordance with the present regulations. Any certificate so issued must contain a statement to the effect that it has been issued at the request of the Government of the State whose flag the ship is or will be entitled to fly and it shall have the same force and receive the same recognition as a certificate issued under regulation 12 of this chapter.

Regulation 14

*Duration and validity of certificates***

(a)   Certificates other than the Cargo Ship Safety Construction Certificate, the Cargo Ship Safety Equipment Certificate and any Exemption Certificate shall be issued for a period not exceeding 12 months. The Cargo Ship Safety Construction Certificate shall be issued for a period not exceeding five years. The Cargo Ship Safety Equipment Certificate shall be issued for a period not exceeding 24 months. Exemption Certificates shall not be valid for longer than the period of the certificates to which they refer.

(b)   No extension of the five-year period of validity of the Cargo Ship Safety Construction Certificate shall be permitted.

(c)   If a survey takes place within two months before the end of the period for which a Cargo Ship Safety Radiotelegraphy Certificate or a Cargo Ship Safety Radiotelephony Certificate issued in respect of cargo ships of 300 tons gross tonnage and upwards, but less than 500 tons gross tonnage, was originally issued, that certificate may be withdrawn, and a new certificate may be issued which shall expire 12 months after the end of the said period.

(d)   If the ship at the time when a certificate, other than that referred to in paragraph (b) of this regulation, expires is not in a port of the State whose flag it is entitled to fly or in which it is to be surveyed, the Administration may extend the certificate, but such extension shall be granted only for the

---

* Reference is made to the circular relating to requests by Parties to the 1978 SOLAS Protocol to Contracting Governments to the 1974 SOLAS Convention which are non-Parties to the Protocol to carry out safety radio surveys (PSLS.2/Circ.3).

** Reference is made to the circular relating to re-validation of certificates issued under the 1974 SOLAS Convention as modified by the 1978 SOLAS Protocol (PSLS.2/Circ.7).

purpose of allowing the ship to complete its voyage to the State whose flag it is entitled to fly or in which it is to be surveyed, and then only in cases where it appears proper and reasonable to do so.

(e)   No certificate shall be extended under the provisions of paragraph (d) of this regulation for a longer period than five months, and a ship to which an extension is granted shall not, on its arrival in the State whose flag it is entitled to fly or the port in which it is to be surveyed, be entitled by virtue of such extension to leave that port or State without having obtained a new certificate.

(f)   A certificate, other than that referred to in paragraph (b) of this regulation, which has not been extended under the foregoing provisions of this regulation, may be extended by the Administration for a period of grace up to one month from the date of expiry stated on it.

(g)   A certificate shall cease to be valid:

   (i)   if the inspections and surveys are not carried out within the periods specified under regulations 7(a), 8, 9 and 10(a) of this chapter or as they may have been extended in accordance with paragraphs (d), (e) or (f) of this regulation, or

  (ii)   upon transfer of the ship to the flag of another Government. A new certificate shall only be issued when the Government issuing the new certificate is fully satisfied that the ship is in compliance with the requirements of regulation 11(a) and (b) of this chapter. In the case of a transfer between Parties, if requested within three months after the transfer has taken place, the Government of the Party whose flag the ship was formerly entitled to fly shall, as soon as possible, transmit to the Administration copies of the certificates carried by the ship before the transfer and, if available, copies of the relevant survey reports.

Regulation 15

Form of certificates

(a)   All certificates shall be drawn up in the official language or languages of the country by which they are issued.

(b)   The form of the certificates shall be that of the models given in the appendix to the present regulations. The arrangement of the printed part of the model certificates shall be exactly reproduced in the certificates issued, or in certified copies thereof, and the particulars inserted in the certificates issued, or in certified copies thereof, shall be in Roman characters and Arabic figures.

28

Regulation 16

Posting up of certificates

All certificates or certified copies thereof issued under the present regulations shall be posted up in a prominent and accessible place in the ship.

Regulation 17

Acceptance of certificates

Certificates issued under the authority of a Contracting Government shall be accepted by the other Contracting Governments for all purposes covered by the present Convention. They shall be regarded by the other Contracting Governments as having the same force as certificates issued by them.

Regulation 18

Qualification of certificates

(a)   If in the course of a particular voyage a ship has on board a number of persons less than the total number stated in the Passenger Ship Safety Certificate and is in consequence, in accordance with the provisions of the present regulations, free to carry a smaller number of lifeboats and other life-saving appliances than that stated in the certificate, an annex may be issued by the Government, person or organization referred to in regulation 12 or 13 of this chapter.

(b)   This annex shall state that in the circumstances there is no infringement of the provisions of the present regulations. It shall be annexed to the certificate and shall be substituted for it in so far as the life-saving appliances are concerned. It shall be valid only for the particular voyage for which it is issued.

Regulation 19 $\boxed{\text{P}}$

*Control**

(a)   Every ship when in a port of another Party is subject to control by officers duly authorized by such Government in so far as this control is directed

---

* Reference is made to Procedures for the Control of Ships (resolution A.466(XII)).

towards verifying that the certificates issued under regulation 12 or regulation 13 of this chapter are valid.

(b)   Such certificates, if valid, shall be accepted unless there are clear grounds for believing that the condition of the ship or of its equipment does not correspond substantially with the particulars of any of the certificates or that the ship and its equipment are not in compliance with the provisions of regulation 11(a) and (b) of this chapter.

(c)   In the circumstances given in paragraph (b) of this regulation or where a certificate has expired or ceased to be valid, the officer carrying out the control shall take steps to ensure that the ship shall not sail until it can proceed to sea or leave the port for the purpose of proceeding to the appropriate repair yard without danger to the ship or persons on board.

(d)   In the event of this control giving rise to an intervention of any kind, the officer carrying out the control shall forthwith inform, in writing, the Consul or, in his absence, the nearest diplomatic representative of the State whose flag the ship is entitled to fly of all the circumstances in which intervention was deemed necessary. In addition, nominated surveyors or recognized organizations responsible for the issue of the certificates shall also be notified. The facts concerning the intervention shall be reported to the Organization.

(e)   The port State authority concerned shall notify all relevant information about the ship to the authorities of the next port of call, in addition to parties mentioned in paragraph (d) of this regulation, if it is unable to take action as specified in paragraphs (c) and (d) of this regulation or if the ship has been allowed to proceed to the next port of call.

(f)   When exercising control under this regulation all possible efforts shall be made to avoid a ship being unduly detained or delayed. If a ship is thereby unduly detained or delayed it shall be entitled to compensation for any loss or damage suffered.

Regulation 20

Privileges

The privileges of the present Convention may not be claimed in favour of any ship unless it holds appropriate valid certificates.

PART C – CASUALTIES

Regulation 21

Casualties

(a)   Each Administration undertakes to conduct an investigation of any casualty occurring to any of its ships subject to the provisions of the present Convention when it judges that such an investigation may assist in determining what changes in the present regulations might be desirable.*

(b)   Each Contracting Government undertakes to supply the Organization with pertinent information concerning the findings of such investigations. No reports or recommendations of the Organization based upon such information shall disclose the identity or nationality of the ships concerned or in any manner fix or imply responsibility upon any ship or person.

---

* Reference is made to the recommendations on "Exchange of information for investigations into marine casualties" and on "Personnel and material resource needs of Administrations for the investigation of casualties and contraventions of conventions" adopted by the Organization by resolutions A.440(XI) and A.442(XI).

Chapter II–1

CONSTRUCTION – SUBDIVISION AND STABILITY, MACHINERY AND ELECTRICAL INSTALLATIONS

Page

PART A – GENERAL

1 Application 36
2 Definitions 37
3 Definitions relating to parts C, D and E 38

PART B – SUBDIVISION AND STABILITY

4 Floodable length in passenger ships 41
5 Permeability in passenger ships 42
6 Permissible length of compartments in passenger ships 44
7 Special requirements concerning passenger ship subdivision 48
8 Stability of passenger ships in damaged condition 50
9 Ballasting of passenger ships 52
10 Peak and machinery space bulkheads, shaft tunnels, etc. in
   passenger ships 53
11 Collision bulkheads in cargo ships 54
12 Double bottoms in passenger ships 55
13 Assigning, marking and recording of subdivision load lines
   for passenger ships 56
14 Construction and initial testing of watertight bulkheads, etc.
   in passenger ships and cargo ships 57
15 Openings in watertight bulkheads in passenger ships 58
16 Passenger ships carrying goods vehicles and
   accompanying personnel 62
17 Openings in the shell plating of passenger ships
   below the margin line 63
18 Construction and initial tests of watertight doors,
   sidescuttles, etc. in passenger ships and cargo ships 66
19 Construction and initial tests of watertight decks, trunks, etc.
   in passenger ships and cargo ships 66
20 Watertight integrity of passenger ships above the margin line 67

21 Bilge pumping arrangements 67
22 Stability information for passenger ships and cargo ships 71
23 Damage control plans in passenger ships 71
24 Marking, periodical operation and inspection of
    watertight doors, etc. in passenger ships 72
25 Entries in log of passenger ships 72

PART C – MACHINERY INSTALLATIONS

26 General 73
27 Machinery 74
28 Means of going astern 75
29 Steering gear 75
30 Additional requirements for electric and electrohydraulic
    steering gear 81
31 Machinery controls 82
32 Steam boilers and boiler feed systems 84
33 Steam pipe systems 84
34 Air pressure systems 85
35 Ventilating systems in machinery spaces 85
36 Protection against noise 85
37 Communication between navigating bridge and
    machinery space 86
38 Engineers' alarm 86
39 Location of emergency installations in passenger ships 86

PART D – ELECTRICAL INSTALLATIONS

40 General 87
41 Main source of electrical power and lighting systems 87
42 Emergency source of electrical power in passenger ships 89
43 Emergency source of electrical power in cargo ships 93
44 Starting arrangements for emergency generating sets 96
45 Precautions against shock, fire and other hazards of
    electrical origin 97

PART E – ADDITIONAL REQUIREMENTS FOR PERIODICALLY UNATTENDED MACHINERY SPACES

46	General	100
47	Fire precautions	101
48	Protection against flooding	101
49	Control of propulsion machinery from the navigating bridge	102
50	Communication	103
51	Alarm system	103
52	Safety systems	104
53	Special requirements for machinery, boiler and electrical installations	104
54	Special consideration in respect of passenger ships	105

PART A – GENERAL

Regulation 1

Application

1.1 Unless expressly provided otherwise, this chapter shall apply to ships the keels of which are laid or which are at a similar stage of construction on or after 1 July 1986.

1.2 For the purpose of this chapter, the term "a similar stage of construction" means the stage at which:

.1 construction identifiable with a specific ship begins; and

.2 assembly of that ship has commenced comprising at least 50 tonnes or one per cent of the estimated mass of all structural material, whichever is less.

1.3 For the purpose of this chapter:

.1 the expression "ships constructed" means "ships the keels of which are laid or which are at a similar stage of construction";

.2 the expression "all ships" means "ships constructed before, on or after 1 July 1986";

.3 a cargo ship, whenever built, which is converted to a passenger ship shall be treated as a passenger ship constructed on the date on which such a conversion commences.

2 Unless expressly provided otherwise, for ships constructed before 1 July 1986 the Administration shall ensure that the requirements which are applicable under chapter II–1 of the International Convention for the Safety of Life at Sea, 1974, as amended by resolution MSC.1(XLV), are complied with.

3 All ships which undergo repairs, alterations, modifications and outfitting related thereto shall continue to comply with at least the requirements previously applicable to these ships. Such ships if constructed before 1 July 1986 shall, as a rule, comply with the requirements for ships constructed on or after that date to at least the same extent as they did before undergoing such repairs, alterations, modifications or outfitting. Repairs, alterations and modifications of a major character and outfitting related thereto shall meet the requirements for ships constructed on or after 1 July 1986 in so far as the Administration deems reasonable and practicable.

4 The Administration of a State may, if it considers that the sheltered nature and conditions of the voyage are such as to render the application

of any specific requirements of this chapter unreasonable or unnecessary, exempt from those requirements individual ships or classes of ships entitled to fly the flag of that State which, in the course of their voyage, do not proceed more than 20 miles from the nearest land.

5   In the case of passenger ships which are employed in special trades for the carriage of large numbers of special trade passengers, such as the pilgrim trade, the Administration of the State whose flag such ships are entitled to fly, if satisfied that it is impracticable to enforce compliance with the requirements of this chapter, may exempt such ships from those requirements, provided that they comply fully with the provisions of:

   .1   the rules annexed to the Special Trade Passenger Ships Agreement, 1971; and

   .2   the rules annexed to the Protocol on Space Requirements for Special Trade Passenger Ships, 1973.

Regulation 2

Definitions

For the purpose of this chapter, unless expressly provided otherwise:

1.1   *Subdivision load line* is a waterline used in determining the subdivision of the ship.

1.2   *Deepest subdivision load line* is the waterline which corresponds to the greatest draught permitted by the subdivision requirements which are applicable.

2   *Length of the ship* is the length measured between perpendiculars taken at the extremities of the deepest subdivision load line.

3   *Breadth of the ship* is the extreme width from outside of frame to outside of frame at or below the deepest subdivision load line.

4   *Draught* is the vertical distance from the moulded base line amidships to the subdivision load line in question.

5   *Bulkhead deck* is the uppermost deck up to which the transverse watertight bulkheads are carried.

6   *Margin line* is a line drawn at least 76 mm below the upper surface of the bulkhead deck at side.

7   *Permeability of a space* is the percentage of that space which can be

occupied by water. The volume of a space which extends above the margin line shall be measured only to the height of that line.

8   *Machinery space* is to be taken as extending from the moulded base line to the margin line and between the extreme main transverse watertight bulkheads, bounding the spaces containing the main and auxiliary propulsion machinery, boilers serving the needs of propulsion, and all permanent coal bunkers. In the case of unusual arrangements, the Administration may define the limits of the machinery spaces.

9   *Passenger spaces* are those spaces which are provided for the accommodation and use of passengers, excluding baggage, store, provision and mail rooms. For the purposes of regulations 5 and 6, spaces provided below the margin line for the accommodation and use of the crew shall be regarded as passenger spaces.

10   In all cases volumes and areas shall be calculated to moulded lines.

11   *Weathertight* means that in any sea conditions water will not penetrate into the ship.

Regulation 3

Definitions relating to parts C, D and E

For the purpose of parts C, D and E, unless expressly provided otherwise:

1   *Steering gear control system* is the equipment by which orders are transmitted from the navigating bridge to the steering gear power units. Steering gear control systems comprise transmitters, receivers, hydraulic control pumps and their associated motors, motor controllers, piping and cables.

2   *Main steering gear* is the machinery, rudder actuators, steering gear power units, if any, and ancillary equipment and the means of applying torque to the rudder stock (e.g. tiller or quadrant) necessary for effecting movement of the rudder for the purpose of steering the ship under normal service conditions.

3   *Steering gear power unit* is:

.1   in the case of electric steering gear, an electric motor and its associated electrical equipment;

.2   in the case of electrohydraulic steering gear, an electric motor and its associated electrical equipment and connected pump;

.3   in the case of other hydraulic steering gear, a driving engine and connected pump.

4   *Auxiliary steering gear* is the equipment other than any part of the main steering gear necessary to steer the ship in the event of failure of the main steering gear but not including the tiller, quadrant or components serving the same purpose.

5   *Normal operational and habitable condition* is a condition under which the ship as a whole, the machinery, services, means and aids ensuring propulsion, ability to steer, safe navigation, fire and flooding safety, internal and external communications and signals, means of escape, and emergency boat winches, as well as the designed comfortable conditions of habitability are in working order and functioning normally.

6   *Emergency condition* is a condition under which any services needed for normal operational and habitable conditions are not in working order due to failure of the main source of electrical power.

7   *Main source of electrical power* is a source intended to supply electrical power to the main switchboard for distribution to all services necessary for maintaining the ship in normal operational and habitable conditions.

8   *Dead ship condition* is the condition under which the main propulsion plant, boilers and auxiliaries are not in operation due to the absence of power.

9   *Main generating station* is the space in which the main source of electrical power is situated.

10   *Main switchboard* is a switchboard which is directly supplied by the main source of electrical power and is intended to distribute electrical energy to the ship's services.

11   *Emergency switchboard* is a switchboard which in the event of failure of the main electrical power supply system is directly supplied by the emergency source of electrical power or the transitional source of emergency power and is intended to distribute electrical energy to the emergency services.

12   *Emergency source of electrical power* is a source of electrical power, intended to supply the emergency switchboard in the event of failure of the supply from the main source of electrical power.

13   *Power actuating system* is the hydraulic equipment provided for supplying power to turn the rudder stock, comprising a steering gear power unit or units, together with the associated pipes and fittings, and a rudder actuator. The power actuating systems may share common mechanical components, i.e., tiller, quadrant and rudder stock, or components serving the same purpose.

14   *Maximum ahead service speed* is the greatest speed which the ship is designed to maintain in service at sea at the deepest seagoing draught.

15   *Maximum astern speed* is the speed which it is estimated the ship can attain at the designed maximum astern power at the deepest seagoing draught.

16   *Machinery spaces* are all machinery spaces of category A and all other spaces containing propelling machinery, boilers, oil fuel units, steam and internal combustion engines, generators and major electrical machinery, oil filling stations, refrigerating, stabilizing, ventilation and air conditioning machinery, and similar spaces, and trunks to such spaces.

17   *Machinery spaces of category A* are those spaces and trunks to such spaces which contain:

.1   internal combustion machinery used for main propulsion; or

.2   internal combustion machinery used for purposes other than main propulsion where such machinery has in the aggregate a total power output of not less than 375 kW; or

.3   any oil-fired boiler or oil fuel unit.

18   *Control stations* are those spaces in which the ship's radio or main navigating equipment or the emergency source of power is located or where the fire recording or fire control equipment is centralized.

19   *Chemical tanker* is a cargo ship constructed or adapted and used for the carriage in bulk of any liquid product listed in either:

.1   chapter 17 of the International Code for the Construction and Equipment of Ships Carrying Dangerous Chemicals in Bulk adopted by the Maritime Safety Committee by resolution MSC.4(48) hereinafter referred to as "the International Bulk Chemical Code", as may be amended by the Organization; or

.2   chapter VI of the Code for the Construction and Equipment of Ships Carrying Dangerous Chemicals in Bulk adopted by the Assembly of the Organization by resolution A.212(VII), hereinafter referred to as "the Bulk Chemical Code", as has been or may be amended by the Organization;

whichever is applicable.

20   *Gas carrier* is a cargo ship constructed or adapted and used for the carriage in bulk of any liquefied gas or other products listed in either:

.1   chapter 19 of the International Code for the Construction and Equipment of Ships Carrying Liquefied Gases in Bulk adopted by the Maritime Safety Committee by resolution MSC.5(48) hereinafter referred to as "the International Gas Carrier Code", as may be amended by the Organization; or

.2   chapter XIX of the Code for the Construction and Equipment of Ships Carrying Liquefied Gases in Bulk adopted by the Organization by resolution A.328(IX), hereinafter referred to as "the Gas Carrier Code", as has been or may be amended by the Organization; whichever is applicable.

21   *Deadweight* is the difference in tonnes between the displacement of a ship in water of a specific gravity of 1.025 at the load waterline corresponding to the assigned summer freeboard and the lightweight of the ship.

22   *Lightweight* is the displacement of a ship in tonnes without cargo, fuel, lubricating oil, ballast water, fresh water and feedwater in tanks, consumable stores, and passengers and crew and their effects.

PART B – SUBDIVISION AND STABILITY*

(Part B applies to passenger ships and to cargo ships, as indicated in the regulations)

Regulation 4

Floodable length in passenger ships

1   The floodable length at any point of the length of a ship shall be determined by a method of calculation which takes into consideration the form, draught and other characteristics of the ship in question.

2   In a ship with a continuous bulkhead deck, the floodable length at a given point is the maximum portion of the length of the ship, having its centre at the point in question, which can be flooded under the definite assumptions set forth in regulation 5 without the ship being submerged beyond the margin line.

3.1   In the case of a ship not having a continuous bulkhead deck, the floodable length at any point may be determined to an assumed continuous margin line which at no point is less than 76 mm below the top of the deck (at side) to which the bulkheads concerned and the shell are carried watertight.

---

* Instead of the requirements in this part, the Regulations on Subdivision and Stability of Passenger Ships as an Equivalent to part B of chapter II of the International Convention for the Safety of Life at Sea, 1960, adopted by the Organization by resolution A.265(VIII), may be used, if applied in their entirety.

3.2   Where a portion of an assumed margin line is appreciably below the deck to which bulkheads are carried, the Administration may permit a limited relaxation in the watertightness of those portions of the bulkheads which are above the margin line and immediately under the higher deck.

Regulation 5

Permeability in passenger ships

1.1   The definite assumptions referred to in regulation 4 relate to the permeability of the spaces below the margin line.

1.2   In determining the floodable length, a uniform average permeability shall be used throughout the whole length of each of the following portions of the ship below the margin line:

.1   the machinery space as defined in regulation 2;

.2   the portion forward of the machinery space; and

.3   the portion abaft the machinery space.

2.1   The uniform average permeability throughout the machinery space shall be determined from the formula:

$$85 + 10\left(\frac{a - c}{v}\right)$$

where:

a = the volume of the passenger spaces, as defined in regulation 2, which are situated below the margin line within the limits of the machinery space;

c = the volume of between-deck spaces below the margin line within the limits of the machinery space which are appropriated to cargo, coal or stores;

v = the whole volume of the machinery space below the margin line.

2.2   Where it is shown to the satisfaction of the Administration that the average permeability as determined by detailed calculation is less than that given by the formula, the detailed calculated value may be used. For the purpose of such calculation, the permeability of passenger spaces, as defined in regulation 2, shall be taken as 95, that of all cargo, coal and store spaces as 60, and that of double bottom, oil fuel and other tanks at such value as may be approved in each case.

3   Except as provided in paragraph 4, the uniform average permeability throughout the portion of the ship forward of or abaft the machinery space shall be determined from the formula:

$$63 + 35\frac{a}{v}$$

where:

a = the volume of the passenger spaces, as defined in regulation 2, which are situated below the margin line, forward of or abaft the machinery space; and

v = the whole volume of the portion of the ship below the margin line forward of or abaft the machinery space.

4.1   In the case of special subdivision required in regulation 6.5, the uniform average permeability throughout the portion of the ship forward of or abaft the machinery space shall be 95–35 b/v where:

b = the volume of the spaces below the margin line and above the tops of floors, inner bottom, or peak tanks, as the case may be, which are appropriated to and used as cargo spaces, coal or oil fuel bunkers, store-rooms, baggage and mail rooms, chain lockers and fresh water tanks, forward of or abaft the machinery space; and

v = the whole volume of the portion of the ship below the margin line forward of or abaft the machinery space.

4.2   In the case of ships engaged on services where the cargo holds are not generally occupied by any substantial quantities of cargo, no part of the cargo spaces is to be included in calculating "b".

5   In the case of unusual arrangements the Administration may allow, or require, a detailed calculation of average permeability for the portions forward of or abaft the machinery space. For the purpose of such calculation, the permeability of passenger spaces as defined in regulation 2 shall be taken as 95, that of spaces containing machinery as 85, that of all cargo, coal and store spaces as 60, and that of double bottom, oil fuel and other tanks at such value as may be approved in each case.

6   Where a between-deck compartment between two watertight transverse bulkheads contains any passenger or crew space, the whole of that compartment, less any space completely enclosed within permanent steel bulkheads and appropriated to other purposes, shall be regarded as passenger space. Where, however, the passenger or crew space in question is completely enclosed within permanent steel bulkheads, only the space so enclosed need be considered as passenger space.

Regulation 6

Permissible length of compartments in passenger ships

1   Ships shall be as efficiently subdivided as is possible having regard to the nature of the service for which they are intended. The degree of subdivision shall vary with the length of the ship and with the service, in such manner that the highest degree of subdivision corresponds with the ships of greatest length, primarily engaged in the carriage of passengers.

2   *Factor of subdivision*

2.1   The maximum permissible length of a compartment having its centre at any point in the ship's length is obtained from the floodable length by multiplying the latter by an appropriate factor called the factor of subdivision.

2.2   The factor of subdivision shall depend on the length of the ship, and for a given length shall vary according to the nature of the service for which the ship is intended. It shall decrease in a regular and continuous manner.

.1   as the length of the ship increases, and

.2   from a factor A, applicable to ships primarily engaged in the carriage of cargo, to a factor B, applicable to ships primarily engaged in the carriage of passengers.

2.3   The variations of the factors A and B shall be expressed by the following formulae (1) and (2) where L is the length of the ship as defined in regulation 2:

$$A = \frac{58.2}{L - 60} + .18\,(L = 131\text{ m and upwards})\tag{1}$$

$$B = \frac{30.3}{L - 42} + .18\,(L = 79\text{ m and upwards})\tag{2}$$

3   *Criterion of service*

3.1   For a ship of given length the appropriate factor of subdivision shall be determined by the criterion of service numeral (hereinafter called the criterion numeral) as given by the following formulae (3) and (4) where:

C_s = the criterion numeral;

L = the length of the ship (metres), as defined in regulation 2;

M = the volume of the machinery space (cubic metres), as defined in regulation 2; with the addition thereto of the volume of any permanent oil fuel bunkers which may be situated above the inner bottom and forward of or abaft the machinery space;

P = the whole volume of the passenger spaces below the margin line (cubic metres), as defined in regulation 2;

V = the whole volume of the ship below the margin line (cubic metres);

P_1 = KN where:

N = the number of passengers for which the ship is to be certified, and

K = 0.056L

3.2   Where the value of KN is greater than the sum of P and the whole volume of the actual passenger spaces above the margin line, the figure to be taken as P_1 is that sum or two-thirds KN, whichever is the greater.

When P_1 is greater than P –

$$C_s = 72\frac{M + 2P_1}{V + P_1 - P} \tag{3}$$

and in other cases –

$$C_s = 72\frac{M + 2P}{V} \tag{4}$$

3.3   For ships not having a continuous bulkhead deck the volumes are to be taken up to the actual margin lines used in determining the floodable lengths.

4   *Rules for subdivision of ships other than those covered by paragraph 5*

4.1   The subdivision abaft the forepeak of ships of 131 m in length and upwards having a criterion numeral of 23 or less shall be governed by the factor A given by formula (1); of those having a criterion numeral of 123 or more by the factor B given by formula (2); and of those having a criterion numeral between 23 and 123 by the factor F obtained by linear interpolation between the factors A and B, using the formula:

$$F = A - \frac{(A - B)(C_s - 23)}{100} \tag{5}$$

Nevertheless, where the criterion numeral is equal to 45 or more and simultaneously the computed factor of subdivision as given by formula (5) is .65 or less, but more than .50, the subdivision abaft the forepeak shall be governed by the factor .50.

4.2   Where the factor F is less than .40 and it is shown to the satisfaction of the Administration to be impracticable to comply with the factor F in a machinery compartment of the ship, the subdivision of such compartment may be governed by an increased factor, which, however, shall not exceed .40.

4.3   The subdivision abaft the forepeak of ships of less than 131 m but not less than 79 m in length having a criterion numeral equal to S, where:

$$S = \frac{3{,}574 - 25L}{13}$$

shall be governed by the factor unity; of those having a criterion numeral of 123 or more by the factor B given by the formula (2); of those having a criterion numeral between S and 123 by the factor F obtained by linear interpolation between unity and the factor B using the formula:

$$F = 1 - \frac{(1 - B)(C_s - S)}{123 - S} \qquad (6)$$

4.4   The subdivision abaft the forepeak of ships of less than 131 m but not less than 79 m in length and having a criterion numeral less than S, and of ships of less than 79 m in length shall be governed by the factor unity, unless, in either case, it is shown to the satisfaction of the Administration to be impracticable to comply with this factor in any part of the ship, in which case the Administration may allow such relaxation as may appear to be justified, having regard to all the circumstances.

4.5   The provisions of paragraph 4.4 shall apply also to ships of whatever length, which are to be certified to carry a number of passengers exceeding 12 but not exceeding –

$$\frac{L^2}{650} \text{, or 50, whichever is the less.}$$

5   *Special subdivision standards for ships complying with regulation III/20.1.2*

5.1.1   In the case of ships primarily engaged in the carriage of passengers, the subdivision abaft the forepeak shall be governed by a factor of .50 or by the factor determined according to paragraphs 3 and 4, if less than .50.

5.1.2   In the case of such ships of less than 91.5 m in length, if the Administration is satisfied that compliance with such factor would be impracticable in a compartment, it may allow the length of that compartment to be governed by a higher factor provided the factor used is the lowest that is practicable and reasonable in the circumstances.

5.2   Where, in the case of any ship whether of less than 91.5 m or not, the necessity of carrying appreciable quantities of cargo makes it impracticable to require the subdivision abaft the forepeak to be governed by a factor not exceeding .50, the standard of subdivision to be applied shall be determined in accordance with the following subparagraphs .1 to .5, subject to the condition that where the Administration is satisfied that insistence on strict compliance in any respect would be unreasonable, it may allow such alternative arrangement of the watertight bulkheads as appears to be justified on merits and will not diminish the general effectiveness of the subdivision.

.1 The provisions of paragraph 3 relating to the criterion numeral shall apply with the exception that in calculating the value of P_1 for berthed passengers K is to have the value defined in paragraph 3, or $3.5 \, m^3$, whichever is the greater, and for unberthed passengers K is to have the value $3.5 \, m^3$.

.2 The factor B in paragraph 2 shall be replaced by the factor BB determined by the following formula:

$$BB = \frac{17.6}{L - 33} + .20 \ (L = 55 \, m \text{ and upwards})$$

.3 The subdivision abaft the forepeak of ships of 131 m in length and upwards having a criterion numeral of 23 or less shall be governed by the factor A given by formula (1) in paragraph 2.3; of those having a criterion numeral of 123 or more by the factor BB given by the formula in paragraph 5.2.2; and of those having a criterion numeral between 23 and 123 by the factor F obtained by linear interpolation between the factors A and BB, using the formula:

$$F = A - \frac{(A - BB)(C_s - 23)}{100}$$

except that if the factor F so obtained is less than .50 the factor to be used shall be either .50 or the factor calculated according to the provisions of paragraph 4.1, whichever is the smaller.

.4 The subdivision abaft the forepeak of ships of less than 131 m but not less than 55 m in length having a criterion numeral equal to S_1 where –

$$S_1 = \frac{3,712 - 25L}{19}$$

shall be governed by the factor unity; of those having a criterion numeral of 123 or more by the factor BB given by the formula in paragraph 5.2.2; of those having a criterion numeral between S_1 and 123 by the factor F obtained by linear interpolation between unity and the factor BB using the formula:

$$F = 1 - \frac{(1 - BB)(C_s - S_1)}{123 - S_1}$$

except that in either of the two latter cases if the factor so obtained is less than .50 the subdivision may be governed by a factor not exceeding .50.

.5 The subdivision abaft the forepeak of ships of less than 131 m but not less than 55 m in length and having a criterion numeral less than S_1 and of ships of less than 55 m in length shall be governed by the factor unity, unless it is shown to the satisfaction of the Administration to be impracticable to comply with this factor in particular compartments, in which event the Administration may allow such relaxations in respect of those compartments as appear to be justified, having regard to all the circumstances, provided that the aftermost compartment and as many as possible of the forward compartments (between the forepeak and the after end of the machinery space) shall be kept within the floodable length.

5.3   The special provisions regarding permeability given in regulation 5.4 shall be employed when calculating the floodable length curves.

5.4   Where the Administration is satisfied that, having regard to the nature and conditions of the intended voyages compliance with the other provisions of this chapter and of chapter II–2 is sufficient, the requirements of this paragraph need not be complied with.

Regulation 7

Special requirements concerning passenger ship subdivision

1   Where in a portion or portions of a ship the watertight bulkheads are carried to a higher deck than in the remainder of the ship and it is desired to take advantage of this higher extension of the bulkheads in calculating the floodable length, separate margin lines may be used for each such portion of the ship provided that:

.1   the sides of the ship are extended throughout the ship's length to the deck corresponding to the upper margin line and all openings in the shell plating below this deck throughout the length of the ship are treated as being below a margin line, for the purposes of regulation 17; and

.2   the two compartments adjacent to the "step" in the bulkhead deck are each within the permissible length corresponding to their respective margin lines, and, in addition, their combined length does not exceed twice the permissible length based on the lower margin line.

2.1   A compartment may exceed the permissible length determined by the rules of regulation 6 provided the combined length of each pair of adjacent compartments to which the compartment in question is common does not exceed either the floodable length or twice the permissible length, whichever is the less.

2.2   If one of the two adjacent compartments is situated inside the machinery space, and the second is situated outside the machinery space, and the average permeability of the portion of the ship in which the second is situated differs from that of the machinery space, the combined length of the two compartments shall be adjusted to the mean average permeability of the two portions of the ship in which the compartments are situated.

2.3 Where the two adjacent compartments have different factors of subdivision, the combined length of the two compartments shall be determined proportionately.

3 In ships of 100 m in length and upwards, one of the main transverse bulkheads abaft the forepeak shall be fitted at a distance from the forward perpendicular which is not greater than the permissible length.

4 A main transverse bulkhead may be recessed provided that all parts of the recess lie inboard of vertical surfaces on both sides of the ship, situated at a distance from the shell plating equal to one-fifth the breadth of the ship, as defined in regulation 2, and measured at right angles to the centreline at the level of the deepest subdivision load line. Any part of a recess which lies outside these limits shall be dealt with as a step in accordance with paragraph 5.

5 A main transverse bulkhead may be stepped provided that it meets one of the following conditions:

.1 the combined length of the two compartments, separated by the bulkhead in question, does not exceed either 90 per cent of the floodable length or twice the permissible length, except that, in ships having a factor of subdivision greater than .9, the combined length of the two compartments in question shall not exceed the permissible length;

.2 additional subdivision is provided in way of the step to maintain the same measure of safety as that secured by a plane bulkhead;

.3 the compartment over which the step extends does not exceed the permissible length corresponding to a margin line taken 76 mm below the step.

6 Where a main transverse bulkhead is recessed or stepped, an equivalent plane bulkhead shall be used in determining the subdivision.

7 If the distance between two adjacent main transverse bulkheads, or their equivalent plane bulkheads, or the distance between the transverse planes passing through the nearest stepped portions of the bulkheads, is less than 3.0 m plus 3 per cent of the length of the ship, or 11.0 m whichever is the less, only one of these bulkheads shall be regarded as forming part of the subdivision of the ship in accordance with the provisions of regulation 6.

8 Where a main transverse watertight compartment contains local subdivision and it can be shown to the satisfaction of the Administration that, after

any assumed side damage extending over a length of 3.0 m plus 3 per cent of the length of the ship, or 11.0 m whichever is the less, the whole volume of the main compartment will not be flooded, a proportionate allowance may be made in the permissible length otherwise required for such compartment. In such a case the volume of effective buoyancy assumed on the undamaged side shall not be greater than that assumed on the damaged side.

9   Where the required factor of subdivision is .50 or less, the combined length of any two adjacent compartments shall not exceed the floodable length.

Regulation 8

Stability of passenger ships in damaged condition

1.1   Sufficient intact stability shall be provided in all service conditions so as to enable the ship to withstand the final stage of flooding of any one main compartment which is required to be within the floodable length.

1.2   Where two adjacent main compartments are separated by a bulkhead which is stepped under the conditions of regulation 7.5.1 the intact stability shall be adequate to withstand the flooding of those two adjacent main compartments.

1.3   Where the required factor of subdivision is .50 or less but more than .33 intact stability shall be adequate to withstand the flooding of any two adjacent main compartments.

1.4   Where the required factor of subdivision is .33 or less the intact stability shall be adequate to withstand the flooding of any three adjacent main compartments.

2.1   The requirements of paragraph 1 shall be determined by calculations which are in accordance with paragraphs 3, 4 and 6 and which take into consideration the proportions and design characteristics of the ship and the arrangement and configuration of the damaged compartments. In making these calculations the ship is to be assumed in the worst anticipated service condition as regards stability.

2.2   Where it is proposed to fit decks, inner skins or longitudinal bulkheads of sufficient tightness to seriously restrict the flow of water, the Administration shall be satisfied that proper consideration is given to such restrictions in the calculations.

2.3   In cases where the Administration considers the range of stability in the damaged condition to be doubtful, it may require investigation thereof.

3   For the purpose of making damage stability calculations the volume and surface permeabilities shall be in general as follows:

Spaces	Permeability
Appropriated to cargo, coal or stores	60
Occupied by accommodation	95
Occupied by machinery	85
Intended for liquids	0 or 95*

* Whichever results in the more severe requirements.

Higher surface permeabilities are to be assumed in respect of spaces which, in the vicinity of the damage waterplane, contain no substantial quantity of accommodation or machinery and spaces which are not generally occupied by any substantial quantity of cargo or stores.

4   Assumed extent of damage shall be as follows:

.1   longitudinal extent: 3.0 m plus 3 per cent of the length of the ship, or 11.0 m whichever is the less. Where the required factor of subdivision is .33 or less the assumed longitudinal extent of damage shall be increased as necessary so as to include any two consecutive main transverse watertight bulkheads;

.2   transverse extent (measured inboard from the ship's side, at right angles to the centreline at the level of the deepest subdivision load line): a distance of one fifth of the breadth of the ship, as defined in regulation 2; and

.3   vertical extent: from the base line upwards without limit;

.4   if any damage of lesser extent than that indicated in paragraphs 4.1, 4.2 and 4.3 would result in a more severe condition regarding heel or loss of metacentric height, such damage shall be assumed in the calculations.

5   Unsymmetrical flooding is to be kept to a minimum consistent with efficient arrangements. Where it is necessary to correct large angles of heel, the means adopted shall, where practicable, be self-acting, but in any case where controls to cross-flooding fittings are provided they shall be operable from above the bulkhead deck. These fittings together with their controls as well as the maximum heel before equalization shall be acceptable to the Administration. Where cross-flooding fittings are required the time for equalization shall not exceed 15 minutes. Suitable information concerning the use of cross-flooding fittings shall be supplied to the master of the ship.*

---

* Reference is made to the Recommendation on a Standard Method for Establishing Compliance with the Requirements for Cross-Flooding Arrangements in Passenger Ships, adopted by the Organization by resolution A.266(VIII).

6   The final conditions of the ship after damage and, in the case of unsymmetrical flooding, after equalization measures have been taken shall be as follows:

.1   in the case of symmetrical flooding there shall be a positive residual metacentric height of at least 50 mm as calculated by the constant displacement method;

.2   in the case of unsymmetrical flooding the total heel shall not exceed 7°, except that, in special cases, the Administration may allow additional heel due to the unsymmetrical moment, but in no case shall the final heel exceed 15°;

.3   in no case shall the margin line be submerged in the final stage of flooding. If it is considered that the margin line may become submerged during an intermediate stage of flooding, the Administration may require such investigations and arrangements as it considers necessary for the safety of the ship.

7   The master of the ship shall be supplied with the data necessary to maintain sufficient intact stability under service conditions to enable the ship to withstand the critical damage. In the case of ships requiring cross-flooding the master of the ship shall be informed of the conditions of stability on which the calculations of heel are based and be warned that excessive heeling might result should the ship sustain damage when in a less favourable condition.

8.1   No relaxation from the requirements for damage stability may be considered by the Administration unless it is shown that the intact metacentric height in any service condition necessary to meet these requirements is excessive for the service intended.

8.2   Relaxations from the requirements for damage stability shall be permitted only in exceptional cases and subject to the condition that the Administration is to be satisfied that the proportions, arrangements and other characteristics of the ship are the most favourable to stability after damage which can practically and reasonably be adopted in the particular circumstances.

Regulation 9

Ballasting of passenger ships

1   Water ballast should not in general be carried in tanks intended for oil fuel. In ships in which it is not practicable to avoid putting water in oil fuel tanks, oily-water separating equipment to the satisfaction of the Administration shall be fitted, or other alternative means, such as discharge to shore

facilities, acceptable to the Administration shall be provided for disposing of the oily-water ballast.

2   The provisions of this regulation are without prejudice to the provisions of the International Convention for the Prevention of Pollution from Ships in force.

Regulation 10

Peak and machinery space bulkheads, shaft tunnels, etc. in passenger ships

1   A forepeak or collision bulkhead shall be fitted which shall be watertight up to the bulkhead deck. This bulkhead shall be located at a distance from the forward perpendicular of not less than 5 per cent of the length of the ship and not more than 3 m plus 5 per cent of the length of the ship.

2   Where any part of the ship below the waterline extends forward of the forward perpendicular, e.g. a bulbous bow, the distances stipulated in paragraph 1 shall be measured from a point either:

.1   at the mid-length of such extension; or

.2   at a distance 1.5 per cent of the length of the ship forward of the forward perpendicular; or

.3   at a distance 3 m forward of the forward perpendicular;

whichever gives the smallest measurement.

3   Where a long forward superstructure is fitted, the forepeak or collision bulkhead shall be extended weathertight to the deck next above the bulkhead deck. The extension need not be fitted directly above the bulkhead below provided it is located within the limits specified in paragraph 1 or 2 with the exemption permitted by paragraph 4 and the part of the deck which forms the step is made effectively weathertight.

4   Where bow doors are fitted and a sloping loading ramp forms part of the extension of the collision bulkhead above the bulkhead deck the part of the ramp which is more than 2.3 m above the bulkhead deck may extend forward of the limit specified in paragraphs 1 and 2. The ramp shall be weathertight over its complete length.

5   An afterpeak bulkhead, and bulkheads dividing the machinery space, as defined in regulation 2, from the cargo and passenger spaces forward and aft, shall also be fitted and made watertight up to the bulkhead deck. The afterpeak bulkhead may, however, be stepped below the bulkhead deck, provided the degree of safety of the ship as regards subdivision is not thereby diminished.

6   In all cases stern tubes shall be enclosed in watertight spaces of moderate volume. The stern gland shall be situated in a watertight shaft tunnel or other watertight space separate from the stern tube compartment and of such volume that, if flooded by leakage through the stern gland, the margin line will not be submerged.

Regulation 11 $\boxed{\text{F}}$

Collision bulkheads in cargo ships

1   For the purpose of this regulation "freeboard deck", "length of ship" and "forward perpendicular" have the meanings as defined in the International Convention on Load Lines in force.

2   A collision bulkhead shall be fitted which shall be watertight up to the freeboard deck. This bulkhead shall be located at a distance from the forward perpendicular of not less than 5 per cent of the length of the ship or 10 m, whichever is the less, and, except as may be permitted by the Administration, not more than 8 per cent of the length of the ship.

3   Where any part of the ship below the waterline extends forward of the forward perpendicular, e.g. a bulbous bow, the distances stipulated in paragraph 2 shall be measured from a point either:

.1   at the mid-length of such extension; or

.2   at a distance 1.5 per cent of the length of the ship forward of the forward perpendicular; or

.3   at a distance 3 m forward of the forward perpendicular;

whichever gives the smallest measurement.

4   The bulkhead may have steps or recesses provided they are within the limits prescribed in paragraph 2 or 3. Pipes piercing the collision bulkhead shall be fitted with suitable valves operable from above the freeboard deck and the valve chest shall be secured at the bulkhead inside the forepeak. The valves may be fitted on the after side of the collision bulkhead provided that the valves are readily accessible under all service conditions and the space in which they are located is not a cargo space. All valves shall be of steel, bronze or other approved ductile material. Valves of ordinary cast iron or similar material are not acceptable. No door, manhole, ventilation duct or any other opening shall be fitted in this bulkhead.

5   Where a long forward superstructure is fitted the collision bulkhead shall be extended weathertight to the deck next above the freeboard deck. The

---

$\boxed{\text{F}}$ See Annex 2.

extension need not be fitted directly above the bulkhead below provided it is located within the limits prescribed in paragraph 2 or 3 with the exemption permitted by paragraph 6 and the part of the deck which forms the step is made effectively weathertight.

6   Where bow doors are fitted and a sloping loading ramp forms part of the extension of the collision bulkhead above the freeboard deck the part of the ramp which is more than 2.3 m above the freeboard deck may extend forward of the limit specified in paragraph 2 or 3. The ramp shall be weathertight over its complete length.

7   The number of openings in the extension of the collision bulkhead above the freeboard deck shall be restricted to the minimum compatible with the design and normal operation of the ship. All such openings shall be capable of being closed weathertight.

Regulation 12

Double bottoms in passenger ships

1   A double bottom shall be fitted extending from the forepeak bulkhead to the afterpeak bulkhead as far as this is practicable and compatible with the design and proper working of the ship.

.1   In ships of 50 m and upwards but less than 61 m in length a double bottom shall be fitted at least from the machinery space to the forepeak bulkhead, or as near thereto as practicable.

.2   In ships of 61 m and upwards but less than 76 m in length a double bottom shall be fitted at least outside the machinery space, and shall extend to the fore and after peak bulkheads, or as near thereto as practicable.

.3   In ships of 76 m in length and upwards, a double bottom shall be fitted amidships, and shall extend to the fore and after peak bulkheads, or as near thereto as practicable.

2   Where a double bottom is required to be fitted its depth shall be to the satisfaction of the Administration and the inner bottom shall be continued out to the ship's sides in such a manner as to protect the bottom to the turn of the bilge. Such protection will be deemed satisfactory if the line of intersection of the outer edge of the margin plate with the bilge plating is not lower at any part than a horizontal plane passing through the point of intersection with the frame line amidships of a transverse diagonal line inclined at 25° to the base line and cutting it at a point one-half the ship's moulded breadth from the middle line.

3   Small wells constructed in the double bottom in connection with drainage arrangements of holds, etc., shall not extend downwards more than necessary. The depth of the well shall in no case be more than the depth less 460 mm of the double bottom at the centreline, nor shall the well extend below the horizontal plane referred to in paragraph 2. A well extending to the outer bottom is, however, permitted at the after end of the shaft tunnel. Other wells (e.g., for lubricating oil under main engines) may be permitted by the Administration if satisfied that the arrangements give protection equivalent to that afforded by a double bottom complying with this regulation.

4   A double bottom need not be fitted in way of watertight compartments of moderate size used exclusively for the carriage of liquids, provided the safety of the ship, in the event of bottom or side damage, is not, in the opinion of the Administration, thereby impaired.

5   In the case of ships to which the provisions of regulation 1.5 apply and which are engaged on regular service within the limits of a short international voyage as defined in regulation III/3.16, the Administration may permit a double bottom to be dispensed with in any part of the ship which is subdivided by a factor not exceeding .50, if satisfied that the fitting of a double bottom in that part would not be compatible with the design and proper working of the ship.

Regulation 13

*Assigning, marking and recording of subdivision load lines
for passenger ships*

1   In order that the required degree of subdivision shall be maintained, a load line corresponding to the approved subdivision draught shall be assigned and marked on the ship's sides. A ship having spaces which are specially adapted for the accommodation of passengers and the carriage of cargo alternatively may, if the owners desire, have one or more additional load lines assigned and marked to correspond with the subdivision draughts which the Administration may approve for the alternative service conditions.

2   The subdivision load lines assigned and marked shall be recorded in the Passenger Ship Safety Certificate, and shall be distinguished by the notation C.1 for the principal passenger condition, and C.2, C.3, etc., for the alternative conditions.

3   The freeboard corresponding to each of these load lines shall be measured at the same position and from the same deck line as the freeboards determined in accordance with the International Convention on Load Lines in force.

4   The freeboard corresponding to each approved subdivision load line and the conditions of service for which it is approved, shall be clearly indicated on the Passenger Ship Safety Certificate.

5   In no case shall any subdivision load line mark be placed above the deepest load line in salt water as determined by the strength of the ship or the International Convention on Load Lines in force.

6   Whatever may be the position of the subdivision load line marks, a ship shall in no case be loaded so as to submerge the load line mark appropriate to the season and locality as determined in accordance with the International Convention on Load Lines in force.

7   A ship shall in no case be so loaded that when it is in salt water the subdivision load line mark appropriate to the particular voyage and condition of service is submerged.

Regulation 14

Construction and initial testing of watertight bulkheads, etc. in passenger ships and cargo ships

1   Each watertight subdivision bulkhead, whether transverse or longitudinal, shall be constructed in such a manner that it shall be capable of supporting, with a proper margin of resistance, the pressure due to the maximum head of water which it might have to sustain in the event of damage to the ship but at least the pressure due to a head of water up to the margin line. The construction of these bulkheads shall be to the satisfaction of the Administration.

2.1   Steps and recesses in bulkheads shall be watertight and as strong as the bulkhead at the place where each occurs.

2.2   Where frames or beams pass through a watertight deck or bulkhead, such deck or bulkhead shall be made structurally watertight without the use of wood or cement.

3   Testing main compartments by filling them with water is not compulsory. When testing by filling with water is not carried out, a hose test is compulsory; this test shall be carried out in the most advanced stage of the fitting out of the ship. In any case, a thorough inspection of the watertight bulkheads shall be carried out.

4   The forepeak, double bottoms (including duct keels) and inner skins shall be tested with water to a head corresponding to the requirements of paragraph 1.

5   Tanks which are intended to hold liquids, and which form part of the subdivision of the ship, shall be tested for tightness with water to a head up to the deepest subdivision load line or to a head corresponding to two-thirds of the depth from the top of keel to the margin line in way of the tanks, whichever is the greater; provided that in no case shall the test head be less than 0.9 m above the top of the tank.

6   The tests referred to in paragraphs 4 and 5 are for the purpose of ensuring that the subdivision structural arrangements are watertight and are not to be regarded as a test of the fitness of any compartment for the storage of oil fuel or for other special purposes for which a test of a superior character may be required depending on the height to which the liquid has access in the tank or its connections.

Regulation 15

Openings in watertight bulkheads in passenger ships

1   The number of openings in watertight bulkheads shall be reduced to the minimum compatible with the design and proper working of the ship; satisfactory means shall be provided for closing these openings.

2.1   Where pipes, scuppers, electric cables, etc., are carried through watertight subdivision bulkheads, arrangements shall be made to ensure the watertight integrity of the bulkheads.

2.2   Valves not forming part of a piping system shall not be permitted in watertight subdivision bulkheads.

2.3   Lead or other heat sensitive materials shall not be used in systems which penetrate watertight subdivision bulkheads, where deterioration of such systems in the event of fire would impair the watertight integrity of the bulkheads.

3.1   No doors, manholes, or access openings are permitted:

    .1   in the collision bulkhead below the margin line;

    .2   in watertight transverse bulkheads dividing a cargo space from an adjoining cargo space or from a permanent or reserve bunker, except as provided in paragraph 12 and in regulation 16.

3.2   Except as provided in paragraph 3.3 the collision bulkhead may be pierced below the margin line by not more than one pipe for dealing with fluid in the forepeak tank, provided that the pipe is fitted with a screwdown valve capable of being operated from above the bulkhead deck, the valve chest being secured inside the forepeak to the collision bulkhead.

3.3   If the forepeak is divided to hold two different kinds of liquids the Administration may allow the collision bulkhead to be pierced below the margin line by two pipes, each of which is fitted as required by paragraph 3.2, provided the Administration is satisfied that there is no practical alternative to the fitting of such a second pipe and that, having regard to the additional subdivision provided in the forepeak, the safety of the ship is maintained.

4.1   Watertight doors fitted in bulkheads between permanent and reserve bunkers shall be always accessible, except as provided in paragraph 11.2 for between-deck bunker doors.

4.2   Satisfactory arrangements shall be made by means of screens or otherwise to prevent the coal from interfering with the closing of watertight bunker doors.

5   Within spaces containing the main and auxiliary propulsion machinery including boilers serving the needs of propulsion and all permanent bunkers, not more than one door apart from the doors to bunkers and shaft tunnels may be fitted in each main transverse bulkhead. Where two or more shafts are fitted the tunnels shall be connected by an intercommunicating passage. There shall be only one door between the machinery space and the tunnel spaces where two shafts are fitted and only two doors where there are more than two shafts. All these doors shall be of the sliding type and shall be so located as to have their sills as high as practicable. The hand gear for operating these doors from above the bulkhead deck shall be situated outside the spaces containing the machinery if this is consistent with a satisfactory arrangement of the necessary gearing.

6.1   Watertight doors shall be sliding doors or hinged doors or doors of an equivalent type. Plate doors secured only by bolts and doors required to be closed by dropping or by the action of a dropping weight are not permitted.

6.2   Sliding doors may be either:

hand-operated only, or

power-operated as well as hand-operated.

6.3   Authorized watertight doors may therefore be divided into three classes:

class 1 – hinged doors;

class 2 – hand-operated sliding doors;

class 3 – sliding doors which are power-operated as well as hand-operated.

6.4   The means of operation of any watertight door whether power-operated or not shall be capable of closing the door with the ship listed to 15° either way.

6.5 In all classes of watertight doors indicators shall be fitted which show, at all operating stations from which the doors are not visible, whether the doors are open or closed. If any of the watertight doors, of whatever class, is not fitted so as to enable it to be closed from a central control station, it shall be provided with a mechanical, electrical, telephonic, or any other suitable direct means of communication, enabling the officer of the watch promptly to contact the person who is responsible for closing the door in question, under previous orders.

7 Hinged doors (class 1) shall be fitted with quick action closing devices, such as catches, workable from each side of the bulkhead.

8 Hand-operated sliding doors (class 2) may have a horizontal or vertical motion. It shall be possible to operate the mechanism at the door itself from either side, and in addition, from an accessible position above the bulkhead deck, with an all round crank motion, or some other movement providing the same guarantee of safety and of an approved type. Departures from the requirement of operation on both sides may be allowed, if this requirement is impossible owing to the layout of the spaces. When operating a hand gear the time necessary for the complete closure of the door with the vessel upright, shall not exceed 90 seconds.

9.1 Power-operated sliding doors (class 3) may have a vertical or horizontal motion. If a door is required to be power-operated from a central control, the gearing shall be so arranged that the door can be operated by power also at the door itself from both sides. The arrangement shall be such that the door will close automatically if opened by local control after being closed from the central control, and also such that any door can be kept closed by local systems which will prevent the door from being opened from the upper control. Local control handles in connection with the power gear shall be provided each side of the bulkhead and shall be so arranged as to enable persons passing through the doorway to hold both handles in the open position without being able to set the closing mechanism in operation accidentally. Power-operated sliding doors shall be provided with hand gear workable at the door itself on either side and from an accessible position above the bulkhead deck, with an all round crank motion or some other movement providing the same guarantee of safety and of an approved type. Provision shall be made to give warnings by sound signal that the door has begun to close and will continue to move until it is completely closed. The door shall take a sufficient time to close to ensure safety.

9.2 There shall be at least two independent power sources capable of opening and closing all the doors under control, each of them capable of operating all the doors simultaneously. The two power sources shall be controlled from the central station on the navigating bridge provided with all the necessary indicators for checking that each of the two power sources is capable of giving the required service satisfactorily.

9.3 In the case of hydraulic operation, each power source shall consist of a pump capable of closing all doors in not more than 60 seconds. In addition, there shall be for the whole installation hydraulic accumulators of sufficient capacity to operate all the doors at least three times, i.e., closed-open-closed. The fluid used shall be one which does not freeze at any of the temperatures liable to be encountered by the ship during its service.

10.1 Hinged watertight doors (class 1) in passenger, crew and working spaces are only permitted above a deck the underside of which, at its lowest point at side, is at least 2.0 m above the deepest subdivision load line.

10.2 Watertight doors, the sills of which are above the deepest load line and below the line specified in paragraph 10.1 shall be sliding doors and may be hand-operated (class 2), except in vessels engaged on short international voyages and required to have a factor of subdivision of .50 or less in which all such doors shall be power-operated. When trunkways in connection with refrigerated cargo and ventilation or forced draught ducts are carried through more than one main watertight subdivision bulkhead, the doors at such openings shall be operated by power.

11.1 Watertight doors which may sometimes be opened at sea, and the sills of which are below the deepest subdivision load line shall be sliding doors. The following rules shall apply:

.1 when the number of such doors (excluding doors at entrances to shaft tunnels) exceeds five, all of these doors and those at the entrance to shaft tunnels or ventilation or forced draught ducts, shall be power-operated (class 3) and shall be capable of being simultaneously closed from a central station situated on the navigating bridge;

.2 when the number of such doors (excluding doors at entrances to shaft tunnels) is greater than one, but does not exceed five;

.2.1 where the ship has no passenger spaces below the bulkhead deck, all the above-mentioned doors may be hand-operated (class 2);

.2.2 where the ship has passenger spaces below the bulkhead deck all the above-mentioned doors shall be power-operated (class 3) and shall be capable of being simultaneously closed from a central station situated on the navigating bridge;

.3 in any ship where there are only two such watertight doors and they are situated in the machinery space or in the bulkheads bounding such space, the Administration may allow these two doors to be hand-operated only (class 2).

11.2 If sliding watertight doors which have sometimes to be open at sea for the purpose of trimming coal are fitted between bunkers in the between-decks below the bulkhead deck, these doors shall be operated by power. The opening and closing of these doors shall be recorded in such log-book as may be prescribed by the Administration.

12.1 If the Administration is satisfied that such doors are essential, watertight doors of satisfactory construction may be fitted in watertight bulkheads dividing cargo between deck spaces. Such doors may be hinged, rolling or sliding doors but shall not be remotely controlled. They shall be fitted at the highest level and as far from the shell plating as practicable, but in no case shall the outboard vertical edges be situated at a distance from the shell plating which is less than one fifth of the breadth of the ship, as defined in regulation 2, such distance being measured at right angles to the centreline of the ship at the level of the deepest subdivision load line.

12.2 Such doors shall be closed before the voyage commences and shall be kept closed during navigation; the time of opening such doors in port and of closing them before the ship leaves port shall be entered in the log-book. Should any of the doors be accessible during the voyage, they shall be fitted with a device which prevents unauthorized opening. When it is proposed to fit such doors, the number and arrangements shall receive the special consideration of the Administration.

13 Portable plates on bulkheads shall not be permitted except in machinery spaces. Such plates shall always be in place before the ship leaves port, and shall not be removed during navigation except in case of urgent necessity. The necessary precautions shall be taken in replacing them to ensure that the joints shall be watertight.

14 All watertight doors shall be kept closed during navigation except when necessarily opened for the working of the ship, in which case they shall always be ready to be immediately closed.

15.1 Where trunkways or tunnels for access from crew accommodation to the stokehold, for piping, or for any other purpose are carried through main transverse watertight bulkheads, they shall be watertight and in accordance with the requirements of regulation 19. The access to at least one end of each such tunnel or trunkway, if used as a passage at sea, shall be through a trunk extending watertight to a height sufficient to permit access above the margin line. The access to the other end of the trunkway or tunnel may be through a watertight door of the type required by its location in the ship. Such trunkways or tunnels shall not extend through the first subdivision bulkhead abaft the collision bulkhead.

15.2 Where it is proposed to fit tunnels or trunkways for forced draught, piercing main transverse watertight bulkheads, these shall receive the special consideration of the Administration.

Regulation 16

Passenger ships carrying goods vehicles and accompanying personnel

1 This regulation applies to passenger ships regardless of the date of construction designed or adapted for the carriage of goods vehicles and

accompanying personnel where the total number of persons on board, other than those specified in regulation I/2(e)(i) and (ii), exceeds 12.

2   If in such a ship the total number of passengers which include personnel accompanying vehicles does not exceed $N = 12 + A/25$, where $A =$ total deck area (square metres) of spaces available for the stowage of goods vehicles and where the clear height at the stowage position and at the entrance to such spaces is not less than 4 m, the provisions of regulation 15.12 in respect of watertight doors apply except that the doors may be fitted at any level in watertight bulkheads dividing cargo spaces. Additionally, indicators are required on the navigating bridge to show automatically when each door is closed and all door fastenings are secured.

3   When applying the provisions of this chapter to such a ship, N shall be taken as the maximum number of passengers for which the ship may be certified in accordance with this regulation.

4   In applying regulation 8 for the worst operating conditions, the permeability for cargo spaces intended for the stowage of goods vehicles and containers shall be derived by calculation in which the goods vehicles and containers shall be assumed to be non-watertight and their permeability taken as 65. For ships engaged in dedicated services the actual value of permeability for goods vehicles or containers may be applied. In no case shall the permeability of the cargo spaces in which the goods vehicles and containers are carried be taken as less than 60.

Regulation 17

Openings in the shell plating of passenger ships below the margin line

1   The number of openings in the shell plating shall be reduced to the minimum compatible with the design and proper working of the ship.

2   The arrangement and efficiency of the means for closing any opening in the shell plating shall be consistent with its intended purpose and the position in which it is fitted and generally to the satisfaction of the Administration.

3.1   Subject to the requirements of the International Convention on Load Lines in force, no sidescuttle shall be fitted in such a position that its sill is below a line drawn parallel to the bulkhead deck at side and having its lowest point 2.5 per cent of the breadth of the ship above the deepest subdivision load line, or 500 mm, whichever is the greater.

3.2   All sidescuttles the sills of which are below the margin line, as permitted by paragraph 3.1 shall be of such construction as will effectively prevent any person opening them without the consent of the master of the ship.

3.3.1   Where in a between-decks, the sills of any of the sidescuttles referred to in paragraph 3.2 are below a line drawn parallel to the bulkhead deck at side and having its lowest point 1.4 m plus 2.5 per cent of the breadth of the ship above the water when the ship departs from any port, all the sidescuttles in that between-decks shall be closed watertight and locked before the ship leaves port, and they shall not be opened before the ship arrives at the next port. In the application of this paragraph the appropriate allowance for fresh water may be made when applicable.

3.3.2   The time of opening such sidescuttles in port and of closing and locking them before the ship leaves port shall be entered in such log-book as may be prescribed by the Administration.

3.3.3   For any ship that has one or more sidescuttles so placed that the requirements of paragraph 3.3.1 would apply when it was floating at its deepest subdivision load line, the Administration may indicate the limiting mean draught at which these sidescuttles will have their sills above the line drawn parallel to the bulkhead deck at side, and having its lowest point 1.4 m plus 2.5 per cent of the breadth of the ship above the waterline corresponding to the limiting mean draught, and at which it will therefore be permissible to depart from port without previously closing and locking them and to open them at sea on the responsibility of the master during the voyage to the next port. In tropical zones as defined in the International Convention on Load Lines in force, this limiting draught may be increased by 0.3 m.

4   Efficient hinged inside deadlights so arranged that they can be easily and effectively closed and secured watertight, shall be fitted to all sidescuttles except that abaft one eighth of the ship's length from the forward perpendicular and above a line drawn parallel to the bulkhead deck at side and having its lowest point at a height of 3.7 m plus 2.5 per cent of the breadth of the ship above the deepest subdivision load line, the deadlights may be portable in passenger accommodation other than that for steerage passengers, unless the deadlights are required by the International Convention on Load Lines in force to be permanently attached in their proper positions. Such portable deadlights shall be stowed adjacent to the sidescuttles they serve.

5   Sidescuttles and their deadlights which will not be accessible during navigation shall be closed and secured before the ship leaves port.

6.1   No sidescuttles shall be fitted in any spaces which are appropriated exclusively to the carriage of cargo or coal.

6.2   Sidescuttles may, however, be fitted in spaces appropriated alternatively to the carriage of cargo or passengers, but they shall be of such construction as will effectively prevent any person opening them or their deadlights without the consent of the master.

6.3   If cargo is carried in such spaces, the sidescuttles and their deadlights shall be closed watertight and locked before the cargo is shipped and such closing and locking shall be recorded in such log-book as may be prescribed by the Administration.

7   Automatic ventilating sidescuttles shall not be fitted in the shell plating below the margin line without the special sanction of the Administration.

8   The number of scuppers, sanitary discharges and other similar openings in the shell plating shall be reduced to the minimum either by making each discharge serve for as many as possible of the sanitary and other pipes, or in any other satisfactory manner.

9.1   All inlets and discharges in the shell plating shall be fitted with efficient and accessible arrangements for preventing the accidental admission of water into the ship.

9.2.1   Subject to the requirements of the International Convention on Load Lines in force, and except as provided in paragraph 9.3, each separate discharge led through the shell plating from spaces below the margin line shall be provided with either one automatic nonreturn valve fitted with a positive means of closing it from above the bulkhead deck or with two automatic nonreturn valves without positive means of closing, provided that the inboard valve is situated above the deepest subdivision load line and is always accessible for examination under service conditions. Where a valve with positive means of closing is fitted, the operating position above the bulkhead deck shall always be readily accessible and means shall be provided for indicating whether the valve is open or closed.

9.2.2   The requirements of the International Convention on Load Lines in force shall apply to discharges led through the shell plating from spaces above the margin line.

9.3   Machinery space main and auxiliary sea inlets and discharges in connection with the operation of machinery shall be fitted with readily accessible valves between the pipes and the shell plating or between the pipes and fabricated boxes attached to the shell plating. The valves may be controlled locally and shall be provided with indicators showing whether they are open or closed.

9.4   All shell fittings and valves required by this regulation shall be of steel, bronze or other approved ductile material. Valves of ordinary cast iron or similar material are not acceptable. All pipes to which this regulation refers shall be of steel or other equivalent material to the satisfaction of the Administration.

10.1 Gangway, cargo and coaling ports fitted below the margin line shall be of sufficient strength. They shall be effectively closed and secured watertight before the ship leaves port, and shall be kept closed during navigation.

10.2 Such ports shall in no case be so fitted as to have their lowest point below the deepest subdivision load line.

11.1 The inboard opening of each ash-chute, rubbish-chute, etc. shall be fitted with an efficient cover.

11.2 If the inboard opening is situated below the margin line, the cover shall be watertight, and in addition an automatic nonreturn valve shall be fitted in the chute in an easily accessible position above the deepest subdivision load line. When the chute is not in use both the cover and the valve shall be kept closed and secured.

Regulation 18

Construction and initial tests of watertight doors, sidescuttles, etc. in passenger ships and cargo ships

1   In passenger ships:

.1   the design, materials and construction of all watertight doors, side-scuttles, gangway, cargo and coaling ports, valves, pipes, ash-chutes and rubbish-chutes referred to in these regulations shall be to the satisfaction of the Administration;

.2   the frames of vertical watertight doors shall have no groove at the bottom in which dirt might lodge and prevent the door closing properly.

2   In passenger ships and cargo ships each watertight door shall be tested by water pressure to a head up to the bulkhead deck or freeboard deck respectively. The test shall be made before the ship is put into service, either before or after the door is fitted.

Regulation 19

Construction and initial tests of watertight decks, trunks, etc. in passenger ships and cargo ships

1   Watertight decks, trunks, tunnels, duct keels and ventilators shall be of the same strength as watertight bulkheads at corresponding levels. The means used for making them watertight, and the arrangements adopted for closing openings in them, shall be to the satisfaction of the Administration. Watertight ventilators and trunks shall be carried at least up to the bulkhead deck in passenger ships and up to the freeboard deck in cargo ships.

2   After completion, a hose or flooding test shall be applied to watertight decks and a hose test to watertight trunks, tunnels and ventilators.

Regulation 20

Watertight integrity of passenger ships above the margin line

1   The Administration may require that all reasonable and practicable measures shall be taken to limit the entry and spread of water above the bulkhead deck. Such measures may include partial bulkheads or webs. When partial watertight bulkheads and webs are fitted on the bulkhead deck, above or in the immediate vicinity of main subdivision bulkheads, they shall have watertight shell and bulkhead deck connections so as to restrict the flow of water along the deck when the ship is in a heeled damaged condition. Where the partial watertight bulkhead does not line up with the bulkhead below, the bulkhead deck between shall be made effectively watertight.

2   The bulkhead deck or a deck above it shall be weathertight. All openings in the exposed weather deck shall have coamings of ample height and strength and shall be provided with efficient means for expeditiously closing them weathertight. Freeing ports, open rails and scuppers shall be fitted as necessary for rapidly clearing the weather deck of water under all weather conditions.

3   Sidescuttles, gangway, cargo and coaling ports and other means for closing openings in the shell plating above the margin line shall be of efficient design and construction and of sufficient strength having regard to the spaces in which they are fitted and their positions relative to the deepest subdivision load line.

4   Efficient inside deadlights, so arranged that they can be easily and effectively closed and secured watertight, shall be provided for all sidescuttles to spaces below the first deck above the bulkhead deck.

Regulation 21 F

Bilge pumping arrangements

1   *Passenger ships and cargo ships*

1.1   An efficient bilge pumping system shall be provided, capable of pumping from and draining any watertight compartment other than a space permanently appropriated for the carriage of fresh water, water ballast, oil fuel or liquid cargo and for which other efficient means of pumping are provided, under all practical conditions. Efficient means shall be provided for draining water from insulated holds.

F   See Annex 2.

1.2   Sanitary, ballast and general service pumps may be accepted as independent power bilge pumps if fitted with the necessary connections to the bilge pumping system.

1.3   All bilge pipes used in or under coal bunkers or fuel storage tanks or in boiler or machinery spaces, including spaces in which oil-settling tanks or oil fuel pumping units are situated, shall be of steel or other suitable material.

1.4   The arrangement of the bilge and ballast pumping system shall be such as to prevent the possibility of water passing from the sea and from water ballast spaces into the cargo and machinery spaces, or from one compartment to another. Provision shall be made to prevent any deep tank having bilge and ballast connections being inadvertently flooded from the sea when containing cargo, or being discharged through a bilge pump when containing water ballast.

1.5   All distribution boxes and manually operated valves in connection with the bilge pumping arrangements shall be in positions which are accessible under ordinary circumstances.

2   *Passenger ships*

2.1   The bilge pumping system required by paragraph 1.1 shall be capable of operation under all practicable conditions after a casualty whether the ship is upright or listed. For this purpose wing suctions shall generally be fitted except in narrow compartments at the end of the ship where one suction may be sufficient. In compartments of unusual form, additional suctions may be required. Arrangements shall be made whereby water in the compartment may find its way to the suction pipes. Where, for particular compartments, the Administration is satisfied that the provision of drainage may be undesirable, it may allow such provision to be dispensed with if calculations made in accordance with the conditions laid down in regulation 8.2.1 to 8.2.3 show that the survival capability of the ship will not be impaired.

2.2   At least three power pumps shall be fitted connected to the bilge main, one of which may be driven by the propulsion machinery. Where the criterion numeral is 30 or more, one additional independent power pump shall be provided.

2.3   Where practicable, the power bilge pumps shall be placed in separate watertight compartments and so arranged or situated that these compartments will not be flooded by the same damage. If the main propulsion machinery, auxiliary machinery and boilers are in two or more watertight compartments, the pumps available for bilge service shall be distributed as far as is possible throughout these compartments.

2.4   On a ship of 91.5 m in length and upwards or having a criterion numeral of 30 or more, the arrangements shall be such that at least one power bilge pump shall be available for use in all flooding conditions which the ship is required to withstand, as follows:

.1 one of the required bilge pumps shall be an emergency pump of a reliable submersible type having a source of power situated above the bulkhead deck; or

.2 the bilge pumps and their sources of power shall be so distributed throughout the length of the ship that at least one pump in an undamaged compartment will be available.

2.5   With the exception of additional pumps which may be provided for peak compartments only, each required bilge pump shall be so arranged as to draw water from any space required to be drained by paragraph 1.1.

2.6   Each power bilge pump shall be capable of pumping water through the required main bilge pipe at a speed of not less than 2 m/sec. Independent power bilge pumps situated in machinery spaces shall have direct suctions from these spaces, except that not more than two such suctions shall be required in any one space. Where two or more such suctions are provided there shall be at least one on each side of the ship. The Administration may require independent power bilge pumps situated in other spaces to have separate direct suctions. Direct suctions shall be suitably arranged and those in a machinery space shall be of a diameter not less than that required for the bilge main.

2.7.1   In addition to the direct bilge suction or suctions required by paragraph 2.6 a direct suction from the main circulating pump leading to the drainage level of the machinery space and fitted with a nonreturn valve shall be provided in the machinery space. The diameter of this direct suction pipe shall be at least two thirds of the diameter of the pump inlet in the case of steamships, and of the same diameter as the pump inlet in the case of motorships.

2.7.2   Where in the opinion of the Administration the main circulating pump is not suitable for this purpose, a direct emergency bilge suction shall be led from the largest available independent power driven pump to the drainage level of the machinery space; the suction shall be of the same diameter as the main inlet of the pump used. The capacity of the pump so connected shall exceed that of a required bilge pump by an amount deemed satisfactory by the Administration.

2.7.3   The spindles of the sea inlet and direct suction valves shall extend well above the engine-room platform.

2.8   All bilge suction piping up to the connection to the pumps shall be independent of other piping.

2.9   The diameter d of the bilge main shall be calculated according to the following formula. However, the actual internal diameter of the bilge main may be rounded off to the nearest standard size acceptable to the

Administration:

$$d = 25 + 1.68 \sqrt{L(B + D)}$$

where d is the internal diameter of the bilge main (millimetres);

L and B are the length and the breadth of the ship (metres) as defined in regulation 2; and

D is the moulded depth of the ship to bulkhead deck (metres).

The diameter of the bilge branch pipes shall meet the requirements of the Administration.

2.10 Provision shall be made to prevent the compartment served by any bilge suction pipe being flooded in the event of the pipe being severed or otherwise damaged by collision or grounding in any other compartment. For this purpose, where the pipe is at any part situated nearer the side of the ship than one fifth of the breadth of the ship (as defined in regulation 2 and measured at right angles to the centreline at the level of the deepest subdivision load line), or is in a duct keel, a nonreturn valve shall be fitted to the pipe in the compartment containing the open end.

2.11 Distribution boxes, cocks and valves in connection with the bilge pumping system shall be so arranged that, in the event of flooding, one of the bilge pumps may be operative on any compartment; in addition, damage to a pump or its pipe connecting to the bilge main outboard of a line drawn at one fifth of the breadth of the ship shall not put the bilge system out of action. If there is only one system of pipes common to all the pumps, the necessary valves for controlling the bilge suctions must be capable of being operated from above the bulkhead deck. Where in addition to the main bilge pumping system an emergency bilge pumping system is provided, it shall be independent of the main system and so arranged that a pump is capable of operating on any compartment under flooding condition as specified in paragraph 2.1; in that case only the valves necessary for the operation of the emergency system need be capable of being operated from above the bulkhead deck.

2.12 All cocks and valves referred to in paragraph 2.11 which can be operated from above the bulkhead deck shall have their controls at their place of operation clearly marked and shall be provided with means to indicate whether they are open or closed.

3   *Cargo ships*

At least two power pumps connected to the main bilge system shall be provided, one of which may be driven by the propulsion machinery. If the Administration is satisfied that the safety of the ship is not impaired, bilge pumping arrangements may be dispensed with in particular compartments.

Regulation 22

*Stability information for passenger ships and cargo ships**

1   Every passenger ship regardless of size and every cargo ship having a length, as defined in the International Convention on Load Lines in force, of 24 m and upwards, shall be inclined upon its completion and the elements of its stability determined. The master shall be supplied with such information satisfactory to the Administration as is necessary to enable him by rapid and simple processes to obtain accurate guidance as to the stability of the ship under varying conditions of service. A copy of the stability information shall be furnished to the Administration.

2   Where any alterations are made to a ship so as to materially affect the stability information supplied to the master, amended stability information shall be provided. If necessary the ship shall be re-inclined.

3   The Administration may allow the inclining test of an individual ship to be dispensed with provided basic stability data are available from the inclining test of a sister ship and it is shown to the satisfaction of the Administration that reliable stability information for the exempted ship can be obtained from such basic data.

4   The Administration may also allow the inclining test of an individual ship or class of ships especially designed for the carriage of liquids or ore in bulk to be dispensed with when reference to existing data for similar ships clearly indicates that due to the ship's proportions and arrangements more than sufficient metacentric height will be available in all probable loading conditions.

Regulation 23

Damage control plans in passenger ships

There shall be permanently exhibited, for the guidance of the officer in charge of the ship, plans showing clearly for each deck and hold the boundaries of the watertight compartments, the openings therein with the means of closure and position of any controls thereof, and the arrangements for the correction of any list due to flooding. In addition, booklets containing the aforementioned information shall be made available to the officers of the ship.

---

* Reference is made to the Recommendation on Intact Stability for Passenger and Cargo Ships under 100 metres in length, adopted by the Organization by resolution A.167(ES.IV) and amendments to this Recommendation, adopted by the Organization by resolution A.206(VII) and Recommendation on a severe wind and rolling criterion (weather criterion) for the intact stability of passenger and cargo ships over 24 metres in length (MSC/Circ.346 and MSC/Circ.346/ Corr.1)

Regulation 23–1 F

Damage control in dry cargo ships

Regulation 24

Marking, periodical operation and inspection of watertight doors, etc. in passenger ships

1   This regulation applies to all ships.

2.1   Drills for the operating of watertight doors, sidescuttles, valves and closing mechanisms of scuppers, ash-chutes and rubbish-chutes shall take place weekly. In ships in which the voyage exceeds one week in duration a complete drill shall be held before leaving port, and others thereafter at least once a week during the voyage.

2.2   All watertight doors, both hinged and power operated, in main transverse bulkheads, in use at sea, shall be operated daily.

3.1   The watertight doors and all mechanisms and indicators connected therewith, all valves, the closing of which is necessary to make a compartment watertight, and all valves the operation of which is necessary for damage control cross-connections shall be periodically inspected at sea at least once a week.

3.2   Such valves, doors and mechanisms shall be suitably marked to ensure that they may be properly used to provide maximum safety.

Regulation 25

Entries in log of passenger ships

1   This regulation applies to all ships.

2   Hinged doors, portable plates, sidescuttles, gangway, cargo and coaling ports and other openings, which are required by these regulations to be kept closed during navigation, shall be closed before the ship leaves port. The time of closing and the time of opening (if permissible under these regulations) shall be recorded in such log-book as may be prescribed by the Administration.

3   A record of all drills and inspections required by regulation 24 shall be entered in the log-book with an explicit record of any defects which may be disclosed.

F   See Annex 2.

PART C – MACHINERY INSTALLATIONS

(Except where expressly provided otherwise part C applies to passenger ships and cargo ships)

Regulation 26

General

1   The machinery, boilers and other pressure vessels, associated piping systems and fittings shall be of a design and construction adequate for the service for which they are intended and shall be so installed and protected as to reduce to a minimum any danger to persons on board, due regard being paid to moving parts, hot surfaces and other hazards. The design shall have regard to materials used in construction, the purpose for which the equipment is intended, the working conditions to which it will be subjected and the environmental conditions on board.

2   The Administration shall give special consideration to the reliability of single essential propulsion components and may require a separate source of propulsion power sufficient to give the ship a navigable speed, especially in the case of unconventional arrangements.

3   Means shall be provided whereby normal operation of propulsion machinery can be sustained or restored even though one of the essential auxiliaries becomes inoperative. Special consideration shall be given to the malfunctioning of:

.1   a generating set which serves as a main source of electrical power;

.2   the sources of steam supply;

.3   the boiler feedwater systems;

.4   the fuel oil supply systems for boilers or engines;

.5   the sources of lubricating oil pressure;

.6   the sources of water pressure;

.7   a condensate pump and the arrangements to maintain vacuum in condensers;

.8   the mechanical air supply for boilers;

.9   an air compressor and receiver for starting or control purposes;

.10   the hydraulic, pneumatic or electrical means for control in main propulsion machinery including controllable pitch propellers.

However, the Administration, having regard to overall safety considerations, may accept a partial reduction in propulsion capability from normal operation.

4   Means shall be provided to ensure that the machinery can be brought into operation from the dead ship condition without external aid.

5   All boilers, all parts of machinery, all steam, hydraulic, pneumatic and other systems and their associated fittings which are under internal pressure shall be subjected to appropriate tests including a pressure test before being put into service for the first time.

6   Main propulsion machinery and all auxiliary machinery essential to the propulsion and the safety of the ship shall, as fitted in the ship, be designed to operate when the ship is upright and when inclined at any angle of list up to and including 15° either way under static conditions and 22.5° under dynamic conditions (rolling) either way and simultaneously inclined dynamically (pitching) 7.5° by bow or stern. The Administration may permit deviation from these angles, taking into consideration the type, size and service conditions of the ship.

7   Provision shall be made to facilitate cleaning, inspection and maintenance of main propulsion and auxiliary machinery including boilers and pressure vessels.

8   Special consideration shall be given to the design, construction and installation of propulsion machinery systems so that any mode of their vibrations shall not cause undue stresses in this machinery in the normal operating ranges.

Regulation 27

Machinery

1   Where risk from overspeeding of machinery exists, means shall be provided to ensure that the safe speed is not exceeded.

2   Where main or auxiliary machinery including pressure vessels or any parts of such machinery are subject to internal pressure and may be subject to dangerous overpressure, means shall be provided where practicable to protect against such excessive pressure.

3   All gearing and every shaft and coupling used for transmission of power to machinery essential for the propulsion and safety of the ship or for the safety of persons on board shall be so designed and constructed that they will withstand the maximum working stresses to which they may be subjected in all service conditions, and due consideration shall be given to the type of engines by which they are driven or of which they form part.

4   Internal combustion engines of a cylinder diameter of 200 mm or a crankcase volume of 0.6 m^3 and above shall be provided with crankcase explosion

relief valves of a suitable type with sufficient relief area. The relief valves shall be arranged or provided with means to ensure that discharge from them is so directed as to minimize the possibility of injury to personnel.

5   Main turbine propulsion machinery and, where applicable, main internal combustion propulsion machinery and auxiliary machinery shall be provided with automatic shutoff arrangements in the case of failures such as lubricating oil supply failure which could lead rapidly to complete breakdown, serious damage or explosion. The Administration may permit provisions for overriding automatic shutoff devices.

Regulation 28

Means of going astern

1   Sufficient power for going astern shall be provided to secure proper control of the ship in all normal circumstances.

2   The ability of the machinery to reverse the direction of thrust of the propeller in sufficient time, and so to bring the ship to rest within a reasonable distance from maximum ahead service speed, shall be demonstrated and recorded.*

3   The stopping times, ship headings and distances recorded on trials, together with the results of trials to determine the ability of ships having multiple propellers to navigate and manoeuvre with one or more propellers inoperative, shall be available on board for the use of the master or designated personnel.*

4   Where the ship is provided with supplementary means for manoeuvring or stopping, the effectiveness of such means shall be demonstrated and recorded as referred to in paragraphs 2 and 3.

Regulation 29

Steering gear

1   Unless expressly provided otherwise, every ship shall be provided with a main steering gear and an auxiliary steering gear to the satisfaction of the

---

* Reference is made to the Recommendation on Information to be Included in the Manoeuvring Booklets adopted by the Organization by resolution A.209(VII).

Administration. The main steering gear and the auxiliary steering gear shall be so arranged that the failure of one of them will not render the other one inoperative.

2.1 All the steering gear components and the rudder stock shall be of sound and reliable construction to the satisfaction of the Administration. Special consideration shall be given to the suitability of any essential component which is not duplicated. Any such essential component shall, where appropriate, utilize antifriction bearings such as ball-bearings, roller-bearings or sleeve-bearings which shall be permanently lubricated or provided with lubrication fittings.

2.2 The design pressure for calculations to determine the scantlings of piping and other steering gear components subjected to internal hydraulic pressure shall be at least 1.25 times the maximum working pressure to be expected under the operational conditions specified in paragraph 3.2, taking into account any pressure which may exist in the low-pressure side of the system. At the discretion of the Administration, fatigue criteria shall be applied for the design of piping and components, taking into account pulsating pressures due to dynamic loads.

2.3 Relief valves shall be fitted to any part of the hydraulic system which can be isolated and in which pressure can be generated from the power source or from external forces. The setting of the relief valves shall not exceed the design pressure. The valves shall be of adequate size and so arranged as to avoid an undue rise in pressure above the design pressure.

3 The main steering gear and rudder stock shall be:

.1 of adequate strength and capable of steering the ship at maximum ahead service speed which shall be demonstrated;

.2 capable of putting the rudder over from 35° on one side to 35° on the other side with the ship at its deepest seagoing draught and running ahead at maximum ahead service speed and, under the same conditions, from 35° on either side to 30° on the other side in not more than 28 seconds;

.3 operated by power where necessary to meet the requirements of paragraph 3.2 and in any case when the Administration requires a rudder stock of over 120 mm diameter in way of the tiller, excluding strengthening for navigation in ice; and

.4 so designed that they will not be damaged at maximum astern speed; however, this design requirement need not be proved by trials at maximum astern speed and maximum rudder angle.

4 The auxiliary steering gear shall be:

.1 of adequate strength and capable of steering the ship at navigable speed and of being brought speedily into action in an emergency;

.2 capable of putting the rudder over from 15° on one side to 15° on the other side in not more than 60 seconds with the ship at its deepest seagoing draught and running ahead at one half of the maximum ahead service speed or 7 knots, whichever is the greater; and

.3 operated by power where necessary to meet the requirements of paragraph 4.2 and in any case when the Administration requires a rudder stock of over 230 mm diameter in way of the tiller, excluding strengthening for navigation in ice.

5   Main and auxiliary steering gear power units shall be:

.1 arranged to restart automatically when power is restored after a power failure; and

.2 capable of being brought into operation from a position on the navigating bridge. In the event of a power failure to any one of the steering gear power units, an audible and visual alarm shall be given on the navigating bridge.

6.1   Where the main steering gear comprises two or more identical power units, an auxiliary steering gear need not be fitted, provided that:

.1 in a passenger ship, the main steering gear is capable of operating the rudder as required by paragraph 3.2 while any one of the power units is out of operation;

.2 in a cargo ship, the main steering gear is capable of operating the rudder as required by paragraph 3.2 while operating with all power units;

.3 the main steering gear is so arranged that after a single failure in its piping system or in one of the power units the defect can be isolated so that steering capability can be maintained or speedily regained.

6.2   The Administration may, until 1 September 1986, accept the fitting of a steering gear which has a proven record of reliability but does not comply with the requirements of paragraph 6.1.3 for a hydraulic system.

6.3   Steering gears, other than of the hydraulic type, shall achieve standards equivalent to the requirements of this paragraph to the satisfaction of the Administration.

7   Steering gear control shall be provided:

.1 for the main steering gear, both on the navigating bridge and in the steering gear compartment;

.2 where the main steering gear is arranged in accordance with paragraph 6, by two independent control systems, both operable from the navigating bridge. This does not require duplication of the steering wheel or steering lever. Where the control system consists of an hydraulic telemotor, a second independent system need not be fitted, except in a tanker, chemical tanker or gas carrier of 10,000 tons gross tonnage and upwards;

.3 for the auxiliary steering gear, in the steering gear compartment and, if power-operated, it shall also be operable from the navigating bridge and shall be independent of the control system for the main steering gear.

8 Any main and auxiliary steering gear control system operable from the navigating bridge shall comply with the following:

.1 if electric, it shall be served by its own separate circuit supplied from a steering gear power circuit from a point within the steering gear compartment, or directly from switchboard busbars supplying that steering gear power circuit at a point on the switchboard adjacent to the supply to the steering gear power circuit;

.2 means shall be provided in the steering gear compartment for disconnecting any control system operable from the navigating bridge from the steering gear it serves;

.3 the system shall be capable of being brought into operation from a position on the navigating bridge;

.4 in the event of a failure of electrical power supply to the control system, an audible and visual alarm shall be given on the navigating bridge; and

.5 short circuit protection only shall be provided for steering gear control supply circuits.

9 The electric power circuits and the steering gear control systems with their associated components, cables and pipes required by this regulation and by regulation 30 shall be separated as far as is practicable throughout their length.

10 A means of communication shall be provided between the navigating bridge and the steering gear compartment.

11 The angular position of the rudder shall:

.1 if the main steering gear is power-operated, be indicated on the navigating bridge. The rudder angle indication shall be independent of the steering gear control system;

.2 be recognizable in the steering gear compartment.

12 Hydraulic power-operated steering gear shall be provided with the following:

.1 arrangements to maintain the cleanliness of the hydraulic fluid taking into consideration the type and design of the hydraulic system;

.2   a low-level alarm for each hydraulic fluid reservoir to give the earliest practicable indication of hydraulic fluid leakage. Audible and visual alarms shall be given on the navigating bridge and in the machinery space where they can be readily observed; and

.3   a fixed storage tank having sufficient capacity to recharge at least one power actuating system including the reservoir, where the main steering gear is required to be power-operated. The storage tank shall be permanently connected by piping in such a manner that the hydraulic systems can be readily recharged from a position within the steering gear compartment and shall be provided with a contents gauge.

13   The steering gear compartment shall be:

.1   readily accessible and, as far as practicable, separated from machinery spaces; and

.2   provided with suitable arrangements to ensure working access to steering gear machinery and controls. These arrangements shall include handrails and gratings or other nonslip surfaces to ensure suitable working conditions in the event of hydraulic fluid leakage.

14   Where the rudder stock is required to be over 230 mm diameter in way of the tiller, excluding strengthening for navigation in ice, an alternative power supply, sufficient at least to supply the steering gear power unit which complies with the requirements of paragraph 4.2 and also its associated control system and the rudder angle indicator, shall be provided automatically, within 45 seconds, either from the emergency source of electrical power or from an independent source of power located in the steering gear compartment. This independent source of power shall be used only for this purpose. In every ship of 10,000 tons gross tonnage and upwards, the alternative power supply shall have a capacity for at least 30 minutes of continuous operation and in any other ship for at least 10 minutes.

15   In every tanker, chemical tanker or gas carrier of 10,000 tons gross tonnage and upwards and in every other ship of 70,000 tons gross tonnage and upwards, the main steering gear shall comprise two or more identical power units complying with the provisions of paragraph 6.

16   Every tanker, chemical tanker or gas carrier of 10,000 tons gross tonnage and upwards shall, subject to paragraph 17, comply with the following:

.1   the main steering gear shall be so arranged that in the event of loss of steering capability due to a single failure in any part of one of the power actuating systems of the main steering gear, excluding the tiller, quadrant or components serving the same purpose, or seizure of the rudder actuators, steering capability shall be regained in not more than 45 seconds after the loss of one power actuating system;

.2 the main steering gear shall comprise either:

.2.1 two independent and separate power actuating systems, each capable of meeting the requirements of paragraph 3.2; or

.2.2 at least two identical power actuating systems which, acting simultaneously in normal operation, shall be capable of meeting the requirements of paragraph 3.2. Where necessary to comply with this requirement, interconnection of hydraulic power actuating systems shall be provided. Loss of hydraulic fluid from one system shall be capable of being detected and the defective system automatically isolated so that the other actuating system or systems shall remain fully operational;

.3 steering gears other than of the hydraulic type shall achieve equivalent standards.

17   For tankers, chemical tankers or gas carriers of 10,000 tons gross tonnage and upwards, but of less than 100,000 tonnes deadweight, solutions other than those set out in paragraph 16, which need not apply the single failure criterion to the rudder actuator or actuators, may be permitted provided that an equivalent safety standard is achieved and that:

.1 following loss of steering capability due to a single failure of any part of the piping system or in one of the power units, steering capability shall be regained within 45 seconds; and

.2 where the steering gear includes only a single rudder actuator, special consideration is given to stress analysis for the design including fatigue analysis and fracture mechanics analysis, as appropriate, to the material used, to the installation of sealing arrangements and to testing and inspection and to the provision of effective maintenance. In consideration of the foregoing, the Administration shall adopt regulations which include the provisions of the Guidelines for Acceptance of Non-Duplicated Rudder Actuators for Tankers, Chemical Tankers and Gas Carriers of 10,000 Tons Gross Tonnage and Above but Less than 100,000 Tonnes Deadweight, adopted by the Organization. *

18   For a tanker, chemical tanker or gas carrier of 10,000 tons gross tonnage and upwards, but less than 70,000 tonnes deadweight, the Administration may, until 1 September 1986, accept a steering gear system with a proven record of reliability which does not comply with the single failure criterion required for a hydraulic system in paragraph 16.

19   Every tanker, chemical tanker or gas carrier of 10,000 tons gross tonnage and upwards, constructed before 1 September 1984, shall comply, not later

---

* Reference is made to the Guidelines for Acceptance of Non-Duplicated Rudder Actuators for Tankers, Chemical Tankers and Gas Carriers of 10,000 Tons Gross Tonnage and Above but Less than 100,000 Tonnes Deadweight, adopted by the Organization by resolution A.467(XII).

than 1 September 1986, with the following:

.1 the requirements of paragraphs 7.1, 8.2, 8.4, 10, 11, 12.2, 12.3 and 13.2;

.2 two independent steering gear control systems shall be provided each of which can be operated from the navigating bridge. This does not require duplication of the steering wheel or steering lever;

.3 if the steering gear control system in operation fails, the second system shall be capable of being brought into immediate operation from the navigating bridge; and

.4 each steering gear control system, if electric, shall be served by its own separate circuit supplied from the steering gear power circuit or directly from switchboard busbars supplying that steering gear power circuit at a point on the switchboard adjacent to the supply to the steering gear power circuit.

20   In addition to the requirements of paragraph 19, in every tanker, chemical tanker or gas carrier of 40,000 tons gross tonnage and upwards, constructed before 1 September 1984, the steering gear shall, not later than 1 September 1988, be so arranged that, in the event of a single failure of the piping or of one of the power units, steering capability can be maintained or the rudder movement can be limited so that steering capability can be speedily regained. This shall be achieved by:

.1 an independent means of restraining the rudder; or

.2 fast-acting valves which may be manually operated to isolate the actuator or actuators from the external hydraulic piping together with a means of directly refilling the actuators by a fixed independent power-operated pump and piping system; or

.3 an arrangement such that, where hydraulic power systems are interconnected, loss of hydraulic fluid from one system shall be detected and the defective system isolated either automatically or from the navigating bridge so that the other system remains fully operational.

Regulation 30

Additional requirements for electric and electrohydraulic steering gear

1   Means for indicating that the motors of electric and electrohydraulic steering gear are running shall be installed on the navigating bridge and at a suitable main machinery control position.

2   Each electric or electrohydraulic steering gear comprising one or more power units shall be served by at least two exclusive circuits fed directly from

the main switchboard; however, one of the circuits may be supplied through the emergency switchboard. An auxiliary electric or electrohydraulic steering gear associated with a main electric or electrohydraulic steering gear may be connected to one of the circuits supplying this main steering gear. The circuits supplying an electric or electrohydraulic steering gear shall have adequate rating for supplying all motors which can be simultaneously connected to them and may be required to operate simultaneously.

3   Short circuit protection and an overload alarm shall be provided for such circuits and motors. Protection against excess current, including starting current, if provided, shall be for not less than twice the full load current of the motor or circuit so protected, and shall be arranged to permit the passage of the appropriate starting currents. Where a three-phase supply is used an alarm shall be provided that will indicate failure of any one of the supply phases. The alarms required in this paragraph shall be both audible and visual and shall be situated in a conspicuous position in the main machinery space or control room from which the main machinery is normally controlled and as may be required by regulation 51.

4   When in a ship of less than 1,600 tons gross tonnage an auxiliary steering gear which is required by regulation 29.4.3 to be operated by power is not electrically powered or is powered by an electric motor primarily intended for other services, the main steering gear may be fed by one circuit from the main switchboard. Where such an electric motor primarily intended for other services is arranged to power such an auxiliary steering gear, the requirement of paragraph 3 may be waived by the Administration if satisfied with the protection arrangement together with the requirements of regulation 29.5.1 and .2 and 29.7.3 applicable to auxiliary steering gear.

Regulation 31

Machinery controls

1   Main and auxiliary machinery essential for the propulsion and safety of the ship shall be provided with effective means for its operation and control.

2   Where remote control of propulsion machinery from the navigating bridge is provided and the machinery spaces are intended to be manned, the following shall apply:

.1   the speed, direction of thrust and, if applicable, the pitch of the propeller shall be fully controllable from the navigating bridge under all sailing conditions, including manoeuvring;

.2   the remote control shall be performed, for each independent propeller, by a control device so designed and constructed that its operation does not require particular attention to the operational details of the machinery. Where multiple propellers are designed to operate simultaneously, they may be controlled by one control device;

.3 the main propulsion machinery shall be provided with an emergency stopping device on the navigating bridge which shall be independent of the navigating bridge control system;

.4 propulsion machinery orders from the navigating bridge shall be indicated in the main machinery control room or at the manoeuvring platform as appropriate;

.5 remote control of the propulsion machinery shall be possible only from one location at a time; at such locations interconnected control positions are permitted. At each location there shall be an indicator showing which location is in control of the propulsion machinery. The transfer of control between the navigating bridge and machinery spaces shall be possible only in the main machinery space or the main machinery control room. This system shall include means to prevent the propelling thrust from altering significantly when transferring control from one location to another;

.6 it shall be possible to control the propulsion machinery locally, even in the case of failure in any part of the remote control system;

.7 the design of the remote control system shall be such that in case of its failure an alarm will be given. Unless the Administration considers it impracticable the preset speed and direction of thrust of the propeller shall be maintained until local control is in operation;

.8 indicators shall be fitted on the navigating bridge for:

.8.1 propeller speed and direction of rotation in the case of fixed pitch propellers;

.8.2 propeller speed and pitch position in the case of controllable pitch propellers;

.9 an alarm shall be provided on the navigating bridge and in the machinery space to indicate low starting air pressure which shall be set at a level to permit further main engine starting operations. If the remote control system of the propulsion machinery is designed for automatic starting, the number of automatic consecutive attempts which fail to produce a start shall be limited in order to safeguard sufficient starting air pressure for starting locally.

3   Where the main propulsion and associated machinery, including sources of main electrical supply, are provided with various degrees of automatic or remote control and are under continuous manual supervision from a control room the arrangements and controls shall be so designed, equipped and installed that the machinery operation will be as safe and effective as if it were under direct supervision; for this purpose regulations 46 to 50 shall apply as appropriate. Particular consideration shall be given to protect such spaces against fire and flooding.

4   In general, automatic starting, operational and control systems shall include provisions for manually overriding the automatic controls. Failure of any part of such systems shall not prevent the use of the manual override.

Regulation 32

Steam boilers and boiler feed systems

1   Every steam boiler and every unfired steam generator shall be provided with not less than two safety valves of adequate capacity. However, having regard to the output or any other features of any boiler or unfired steam generator, the Administration may permit only one safety valve to be fitted if it is satisfied that adequate protection against overpressure is thereby provided.

2   Each oil-fired boiler which is intended to operate without manual supervision shall have safety arrangements which shut off the fuel supply and give an alarm in the case of low water level, air supply failure or flame failure.

3   Water tube boilers serving turbine propulsion machinery shall be fitted with a high-water-level alarm.

4   Every steam generating system which provides services essential for the safety of the ship, or which could be rendered dangerous by the failure of its feedwater supply, shall be provided with not less than two separate feedwater systems from and including the feed pumps, noting that a single penetration of the steam drum is acceptable. Unless overpressure is prevented by the pump characteristics means shall be provided which will prevent overpressure in any part of the systems.

5   Boilers shall be provided with means to supervise and control the quality of the feedwater. Suitable arrangements shall be provided to preclude, as far as practicable, the entry of oil or other contaminants which may adversely affect the boiler.

6   Every boiler essential for the safety of the ship and designed to contain water at a specified level shall be provided with at least two means for indicating its water level, at least one of which shall be a direct reading gauge glass.

Regulation 33

Steam pipe systems

1   Every steam pipe and every fitting connected thereto through which steam may pass shall be so designed, constructed and installed as to withstand the maximum working stresses to which it may be subjected.

2   Means shall be provided for draining every steam pipe in which dangerous water hammer action might otherwise occur.

3   If a steam pipe or fitting may receive steam from any source at a higher

pressure than that for which it is designed a suitable reducing valve, relief valve and pressure gauge shall be fitted.

Regulation 34

Air pressure systems

1   In every ship means shall be provided to prevent overpressure in any part of compressed air systems and wherever water jackets or casings of air compressors and coolers might be subjected to dangerous overpressure due to leakage into them from air pressure parts. Suitable pressure relief arrangements shall be provided for all systems.

2   The main starting air arrangements for main propulsion internal combustion engines shall be adequately protected against the effects of backfiring and internal explosion in the starting air pipes.

3   All discharge pipes from starting air compressors shall lead directly to the starting air receivers, and all starting pipes from the air receivers to main or auxiliary engines shall be entirely separate from the compressor discharge pipe system.

4   Provision shall be made to reduce to a minimum the entry of oil into the air pressure systems and to drain these systems.

Regulation 35

Ventilating systems in machinery spaces

Machinery spaces of category A shall be adequately ventilated so as to ensure that when machinery or boilers therein are operating at full power in all weather conditions including heavy weather, an adequate supply of air is maintained to the spaces for the safety and comfort of personnel and the operation of the machinery. Any other machinery space shall be adequately ventilated appropriate for the purpose of that machinery space.

Regulation 36

*Protection against noise**

Measures shall be taken to reduce machinery noise in machinery spaces to acceptable levels as determined by the Administration. If this noise cannot

---

* Reference is made to the Code on Noise Levels on Board Ships, adopted by the Organization by resolution A.468(XII).

be sufficiently reduced the source of excessive noise shall be suitably insulated or isolated or a refuge from noise shall be provided if the space is required to be manned. Ear protectors shall be provided for personnel required to enter such spaces, if necessary.

Regulation 37

Communication between navigating bridge and machinery space

At least two independent means shall be provided for communicating orders from the navigating bridge to the position in the machinery space or in the control room from which the engines are normally controlled: one of these shall be an engine-room telegraph which provides visual indication of the orders and responses both in the machinery space and on the navigating bridge. Appropriate means of communication shall be provided to any other positions from which the engines may be controlled.

Regulation 38

Engineers' alarm

An engineers' alarm shall be provided to be operated from the engine control room or at the manoeuvring platform as appropriate, and shall be clearly audible in the engineers' accommodation.

Regulation 39

Location of emergency installations in passenger ships

Emergency sources of electrical power, fire pumps, bilge pumps except those specifically serving the spaces forward of the collision bulkhead, any fixed fire-extinguishing system required by chapter II-2 and other emergency installations which are essential for the safety of the ship, except anchor windlasses, shall not be installed forward of the collision bulkhead.

PART D – ELECTRICAL INSTALLATIONS

(Except where expressly provided otherwise part D applies to passenger ships and cargo ships)

Regulation 40

General

1   Electrical installations shall be such that:

.1   all electrical auxiliary services necessary for maintaining the ship in normal operational and habitable conditions will be ensured without recourse to the emergency source of electrical power;

.2   electrical services essential for safety will be ensured under various emergency conditions; and

.3   the safety of passengers, crew and ship from electrical hazards will be ensured.

2   The Administration shall take appropriate steps to ensure uniformity in the implementation and application of the provisions of this part in respect of electrical installations.*

Regulation 41

Main source of electrical power and lighting systems

1.1   A main source of electrical power of sufficient capacity to supply all those services mentioned in regulation 40.1.1 shall be provided. This main source of electrical power shall consist of at least two generating sets.

1.2   The capacity of these generating sets shall be such that in the event of any one generating set being stopped it will still be possible to supply those services necessary to provide normal operational conditions of propulsion and safety. Minimum comfortable conditions of habitability shall also be ensured which include at least adequate services for cooking, heating, domestic refrigeration, mechanical ventilation, sanitary and fresh water.

1.3   The arrangements of the ship's main source of electrical power shall

---

* Reference is made to the Recommendations published by the International Electrotechnical Commission and, in particular, Publication 92 – Electrical Installations in Ships.

be such that the services referred to in regulation 40.1.1 can be maintained regardless of the speed and direction of rotation of the propulsion machinery or shafting.

1.4   In addition, the generating sets shall be such as to ensure that with any one generator or its primary source of power out of operation, the remaining generating sets shall be capable of providing the electrical services necessary to start the main propulsion plant from a dead ship condition. The emergency source of electrical power may be used for the purpose of starting from a dead ship condition if its capability either alone or combined with that of any other source of electrical power is sufficient to provide at the same time those services required to be supplied by regulations 42.2.1 to 42.2.3 or 43.2.1 to 43.2.4.

1.5   Where transformers constitute an essential part of the electrical supply system required by this paragraph, the system shall be so arranged as to ensure the same continuity of the supply as is stated in this paragraph.

2.1   A main electric lighting system which shall provide illumination throughout those parts of the ship normally accessible to and used by passengers or crew shall be supplied from the main source of electrical power.

2.2   The arrangement of the main electric lighting system shall be such that a fire or other casualty in spaces containing the main source of electrical power, associated transforming equipment, if any, the main switchboard and the main lighting switchboard, will not render the emergency electric lighting system required by regulations 42.2.1 and 42.2.2 or 43.2.1, 43.2.2 and 43.2.3 inoperative.

2.3   The arrangement of the emergency electric lighting system shall be such that a fire or other casualty in spaces containing the emergency source of electrical power, associated transforming equipment, if any, the emergency switchboard and the emergency lighting switchboard will not render the main electric lighting system required by this regulation inoperative.

3   The main switchboard shall be so placed relative to one main generating station that, as far as is practicable, the integrity of the normal electrical supply may be affected only by a fire or other casualty in one space. An environmental enclosure for the main switchboard, such as may be provided by a machinery control room situated within the main boundaries of the space, is not to be considered as separating the switchboards from the generators.

4   Where the total installed electrical power of the main generating sets is in excess of 3 MW, the main busbars shall be subdivided into at least two parts which shall normally be connected by removable links or other approved means; so far as is practicable, the connection of generating sets and any other duplicated equipment shall be equally divided between the parts. Equivalent arrangements may be permitted to the satisfaction of the Administration.

Regulation 42

Emergency source of electrical power in passenger ships

1.1   A self-contained emergency source of electrical power shall be provided.

1.2   The emergency source of electrical power, associated transforming equipment, if any, transitional source of emergency power, emergency switchboard and emergency lighting switchboard shall be located above the uppermost continuous deck and shall be readily accessible from the open deck. They shall not be located forward of the collision bulkhead.

1.3   The location of the emergency source of electrical power and associated transforming equipment, if any, the transitional source of emergency power, the emergency switchboard and the emergency electric lighting switchboards in relation to the main source of electrical power, associated transforming equipment, if any, and the main switchboard shall be such as to ensure to the satisfaction of the Administration that a fire or other casualty in spaces containing the main source of electrical power, associated transforming equipment, if any, and the main switchboard or in any machinery space of category A will not interfere with the supply, control and distribution of emergency electrical power. As far as practicable, the space containing the emergency source of electrical power, associated transforming equipment, if any, the transitional source of emergency electrical power and the emergency switchboard shall not be contiguous to the boundaries of machinery spaces of category A or those spaces containing the main source of electrical power, associated transforming equipment, if any, or the main switchboard.

1.4   Provided that suitable measures are taken for safeguarding independent emergency operation under all circumstances, the emergency generator may be used exceptionally, and for short periods, to supply non-emergency circuits.

2   The electrical power available shall be sufficient to supply all those services that are essential for safety in an emergency, due regard being paid to such services as may have to be operated simultaneously. The emergency source of electrical power shall be capable, having regard to starting currents and the transitory nature of certain loads, of supplying simultaneously at least the following services for the periods specified hereinafter, if they depend upon an electrical source for their operation:

2.1   For a period of 36 hours, emergency lighting:

   .1   at every muster and embarkation station and over the sides as required by regulations III/11.4 and III/15.7;

   .2   in alleyways, stairways and exits giving access to the muster and embarkation stations, as required by regulation III/11.5;

   .3   in all service and accommodation alleyways, stairways and exits, personnel lift cars;

.4　in the machinery spaces and main generating stations including their control positions;

.5　in all control stations, machinery control rooms, and at each main and emergency switchboard;

.6　at all stowage positions for firemen's outfits;

.7　at the steering gear; and

.8　at the fire pump, the sprinkler pump and the emergency bilge pump referred to in paragraph 2.4 and at the starting position of their motors.

2.2　For a period of 36 hours, the navigation lights and other lights required by the International Regulations for Preventing Collisions at Sea in force. $\boxed{\text{F}}$

2.3　For a period of 36 hours:

.1　all internal communication equipment required in an emergency;

.2　the navigational aids as required by regulation V/12; where such provision is unreasonable or impracticable the Administration may waive this requirement for ships of less than 5,000 tons gross tonnage;

.3　the fire detection and fire alarm system, and the fire door holding and release system; and

.4　for intermittent operation of the daylight signalling lamp, the ship's whistle, the manually operated call points, and all internal signals that are required in an emergency;

unless such services have an independent supply for the period of 36 hours from an accumulator battery suitably located for use in an emergency.

2.4　For a period of 36 hours:

.1　one of the fire pumps required by regulation II-2/4.3.1 and 4.3.3;

.2　the automatic sprinkler pump, if any; and

.3　the emergency bilge pump and all the equipment essential for the operation of electrically powered remote controlled bilge valves.

2.5　For the period of time required by regulation 29.14 the steering gear if required to be so supplied by that regulation.

2.6　For a period of half an hour:

.1　any watertight doors required by regulation 15 to be power-operated together with their indicators and warning signals. Provided the requirements of regulation 15.9.2 are complied with, sequential

---

$\boxed{\text{F}}$　See Annex 2.

operation of the doors may be permitted providing all doors can be closed in 60 seconds;

.2 the emergency arrangements to bring the lift cars to deck level for the escape of persons. The passenger lift cars may be brought to deck level sequentially in an emergency.

2.7 In a ship engaged regularly on voyages of short duration, the Administration if satisfied that an adequate standard of safety would be attained may accept a lesser period than the 36 hour period specified in paragraphs 2.1 to 2.5 but not less than 12 hours.

3 The emergency source of electrical power may be either a generator or an accumulator battery, which shall comply with the following:

3.1 Where the emergency source of electrical power is a generator, it shall be:

.1 driven by a suitable prime mover with an independent supply of fuel having a flashpoint (closed cup test) of not less than 43°C;

.2 started automatically upon failure of the electrical supply from the main source of electrical power and shall be automatically connected to the emergency switchboard; those services referred to in paragraph 4 shall then be transferred automatically to the emergency generating set. The automatic starting system and the characteristic of the prime mover shall be such as to permit the emergency generator to carry its full rated load as quickly as is safe and practicable, subject to a maximum of 45 seconds; unless a second independent means of starting the emergency generating set is provided, the single source of stored energy shall be protected to preclude its complete depletion by the automatic starting system; and

.3 provided with a transitional source of emergency electrical power according to paragraph 4.

3.2 Where the emergency source of electrical power is an accumulator battery, it shall be capable of:

.1 carrying the emergency electrical load without recharging while maintaining the voltage of the battery throughout the discharge period within 12 per cent above or below its nominal voltage;

.2 automatically connecting to the emergency switchboard in the event of failure of the main source of electrical power; and

.3 immediately supplying at least those services specified in paragraph 4.

4 The transitional source of emergency electrical power required by paragraph 3.1.3 shall consist of an accumulator battery suitably located for use in an emergency which shall operate without recharging while maintaining

the voltage of the battery throughout the discharge period within 12 per cent above or below its nominal voltage and be of sufficient capacity and so arranged as to supply automatically in the event of failure of either the main or emergency source of electrical power at least the following services, if they depend upon an electrical source for their operation:

4.1 For half an hour:

.1 the lighting required by paragraphs 2.1 and 2.2;

.2 all services required by paragraphs 2.3.1, 2.3.3 and 2.3.4 unless such services have an independent supply for the period specified from an accumulator battery suitably located for use in an emergency.

4.2 Power to close the watertight doors but not necessarily all of them simultaneously, together with their indicators and warning signals as required by paragraph 2.6.1.

5.1 The emergency switchboard shall be installed as near as is practicable to the emergency source of electrical power.

5.2 Where the emergency source of electrical power is a generator, the emergency switchboard shall be located in the same space unless the operation of the emergency switchboard would thereby be impaired.

5.3 No accumulator battery fitted in accordance with this regulation shall be installed in the same space as the emergency switchboard. An indicator shall be mounted in a suitable place on the main switchboard or in the machinery control room to indicate when the batteries constituting either the emergency source of electrical power or the transitional source of emergency electrical power referred to in paragraph 3.1.3 or 4 are being discharged.

5.4 The emergency switchboard shall be supplied during normal operation from the main switchboard by an interconnector feeder which is to be adequately protected at the main switchboard against overload and short circuit and which is to be disconnected automatically at the emergency switchboard upon failure of the main source of electrical power. Where the system is arranged for feedback operation, the interconnector feeder is also to be protected at the emergency switchboard at least against short circuit.

5.5 In order to ensure ready availability of the emergency source of electrical power, arrangements shall be made where necessary to disconnect automatically non-emergency circuits from the emergency switchboard to ensure that power shall be available to the emergency circuits.

6 The emergency generator and its prime mover and any emergency accumulator battery shall be so designed and arranged as to ensure that they will function at full rated power when the ship is upright and when inclined at any angle of list up to 22.5° or when inclined up to 10° either in the fore or aft direction, or is in any combination of angles within those limits.

7   Provision shall be made for the periodic testing of the complete emergency system and shall include the testing of automatic starting arrangements.

Regulation 43

Emergency source of electrical power in cargo ships

1.1   A self-contained emergency source of electrical power shall be provided.

1.2   The emergency source of electrical power, associated transforming equipment, if any, transitional source of emergency power, emergency switchboard and emergency lighting switchboard shall be located above the uppermost continuous deck and shall be readily accessible from the open deck. They shall not be located forward of the collision bulkhead, except where permitted by the Administration in exceptional circumstances.

1.3   The location of the emergency source of electrical power, associated transforming equipment, if any, the transitional source of emergency power, the emergency switchboard and the emergency lighting switchboard in relation to the main source of electrical power, associated transforming equipment, if any, and the main switchboard shall be such as to ensure to the satisfaction of the Administration that a fire or other casualty in the space containing the main source of electrical power, associated transforming equipment, if any, and the main switchboard, or in any machinery space of category A will not interfere with the supply, control and distribution of emergency electrical power. As far as practicable the space containing the emergency source of electrical power, associated transforming equipment, if any, the transitional source of emergency electrical power and the emergency switchboard shall not be contiguous to the boundaries of machinery spaces of category A or those spaces containing the main source of electrical power, associated transforming equipment, if any, and the main switchboard.

1.4   Provided that suitable measures are taken for safeguarding independent emergency operation under all circumstances, the emergency generator may be used, exceptionally, and for short periods, to supply non-emergency circuits.

2   The electrical power available shall be sufficient to supply all those services that are essential for safety in an emergency, due regard being paid to such services as may have to be operated simultaneously. The emergency source of electrical power shall be capable, having regard to starting currents and the transitory nature of certain loads, of supplying simultaneously at least the following services for the periods specified hereinafter, if they depend upon an electrical source for their operation:

2.1   For a period of 3 hours, emergency lighting at every muster and embarkation station and over the sides as required by regulations III/11.4 and III/15.7.

2.2   For a period of 18 hours, emergency lighting:

.1   in all service and accommodation alleyways, stairways and exits, personnel lift cars and personnel lift trunks;

.2   in the machinery spaces and main generating stations including their control positions;

.3   in all control stations, machinery control rooms, and at each main and emergency switchboard;

.4   at all stowage positions for firemen's outfits;

.5   at the steering gear; and

.6   at the fire pump referred to in paragraph 2.5, at the sprinkler pump, if any, and at the emergency bilge pump, if any, and at the starting positions of their motors.

2.3   For a period of 18 hours, the navigation lights and other lights required by the International Regulations for Preventing Collisions at Sea in force. $\boxed{\text{F}}$

2.4   For a period of 18 hours:

.1   all internal communication equipment as required in an emergency;

.2   the navigational aids as required by regulation $V/12$; where such provision is unreasonable or impracticable the Administration may waive this requirement for ships of less than 5,000 tons gross tonnage; $\boxed{\text{F}}$

.3   the fire detection and fire alarm system; and

.4   intermittent operation of the daylight signalling lamp, the ship's whistle, the manually operated call points and all internal signals that are required in an emergency;

unless such services have an independent supply for the period of 18 hours from an accumulator battery suitably located for use in an emergency.

2.5   For a period of 18 hours one of the fire pumps required by regulation II-2/4.3.1 and 4.3.3 if dependent upon the emergency generator for its source of power.

2.6.1   For the period of time required by regulation 29.14 the steering gear where it is required to be so supplied by that regulation.

2.6.2   In a ship engaged regularly in voyages of short duration, the Administration if satisfied that an adequate standard of safety would be attained may accept a lesser period than the 18 hour period specified in paragraphs 2.2 to 2.5 but not less than 12 hours.

3   The emergency source of electrical power may be either a generator or an accumulator battery, which shall comply with the following:

$\boxed{\text{F}}$ See Annex 2.

3.1   Where the emergency source of electrical power is a generator, it shall be:

.1   driven by a suitable prime mover with an independent supply of fuel, having a flashpoint (closed cup test) of not less than 43°C;

.2   started automatically upon failure of the main source of electrical power supply unless a transitional source of emergency electrical power in accordance with paragraph 3.1.3 is provided; where the emergency generator is automatically started, it shall be automatically connected to the emergency switchboard; those services referred to in paragraph 4 shall then be connected automatically to the emergency generator; and unless a second independent means of starting the emergency generator is provided the single source of stored energy shall be protected to preclude its complete depletion by the automatic starting system; and

.3   provided with a transitional source of emergency electrical power as specified in paragraph 4 unless an emergency generator is provided capable both of supplying the services mentioned in that paragraph and of being automatically started and supplying the required load as quickly as is safe and practicable subject to a maximum of 45 seconds.

3.2   Where the emergency source of electrical power is an accumulator battery it shall be capable of:

.1   carrying the emergency electrical load without recharging while maintaining the voltage of the battery throughout the discharge period within 12 per cent above or below its nominal voltage;

.2   automatically connecting to the emergency switchboard in the event of failure of the main source of electrical power; and

.3   immediately supplying at least those services specified in paragraph 4.

4   The transitional source of emergency electrical power where required by paragraph 3.1.3 shall consist of an accumulator battery suitably located for use in an emergency which shall operate without recharging while maintaining the voltage of the battery throughout the discharge period within 12 per cent above or below its nominal voltage and be of sufficient capacity and shall be so arranged as to supply automatically in the event of failure of either the main or the emergency source of electrical power for half an hour at least the following services if they depend upon an electrical source for their operation:

.1   the lighting required by paragraphs 2.1, 2.2 and 2.3. For this transitional phase, the required emergency electric lighting, in respect of the machinery space and accommodation and service spaces may be provided by permanently fixed, individual, automatically charged, relay operated accumulator lamps; and

.2   all services required by paragraphs 2.4.1, 2.4.3 and 2.4.4 unless such services have an independent supply for the period specified from an accumulator battery suitably located for use in an emergency.

5.1   The emergency switchboard shall be installed as near as is practicable to the emergency source of electrical power.

5.2   Where the emergency source of electrical power is a generator, the emergency switchboard shall be located in the same space unless the operation of the emergency switchboard would thereby be impaired.

5.3   No accumulator battery fitted in accordance with this regulation shall be installed in the same space as the emergency switchboard. An indicator shall be mounted in a suitable place on the main switchboard or in the machinery control room to indicate when the batteries constituting either the emergency source of electrical power or the transitional source of electrical power referred to in paragraph 3.2 or 4 are being discharged.

5.4   The emergency switchboard shall be supplied during normal operation from the main switchboard by an interconnector feeder which is to be adequately protected at the main switchboard against overload and short circuit and which is to be disconnected automatically at the emergency switchboard upon failure of the main source of electrical power. Where the system is arranged for feedback operation, the interconnector feeder is also to be protected at the emergency switchboard at least against short circuit.

5.5   In order to ensure ready availability of the emergency source of electrical power, arrangements shall be made where necessary to disconnect automatically non-emergency circuits from the emergency switchboard to ensure that electrical power shall be available automatically to the emergency circuits.

6   The emergency generator and its prime mover and any emergency accumulator battery shall be so designed and arranged as to ensure that they will function at full rated power when the ship is upright and when inclined at any angle of list up to 22.5° or when inclined up to 10° either in the fore or aft direction, or is in any combination of angles within those limits.

7   Provision shall be made for the periodic testing of the complete emergency system and shall include the testing of automatic starting arrangements.

Regulation 44

Starting arrangements for emergency generating sets

1   Emergency generating sets shall be capable of being readily started in their cold condition at a temperature of 0°C. If this is impracticable, or if

lower temperatures are likely to be encountered, provision acceptable to the Administration shall be made for the maintenance of heating arrangements, to ensure ready starting of the generating sets.

2   Each emergency generating set arranged to be automatically started shall be equipped with starting devices approved by the Administration with a stored energy capability of at least three consecutive starts. A second source of energy shall be provided for an additional three starts within 30 minutes unless manual starting can be demonstrated to be effective.

3   The stored energy shall be maintained at all times, as follows:

.1   electrical and hydraulic starting systems shall be maintained from the emergency switchboard;

.2   compressed air starting systems may be maintained by the main or auxiliary compressed air receivers through a suitable nonreturn valve or by an emergency air compressor which, if electrically driven, is supplied from the emergency switchboard;

.3   all of these starting, charging and energy storing devices shall be located in the emergency generator space; these devices are not to be used for any purpose other than the operation of the emergency generating set. This does not preclude the supply to the air receiver of the emergency generating set from the main or auxiliary compressed air system through the nonreturn valve fitted in the emergency generator space.

4.1   Where automatic starting is not required, manual starting is permissible, such as manual cranking, inertia starters, manually charged hydraulic accumulators, or powder charge cartridges, where they can be demonstrated as being effective.

4.2   When manual starting is not practicable, the requirements of paragraphs 2 and 3 shall be complied with except that starting may be manually initiated.

Regulation 45

Precautions against shock, fire and other hazards of electrical origin

1.1   Exposed metal parts of electrical machines or equipment which are not intended to be live but which are liable under fault conditions to become live shall be earthed unless the machines or equipment are:

.1   supplied at a voltage not exceeding 55 V direct current or 55 V, root mean square between conductors; auto-transformers shall not be used for the purpose of achieving this voltage; or

.2 supplied at a voltage not exceeding 250 V by safety isolating transformers supplying only one consuming device; or

.3 constructed in accordance with the principle of double insulation.

1.2 The Administration may require additional precautions for portable electrical equipment for use in confined or exceptionally damp spaces where particular risks due to conductivity may exist.

1.3 All electrical apparatus shall be so constructed and so installed as not to cause injury when handled or touched in the normal manner.

2 Main and emergency switchboards shall be so arranged as to give easy access as may be needed to apparatus and equipment, without danger to personnel. The sides and the rear and, where necessary, the front of switchboards shall be suitably guarded. Exposed live parts having voltages to earth exceeding a voltage to be specified by the Administration shall not be installed on the front of such switchboards. Where necessary, nonconducting mats or gratings shall be provided at the front and rear of the switchboard.

3.1 The hull return system of distribution shall not be used for any purpose in a tanker, or for power, heating, or lighting in any other ship of 1,600 tons gross tonnage and upwards.

3.2 The requirement of paragraph 3.1 does not preclude under conditions approved by the Administration the use of:

.1 impressed current cathodic protective systems;

.2 limited and locally earthed systems; or

.3 insulation level monitoring devices provided the circulation current does not exceed 30 mA under the most unfavourable conditions.

3.3 Where the hull return system is used, all final subcircuits, i.e. all circuits fitted after the last protective device, shall be two-wire and special precautions shall be taken to the satisfaction of the Administration.

4.1 Earthed distribution systems shall not be used in a tanker. The Administration may exceptionally permit in a tanker the earthing of the neutral for alternating current power networks of 3,000 V (line to line) and over, provided that any possible resulting current does not flow directly through any of the dangerous spaces.

4.2 When a distribution system, whether primary or secondary, for power, heating or lighting, with no connection to earth is used, a device capable of continuously monitoring the insulation level to earth and of giving an audible or visual indication of abnormally low insulation values shall be provided.

5.1 Except as permitted by the Administration in exceptional circumstances, all metal sheaths and armour of cables shall be electrically continuous and shall be earthed.

5.2　All electric cables and wiring external to equipment shall be at least of a flame-retardant type and shall be so installed as not to impair their original flame-retarding properties. Where necessary for particular applications the Administration may permit the use of special types of cables such as radio frequency cables, which do not comply with the foregoing.

5.3　Cables and wiring serving essential or emergency power, lighting, internal communications or signals shall so far as practicable be routed clear of galleys, laundries, machinery spaces of category A and their casings and other high fire risk areas. Cables connecting fire pumps to the emergency switchboard shall be of a fire-resistant type where they pass through high fire risk areas. Where practicable all such cables should be run in such a manner as to preclude their being rendered unserviceable by heating of the bulkheads that may be caused by a fire in an adjacent space.

5.4　Where cables which are installed in hazardous areas introduce the risk of fire or explosion in the event of an electrical fault in such areas, special precautions against such risks shall be taken to the satisfaction of the Administration.

5.5　Cables and wiring shall be installed and supported in such a manner as to avoid chafing or other damage.

5.6　Terminations and joints in all conductors shall be so made as to retain the original electrical, mechanical, flame-retarding and, where necessary, fire-resisting properties of the cable.

6.1　Each separate circuit shall be protected against short circuit and against overload, except as permitted in regulations 29 and 30 or where the Administration may exceptionally otherwise permit.

6.2　The rating or appropriate setting of the overload protective device for each circuit shall be permanently indicated at the location of the protective device.

7　Lighting fittings shall be so arranged as to prevent temperature rises which could damage the cables and wiring, and to prevent surrounding material from becoming excessively hot.

8　All lighting and power circuits terminating in a bunker or cargo space shall be provided with a multiple-pole switch outside the space for disconnecting such circuits.

9.1　Accumulator batteries shall be suitably housed, and compartments used primarily for their accommodation shall be properly constructed and efficiently ventilated.

9.2　Electrical or other equipment which may constitute a source of ignition of flammable vapours shall not be permitted in these compartments except as permitted in paragraph 10.

9.3 Accumulator batteries shall not be located in sleeping quarters except where hermetically sealed to the satisfaction of the Administration.

10 No electrical equipment shall be installed in any space where flammable mixtures are liable to collect including those on board tankers or in compartments assigned principally to accumulator batteries, in paint lockers, acetylene stores or similar spaces, unless the Administration is satisfied that such equipment is:

.1 essential for operational purposes;

.2 of a type which will not ignite the mixture concerned;

.3 appropriate to the space concerned; and

.4 appropriately certified for safe usage in the dusts, vapours or gases likely to be encountered.

11 In a passenger ship, distribution systems shall be so arranged that fire in any main vertical zone as is defined in regulation II-2/3.9 will not interfere with services essential for safety in any other such zone. This requirement will be met if main and emergency feeders passing through any such zone are separated both vertically and horizontally as widely as is practicable.

PART E – ADDITIONAL REQUIREMENTS FOR PERIODICALLY UNATTENDED MACHINERY SPACES

(Part E applies to cargo ships except that regulation 54
refers to passenger ships)

Regulation 46

General

1 The arrangements provided shall be such as to ensure that the safety of the ship in all sailing conditions, including manoeuvring, is equivalent to that of a ship having the machinery spaces manned.

2 Measures shall be taken to the satisfaction of the Administration to ensure that the equipment is functioning in a reliable manner and that satisfactory arrangements are made for regular inspections and routine tests to ensure continuous reliable operation.

3   Every ship shall be provided with documentary evidence, to the satisfaction of the Administration, of its fitness to operate with periodically unattended machinery spaces.

Regulation 47

Fire precautions

1   Means shall be provided to detect and give alarms at an early stage in case of fires:

.1   in boiler air supply casings and exhausts (uptakes); and

.2   in scavenging air belts of propulsion machinery,

unless the Administration considers this to be unnecessary in a particular case.

2   Internal combustion engines of 2250 kW and above or having cylinders of more than 300 mm bore shall be provided with crankcase oil mist detectors or engine bearing temperature monitors or equivalent devices.

Regulation 48

Protection against flooding

1   Bilge wells in periodically unattended machinery spaces shall be located and monitored in such a way that the accumulation of liquids is detected at normal angles of trim and heel, and shall be large enough to accommodate easily the normal drainage during the unattended period.

2   Where the bilge pumps are capable of being started automatically, means shall be provided to indicate when the influx of liquid is greater than the pump capacity or when the pump is operating more frequently than would normally be expected. In these cases, smaller bilge wells to cover a reasonable period of time may be permitted. Where automatically controlled bilge pumps are provided, special attention shall be given to oil pollution prevention requirements.

3   The location of the controls of any valve serving a sea inlet, a discharge below the waterline or a bilge injection system shall be so sited as to allow adequate time for operation in case of influx of water to the space, having regard to the time likely to be required in order to reach and operate such controls. If the level to which the space could become flooded with the ship

in the fully loaded condition so requires, arrangements shall be made to operate the controls from a position above such level.

Regulation 49

Control of propulsion machinery from the navigating bridge

1   Under all sailing conditions, including manoeuvring, the speed, direction of thrust and, if applicable, the pitch of the propeller shall be fully controllable from the navigating bridge.

1.1   Such remote control shall be performed by a single control device for each independent propeller, with automatic performance of all associated services, including, where necessary, means of preventing overload of the propulsion machinery.

1.2   The main propulsion machinery shall be provided with an emergency stopping device on the navigating bridge which shall be independent of the navigating bridge control system.

2   Propulsion machinery orders from the navigating bridge shall be indicated in the main machinery control room or at the propulsion machinery control position as appropriate.

3   Remote control of the propulsion machinery shall be possible only from one location at a time; at such locations interconnected control positions are permitted. At each location there shall be an indicator showing which location is in control of the propulsion machinery. The transfer of control between the navigating bridge and machinery spaces shall be possible only in the main machinery space or in the main machinery control room. The system shall include means to prevent the propelling thrust from altering significantly when transferring control from one location to another.

4   It shall be possible for all machinery essential for the safe operation of the ship to be controlled from a local position, even in the case of failure in any part of the automatic or remote control systems.

5   The design of the remote automatic control system shall be such that in case of its failure an alarm will be given. Unless the Administration considers it impracticable, the preset speed and direction of thrust of the propeller shall be maintained until local control is in operation.

6   Indicators shall be fitted on the navigating bridge for:

.1   propeller speed and direction of rotation in the case of fixed pitch propellers; or

.2   propeller speed and pitch position in the case of controllable pitch propellers.

7   The number of consecutive automatic attempts which fail to produce a start shall be limited to safeguard sufficient starting air pressure. An alarm shall be provided to indicate low starting air pressure set at a level which still permits starting operations of the propulsion machinery.

Regulation 50

Communication

A reliable means of vocal communication shall be provided between the main machinery control room or the propulsion machinery control position as appropriate, the navigating bridge and the engineer officers' accommodation.

Regulation 51

Alarm system

1   An alarm system shall be provided indicating any fault requiring attention and shall:

.1   be capable of sounding an audible alarm in the main machinery control room or at the propulsion machinery control position, and indicate visually each separate alarm function at a suitable position;

.2   have a connection to the engineers' public rooms and to each of the engineers' cabins through a selector switch, to ensure connection to at least one of those cabins. Administrations may permit equivalent arrangements;

.3   activate an audible and visual alarm on the navigating bridge for any situation which requires action by or attention of the officer on watch;

.4   as far as is practicable be designed on the fail-to-safety principle; and

.5   activate the engineers' alarm required by regulation 38 if an alarm function has not received attention locally within a limited time.

2.1   The alarm system shall be continuously powered and shall have an automatic change-over to a stand-by power supply in case of loss of normal power supply.

2.2   Failure of the normal power supply of the alarm system shall be indicated by an alarm.

3.1   The alarm system shall be able to indicate at the same time more than one fault and the acceptance of any alarm shall not inhibit another alarm.

3.2   Acceptance at the position referred to in paragraph 1 of any alarm condition shall be indicated at the positions where it was shown. Alarms shall be maintained until they are accepted and the visual indications of individual alarms shall remain until the fault has been corrected, when the alarm system shall automatically reset to the normal operating condition.

Regulation 52

Safety systems

A safety system shall be provided to ensure that serious malfunction in machinery or boiler operations, which presents an immediate danger, shall initiate the automatic shutdown of that part of the plant and that an alarm shall be given. Shutdown of the propulsion system shall not be automatically activated except in cases which could lead to serious damage, complete breakdown, or explosion. Where arrangements for overriding the shutdown of the main propelling machinery are fitted, these shall be such as to preclude inadvertent operation. Visual means shall be provided to indicate when the override has been activated.

Regulation 53

Special requirements for machinery, boiler and electrical installations

1   The special requirements for the machinery, boiler and electrical installations shall be to the satisfaction of the Administration and shall include at least the requirements of this regulation.

2   The main source of electrical power shall comply with the following:

2.1   Where the electrical power can normally be supplied by one generator, suitable load-shedding arrangements shall be provided to ensure the integrity of supplies to services required for propulsion and steering as well as the safety of the ship. In the case of loss of the generator in operation, adequate provision shall be made for automatic starting and connecting to the main switchboard of a stand-by generator of sufficient capacity to permit propulsion and steering and to ensure the safety of the ship with automatic restarting of the essential auxiliaries including, where necessary, sequential operations. The Administration may dispense with this requirement for a ship of less than 1,600 tons gross tonnage, if it is considered impracticable.

2.2   If the electrical power is normally supplied by more than one generator simultaneously in parallel operation, provision shall be made, for instance by load shedding, to ensure that, in case of loss of one of these generating sets, the remaining ones are kept in operation without overload to permit propulsion and steering, and to ensure the safety of the ship.

3   Where stand-by machines are required for other auxiliary machinery essential to propulsion, automatic change-over devices shall be provided.

4   *Automatic control and alarm system*

4.1   The control system shall be such that the services needed for the operation of the main propulsion machinery and its auxiliaries are ensured through the necessary automatic arrangements.

4.2   An alarm shall be given on the automatic change-over.

4.3   An alarm system complying with regulation 51 shall be provided for all important pressures, temperatures and fluid levels and other essential parameters.

4.4   A centralized control position shall be arranged with the necessary alarm panels and instrumentation indicating any alarm.

5   Means shall be provided to keep the starting air pressure at the required level where internal combustion engines are used for main propulsion.

Regulation 54

Special consideration in respect of passenger ships

Passenger ships shall be specially considered by the Administration as to whether or not their machinery spaces may be periodically unattended and if so whether additional requirements to those stipulated in these regulations are necessary to achieve equivalent safety to that of normally attended machinery spaces.

Chapter II–2

CONSTRUCTION – FIRE PROTECTION, FIRE DETECTION AND FIRE EXTINCTION

Page

PART A – GENERAL

1	Application	110
2	Basic principles	111
3	Definitions	112
4	Fire pumps, fire mains, hydrants and hoses	117
5	Fixed gas fire-extinguishing systems	123
6	Fire extinguishers	130
7	Fire-extinguishing arrangements in machinery spaces	131
8	Fixed low-expansion foam fire-extinguishing systems in machinery spaces	133
9	Fixed high-expansion foam fire-extinguishing systems in machinery spaces	133
10	Fixed pressure water-spraying fire-extinguishing systems in machinery spaces	134
11	Special arrangements in machinery spaces	135
12	Automatic sprinkler, fire detection and fire alarm systems	136
13	Fixed fire detection and fire alarm systems	140
14	Fixed fire detection and fire alarm systems for periodically unattended machinery spaces	143
15	Arrangements for oil fuel, lubricating oil and other flammable oils	143
16	Ventilation systems in ships other than passenger ships carrying more than 36 passengers	147
17	Fireman's outfit	150
18	Miscellaneous items	151
19	International shore connection	152
20	Fire control plans	153
21	Ready availability of fire-extinguishing appliances	153
22	Acceptance of substitutes	154

PART B – FIRE SAFETY MEASURES FOR PASSENGER SHIPS

23 Structure 154
24 Main vertical zones and horizontal zones...................... 155
25 Bulkheads within a main vertical zone 156
26 Fire integrity of bulkheads and decks in ships carrying more
    than 36 passengers... 157
27 Fire integrity of bulkheads and decks in ships carrying not more
    than 36 passengers... 165
28 Means of escape 169
29 Protection of stairways and lifts in accommodation and service
    spaces 171
30 Openings in "A" class divisions 171
31 Openings in "B" class divisions.............................. 172
32 Ventilation systems.. 173
33 Windows and sidescuttles..................................... 174
34 Restricted use of combustible materials...................... 175
35 Details of construction 176
36 Fixed fire detection and fire alarm systems, automatic sprinkler,
    fire detection and fire alarm systems........................ 176
37 Protection of special category spaces 177
38 Protection of cargo spaces, other than special category spaces,
    intended for the carriage of motor vehicles with fuel in their
    tanks for their own propulsion............................... 180
39 Fixed fire-extinguishing arrangements in cargo spaces........ 182
40 Fire patrols, detection, alarms and public address systems .. 182
41 Special requirements for ships carrying dangerous goods 183

PART C – FIRE SAFETY MEASURES FOR CARGO SHIPS 183

42 Structure 183
43 Bulkheads within the accommodation and service spaces 184
44 Fire integrity of bulkheads and decks 185
45 Means of escape 188
46 Protection of stairways and lift trunks in accommodation spaces,
    service spaces and control stations 190
47 Doors in fire resisting divisions 190
48 Ventilation systems.. 191
49 Restricted use of combustible materials...................... 191
50 Details of construction 192

51 Arrangements for gaseous fuel for domestic purposes   192
52 Fixed fire detection and fire alarm systems, automatic sprinkler,
    fire detection and fire alarm systems   193
53 Fire protection arrangements in cargo spaces   193
54 Special requirements for ships carrying dangerous goods   197

PART D – FIRE SAFETY MEASURES FOR TANKERS

55 Application   203
56 Location and separation of spaces   204
57 Structure, bulkheads within accommodation and service spaces
    and details of construction   206
58 Fire integrity of bulkheads and decks   207
59 Venting, purging, gas-freeing and ventilation   210
60 Cargo tank protection   213
61 Fixed deck foam systems   214
62 Inert gas systems   216
63 Cargo pump-rooms   223

PART A – GENERAL

Regulation 1

Application

1.1 Unless expressly provided otherwise, this chapter shall apply to ships the keels of which are laid or which are at a similar stage of construction on or after 1 July 1986.

1.2 For the purpose of this chapter the term "a similar stage of construction" means the stage at which:

.1 construction identifiable with a specific ship begins; and

.2 assembly of that ship has commenced comprising at least 50 tonnes or one per cent of the estimated mass of all structural material, whichever is less.

1.3 For the purpose of this chapter:

.1 the expression "ships constructed" means "ships the keels of which are laid or which are at a similar stage of construction";

.2 the expression "all ships" means "ships constructed before, on or after 1 July 1986";

.3 a cargo ship, whenever built, which is converted to a passenger ship shall be treated as a passenger ship constructed on the date on which such a conversion commences.

2 Unless expressly provided otherwise, for ships constructed before 1 July 1986 the Administration shall ensure that the requirements which are applicable under chapter II–2 of the International Convention for the Safety of Life at Sea, 1974, as amended by resolution MSC.1(XLV) adopted on 20 November 1981, are complied with.

3 All ships which undergo repairs, alterations, modifications and outfitting related thereto shall continue to comply with at least the requirements previously applicable to these ships. Such ships, if constructed before 1 July 1986 shall, as a rule, comply with the requirements for ships constructed on or after that date to at least the same extent as they did before undergoing such repairs, alterations, modifications or outfitting. Repairs, alterations and

modifications of a major character* and outfitting related thereto shall meet the requirements for ships constructed on or after 1 July 1986 in so far as the Administration deems reasonable and practicable.

4.1   The Administration of a State may, if it considers that the sheltered nature and conditions of the voyage are such as to render the application of any specific requirements of this chapter unreasonable or unnecessary, exempt from those requirements individual ships or classes of ships entitled to fly the flag of that State which, in the course of their voyage, do not proceed more than 20 miles from the nearest land.

4.2   In the case of passenger ships which are employed in special trades for the carriage of large numbers of special trade passengers, such as the pilgrim trade, the Administration of the State whose flag such ships are entitled to fly, if satisfied that it is impracticable to enforce compliance with the requirements of this chapter, may exempt such ships from those requirements, provided that they comply fully with provisions of:

   .1   the rules annexed to the Special Trade Passenger Ships Agreement, 1971; and

   .2   the rules annexed to the Protocol on Space Requirements for Special Trade Passenger Ships, 1973.

Regulation 2

Basic principles

1   The purpose of this chapter is to require the fullest practicable degree of fire protection, fire detection and fire extinction in ships.

2   The following basic principles underlie the regulations in this chapter and are embodied in the regulations as appropriate, having regard to the type of ships and the potential fire hazard involved:

---

* The following repairs, alterations and modifications should be recognized as being of a "major character":

1   Any change that substantially alters the dimensions of a ship.
    Example – Lengthening by adding new midbody.
    New midbody should comply with chapter II–2 of SOLAS 1974 as amended.

2   Any change that substantially alters the passenger carrying capacity of a ship.
    Example – Vehicle deck converted to passenger accommodation.
    New accommodation should comply with chapter II–2 of SOLAS 1974 as amended.

3   Any change that substantially increases a ship's service life.
    Example – Renewal of passenger accommodation on one entire deck.
    Renewed accommodation should comply with chapter II–2 of SOLAS 1974 as amended.
    (Interpretation approved by the Maritime Safety Committee at its forty-eighth session.)

.1   division of ship into main vertical zones by thermal and structural boundaries;

.2   separation of accommodation spaces from the remainder of the ship by thermal and structural boundaries;

.3   restricted use of combustible materials;

.4   detection of any fire in the zone of origin;

.5   containment and extinction of any fire in the space of origin;

.6   protection of means of escape or access for fire fighting;

.7   ready availability of fire-extinguishing appliances;

.8   minimization of possibility of ignition of flammable cargo vapour.

Regulation 3

Definitions

For the purpose of this chapter, unless expressly provided otherwise:

1   *Non-combustible material** is a material which neither burns nor gives off flammable vapours in sufficient quantity for self-ignition when heated to approximately 750°C, this being determined to the satisfaction of the Administration by an established test procedure.** Any other material is a combustible material.

2   *A standard fire test* is one in which specimens of the relevant bulkheads or decks are exposed in a test furnace to temperatures corresponding approximately to the standard time-temperature curve. The specimen shall have an exposed surface of not less than 4.65 m² and height (or length of deck) of 2.44 m, resembling as closely as possible the intended construction and including where appropriate at least one joint. The standard time-temperature curve is defined by a smooth curve drawn through the following temperature points measured above the initial furnace temperature:

at the end of the first	5 minutes	556°C
" " " " " "	10 minutes	659°C
" " " " " "	15 minutes	718°C
" " " " " "	30 minutes	821°C
" " " " " "	60 minutes	925°C

---

* If a material passes the test as specified in resolution A.270(VIII) it should be considered as "non-combustible" even if it consists of a mixture of inorganic and organic substances. (Interpretation approved by the MSC at its forty-sixth session, SLS 14/Circ. 17.)

** Reference is made to Improved Recommendation on Test Method for Qualifying Marine Construction Materials as Non-Combustible, adopted by the Organization by resolution A.472(XII).

3   *"A" class divisions* are those divisions formed by bulkheads and decks which comply with the following:

.1 they shall be constructed of steel or other equivalent material;

.2 they shall be suitably stiffened;

.3 they shall be so constructed as to be capable of preventing the passage of smoke and flame to the end of the one-hour standard fire test;

.4 they shall be insulated with approved non-combustible materials such that the average temperature of the unexposed side will not rise more than 139°C above the original temperature, nor will the temperature, at any one point, including any joint, rise more than 180°C above the original temperature, within the time listed below:

class "A-60"	60 minutes
class "A-30"	30 minutes
class "A-15"	15 minutes
class "A-0"	0 minutes

.5 the Administration may require a test of a prototype bulkhead or deck to ensure that it meets the above requirements for integrity and temperature rise.*

4   *"B" class divisions* are those divisions formed by bulkheads, decks, ceilings or linings which comply with the following:

.1 they shall be so constructed as to be capable of preventing the passage of flame to the end of the first half hour of the standard fire test;

.2 they shall have an insulation value such that the average temperature of the unexposed side will not rise more than 139°C above the original temperature, nor will the temperature at any one point, including any joint, rise more than 225°C above the original temperature, within the time listed below:

class "B-15"	15 minutes
class "B-0"	0 minutes

.3 they shall be constructed of approved non-combustible materials and all materials entering into the construction and erection of "B" class divisions shall be non-combustible, with the exception that combustible veneers may be permitted provided they meet other requirements of this chapter;

.4 the Administration may require a test of a prototype division to ensure that it meets the above requirements for integrity and temperature rise.*

---

* Reference is made to Recommendation on Fire Test Procedures for "A", "B" and "F" Class Divisions, adopted by the Organization by resolution A.517(13).

5   *"C" class divisions* are divisions constructed of approved non-combustible materials. They need meet neither requirements relative to the passage of smoke and flame nor limitations relative to the temperature rise. Combustible veneers are permitted provided they meet other requirements of this chapter.

6   *Continuous "B" class ceilings or linings* are those "B" class ceilings or linings which terminate only at an "A" or "B" class division.

7   *Steel or other equivalent material.* Where the words "steel or other equivalent material" occur, "equivalent material" means any non-combustible material which, by itself or due to insulation provided, has structural and integrity properties equivalent to steel at the end of the applicable exposure to the standard fire test (e.g. aluminium alloy with appropriate insulation).

8   *Low flame spread* means that the surface thus described will adequately restrict the spread of flame, this being determined to the satisfaction of the Administration by an established test procedure.

9   *Main vertical zones* are those sections into which the hull, superstructure, and deckhouses are divided by "A" class divisions, the mean length of which on any deck does not in general exceed 40 m.

10   *Accommodation spaces* are those spaces used for public spaces, corridors, lavatories, cabins, offices, hospitals, cinemas, games and hobbies rooms, barber shops, pantries containing no cooking appliances and similar spaces.

11   *Public spaces* are those portions of the accommodation which are used for halls, dining rooms, lounges and similar permanently enclosed spaces.

12   *Service spaces* are those spaces used for galleys, pantries containing cooking appliances, lockers, mail and specie rooms, store-rooms, workshops other than those forming part of the machinery spaces, and similar spaces and trunks to such spaces.

13   *Cargo spaces* are all spaces used for cargo (including cargo oil tanks) and trunks to such spaces.

14   *Ro–ro cargo spaces* are spaces not normally subdivided in any way and extending to either a substantial length or the entire length of the ship in which goods (packaged or in bulk, in or on rail or road cars, vehicles (including road or rail tankers), trailers, containers, pallets, demountable tanks or in or on similar stowage units or other receptacles) can be loaded and unloaded normally in a horizontal direction.

15   *Open ro–ro cargo spaces* are ro–ro cargo spaces either open at both ends, or open at one end and provided with adequate natural ventilation effective over their entire length through permanent openings in the side plating or deckhead to the satisfaction of the Administration.

16   *Closed ro–ro cargo spaces* are ro–ro cargo spaces which are neither open ro–ro cargo spaces nor weather decks.

17   *Weather deck* is a deck which is completely exposed to the weather from above and from at least two sides.

18   *Special category spaces* are those enclosed spaces above or below the bulkhead deck intended for the carriage of motor vehicles with fuel in their tanks for their own propulsion, into and from which such vehicles can be driven and to which passengers have access.

19   *Machinery spaces of category A* are those spaces and trunks to such spaces which contain:

.1   internal combustion machinery used for main propulsion; or

.2   internal combustion machinery used for purposes other than main propulsion where such machinery has in the aggregate a total power output of not less than 375 kW; or

.3   any oil-fired boiler or oil fuel unit.

20   *Machinery spaces* are all machinery spaces of category A and all other spaces containing propulsion machinery, boilers, oil fuel units, steam and internal combustion engines, generators and major electrical machinery, oil filling stations, refrigerating, stabilizing, ventilation and air-conditioning machinery, and similar spaces, and trunks to such spaces.

21   *Oil fuel unit* is the equipment used for the preparation of oil fuel for delivery to an oil-fired boiler, or equipment used for the preparation for delivery of heated oil to an internal combustion engine, and includes any oil pressure pumps, filters and heaters dealing with oil at a pressure of more than 0.18 N/mm².

22   *Control stations* are those spaces in which the ship's radio or main navigating equipment or the emergency source of power is located or where the fire recording or fire control equipment is centralized.

23   *Rooms containing furniture and furnishings of restricted fire risk* are, for the purpose of regulation 26, those rooms containing furniture and furnishings of restricted fire risk (whether cabins, public spaces, offices or other types of accommodation) in which:

.1   all case furniture such as desks, wardrobes, dressing tables, bureaux, dressers, is constructed entirely of approved non-combustible materials, except that a combustible veneer not exceeding 2 mm may be used on the working surface of such articles;

.2   all free-standing furniture such as chairs, sofas, tables, is constructed with frames of non-combustible materials;

.3   all draperies, curtains and other suspended textile materials have, to the satisfaction of the Administration, qualities of resistance to the propagation of flame not inferior to those of wool of mass $0.8\,kg/m^2$;*

.4 all floor coverings have, to the satisfaction of the Administration, qualities of resistance to the propagation of flame not inferior to those of an equivalent woollen material used for the same purpose;

.5 all exposed surfaces of bulkheads, linings and ceilings have low flame-spread characteristics; and

.6 all upholstered furniture has qualities of resistance to the ignition and propagation of flame to the satisfaction of the Administration.

24   *Bulkhead deck* is the uppermost deck up to which the transverse watertight bulkheads are carried.

25   *Deadweight* is the difference in tonnes between the displacement of a ship in water of a specific gravity of 1.025 at the load waterline corresponding to the assigned summer freeboard and the lightweight of the ship.

26   *Lightweight* is the displacement of a ship in tonnes without cargo, fuel, lubricating oil, ballast water, fresh water and feedwater in tanks, consumable stores, and passengers and crew and their effects.

27   *Combination carrier* is a tanker designed to carry oil or alternatively solid cargoes in bulk.

28   *Crude oil* is any oil occurring naturally in the earth whether or not treated to render it suitable for transportation and includes:

.1 crude oil from which certain distillate fractions may have been removed; and

.2 crude oil to which certain distillate fractions may have been added.

29   *Dangerous goods* are those goods referred to in regulation VII/2.

30   *Chemical tanker* is a tanker constructed or adapted and used for the carriage in bulk of any liquid product of a flammable nature listed in either:

.1 chapter 17 of the International Code for the Construction and Equipment of Ships Carrying Dangerous Chemicals in Bulk adopted by the Maritime Safety Committee by resolution MSC.4(48), hereinafter referred to as "the International Bulk Chemical Code", as may be amended by the Organization; or

.2 chapter VI of the Code for the Construction and Equipment of Ships

---

* Reference is made to Recommendation on Test Method for Determining the Resistance to Flame of Vertically Supported Textiles and Films, adopted by the Organization by resolution A.471(XII).

Carrying Dangerous Chemicals in Bulk adopted by the Assembly of the Organization by resolution A.212(VII), hereinafter referred to as "the Bulk Chemical Code", as has been or may be amended by the Organization;

whichever is applicable.

31   *Gas carrier* is a tanker constructed or adapted and used for the carriage in bulk of any liquefied gas or other products of a flammable nature listed in either:

.1   chapter 19 of the International Code for the Construction and Equipment of Ships Carrying Liquefied Gases in Bulk adopted by the Maritime Safety Committee by resolution MSC.5(48), hereinafter referred to as "the International Gas Carrier Code", as may be amended by the Organization; or

.2   chapter XIX of the Code for the Construction and Equipment of Ships Carrying Liquefied Gases in Bulk adopted by the Assembly of the Organization by resolution A.328(IX), hereinafter referred to as "the Gas Carrier Code", as has been or may be amended by the Organization;

whichever is applicable.

32   *Cargo area* is that part of the ship that contains cargo tanks, slop tanks and cargo pump-rooms including pump-rooms, cofferdams, ballast and void spaces adjacent to cargo tanks and also deck areas throughout the entire length and breadth of the part of the ship over the above-mentioned spaces.

Regulation 4

Fire pumps, fire mains, hydrants and hoses

1   Every ship shall be provided with fire pumps, fire mains, hydrants and hoses complying as applicable with the requirements of this regulation.

2   *Capacity of fire pumps*

2.1   The required fire pumps shall be capable of delivering for fire-fighting purposes a quantity of water, at the pressure specified in paragraph 4, as follows:

.1   pumps in passenger ships, not less than two thirds of the quantity required to be dealt with by the bilge pumps when employed for bilge pumping; and

.2 pumps in cargo ships, other than any emergency pump, not less than four thirds of the quantity required under regulation II–1/21 to be dealt with by each of the independent bilge pumps in a passenger ship of the same dimension when employed in bilge pumping, provided that in no cargo ship need the total required capacity of the fire pumps exceed 180 m³/hour.

2.2 Each of the required fire pumps (other than any emergency pump required in paragraph 3.3.2 for cargo ships) shall have a capacity not less than 80 per cent of the total required capacity divided by the minimum number of required fire pumps but in any case not less than 25 m³/hour and each such pump shall in any event be capable of delivering at least the two required jets of water. These fire pumps shall be capable of supplying the fire main system under the required conditions. Where more pumps than the minimum of required pumps are installed the capacity of such additional pumps shall be to the satisfaction of the Administration.

3 *Arrangements of fire pumps and of fire mains*

3.1 Ships shall be provided with independently driven fire pumps as follows:

.1 Passenger ships of 4,000 tons gross
    tonnage and upwards   at least three

.2 Passenger ships of less than 4,000 tons
    gross tonnage and cargo ships of 1,000
    tons gross tonnage and upwards   at least two

.3 Cargo ships of less than 1,000 tons   to the satisfaction
    gross tonnage   of the Administration

3.2 Sanitary, ballast, bilge or general service pumps may be accepted as fire pumps, provided that they are not normally used for pumping oil and that if they are subject to occasional duty for the transfer or pumping of oil fuel, suitable change-over arrangements are fitted.

3.3 The arrangement of sea connections, fire pumps and their sources of power shall be such as to ensure that:

.1 In passenger ships of 1,000 tons gross tonnage and upwards, in the event of a fire in any one compartment all the fire pumps will not be put out of action.

.2 In cargo ships of 2,000 tons gross tonnage and upwards if a fire in any one compartment could put all the pumps out of action there shall be an alternative means consisting of a fixed independently driven emergency pump which shall be capable of supplying two jets of water to the satisfaction of the Administration. The pump and its location shall comply with the following requirements:

.2.1 The capacity of the pump shall not be less than 40 per cent of

118

the total capacity of the fire pumps required by this regulation and in any case not less than 25 m³/hour.

.2.2 When the pump is delivering the quantity of water required by paragraph 3.3.2.1 the pressure at any hydrant shall be not less than the minimum pressures given in paragraph 4.2.

.2.3 Any diesel driven power source for the pump shall be capable of being readily started in its cold condition down to a temperature of 0°C by hand (manual) cranking. If this is impracticable, or if lower temperatures are likely to be encountered, consideration is to be given to the provision and maintenance of heating arrangements, acceptable to the Administration, so that ready starting will be assured. If hand (manual) starting is impracticable the Administration may permit other means of starting. These means shall be such as to enable the diesel driven power source to be started at least 6 times within a period of 30 minutes, and at least twice within the first 10 minutes.

.2.4 Any service fuel tank shall contain sufficient fuel to enable the pump to run on full load for at least three hours and sufficient reserves of fuel shall be available outside the main machinery space to enable the pump to be run on full load for an additional 15 hours.

.2.5 The total suction head of the pump shall not exceed 4.5 m under all conditions of list and trim likely to be encountered in service and the suction piping shall be designed to minimize suction losses.

.2.6 The boundaries of the space containing the fire pump shall be insulated to a standard of structural fire protection equivalent to that required for a control station in regulation 44.

.2.7 No direct access shall be permitted between the machinery space and the space containing the emergency fire pump and its source of power. When this is impracticable an Administration may accept an arrangement where the access is by means of an airlock, each of the two doors being self-closing, or through a watertight door capable of being operated from a space remote from the machinery space and the space containing the emergency fire pump and unlikely to be cut off in the event of fire in those spaces. In such cases a second means of access to the space containing the emergency fire pump and its source of power shall be provided.

.2.8 Ventilation arrangements to the space containing the independent source of power for the emergency fire pump shall be such as to preclude, as far as practicable, the possibility of smoke from a machinery space fire entering or being drawn into that space.

.3 In passenger ships of less than 1,000 tons gross tonnage and cargo ships of less than 2,000 tons gross tonnage, if a fire in any one compartment could put all the pumps out of action the alternative means of providing water for fire-fighting purposes are to the satisfaction of the Administration.

.4 In addition, in cargo ships where other pumps, such as general service, bilge and ballast, etc., are fitted in a machinery space, arrangements shall be made to ensure that at least one of these pumps, having the capacity and pressure required by paragraphs 2.2 and 4.2, is capable of providing water to the fire main.

3.4 The arrangements for the ready availability of water supply shall be:

.1 in passenger ships of 1,000 tons gross tonnage and upwards such that at least one effective jet of water is immediately available from any hydrant in an interior location and so as to ensure the continuation of the output of water by the automatic starting of a required fire pump;

.2 in passenger ships of less than 1,000 tons gross tonnage and in cargo ships to the satisfaction of the Administration;

.3 in cargo ships with a periodically unattended machinery space or when only one person is required on watch there shall be immediate water delivery from the fire main system at a suitable pressure, either by remote starting of one of the main fire pumps with remote starting from the navigating bridge and fire control station, if any, or permanent pressurization of the fire main system by one of the main fire pumps, except that the Administration may waive this requirement for cargo ships of less than 1,600 tons gross tonnage if the arrangement of the machinery space access makes it unnecessary;

.4 in passenger ships, if fitted with periodically unattended machinery spaces in accordance with regulation II–1/54, the Administration shall determine provisions for fixed water fire-extinguishing arrangement for such spaces equivalent to those required for normally attended machinery spaces.

3.5 Relief valves shall be provided in conjunction with all fire pumps if the pumps are capable of developing a pressure exceeding the design pressure of the water service pipes, hydrants and hoses. These valves shall be so placed and adjusted as to prevent excessive pressure in any part of the fire main system.

3.6 In tankers isolation valves shall be fitted in the fire main at poop front in a protected position and on the tank deck at intervals of not more than 40 m to preserve the integrity of the fire main system in case of fire or explosion.

4   *Diameter of and pressure in the fire mains*

4.1 The diameter of the fire main and water service pipes shall be sufficient for the effective distribution of the maximum required discharge from two fire pumps operating simultaneously, except that in the case of cargo ships the diameter need only be sufficient for the discharge of 140 m³/hour.

4.2   With the two pumps simultaneously delivering through nozzles specified in paragraph 8 the quantity of water specified in paragraph 4.1, through any adjacent hydrants, the following minimum pressures shall be maintained at all hydrants:

Passenger ships:

4,000 tons gross tonnage and upwards	$0.31\,\text{N}/\text{mm}^2$
1,000 tons gross tonnage and upwards but under 4,000 tons gross tonnage	$0.27\,\text{N}/\text{mm}^2$
Under 1,000 tons gross tonnage	To the satisfaction of the Administration

Cargo ships:

6,000 tons gross tonnage and upwards	$0.27\,\text{N}/\text{mm}^2$
1,000 tons gross tonnage and upwards but under 6,000 tons gross tonnage	$0.25\,\text{N}/\text{mm}^2$
Under 1,000 tons gross tonnage	To the satisfaction of the Administration

4.3   The maximum pressure at any hydrant shall not exceed that at which the effective control of a fire hose can be demonstrated.

5   *Number and position of hydrants*

5.1   The number and position of hydrants shall be such that at least two jets of water not emanating from the same hydrant, one of which shall be from a single length of hose, may reach any part of the ship normally accessible to the passengers or crew while the ship is being navigated and any part of any cargo space when empty, any ro–ro cargo space or any special category space in which latter case the two jets shall reach any part of such space, each from a single length of hose. Furthermore, such hydrants shall be positioned near the accesses to the protected spaces.

5.2   In the accommodation, service and machinery spaces of passenger ships the number and position of hydrants shall be such that the requirements of paragraph 5.1 may be complied with when all watertight doors and all doors in main vertical zone bulkheads are closed.

5.3   Where, in a passenger ship, access is provided to a machinery space of category A at a low level from an adjacent shaft tunnel, two hydrants shall be provided external to, but near the entrance to that machinery space. Where such access is provided from other spaces, in one of those spaces two hydrants shall be provided near the entrance to the machinery space of category A. Such provision need not be made where the tunnel or adjacent spaces are not part of the escape route.

6 Pipes and hydrants

6.1 Materials readily rendered ineffective by heat shall not be used for fire mains and hydrants unless adequately protected. The pipes and hydrants shall be so placed that the fire hoses may be easily coupled to them. The arrangement of pipes and hydrants shall be such as to avoid the possibility of freezing. In ships where deck cargo may be carried, the positions of the hydrants shall be such that they are always readily accessible and the pipes shall be arranged as far as practicable to avoid risk of damage by such cargo. Unless one hose and nozzle is provided for each hydrant in the ship, there shall be complete interchangeability of hose couplings and nozzles.

6.2 A valve shall be fitted to serve each fire hose so that any fire hose may be removed while the fire pumps are at work.

6.3 Isolating valves to separate the section of the fire main within the machinery space containing the main fire pump or pumps from the rest of the fire main shall be fitted in an easily accessible and tenable position outside the machinery spaces. The fire main shall be so arranged that when the isolating valves are shut all the hydrants on the ship, except those in the machinery space referred to above, can be supplied with water by a fire pump not located in this machinery space through pipes which do not enter this space. Exceptionally, the Administration may permit short lengths of the emergency fire pump suction and discharge piping to penetrate the machinery space if it is impracticable to route it externally provided that the integrity of the fire main is maintained by the enclosure of the piping in a substantial steel casing.

7 Fire hoses

7.1 Fire hoses shall be of material approved by the Administration and shall be sufficient in length to project a jet of water to any of the spaces in which they may be required to be used. Their maximum length shall be to the satisfaction of the Administration. Each hose shall be provided with a nozzle and the necessary couplings. Hoses specified in this chapter as "fire hoses" shall together with any necessary fittings and tools be kept ready for use in conspicuous positions near the water service hydrants or connections. Additionally in interior locations in passenger ships carrying more than 36 passengers fire hoses shall be connected to the hydrants at all times.

7.2 Ships shall be provided with fire hoses the number and diameter of which shall be to the satisfaction of the Administration.

7.3 In passenger ships there shall be at least one fire hose for each of the hydrants required by paragraph 5 and these hoses shall be used only for the purposes of extinguishing fires or testing the fire-extinguishing apparatus at fire drills and surveys.

7.4.1 In cargo ships of 1,000 tons gross tonnage and upwards the number of fire hoses to be provided shall be one for each 30 m length of the ship and one spare but in no case less than five in all. This number does not include any hoses required in any engine or boiler room. The Administration may increase the number of hoses required so as to ensure that hoses in sufficient number are available and accessible at all times, having regard to the type of ship and the nature of trade in which the ship is employed.

7.4.2   In cargo ships of less than 1,000 tons gross tonnage the number of fire hoses to be provided shall be to the satisfaction of the Administration.

8   *Nozzles*

8.1   For the purposes of this chapter, standard nozzle sizes shall be 12 mm, 16 mm and 19 mm or as near thereto as possible. Larger diameter nozzles may be permitted at the discretion of the Administration.

8.2   For accommodation and service spaces, a nozzle size greater than 12 mm need not be used.

8.3   For machinery spaces and exterior locations, the nozzle size shall be such as to obtain the maximum discharge possible from two jets at the pressure mentioned in paragraph 4 from the smallest pump, provided that a nozzle size greater than 19 mm need not be used.

8.4   All nozzles shall be of an approved dual-purpose type (i.e. spray/jet type) incorporating a shutoff.

9   *Location and arrangement of water pumps, etc., for other fire-extinguishing systems*

Pumps required for the provision of water for other fire-extinguishing systems required by this chapter, their sources of power and their controls shall be installed outside the space or spaces protected by such systems and shall be so arranged that a fire in the space or spaces protected will not put any such system out of action.

Regulation 5

Fixed gas fire-extinguishing systems

1   *General*

1.1   The use of a fire-extinguishing medium which, in the opinion of the Administration, either by itself or under expected conditions of use gives off toxic gases in such quantities as to endanger persons shall not be permitted.

1.2   The necessary pipes for conveying fire-extinguishing medium into protected spaces shall be provided with control valves so marked as to indicate clearly the spaces to which the pipes are led. Suitable provision shall be made to prevent inadvertent admission of the medium to any space. Where a cargo space fitted with a gas fire-extinguishing system is used as a passenger space the gas connection shall be blanked during such use.

1.3   The piping for the distribution of fire-extinguishing medium shall be arranged and discharge nozzles so positioned that a uniform distribution of medium is obtained.

1.4   Means shall be provided to close all openings which may admit air to or allow gas to escape from a protected space.

1.5   Where the volume of free air contained in air receivers in any space is such that, if released in such space in the event of fire, such release of air within that space would seriously affect the efficiency of the fixed fire-extinguishing system, the Administration shall require the provision of an additional quantity of fire-extinguishing medium.

1.6   Means shall be provided for automatically giving audible warning of the release of fire-extinguishing medium into any space in which personnel normally work or to which they have access. The alarm shall operate for a suitable period before the medium is released.

1.7   The means of control of any fixed gas fire-extinguishing system shall be readily accessible and simple to operate and shall be grouped together in as few locations as possible at positions not likely to be cut off by a fire in a protected space. At each location there shall be clear instructions relating to the operation of the system having regard to the safety of personnel.

1.8   Automatic release of fire-extinguishing medium shall not be permitted, except as permitted by paragraph 3.3.5 and in respect of local automatically operated units referred to in paragraphs 3.4 and 3.5.

1.9   Where the quantity of extinguishing medium is required to protect more than one space, the quantity of medium available need not be more than the largest quantity required for any one space so protected.

1.10 Except as otherwise permitted by paragraphs 3.3, 3.4 or 3:5 pressure containers required for the storage of fire-extinguishing medium, other than steam, shall be located outside protected spaces in accordance with paragraph 1.13.

1.11 Means shall be provided for the crew to safely check the quantity of medium in the containers.

1.12 Containers for the storage of fire-extinguishing medium and associated pressure components shall be designed to pressure codes of practice to the satisfaction of the Administration having regard to their locations and maximum ambient temperatures expected in service.

1.13 When the fire-extinguishing medium is stored outside a protected space, it shall be stored in a room which shall be situated in a safe and readily accessible position and shall be effectively ventilated to the satisfaction of the Administration. Any entrance to such a storage room shall preferably be from the open deck and in any case shall be independent of the protected space. Access doors shall open outwards, and bulkheads and decks including doors and other means of closing any opening therein, which form the boundaries between such rooms and adjoining enclosed spaces shall be gastight. For the purpose of the application of the integrity tables in regulations 26, 27, 44 and 58, such storage rooms shall be treated as control stations.

1.14 Spare parts for the system shall be stored on board and be to the satisfaction of the Administration.

2 Carbon dioxide systems

2.1 For cargo spaces the quantity of carbon dioxide available shall, unless otherwise provided, be sufficient to give a minimum volume of free gas equal to 30 per cent of the gross volume of the largest cargo space so protected in the ship.

2.2 For machinery spaces the quantity of carbon dioxide carried shall be sufficient to give a minimum volume of free gas equal to the larger of the following volumes, either:

.1 40 per cent of the gross volume of the largest machinery space so protected, the volume to exclude that part of the casing above the level at which the horizontal area of the casing is 40 per cent or less of the horizontal area of the space concerned taken midway between the tank top and the lowest part of the casing; or

.2 35 per cent of the gross volume of the largest machinery space protected, including the casing;

provided that the above-mentioned percentages may be reduced to 35 per cent and 30 per cent respectively for cargo ships of less than 2,000 tons gross tonnage; provided also that if two or more machinery spaces are not entirely separate they shall be considered as forming one space.

2.3 For the purpose of this paragraph the volume of free carbon dioxide shall be calculated at $0.56 \, \text{m}^3/\text{kg}$.

2.4 For machinery spaces the fixed piping system shall be such that 85 per cent of the gas can be discharged into the space within 2 minutes.

3 Halogenated hydrocarbon systems

3.1 The use of halogenated hydrocarbons as fire-extinguishing media is only permitted in machinery spaces, pump-rooms and in cargo spaces intended solely for the carriage of vehicles which are not carrying any cargo.

3.2 When halogenated hydrocarbons are used as the fire-extinguishing media in total flooding systems:

.1 The system shall be arranged for manual initiation of power release only.

.2 If the charge of halogenated hydrocarbon is required to supply more than one space, the arrangements for its storage and release shall be such that compliance with paragraphs 3.2.9 or 3.2.10 respectively, is obtained.

.3 Means shall be provided for automatically stopping all ventilation fans serving the protected space before the medium is released.

.4 Means shall be provided to manually close all dampers in the ventilation system serving a protected space.

.5 The discharge arrangements shall be so designed that the minimum quantity of medium required for cargo spaces or machinery spaces in paragraphs 3.2.9 or 3.2.10 respectively can be substantially discharged in a nominal 20 seconds or less based on the discharge of the liquid phase.

.6 The system shall be designed to operate within a temperature range to the satisfaction of the Administration.

.7 The discharge shall not endanger personnel engaged on maintenance of equipment or using the normal access ladders and escapes serving the space.

.8 Means shall be provided for the crew to safely check the pressure within containers.

.9 The quantity of extinguishing medium for cargo spaces intended solely for the carriage of vehicles which are not carrying any cargo shall be calculated in accordance with table 5.1. This quantity shall be based on the gross volume of the protected space. In respect of Halon 1301 and 1211, the quantity shall be calculated on a volumetric ratio basis, and in respect of Halon 2402 on a mass per unit volume basis.

TABLE 5.1

Halon	Minimum	Maximum
1301	5 per cent	7 per cent
1211	5 per cent	5.5 per cent
2402	$0.23 \, kg/m^3$	$0.30 \, kg/m^3$

.10 The quantity of extinguishing media for machinery spaces shall be calculated in accordance with table 5.2. This quantity shall be based on the gross volume of the space in respect of the minimum concentration and the net volume of the space in respect of the maximum concentration, including the casing. In respect of Halon 1301 and 1211, the quantity shall be calculated on a volumetric ratio basis, and in respect of Halon 2402 on a mass per unit volume basis.

TABLE 5.2

Halon	Minimum	Maximum
1301	4.25 per cent	7 per cent
1211	4.25 per cent	5.5 per cent
2402	$0.20\,kg/m^3$	$0.30\,kg/m^3$

.11 For the purpose of paragraphs 3.2.9 and 3.2.10, the volume of Halon 1301 shall be calculated at $0.16\,m^3/kg$ and the volume of Halon 1211 shall be calculated at $0.14\,m^3/kg$.

3.3 Only Halon 1301 may be stored within a protected machinery space. Containers shall be individually distributed throughout that space and the following requirements shall be complied with:

.1 A manually initiated power release, located outside the protected space, shall be provided. Duplicate sources of power shall be provided for this release and shall be located outside the protected space and be immediately available except that for machinery spaces, one of the sources of power may be located inside the protected space.

.2 Electric power circuits connecting the containers shall be monitored for fault conditions and loss of power. Visual and audible alarms shall be provided to indicate this.

.3 Pneumatic or hydraulic power circuits connecting the containers shall be duplicated. The sources of pneumatic or hydraulic pressure shall be monitored for loss of pressure. Visual and audible alarms shall be provided to indicate this.

.4 Within the protected space, electrical circuits essential for the release of the system shall be heat resistant e.g. mineral insulated cable or equivalent. Piping systems essential for the release of systems designed to be operated hydraulically or pneumatically shall be of steel or other equivalent heat-resisting material to the satisfaction of the Administration.

.5 Each pressure container shall be fitted with an automatic overpressure release device which, in the event of the container being exposed to the effects of fire and the system not being operated, will safely vent the contents of the container into the protected space.

.6 The arrangement of containers and the electrical circuits and piping essential for the release of any system shall be such that in the event of damage to any one power release line through fire or explosion in a protected space, i.e. a single fault concept, at least two thirds of the fire-extinguishing charge required by paragraphs 3.2.9 or 3.2.10 for that space can still be discharged having regard to the requirement for uniform distribution of medium throughout the space. The arrangements in respect of systems for spaces requiring only one or two containers shall be to the satisfaction of the Administration.

.7 Not more than two discharge nozzles shall be fitted to any pressure container and the maximum quantity of agent in each container shall be to the satisfaction of the Administration having regard to the requirement for uniform distribution of medium throughout the space.

.8 The containers shall be monitored for decrease in pressure due to leakage and discharge. Visual and audible alarms in the protected area and on the navigating bridge or in the space where the fire control equipment is centralized shall be provided to indicate this condition, except that for cargo spaces, alarms are only required on the navigating bridge or the space where the fire control equipment is centralized.

3.4 Local automatically operated fixed fire-extinguishing units containing Halon 1301 or 1211, fitted in enclosed areas of high fire risk within machinery spaces, in addition to, and independent of, any required fixed fire-extinguishing system may be accepted subject to compliance with the following:

.1 The space in which such additional local protection is provided shall preferably be on one working level and on the same level as the access. At the discretion of the Administration more than one working level may be permitted subject to an access being provided on each level.

.2 The size of the space and arrangements of accesses thereto and machinery therein, shall be such that escape from anywhere in the space can be effected in not more than 10 seconds.

.3 The operation of any unit shall be signalled both visually and audibly outside each access to the machinery space and at the navigating bridge or in the space where the fire control equipment is centralized.

.4 A notice indicating that the space contains one or more automatically operated fire-extinguishing units and stating which medium is used, shall be displayed outside each access thereto.

.5 Discharge nozzles shall be so positioned that the discharge does not endanger personnel using the normal access ladders and escapes serving the compartment. Provision shall also be made to protect personnel engaged in maintenance of machinery from inadvertent discharge of the medium.

.6 The fire-extinguishing units shall be designed to operate within a temperature range to the satisfaction of the Administration.

.7 Means shall be provided for the crew to safely check the pressure within the containers.

.8 The total quantity of extinguishing medium provided in the local automatically operated units shall be such that a concentration of 7 per cent in respect of Halon 1301 and 5.5 per cent in respect of Halon 1211 at 20°C based on the net volume of the enclosed space is not exceeded. This requirement applies when either a local automatically operated unit or a fixed system fitted in compliance with paragraph 3.2 has operated, but not when both have operated. The volume of Halon 1301 shall be calculated at $0.16 \, m^3/kg$ and the volume of Halon 1211 shall be calculated at $0.14 \, m^3/kg$.

.9 The time of discharge of a unit, based on the discharge of the liquid phase, shall be 10 seconds or less.

.10 The arrangement of local automatically operated fire-extinguishing units shall be such that their release does not result in loss of electrical power or reduction of the manoeuvrability of the ship.

3.5 Automatically operated fire-extinguishing units, as described in paragraph 3.4, fitted in machinery spaces over equipment having a high fire risk, in addition to and independent of any required fixed fire-extinguishing system, may be accepted subject to compliance with paragraphs 3.4.3 to 3.4.6, 3.4.9 and 3.4.10 and with the following:

.1 The quantity of medium provided in local automatically operated units shall be such that a vapour in air concentration not greater than 1.25 per cent at 20°C based on the gross volume of the machinery space is obtained in the event of their simultaneous operation.

.2 The volume of Halon 1301 shall be calculated at $0.16 \, m^3/kg$ and the volume of Halon 1211 shall be calculated at $0.14 \, m^3/kg$.

4   *Steam systems*

In general, the Administration shall not permit the use of steam as a fire-extinguishing medium in fixed fire-extinguishing systems. Where the use of steam is permitted by the Administration it shall be used only in restricted areas as an addition to the required fire-extinguishing medium and with the proviso that the boiler or boilers available for supplying steam shall have an evaporation of at least 1.0 kg of steam per hour for each $0.75 \, m^3$ of the gross volume of the largest space so protected. In addition to complying with the foregoing requirements the systems in all respects shall be as determined by, and to the satisfaction of, the Administration.

5   *Other gas systems*

5.1 Where gas other than carbon dioxide or halogenated hydrocarbons, or steam as permitted by paragraph 4 is produced on the ship and is used as a fire-extinguishing medium, it shall be a gaseous product of fuel combustion in which the oxygen content, the carbon monoxide content, the corrosive elements and any solid combustible elements have been reduced to a permissible minimum.

5.2   Where such gas is used as the fire-extinguishing medium in a fixed fire-extinguishing system for the protection of machinery spaces it shall afford protection equivalent to that provided by a fixed system using carbon dioxide as the medium.

5.3   Where such gas is used as a fire-extinguishing medium in a fixed fire-extinguishing system for the protection of cargo spaces, a sufficient quantity of such gas shall be available to supply hourly a volume of free gas at least equal to 25 per cent of the gross volume of the largest space protected in this way for a period of 72 hours.

Regulation 6

Fire extinguishers*

1   All fire extinguishers shall be of approved types and designs.

1.1   The capacity of required portable fluid extinguishers shall be not more than 13.5ℓ and not less than 9ℓ. Other extinguishers shall be at least as portable as the 13.5ℓ fluid extinguisher and shall have a fire-extinguishing capability at least equivalent to that of a 9ℓ fluid extinguisher.

1.2   The Administration shall determine the equivalents of fire extinguishers.

2   Spare charges shall be provided in accordance with requirements to be specified by the Administration.

3   Fire extinguishers containing an extinguishing medium which, in the opinion of the Administration, either by itself or under expected conditions of use gives off toxic gases in such quantities as to endanger persons shall not be permitted.

4   A portable foam applicator unit shall consist of an air-foam nozzle of an inductor type capable of being connected to the fire main by a fire hose, together with a portable tank containing at least 20ℓ of foam-making liquid and one spare tank. The nozzle shall be capable of producing effective foam suitable for extinguishing an oil fire, at the rate of at least 1.5 m³/minute.

---

* Reference is made to the Guidelines for Marine Portable Fire Extinguishers adopted by the Organization by resolution A.518(13).

5   Fire extinguishers shall be periodically examined and subjected to such tests as the Administration may require.

6   One of the portable fire extinguishers intended for use in any space shall be stowed near the entrance to that space.

7   Accommodation spaces, service spaces and control stations shall be provided with portable fire extinguishers of appropriate types and in sufficient number to the satisfaction of the Administration. Ships of 1,000 tons gross tonnage and upwards shall carry at least five portable fire extinguishers.

Regulation 7

Fire-extinguishing arrangements in machinery spaces

1   *Spaces containing oil-fired boilers or oil fuel units*

1.1   Machinery spaces of category A containing oil-fired boilers or oil fuel units shall be provided with any one of the following fixed fire-extinguishing systems:

.1   a gas system complying with the provisions of regulation 5;

.2   a high-expansion foam system complying with the provisions of regulation 9;

.3   a pressure water-spraying system complying with the provisions of regulation 10.

In each case if the engine and boiler rooms are not entirely separate, or if fuel oil can drain from the boiler room into the engine-room, the combined engine and boiler rooms shall be considered as one compartment.

1.2   There shall be in each boiler room at least one set of portable foam applicator unit complying with the provisions of regulation 6.4.

1.3   There shall be at least two portable foam extinguishers or equivalent in each firing space in each boiler room and in each space in which a part of the oil fuel installation is situated. There shall be not less than one approved foam-type extinguisher of at least 135ℓ capacity or equivalent in each boiler room. These extinguishers shall be provided with hoses on reels suitable for reaching any part of the boiler room. In the case of domestic boilers of less than 175 kW in cargo ships the Administration may consider relaxing the requirements of this paragraph.

1.4   In each firing space there shall be a receptacle containing sand, sawdust impregnated with soda, or other approved dry material in such quantity as

131

may be required by the Administration. An approved portable extinguisher may be substituted as an alternative.

2   *Spaces containing internal combustion machinery*

Machinery spaces of category A containing internal combustion machinery shall be provided with:

.1   One of the fire-extinguishing systems required by paragraph 1.1.

.2   At least one set of portable air-foam equipment complying with the provisions of Regulation 6.4.

.3   In each such space approved foam-type fire extinguishers, each of at least 45 ℓ capacity or equivalent, sufficient in number to enable foam or its equivalent to be directed on to any part of the fuel and lubricating oil pressure systems, gearing and other fire hazards. In addition, there shall be provided a sufficient number of portable foam extinguishers or equivalent which shall be so located that no point in the space is more than 10 m walking distance from an extinguisher and that there are at least two such extinguishers in each such space. For smaller spaces of cargo ships the Administration may consider relaxing this requirement.

3   *Spaces containing steam turbines or enclosed steam engines*

In spaces containing steam turbines or enclosed steam engines used either for main propulsion or for other purposes when such machinery has in the aggregate a total power output of not less than 375 kW there shall be provided:

.1   Approved foam fire extinguishers each of at least 45 ℓ capacity or equivalent sufficient in number to enable foam or its equivalent to be directed on to any part of the pressure lubrication system, on to any part of the casings enclosing pressure lubricated parts of the turbines, engines or associated gearing, and any other fire hazards. However, such extinguishers shall not be required if protection at least equivalent to that required by this subparagraph is provided in such spaces by a fixed fire-extinguishing system fitted in compliance with paragraph 1.1.

.2   A sufficient number of portable foam extinguishers or equivalent which shall be so located that no point in the space is more than 10 m walking distance from an extinguisher and that there are at least two such extinguishers in each such space, except that such extinguishers shall not be required in addition to any provided in compliance with paragraph 1.3.

.3   One of the fire-extinguishing systems required by paragraph 1.1, where such spaces are periodically unattended.

4   *Fire-extinguishing appliances in other machinery spaces*

Where, in the opinion of the Administration, a fire hazard exists in any machinery space for which no specific provisions for fire-extinguishing appliances are prescribed in paragraphs 1, 2 and 3, there shall be provided in, or adjacent to, that space such a number of approved portable fire extinguishers or other means of fire extinction as the Administration may deem sufficient.

5 Fixed fire-extinguishing systems not required by this chapter

Where a fixed fire-extinguishing system not required by this chapter is installed, such a system shall be to the satisfaction of the Administration.

6 Machinery spaces of category A in passenger ships

In passenger ships carrying more than 36 passengers each machinery space of category A shall be provided with at least two suitable water fog applicators.*

Regulation 8

Fixed low-expansion foam fire-extinguishing systems in machinery spaces

1 Where in any machinery space a fixed low-expansion foam fire-extinguishing system is fitted in addition to the requirements of regulation 7, such system shall be capable of discharging through fixed discharge outlets in not more than five minutes a quantity of foam sufficient to cover to a depth of 150 mm the largest single area over which oil fuel is liable to spread. The system shall be capable of generating foam suitable for extinguishing oil fires. Means shall be provided for effective distribution of the foam through a permanent system of piping and control valves or cocks to suitable discharge outlets, and for the foam to be effectively directed by fixed sprayers on other main fire hazards in the protected space. The expansion ratio of the foam shall not exceed 12 to 1.

2 The means of control of any such systems shall be readily accessible and simple to operate and shall be grouped together in as few locations as possible at positions not likely to be cut off by a fire in the protected space.

Regulation 9

Fixed high-expansion foam fire-extinguishing systems in machinery spaces

1.1 Any required fixed high-expansion foam system in machinery spaces shall be capable of rapidly discharging through fixed discharge outlets a

---

* A water fog applicator might consist of a metal "L"-shaped pipe, the long limb being about 2 m in length capable of being fitted to a fire hose and the short limb being about 250 mm in length fitted with a fixed water fog nozzle or capable of being fitted with a water spray nozzle.

quantity of foam sufficient to fill the greatest space to be protected at a rate of at least 1 m in depth per minute. The quantity of foam-forming liquid available shall be sufficient to produce a volume of foam equal to five times the volume of the largest space to be protected. The expansion ratio of the foam shall not exceed 1,000 to 1.

1.2 The Administration may permit alternative arrangements and discharge rates provided that it is satisfied that equivalent protection is achieved.

2 Supply ducts for delivering foam, air intakes to the foam generator and the number of foam-producing units shall in the opinion of the Administration be such as will provide effective foam production and distribution.

3 The arrangement of the foam generator delivery ducting shall be such that a fire in the protected space will not affect the foam generating equipment.

4 The foam generator, its sources of power supply, foam-forming liquid and means of controlling the system shall be readily accessible and simple to operate and shall be grouped in as few locations as possible at positions not likely to be cut off by a fire in the protected space.

Regulation 10

Fixed pressure water-spraying fire-extinguishing systems in machinery spaces

1 Any required fixed pressure water-spraying fire-extinguishing system in machinery spaces shall be provided with spraying nozzles of an approved type.

2 The number and arrangement of the nozzles shall be to the satisfaction of the Administration and shall be such as to ensure an effective average distribution of water of at least $5\ell/m^2$ per minute in the spaces to be protected. Where increased application rates are considered necessary, these shall be to the satisfaction of the Administration. Nozzles shall be fitted above bilges, tank tops and other areas over which oil fuel is liable to spread and also above other specific fire hazards in the machinery spaces.

3 The system may be divided into sections, the distribution valves of which shall be operated from easily accessible positions outside the spaces to be protected and will not be readily cut off by a fire in the protected space.

4 The system shall be kept charged at the necessary pressure and the pump supplying the water for the system shall be put automatically into action by a pressure drop in the system.

5 The pump shall be capable of simultaneously supplying at the necessary pressure all sections of the system in any one compartment to be protected. The pump and its controls shall be installed outside the space or spaces to

be protected. It shall not be possible for a fire in the space or spaces protected by the water-spraying system to put the system out of action.

6   The pump may be driven by independent internal combustion machinery but, if it is dependent upon power being supplied from the emergency generator fitted in compliance with the provisions of regulation II–1/44 or regulation II–1/45, as appropriate, that generator shall be so arranged as to start automatically in case of main power failure so that power for the pump required by paragraph 5 is immediately available. When the pump is driven by independent internal combustion machinery it shall be so situated that a fire in the protected space will not affect the air supply to the machinery.

7   Precautions shall be taken to prevent the nozzles from becoming clogged by impurities in the water or corrosion of piping, nozzles, valves and pump.

Regulation 11

Special arrangements in machinery spaces

1   The provisions of this regulation shall apply to machinery spaces of category A and, where the Administration considers it desirable, to other machinery spaces.

2.1   The number of skylights, doors, ventilators, openings in funnels to permit exhaust ventilation and other openings to machinery spaces shall be reduced to a minimum consistent with the needs of ventilation and the proper and safe working of the ship.

2.2   Skylights shall be of steel and shall not contain glass panels. Suitable arrangements shall be made to permit the release of smoke in the event of fire, from the space to be protected.

2.3   In passenger ships, doors other than power-operated watertight doors, shall be so arranged that positive closure is assured in case of fire in the space, by power-operated closing arrangements or by the provision of self-closing doors capable of closing against an inclination of 3.5° opposing closure and having a fail-safe hook-back facility, provided with a remotely operated release device.

3   Windows shall not be fitted in machinery space boundaries. This does not preclude the use of glass in control rooms within the machinery spaces.

4   Means of control shall be provided for:

.1   opening and closure of skylights, closure of openings in funnels which normally allow exhaust ventilation, and closure of ventilator dampers;

.2   permitting the release of smoke;

.3   closing power-operated doors or actuating release mechanism on doors other than power-operated watertight doors;

.4   stopping ventilating fans; and

.5   stopping forced and induced draught fans, oil fuel transfer pumps, oil fuel unit pumps and other similar fuel pumps.

5   The controls required in paragraph 4 and in regulation 15.2.5 shall be located outside the space concerned, where they will not be cut off in the event of fire in the space they serve. In passenger ships such controls and the controls for any required fire-extinguishing system shall be situated at one control position or grouped in as few positions as possible to the satisfaction of the Administration. Such positions shall have a safe access from the open deck.

6   When access to any machinery space of category A is provided at a low level from an adjacent shaft tunnel, there shall be provided in the shaft tunnel, near the watertight door, a light steel fire-screen door operable from each side.

7   For periodically unattended machinery spaces in cargo ships, the Administration shall give special consideration to maintaining fire integrity of the machinery spaces, the location and centralization of the fire-extinguishing system controls, the required shutdown arrangements (e.g. ventilation, fuel pumps, etc.) and may require additional fire-extinguishing appliances and other fire-fighting equipment and breathing apparatus. In passenger ships these requirements shall be at least equivalent to those of machinery spaces normally attended.

8   A fixed fire detection and alarm system complying with the provisions of regulation 14 shall be fitted in any machinery space:

.1   where the installation of automatic and remote control systems and equipment has been approved in lieu of continuous manning of the space; and

.2   where the main propulsion and associated machinery including sources of main electrical supply are provided with various degrees of automatic or remote control and are under continuous manned supervision from a control room.

Regulation 12

Automatic sprinkler, fire detection and fire alarm systems

1.1   Any required automatic sprinkler, fire detection and fire alarm system shall be capable of immediate operation at all times and no action by the crew shall be necessary to set it in operation. It shall be of the wet pipe type but small exposed sections may be of the dry pipe type where in the opinion of the Administration this is a necessary precaution. Any parts of the system which may be subjected to freezing temperatures in service shall be suitably protected against freezing. It shall be kept charged at the necessary pressure and shall have provision for a continuous supply of water as required in this regulation.

1.2   Each section of sprinklers shall include means for giving a visual and audible alarm signal automatically at one or more indicating units whenever any sprinkler comes into operation. Such alarm systems shall be such as to indicate if any fault occurs in the system.

1.2.1   In passenger ships such units shall give an indication of any fire and its location in any space served by the system and shall be centralized on the navigating bridge or in the main fire control station, which shall be so manned or equipped as to ensure that any alarm from the system is immediately received by a responsible member of the crew.

1.2.2   In cargo ships such units shall indicate in which section served by the system fire has occurred and shall be centralized on the navigating bridge and in addition, visible and audible alarms from the unit shall be placed in a position other than on the navigating bridge, so as to ensure that the indication of fire is immediately received by the crew.

2.1   Sprinklers shall be grouped into separate sections, each of which shall contain not more than 200 sprinklers. In passenger ships any section of sprinklers shall not serve more than two decks and shall not be situated in more than one main vertical zone. However, the Administration may permit such a section of sprinklers to serve more than two decks or be situated in more than one main vertical zone, if it is satisfied that the protection of the ship against fire will not thereby be reduced.

2.2   Each section of sprinklers shall be capable of being isolated by one stop valve only. The stop valve in each section shall be readily accessible and its location shall be clearly and permanently indicated. Means shall be provided to prevent the operation of the stop valves by any unauthorized person.

2.3   A gauge indicating the pressure in the system shall be provided at each section stop valve and at a central station.

2.4   The sprinklers shall be resistant to corrosion by marine atmosphere. In accommodation and service spaces the sprinklers shall come into operation within the temperature range from 68° to 79°C, except that in locations such as drying rooms, where high ambient temperatures might be expected, the operating temperature may be increased by not more than 30°C above the maximum deckhead temperature.

2.5   A list or plan shall be displayed at each indicating unit showing the spaces covered and the location of the zone in respect of each section. Suitable instructions for testing and maintenance shall be available.

3   Sprinklers shall be placed in an overhead position and spaced in a suitable pattern to maintain an average application rate of not less than $5\,\ell/m^2$ per minute over the nominal area covered by the sprinklers. However, the Administration may permit the use of sprinklers providing such an alternative amount of water suitably distributed as has been shown to the satisfaction of the Administration to be not less effective.

4.1   A pressure tank having a volume equal to at least twice that of the charge of water specified in this subparagraph shall be provided. The tank shall contain a standing charge of fresh water, equivalent to the amount of water which would be discharged in one minute by the pump referred to in paragraph 5.2, and the arrangements shall provide for maintaining an air pressure in the tank such as to ensure that where the standing charge of fresh water in the tank has been used the pressure will be not less than the working pressure of the sprinkler, plus the pressure exerted by a head of water measured from the bottom of the tank to the highest sprinkler in the system. Suitable means of replenishing the air under pressure and of replenishing the fresh water charge in the tank shall be provided. A glass gauge shall be provided to indicate the correct level of the water in the tank.

4.2   Means shall be provided to prevent the passage of seawater into the tank.

5.1   An independent power pump shall be provided solely for the purpose of continuing automatically the discharge of water from the sprinklers. The pump shall be brought into action automatically by the pressure drop in the system before the standing fresh water charge in the pressure tank is completely exhausted.

5.2   The pump and the piping system shall be capable of maintaining the necessary pressure at the level of the highest sprinkler to ensure a continuous output of water sufficient for the simultaneous coverage of a minimum area of $280\,m^2$ at the application rate specified in paragraph 3.

5.3   The pump shall have fitted on the delivery side a test valve with a short open-ended discharge pipe. The effective area through the valve and pipe shall be adequate to permit the release of the required pump output while maintaining the pressure in the system specified in paragraph 4.1.

5.4   The sea inlet to the pump shall wherever possible be in the space containing the pump and shall be so arranged that when the ship is afloat it will not be necessary to shut off the supply of seawater to the pump for any purpose other than the inspection or repair of the pump.

6   The sprinkler pump and tank shall be situated in a position reasonably remote from any machinery space of category A and shall not be situated in any space required to be protected by the sprinkler system.

7.1   In passenger ships there shall be not less than two sources of power supply for the seawater pump and automatic alarm and detection system. Where the sources of power for the pump are electrical, these shall be a main generator and an emergency source of power. One supply for the pump shall be taken from the main switchboard, and one from the emergency switchboard by separate feeders reserved solely for that purpose. The feeders shall be so arranged as to avoid galleys, machinery spaces and other enclosed spaces of high fire risk except in so far as it is necessary to reach the appropriate switchboards, and shall be run to an automatic change-over switch situated near the sprinkler pump. This switch shall permit the supply of power from the main switchboard so long as a supply is available therefrom, and be so designed that upon failure of that supply it will automatically change over to the supply from the emergency switchboard. The switches on the main switchboard and the emergency switchboard shall be clearly labelled and normally kept closed. No other switch shall be permitted in the feeders concerned. One of the sources of power supply for the alarm and detection system shall be an emergency source. Where one of the sources of power for the pump is an internal combustion engine it shall, in addition to complying with the provisions of paragraph 6, be so situated that a fire in any protected space will not affect the air supply to the machinery.

7.2   In cargo ships there shall not be less than two sources of power supply for the seawater pump and automatic alarm and detection system. If the pump is electrically driven it shall be connected to the main source of electrical power, which shall be capable of being supplied by at least two generators. The feeders shall be so arranged as to avoid galleys, machinery spaces and other enclosed spaces of high fire risk except in so far as it is necessary to reach the appropriate switchboards. One of the sources of power supply for the alarm and detection system shall be an emergency source. Where one of the sources of power for the pump is an internal combustion engine it shall, in addition to complying with the provisions of paragraph 6, be so situated that a fire in any protected space will not affect the air supply to the machinery.

8   The sprinkler system shall have a connection from the ship's fire main by way of a lockable screw-down nonreturn valve at the connection which will prevent a backflow from the sprinkler system to the fire main.

9.1   A test valve shall be provided for testing the automatic alarm for each section of sprinklers by a discharge of water equivalent to the operation of one sprinkler. The test valve for each section shall be situated near the stop valve for that section.

9.2   Means shall be provided for testing the automatic operation of the pump on reduction of pressure in the system.

9.3   Switches shall be provided at one of the indicating positions referred to in paragraph 1.2 which will enable the alarm and the indicators for each section of sprinklers to be tested.

139

10   Spare sprinkler heads shall be provided for each section of sprinklers to the satisfaction of the Administration.

Regulation 13

Fixed fire detection and fire alarm systems

1   *General requirements*

1.1   Any required fixed fire detection and fire alarm system with manually operated call points shall be capable of immediate operation at all times.

1.2   Power supplies and electric circuits necessary for the operation of the system shall be monitored for loss of power or fault conditions as appropriate. Occurrence of a fault condition shall initiate a visual and audible fault signal at the control panel which shall be distinct from a fire signal.

1.3   There shall be not less than two sources of power supply for the electrical equipment used in the operation of the fire detection and fire alarm system, one of which shall be an emergency source. The supply shall be provided by separate feeders reserved solely for that purpose. Such feeders shall run to an automatic change-over switch situated in or adjacent to the control panel for the fire detection system.

1.4   Detectors and manually operated call points shall be grouped into sections. The activation of any detector or manually operated call point shall initiate a visual and audible fire signal at the control panel and indicating units. If the signals have not received attention within two minutes an audible alarm shall be automatically sounded throughout the crew accommodation and service spaces, control stations and machinery spaces of category A. This alarm sounder system need not be an integral part of the detection system.

1.5   The control panel shall be located on the navigating bridge or in the main fire control station.

1.6   Indicating units shall denote the section in which a detector or manually operated call point has operated. At least one unit shall be so located that it is easily accessible to responsible members of the crew at all times, when at sea or in port except when the ship is out of service. One indicating unit shall be located on the navigating bridge if the control panel is located in the main fire control station.

1.7   Clear information shall be displayed on or adjacent to each indicating unit about the spaces covered and the location of the sections.

1.8   No section covering more than one deck within accommodation, service

140

and control stations shall normally be permitted except a section which covers an enclosed stairway. In order to avoid delay in identifying the source of fire, the number of enclosed spaces included in each section shall be limited as determined by the Administration. In no case shall more than fifty enclosed spaces be permitted in any section.

1.9　In passenger ships a section of detectors shall not serve spaces on both sides of the ship nor on more than one deck and neither shall it be situated in more than one main vertical zone except that the Administration, if it is satisfied that the protection of the ship against fire will not thereby be reduced, may permit such a section of detectors to serve both sides of the ship and more than one deck.

1.10　A section of fire detectors which covers a control station, a service space or an accommodation space shall not include a machinery space of category A.

1.11　Detectors shall be operated by heat, smoke or other products of combustion, flame, or any combination of these factors. Detectors operated by other factors indicative of incipient fires may be considered by the Administration provided that they are no less sensitive than such detectors. Flame detectors shall only be used in addition to smoke or heat detectors.

1.12　Suitable instructions and component spares for testing and maintenance shall be provided.

1.13　The function of the detection system shall be periodically tested to the satisfaction of the Administration by means of equipment producing hot air at the appropriate temperature, or smoke or aerosol particles having the appropriate range of density or particle size, or other phenomena associated with incipient fires to which the detector is designed to respond. All detectors shall be of a type such that they can be tested for correct operation and restored to normal surveillance without the renewal of any component.

1.14　The fire detection system shall not be used for any other purpose, except that closing of fire doors and similar functions may be permitted at the control panel.

2　*Installation requirements*

2.1　Manually operated call points shall be installed throughout the accommodation spaces, service spaces and control stations. One manually operated call point shall be located at each exit. Manually operated call points shall be readily accessible in the corridors of each deck such that no part of the corridor is more than 20 m from a manually operated call point.

2.2　Smoke detectors shall be installed in all stairways, corridors and escape routes within accommodation spaces. Consideration shall be given to the installation of special purpose smoke detectors within ventilation ducting.

2.3   Where a fixed fire detection and fire alarm system is required for the protection of spaces other than those specified in paragraph 2.2, at least one detector complying with paragraph 1.11 shall be installed in each such space.

2.4   Detectors shall be located for optimum performance. Positions near beams and ventilation ducts or other positions where patterns of air flow could adversely affect performance and positions where impact or physical damage is likely shall be avoided. In general, detectors which are located on the overhead shall be a minimum distance of 0.5 m away from bulkheads.

2.5   The maximum spacing of detectors shall be in accordance with the table below:

Type of detector	Maximum floor area per detector	Maximum distance apart between centres	Maximum distance away from bulkheads
Heat	37 m²	9 m	4.5 m
Smoke	74 m²	11 m	5.5 m

The Administration may require or permit other spacings based upon test data which demonstrate the characteristics of the detectors.

2.6   Electrical wiring which forms part of the system shall be so arranged as to avoid galleys, machinery spaces of category A, and other enclosed spaces of high fire risk except where it is necessary to provide for fire detection or fire alarm in such spaces or to connect to the appropriate power supply.

3   *Design requirements*

3.1   The system and equipment shall be suitably designed to withstand supply voltage variation and transients, ambient temperature changes, vibration, humidity, shock, impact and corrosion normally encountered in ships.

3.2   Smoke detectors required by paragraph 2.2 shall be certified to operate before the smoke density exceeds 12.5 per cent obscuration per metre, but not until the smoke density exceeds 2 per cent obscuration per metre. Smoke detectors to be installed in other spaces shall operate within sensitivity limits to the satisfaction of the Administration having regard to the avoidance of detector insensitivity or oversensitivity.

3.3   Heat detectors shall be certified to operate before the temperature exceeds 78°C but not until the temperature exceeds 54°C, when the temperature is raised to those limits at a rate less than 1°C per minute. At higher rates of temperature rise, the heat detector shall operate within temperature limits to the satisfaction of the Administration having regard to the avoidance of detector insensitivity or oversensitivity.

3.4   At the discretion of the Administration, the permissible temperature of operation of heat detectors may be increased to 30°C above the maximum deckhead temperature in drying rooms and similar spaces of a normal high ambient temperature.

Regulation 13–1 [F]

Sample extraction smoke detection systems

Regulation 14

Fixed fire detection and fire alarm systems for periodically unattended machinery spaces

1   A fixed fire detection and fire alarm system of an approved type in accordance with the relevant provisions of regulation 13 shall be installed in periodically unattended machinery spaces.

2   This fire detection system shall be so designed and the detectors so positioned as to detect rapidly the onset of fire in any part of those spaces and under any normal conditions of operation of the machinery and variations of ventilation as required by the possible range of ambient temperatures. Except in spaces of restricted height and where their use is specially appropriate, detection systems using only thermal detectors shall not be permitted. The detection system shall initiate audible and visual alarms distinct in both respects from the alarms of any other system not indicating fire, in sufficient places to ensure that the alarms are heard and observed on the navigating bridge and by a responsible engineer officer. When the navigating bridge is unmanned the alarm shall sound in a place where a responsible member of the crew is on duty.

3   After installation the system shall be tested under varying conditions of engine operation and ventilation.

Regulation 15

Arrangements for oil fuel, lubricating oil and other flammable oils

1   *Limitations in the use of oil as fuel*

The following limitations shall apply to the use of oil as fuel:

.1   Except as otherwise permitted by this paragraph, no oil fuel with a flashpoint of less than 60°C shall be used.

[F]   See Annex 2.

.2   In emergency generators oil fuel with a flashpoint of not less than 43°C may be used.

.3   Subject to such additional precautions as it may consider necessary and on condition that the ambient temperature of the space in which such oil fuel is stored or used shall not be allowed to rise to within. 10°C below the flashpoint of the oil fuel, the Administration may permit the general use of oil fuel having a flashpoint of less than 60°C but not less than 43°C.

.4   In cargo ships the use of fuel having a lower flashpoint than otherwise specified in this paragraph, for example crude oil, may be permitted provided that such fuel is not stored in any machinery space and subject to the approval by the Administration of the complete installation.

The flashpoint of oils shall be determined by an approved closed cup method.

2   *Oil fuel arrangements*

In a ship in which oil fuel is used, the arrangements for the storage, distribution and utilization of the oil fuel shall be such as to ensure the safety of the ship and persons on board and shall at least comply with the following provisions:

.1   As far as practicable, parts of the oil fuel system containing heated oil under pressure exceeding $0.18\,\text{N}/\text{mm}^2$ shall not be placed in a concealed position such that defects and leakage cannot readily be observed. The machinery spaces in way of such parts of the oil fuel system shall be adequately illuminated.

.2   The ventilation of machinery spaces shall be sufficient under all normal conditions to prevent accumulation of oil vapour.

.3   As far as practicable, oil fuel tanks shall be part of the ship's structure and shall be located outside machinery spaces of category A. Where oil fuel tanks, other than double bottom tanks, are necessarily located adjacent to or within machinery spaces of category A, at least one of their vertical sides shall be contiguous to the machinery space boundaries, and shall preferably have a common boundary with the double bottom tanks, and the area of the tank boundary common with the machinery spaces shall be kept to a minimum. Where such tanks are situated within the boundaries of machinery spaces of category A they shall not contain oil fuel having a flashpoint of less than 60°C. In general the use of free-standing oil fuel tanks shall be avoided. When such tanks are employed their use shall be prohibited in category A machinery spaces on passenger ships. Where permitted, they shall be placed in an oil-tight spill tray of ample size having a suitable drain pipe leading to a suitably sized spill oil tank.

.4   No oil fuel tank shall be situated where spillage or leakage therefrom can constitute a hazard by falling on heated surfaces. Precautions shall be taken to prevent any oil that may escape under pressure from any pump, filter or heater from coming into contact with heated surfaces.

.5 Every oil fuel pipe, which, if damaged, would allow oil to escape from a storage, settling or daily service tank situated above the double bottom shall be fitted with a cock or valve directly on the tank capable of being closed from a safe position outside the space concerned in the event of a fire occurring in the space in which such tanks are situated. In the special case of deep tanks situated in any shaft or pipe tunnel or similar space, valves on the tank shall be fitted but control in the event of fire may be effected by means of an additional valve on the pipe or pipes outside the tunnel or similar space. If such additional valve is fitted in the machinery space it shall be operated from a position outside this space.

F .6 Safe and efficient means of ascertaining the amount of oil fuel contained in any oil fuel tank shall be provided. Sounding pipes shall not terminate in any space where the risk of ignition of spillage from the sounding pipe might arise. In particular, they shall not terminate in passenger or crew spaces. Other means of ascertaining the amount of oil fuel contained in any oil fuel tank may be permitted:

.6.1 in passenger ships, if such means do not require penetration below the top of the tank, and providing their failure or overfilling of the tanks will not permit release of fuel;

.6.2 in cargo ships, providing the failure of such means or overfilling of the tanks will not permit release of fuel. The use of cylindrical gauge glasses is prohibited. The Administration may permit the use of oil level gauges with flat glasses and self-closing valves between the gauges and oil tanks.

Such other means shall be acceptable to the Administration and shall be maintained in the proper condition to ensure their continued accurate functioning in service.

.7 Provision shall be made to prevent overpressure in any oil tank or in any part of the oil fuel system, including the filling pipes. Any relief valves and air or overflow pipes shall discharge to a position which, in the opinion of the Administration, is safe.

.8 Oil fuel pipes and their valves and fittings shall be of steel or other approved material, except that restricted use of flexible pipes shall be permissible in positions where the Administration is satisfied that they are necessary. Such flexible pipes and end attachments shall be of approved fire-resisting materials of adequate strength and shall be constructed to the satisfaction of the Administration.

F See Annex 2.

3   *Lubricating oil arrangements*

The arrangements for the storage, distribution and utilization of oil used in pressure lubrication systems shall be such as to ensure the safety of the ship and persons on board, and such arrangements in machinery spaces of category A and whenever practicable in other machinery spaces shall at least comply with the provisions of paragraphs 2.1, 2.4, 2.5, 2.6, 2.7 and 2.8, except that this does not preclude the use of sight flow glasses in lubricating systems provided that they are shown by test to have a suitable degree of fire resistance.

4   *Arrangements for other flammable oils*

The arrangements for the storage, distribution and utilization of other flammable oils employed under pressure in power transmission systems, control and activating systems and heating systems shall be such as to ensure the safety of the ship and persons on board. In locations where means of ignition are present, such arrangements shall at least comply with the provisions of paragraphs 2.4 and 2.6, and with the provisions of paragraphs 2.7 and 2.8 in respect of strength and construction.

5   *Periodically unattended machinery spaces*

In addition to the requirements of paragraphs 1 to 4, the oil fuel and lubricating oil systems shall comply with the following:

.1   Where necessary, oil fuel and lubricating oil pipelines shall be screened or otherwise suitably protected to avoid as far as practicable oil spray or oil leakages on to hot surfaces or into machinery air intakes. The number of joints in such piping systems shall be kept to a minimum and, where practicable, leakages from high pressure oil fuel pipes shall be collected and arrangements provided for an alarm to be given.

.2   Where daily service oil fuel tanks are filled automatically, or by remote control, means shall be provided to prevent overflow spillages. Other equipment which treats flammable liquids automatically, e.g. oil fuel purifiers, which, whenever practicable, shall be installed in a special space reserved for purifiers and their heaters, shall have arrangements to prevent overflow spillages.

.3   Where daily service oil fuel tanks or settling tanks are fitted with heating arrangements, a high temperature alarm shall be provided if the flashpoint of the oil fuel can be exceeded.

6   *Prohibition of carriage of flammable oils in forepeak tanks*

Fuel oil, lubrication oil and other flammable oils shall not be carried in forepeak tanks.

F   See Annex 2.

Regulation 16

Ventilation systems in ships other than passenger ships
carrying more than 36 passengers

1   Ventilation ducts shall be of non-combustible material. Short ducts, however, not generally exceeding 2 m in length and with a cross-section not exceeding 0.02 m² need not be non-combustible, subject to the following conditions:

   .1   these ducts shall be of a material which, in the opinion of the Administration, has a low fire risk;

   .2   they may only be used at the end of the ventilation device;

   .3   they shall not be situated less than 600 mm, measured along the duct, from an opening in an "A" or "B" class division including continuous "B" class ceilings.

2   Where the ventilation ducts with a free-sectional area exceeding 0.02 m² pass through class "A" bulkheads or decks, the opening shall be lined with a steel sheet sleeve unless the ducts passing through the bulkheads or decks are of steel in the vicinity of passage through the deck or bulkhead and the ducts and sleeves shall comply in this part with the following:

   .1   The sleeves shall have a thickness of at least 3 mm and a length of at least 900 mm. When passing through bulkheads, this length shall be divided preferably into 450 mm on each side of the bulkhead. These ducts, or sleeves lining such ducts, shall be provided with fire insulation. The insulation shall have at least the same fire integrity as the bulkhead or deck through which the duct passes. Equivalent penetration protection may be provided to the satisfaction of the Administration.

   .2   Ducts with a free cross-sectional area exceeding 0.075 m² shall be fitted with fire dampers in addition to the requirements of paragraph 2.1. The fire damper shall operate automatically but shall also be capable of being closed manually from both sides of the bulkhead or deck. The damper shall be provided with an indicator which shows whether the damper is open or closed. Fire dampers are not required, however, where ducts pass through spaces surrounded by "A" class divisions, without serving those spaces, provided those ducts have the same fire integrity as the divisions which they pierce.

3   Ducts provided for the ventilation of machinery spaces of category A, galleys, car deck spaces, ro–ro cargo spaces or special category spaces shall not pass through accommodation spaces, service spaces or control stations unless they comply with the conditions specified in subparagraphs 1.1 to 1.4 or 2.1 and 2.2 below:

   .1.1   the ducts are constructed of steel having a thickness of at least 3 mm and 5 mm for ducts the widths or diameters of which are

147

up to and including 300 mm and 760 mm and over respectively and, in the case of such ducts, the widths or diameters of which are between 300 mm and 760 mm having a thickness to be obtained by interpolation;

.1.2 the ducts are suitably supported and stiffened;

.1.3 the ducts are fitted with automatic fire dampers close to the boundaries penetrated; and

.1.4 the ducts are insulated to "A-60" standard from the machinery spaces, galleys, car deck spaces, ro–ro cargo spaces or special category spaces to a point at least 5 m beyond each fire damper;

or

.2.1 the ducts are constructed of steel in accordance with paragraphs 3.1.1 and 3.1.2; and

.2.2 the ducts are insulated to "A-60" standard throughout the accommodation spaces, service spaces or control stations;

except that penetrations of main zone divisions shall also comply with the requirements of paragraph 8.

4   Ducts provided for ventilation to accommodation spaces, service spaces or control stations shall not pass through machinery spaces of category A, galleys, car deck spaces, ro–ro cargo spaces or special category spaces unless they comply with the conditions specified in subparagraphs 1.1 to 1.3 or 2.1 and 2.2 below:

.1.1 the ducts where they pass through a machinery space of category A, galley, car deck space, ro–ro cargo space or special category space are constructed of steel in accordance with paragraphs 3.1.1 and 3.1.2;

.1.2 automatic fire dampers are fitted close to the boundaries penetrated; and

.1.3 the integrity of the machinery space, galley, car deck space, ro–ro cargo space or special category space boundaries is maintained at the penetrations;

or

.2.1 the ducts where they pass through a machinery space of category A, galley, car deck space, ro–ro cargo space or special category space are constructed of steel in accordance with paragraphs 3.1.1 and 3.1.2; and

.2.2 the ducts are insulated to "A-60" standard within the machinery space, galley, car deck space, ro–ro cargo space or special category space;

except that penetrations of main zone divisions shall also comply with the requirements of paragraph 8.

148

5   Ventilation ducts with a free cross-sectional area exceeding 0.02 m² passing through "B" class bulkheads shall be lined with steel sheet sleeves of 900 mm in length divided preferably into 450 mm on each side of the bulkheads unless the duct is of steel for this length.

6   Such measures as are practicable shall be taken in respect of control stations outside machinery spaces in order to ensure that ventilation, visibility and freedom from smoke are maintained, so that in the event of fire the machinery and equipment contained therein may be supervised and continue to function effectively. Alternative and separate means of air supply shall be provided; air inlets of the two sources of supply shall be so disposed that the risk of both inlets drawing in smoke simultaneously is minimized. At the discretion of the Administration, such requirements need not apply to control stations situated on, and opening on to, an open deck, or where local closing arrangements would be equally effective.

7   Where they pass through accommodation spaces or spaces containing combustible materials, the exhaust ducts from galley ranges shall be constructed of "A" class divisions. Each exhaust duct shall be fitted with:

.1   a grease trap readily removable for cleaning;

.2   a fire damper located in the lower end of the duct;

.3   arrangements, operable from within the galley, for shutting off the exhaust fans; and

.4   fixed means for extinguishing a fire within the duct.

8   Where in a passenger ship it is necessary that a ventilation duct passes through a main vertical zone division, a fail-safe automatic closing fire damper shall be fitted adjacent to the division. The damper shall also be capable of being manually closed from each side of the division. The operating position shall be readily accessible and be marked in red light-reflecting colour. The duct between the division and the damper shall be of steel or other equivalent material and, if necessary, insulated to comply with the requirements of regulation 18.1.1. The damper shall be fitted on at least one side of the division with a visible indicator showing whether the damper is in the open position.

9   The main inlets and outlets of all ventilation systems shall be capable of being closed from outside the spaces being ventilated.

10   Power ventilation of accommodation spaces, service spaces, cargo spaces, control stations and machinery spaces shall be capable of being stopped from an easily accessible position outside the space being served. This position should not be readily cut off in the event of a fire in the spaces served. The means provided for stopping the power ventilation of the machinery spaces shall be entirely separate from the means provided for stopping ventilation of other spaces.

149

Regulation 17

Fireman's outfit

1   A fireman's outfit shall consist of:

1.1   Personal equipment comprising:

.1   Protective clothing of material to protect the skin from the heat radiating from the fire and from burns and scalding by steam. The outer surface shall be water-resistant.

.2   Boots and gloves of rubber or other electrically nonconducting material.

.3   A rigid helmet providing effective protection against impact.

.4   An electric safety lamp (hand lantern) of an approved type with a minimum burning period of three hours.

.5   An axe to the satisfaction of the Administration.

1.2   A breathing apparatus of an approved type which may be either:

.1   a smoke helmet or smoke mask which shall be provided with a suitable air pump and a length of air hose sufficient to reach from the open deck, well clear of hatch or doorway, to any part of the holds or machinery spaces. If, in order to comply with this subparagraph, an air hose exceeding 36 m in length would be necessary, a self-contained breathing apparatus shall be substituted or provided in addition as determined by the Administration; or

.2   a self-contained compressed-air-operated breathing apparatus, the volume of air contained in the cylinders of which shall be at least 1,200 ℓ, or other self-contained breathing apparatus which shall be capable of functioning for at least 30 minutes. A number of spare charges, suitable for use with the apparatus provided, shall be available on board to the satisfaction of the Administration.

2   For each breathing apparatus a fireproof lifeline of sufficient length and strength shall be provided capable of being attached by means of a snaphook to the harness of the apparatus or to a separate belt in order to prevent the breathing apparatus becoming detached when the lifeline is operated.

3   All ships shall carry at least two fireman's outfits complying with the requirements of paragraph 1.

3.1   In addition, there shall be provided:

.1   in passenger ships for every 80 m, or part thereof, of the aggregate of the lengths of all passenger spaces and service spaces on the deck which carries such spaces or, it there is more than one such deck, on the deck which has the largest aggregate of such lengths, two fireman's outfits and two sets of personal equipment, each set comprising the items stipulated in paragraphs 1.1.1, 1.1.2 and 1.1.3;

.2   in tankers, two fireman's outfits.

3.2   In passenger ships carrying more than 36 passengers for each pair of breathing apparatus there shall be provided one water fog applicator which shall be stored adjacent to such apparatus.

3.3   The Administration may require additional sets of personal equipment and breathing apparatus, having due regard to the size and type of the ship.

4   The fireman's outfits or sets of personal equipment shall be so stored as to be easily accessible and ready for use and, where more than one fireman's outfit or more than one set of personal equipment is carried, they shall be stored in widely separated positions. In passenger ships at least two fireman's outfits and one set of personal equipment shall be available at any one position.

Regulation 18

Miscellaneous items

1.1   Where "A" class divisions are penetrated for the passage of electric cables, pipes, trunks, ducts, etc., or for girders, beams or other structural members, arrangements shall be made to ensure that the fire resistance is not impaired, subject to the provisions of regulation 30.5.

1.2   Where "B" class divisions are penetrated for the passage of electric cables, pipes, trunks, ducts, etc., or for the fitting of ventilation terminals, lighting fixtures and similar devices, arrangements shall be made to ensure that the fire resistance is not impaired.

2.1   Pipes penetrating "A" or "B" class divisions shall be of materials approved by the Administration having regard to the temperature such divisions are required to withstand.

2.2   Where the Administration may permit the conveying of oil and combustible liquids through accommodation and service spaces, the pipes conveying oil or combustible liquids shall be of a material approved by the Administration having regard to the fire risk.

2.3   Materials readily rendered ineffective by heat shall not be used for overboard scuppers, sanitary discharges, and other outlets which are close to the waterline and where the failure of the material in the event of fire would give rise to danger of flooding.

3   Electric radiators, if used, shall be fixed in position and so constructed as to reduce fire risks to a minimum. No such radiators shall be fitted with an element so exposed that clothing, curtains, or other similar materials can be scorched or set on fire by heat from the element.

4   Cellulose-nitrate based films shall not be used for cinematograph installations.

5   All waste-receptacles shall be constructed of non-combustible materials with no openings in the sides or bottom.

6   In spaces where penetration of oil products is possible, the surface of insulation shall be impervious to oil or oil vapours.

Regulation 19

*International shore connection**

1   Ships of 500 tons gross tonnage and upwards shall be provided with at least one international shore connection, complying with provisions of paragraph 3.

2   Facilities shall be available enabling such a connection to be used on either side of the ship.

3   Standard dimensions of flanges for the international shore connection shall be in accordance with the following table:

Description	Dimension
Outside diameter	178 mm
Inside diameter	64 mm
Bolt circle diameter	132 mm
Slots in flange	4 holes 19 mm in diameter spaced equidistantly on a bolt circle of the above diameter, slotted to the flange periphery
Flange thickness	14.5 mm minimum
Bolts and nuts	4, each of 16 mm diameter, 50 mm in length

---

* Reference is made to the recommendation contained in resolution A.470(XII) adopted by the Organization entitled "International shore connexion (shore side)".

4   The connection shall be of steel or other suitable material and shall be designed for $1.0\,\text{N/mm}^2$ services. The flange shall have a flat face on one side and on the other shall be permanently attached to a coupling that will fit the ship's hydrant and hose. The connection shall be kept aboard the ship together with a gasket of any material suitable for $1.0\,\text{N/mm}^2$ services, together with four 16 mm bolts, 50 mm in length and eight washers.

Regulation 20

Fire control plans

1   In all ships general arrangement plans shall be permanently exhibited for the guidance of the ship's officers, showing clearly for each deck the control stations, the various fire sections enclosed by "A" class divisions, the sections enclosed by "B" class divisions together with particulars of the fire detection and fire alarm systems, the sprinkler installation, the fire-extinguishing appliances, means of access to different compartments, decks, etc. and the ventilating system including particulars of the fan control positions, the position of dampers and identification numbers of the ventilating fans serving each section. Alternatively, at the discretion of the Administration, the aforementioned details may be set out in a booklet, a copy of which shall be supplied to each officer, and one copy shall at all times be available on board in an accessible position. Plans and booklets shall be kept up to date, any alterations being recorded thereon as soon as practicable. Description in such plans and booklets shall be in the official language of the flag State. If the language is neither English nor French, a translation into one of those languages shall be included. In addition, instructions concerning the maintenance and operation of all the equipment and installations on board for the fighting and containment of fire shall be kept under one cover, readily available in an accessible position.

2   In all ships a duplicate set of fire control plans or a booklet containing such plans shall be permanently stored in a prominently marked weathertight enclosure outside the deckhouse for the assistance of shoreside fire-fighting personnel.

Regulation 21

Ready availability of fire-extinguishing appliances

In all ships, fire-extinguishing appliances shall be kept in good order and available for immediate use at all times during the voyage.

Regulation 22

Acceptance of substitutes

1   This regulation applies to all ships.

2   Where in this chapter any special type of appliance, apparatus, extinguishing medium or arrangement is specified in any ship, any other type of appliance etc., may be allowed, provided the Administration is satisfied that it is not less effective.

PART B – FIRE SAFETY MEASURES FOR PASSENGER SHIPS

Regulation 23

Structure

1   The hull, superstructure, structural bulkheads, decks and deckhouses shall be constructed of steel or other equivalent material. For the purpose of applying the definition of steel or other equivalent material as given in regulation 3.7 the "applicable fire exposure" shall be according to the integrity and insulation standards given in the tables of regulations 26 and 27. For example where divisions such as decks or sides and ends of deckhouses are permitted to have "B-0" fire integrity, the "applicable fire exposure" shall be half an hour.

2   However, in cases where any part of the structure is of aluminium alloy, the following shall apply:

.1   The insulation of aluminium alloy components of "A" or "B" class divisions, except structure which, in the opinion of the Administration, is non-load-bearing, shall be such that the temperature of the structural core does not rise more than 200°C above the ambient temperature at any time during the applicable fire exposure to the standard fire test.

.2   Special attention shall be given to the insulation of aluminium alloy components of columns, stanchions and other structural members required to support lifeboat and liferaft stowage, launching and embarkation areas, and "A" and "B" class divisions to ensure:

.2.1   that for such members supporting lifeboat and liferaft areas and

"A" class divisions, the temperature rise limitation specified in paragraph 2.1 shall apply at the end of one hour; and

.2.2 that for such members required to support "B" class divisions, the temperature rise limitation specified in paragraph 2.1 shall apply at the end of half an hour.

3   Crowns and casings of machinery spaces of category A shall be of steel construction adequately insulated and openings therein, if any, shall be suitably arranged and protected to prevent the spread of fire.

Regulation 24

Main vertical zones and horizontal zones

1.1   For ships carrying more than 36 passengers, the hull, superstructure and deckhouses shall be subdivided into main vertical zones by "A" class divisions. Steps and recesses shall be kept to a minimum, but where they are necessary they shall also be "A" class divisions. These divisions shall have insulation values in accordance with tables in regulation 26.

1.2   For ships carrying not more than 36 passengers, the hull, superstructure and deckhouses in way of accommodation and service spaces shall be subdivided into main vertical zones by "A" class divisions. These divisions shall have insulation values in accordance with tables in regulation 27.

2   As far as practicable, the bulkheads forming the boundaries of the main vertical zones above the bulkhead deck shall be in line with watertight subdivision bulkheads situated immediately below the bulkhead deck.

3   Such bulkheads shall extend from deck to deck and to the shell or other boundaries.

4   Where a main vertical zone is subdivided by horizontal "A" class divisions into horizontal zones for the purpose of providing an appropriate barrier between sprinklered and non-sprinklered zones of the ship, the divisions shall extend between adjacent main vertical zone bulkheads and to the shell or exterior boundaries of the ship and shall be insulated in accordance with the fire insulation and integrity values given in table 26.3 or in table 27.2.

5.1   On ships designed for special purposes, such as automobile or railroad car ferries, where the provision of main vertical zone bulkheads would defeat the purpose for which the ship is intended, equivalent means for controlling and limiting a fire shall be substituted and specifically approved by the Administration.

5.2   However, in a ship with special category spaces, any such space shall comply with the applicable provisions of regulation 37 and in so far as such compliance would be inconsistent with compliance with other requirements of this part, the requirements of regulation 37 shall prevail.

Regulation 25

Bulkheads within a main vertical zone

1.1   For ships carrying more than 36 passengers all bulkheads which are not required to be "A" class divisions shall be at least "B" class or "C" class divisions as prescribed in the tables in regulation 26.

1.2   For ships carrying not more than 36 passengers all bulkheads within accommodation and service spaces which are not required to be "A" class divisions shall be at least "B" class or "C" class divisions as prescribed in the tables in regulation 27.

1.3   All such divisions may be faced with combustible materials in accordance with the provisions of regulation 34.

2   All corridor bulkheads where not required to be "A" class shall be "B" class divisions which shall extend from deck to deck except:

.1   when continuous "B" class ceilings or linings are fitted on both sides of the bulkhead, the portion of the bulkhead behind the continuous ceiling or lining shall be of material which, in thickness and composition, is acceptable in the construction of "B" class divisions but which shall be required to meet "B" class integrity standards only in so far as is reasonable and practicable in the opinion of the Administration;

.2   in the case of a ship protected by an automatic sprinkler system complying with the provisions of regulation 12 the corridor bulkheads of "B" class materials may terminate at a ceiling in the corridor provided such a ceiling is of material which, in thickness and composition, is acceptable in the construction of "B" class divisions. Notwithstanding the requirements of regulations 26 and 27 such bulkheads and ceilings shall be required to meet "B" class integrity standards only in so far as is reasonable and practicable in the opinion of the Administration. All doors and frames in such bulkheads shall be of non-combustible materials and shall be so constructed and erected as to provide substantial fire resistance to the satisfaction of the Administration.

3   All bulkheads required to be "B" class divisions, except corridor bulkheads, shall extend from deck to deck and to the shell or other boundaries

unless continuous "B" class ceilings or linings are fitted on both sides of the bulkhead, in which case the bulkhead may terminate at the continuous ceiling or lining.

Regulation 26

Fire integrity of bulkheads and decks in ships carrying more than 36 passengers

1   In addition to complying with the specific provisions for fire integrity of bulkheads and decks mentioned elsewhere in this part, the minimum fire integrity of all bulkheads and decks shall be as prescribed in tables 26.1 to 26.4. Where, due to any particular structural arrangements in the ship, difficulty is experienced in determining from the tables the minimum fire integrity value of any divisions, such values shall be determined to the satisfaction of the Administration.

2   The following requirements shall govern application of the tables:

.1   Table 26.1 shall apply to bulkheads bounding main vertical zones or horizontal zones.

Table 26.2 shall apply to bulkheads not bounding either main vertical zones or horizontal zones.

Table 26.3 shall apply to decks forming steps in main vertical zones or bounding horizontal zones.

Table 26.4 shall apply to decks not forming steps in main vertical zones nor bounding horizontal zones.

.2   For determining the appropriate fire integrity standards to be applied to boundaries between adjacent spaces, such spaces are classified according to their fire risk as shown in categories (1) to (14) below. Where the contents and use of a space are such that there is a doubt as to its classification for the purpose of this regulation, it shall be treated as a space within the relevant category having the most stringent boundary requirements. The title of each category is intended to be typical rather than restrictive. The number in parentheses preceding each category refers to the applicable column or row in the tables.

(1)   *Control stations*

Spaces containing emergency sources of power and lighting.

Wheelhouse and chartroom.

Spaces containing the ship's radio equipment.

157

Fire-extinguishing rooms, fire control rooms and fire-recording stations.

Control room for propulsion machinery when located outside the propulsion machinery space.

Spaces containing centralized fire alarm equipment.

Spaces containing centralized emergency public address system stations and equipment.

(2) *Stairways*

Interior stairways, lifts and escalators (other than those wholly contained within the machinery spaces) for passengers and crew and enclosures thereto.

In this connection a stairway which is enclosed at only one level shall be regarded as part of the space from which it is not separated by a fire door.

(3) *Corridors*

Passenger and crew corridors and lobbies.

(4) *Lifeboat and liferaft handling and embarkation stations*

Open deck spaces and enclosed promenades forming lifeboat and liferaft embarkation and lowering stations.

(5) *Open deck spaces*

Open deck spaces and enclosed promenades clear of lifeboat and liferaft embarkation and lowering stations.

Air spaces (the space outside superstructures and deckhouses).

(6) *Accommodation spaces of minor fire risk*

Cabins containing furniture and furnishings of restricted fire risk.

Offices and dispensaries containing furniture and furnishings of restricted fire risk.

Public spaces containing furniture and furnishings of restricted fire risk and having a deck area of less than 50 m².

(7) *Accommodation spaces of moderate fire risk*

Spaces as in category (6) above but containing furniture and furnishings of other than restricted fire risk.

Public spaces containing furniture and furnishings of restricted fire risk and having a deck area of 50 m² or more.

Isolated lockers and small store-rooms in accommodation spaces.

Sale shops.

Motion picture projection and film stowage rooms.

Diet kitchens (containing no open flame).

158

Cleaning gear lockers (in which flammable liquids are not stowed).

Laboratories (in which flammable liquids are not stowed).

Pharmacies.

Small drying rooms (having a deck area of 4 m² or less).

Specie rooms.

(8) *Accommodation spaces of greater fire risk*

Public spaces containing furniture and furnishings of other than restricted fire risk and having a deck area of 50 m² or more.

Barber shops and beauty parlours.

(9) *Sanitary and similar spaces*

Communal sanitary facilities, showers, baths, water closets, etc.

Small laundry rooms.

Indoor swimming pool area.

Operating rooms.

Isolated pantries containing no cooking appliances in accommodation spaces.

Private sanitary facilities shall be considered a portion of the space in which they are located.

(10) *Tanks, voids and auxiliary machinery spaces having little or no fire risk*

Water tanks forming part of the ship's structure.

Voids and cofferdams.

Auxiliary machinery spaces which do not contain machinery having a pressure lubrication system and where storage of combustibles is prohibited, such as:

ventilation and air-conditioning rooms; windlass room; steering gear room; stabilizer equipment room; electrical propulsion motor room; rooms containing section switch-boards and purely electrical equipment other than oil-filled electrical transformers (above 10 kVA); shaft alleys and pipe tunnels; spaces for pumps and refrigeration machinery (not handling or using flammable liquids).

Closed trunks serving the spaces listed above.

Other closed trunks such as pipe and cable trunks.

(11) *Auxiliary machinery spaces, cargo spaces, special category spaces, cargo and other oil tanks and other similar spaces of moderate fire risk*

Cargo oil tanks.

Cargo holds, trunkways and hatchways.

Refrigerated chambers.

Oil fuel tanks (where installed in a separate space with no machinery).

Shaft alleys and pipe tunnels allowing storage of combustibles.

Auxiliary machinery spaces as in category (10) which contain machinery having a pressure lubrication system or where storage of combustibles is permitted.

Oil fuel filling stations.

Spaces containing oil-filled electrical transformers (above 10 kVA).

Spaces containing turbine and reciprocating steam engine driven auxiliary generators and small internal combustion engines of power output up to 110 kW driving emergency generators, sprinkler, drencher or fire pumps, bilge pumps, etc.

Special category spaces (tables 26.1 and 26.3 only apply).

Closed trunks serving the spaces listed above.

(12) *Machinery spaces and main galleys*

Main propulsion machinery rooms (other than electric propulsion motor rooms) and boiler rooms.

Auxiliary machinery spaces other than those in categories (10) and (11) which contain internal combustion machinery or other oil-burning, heating or pumping units.

Main galleys and annexes.

Trunks and casings to the spaces listed above.

(13) *Store-rooms, workshops, pantries, etc.*

Main pantries not annexed to galleys.

Main laundry.

Large drying rooms (having a deck area of more than 4 m²).

Miscellaneous stores.

Mail and baggage rooms.

Garbage rooms.

Workshops (not part of machinery spaces, galleys, etc.)

(14) *Other spaces in which flammable liquids are stowed*

Lamp rooms.

Paint rooms.

Store-rooms containing flammable liquids (including dyes, medicines, etc.).

Laboratories (in which flammable liquids are stowed).

.3   Where a single value is shown for the fire integrity of a boundary between two spaces, that value shall apply in all cases.

TABLE 26.1 ■ BULKHEADS BOUNDING MAIN VERTICAL ZONES OR HORIZONTAL ZONES

Spaces		(1)	(2)	(3)	(4)	(5)	(6)	(7)	(8)	(9)	(10)	(11)	(12)	(13)	(14)
Control stations	(1)	A-60	A-30	A-30	A-0	A-0	A-60	A-60	A-60	A-0	A-0	A-60	A-60	A-60	A-60
Stairways	(2)		A-0	A-0	A-0	A-0	A-15 A-0	A-30 A-0	A-60 A-15	A-0	A-0	A-30	A-60	A-15 A-0	A-60
Corridors	(3)			A-0	A-0	A-0	A-0	A-30 A-0	A-30 A-0	A-0	A-0	A-30 A-0	A-60	A-15 A-0	A-60
Lifeboat and liferaft handling and embarkation stations	(4)				—	—	A-0	A-0	A-0	A-0	A-0	A-0	A-60	A-0	A-60
Open deck spaces	(5)					—	A-0	A-0	A-0	A-0	A-0	A-0	A-0	A-0	A-0
Accommodation spaces of minor fire risk	(6)						A-15 A-0	A-30 A-0	A-30 A-0	A-0	A-0	A-15 A-0	A-30	A-15 A-0	A-30
Accommodation spaces of moderate fire risk	(7)							A-30 A-0	A-60 A-15	A-0	A-0	A-30 A-0	A-60	A-30 A-0	A-60
Accommodation spaces of greater fire risk	(8)								A-60 A-15	A-0	A-0	A-60 A-15	A-60	A-30 A-0	A-60
Sanitary and similar spaces	(9)									A-0	A-0	A-0	A-0	A-0	A-0
Tanks, voids and auxiliary machinery spaces having little or no fire risk	(10)										A-0	A-0	A-0	A-0	A-0
Auxiliary machinery spaces, cargo spaces, special category spaces, cargo and other oil tanks and other similar spaces of moderate fire risk	(11)											A-0	A-60	A-0	A-60
Machinery spaces and main galleys	(12)												A-60	A-30[b] A-15	A-60
Store-rooms, workshops, pantries etc.	(13)													A-0	A-30
Other spaces in which flammable liquids are stowed	(14)														A-60

See notes under table 26.4.

161

TABLE 26.2 – BULKHEADS NOT BOUNDING EITHER MAIN VERTICAL ZONES OR HORIZONTAL ZONES

Spaces	(1)	(2)	(3)	(4)	(5)	(6)	(7)	(8)	(9)	(10)	(11)	(12)	(13)	(14)
Control stations (1)	B-0[a]	A-0	A-0	A-0	A-0 B-0	A-60	A-60	A-60	A-0	A-0	A-60	A-60	A-60	A-60
Stairways (2)		A-0[a]	A-0	A-0	A-0	A-0	A-15 A-0	A-30 A-0	A-0	A-0	A-15	A-30	A-15 A-0	A-30
Corridors (3)			C	A-0	A-0 B-0	B-0	B-15 B-0	B-15 B-0	B-0	A-0	A-15	A-30	A-0	A-30 A-0
Lifeboat and liferaft handling and embarkation stations (4)				—	—	A-0	A-0	A-0	A-0	A-0	A-0	A-15	A-0	A-15 A-0
Open deck spaces (5)					—	A-0 B-0	A-0 B-0	A-0 B-0	A-0 B-0	A-0	A-0	A-0	A-0 B-0	A-0 B-0
Accommodation spaces of minor fire risk (6)						B-0 C	B-15 C	B-15 C	B-0 C	A-0	A-15 A-0	A-30	A-0	A-30 A-0
Accommodation spaces of moderate fire risk (7)							B-15 C	B-15 C	B-0 C	A-0	A-15 A-0	A-60	A-15 A-0	A-60 A-15
Accommodation spaces of greater fire risk (8)								B-15 C	B-0 C	A-0	A-30 A-0	A-60	A-15 A-0	A-60 A-15
Sanitary and similar spaces (9)									C	A-0	A-0	A-0	A-0	A-0
Tanks, voids and auxiliary machinery spaces having little or no fire risk (10)										A-0[a]	A-0	A-0	A-0	A-0
Auxiliary machinery spaces, cargo spaces, cargo and other oil tanks and other similar spaces of moderate fire risk (11)											A-0[a]	A-0	A-0	A-30[b] A-15
Machinery spaces and main galleys (12)												A-0[a]	A-0	A-60
Store-rooms, workshops, pantries etc. (13)													A-0[a]	A-0
Other spaces in which flammable liquids are stowed (14)														A-30[b] A-15

See notes under table 26.4.

162

TABLE 26.3 – DECKS FORMING STEPS IN MAIN VERTICAL ZONES OR BOUNDING HORIZONTAL ZONES

Space below ↓ / Space above →	(1)	(2)	(3)	(4)	(5)	(6)	(7)	(8)	(9)	(10)	(11)	(12)	(13)	(14)
Control stations (1)	A-60	A-60	A-30	A-0	A-0	A-15	A-30	A-60	A-0	A-0	A-30	A-60	A-15	A-60
Stairways (2)	A-15	A-0	A-0	A-0	A-0	A-0	A-15 A-0	A-15 A-0	A-0	A-0	A-0	A-60	A-0	A-60
Corridors (3)	A-30	A-0	A-0	A-0	A-0	A-0	A-15 A-0	A-15 A-0	A-0	A-0	A-0	A-60	A-0	A-60
Lifeboat and liferaft handling and embarkation stations (4)	A-0	A-0	A-0	A-0	A-0	A-0	A-0	A-0	A-0	A-0	A-0	A-0	A-0	A-0
Open deck spaces (5)	A-0	A-0	A-0	A-0	A-0	A-0	A-0	A-0	A-0	A-0	A-0	A-0	A-0	A-0
Accommodation spaces of minor fire risk (6)	A-60	A-30 A-0	A-15 A-0	A-0	A-0	A-0	A-15 A-0	A-30 A-0	A-0	A-0	A-15 A-0	A-15	A-0	A-15
Accommodation spaces of moderate fire risk (7)	A-60	A-60 A-15	A-30 A-0	A-15 A-0	A-0	A-15 A-0	A-30 A-0	A-60 A-15	A-0	A-0	A-30 A-0	A-30	A-0	A-30
Accommodation spaces of greater fire risk (8)	A-60	A-60 A-15	A-60 A-15	A-60 A-15	A-0	A-30 A-0	A-60 A-15	A-60 A-15	A-0	A-0	A-30 A-0	A-60	A-15 A-0	A-60
Sanitary and similar spaces (9)	A-0	A-0	A-0	A-0	A-0	A-0	A-0	A-0	A-0	A-0	A-0	A-0	A-0	A-0
Tanks, voids and auxiliary machinery spaces having little or no fire risk (10)	A-0	A-0	A-0	A-0	A-0	A-0	A-0	A-0	A-0	A-0	A-0	A-0	A-0	A-0
Auxiliary machinery spaces, cargo spaces, special category spaces, cargo and other oil tanks and other similar spaces of moderate fire risk (11)	A-60	A-60	A-60	A-60	A-0	A-30 A-0	A-60 A-15	A-60 A-15	A-0	A-0	A-0	A-30	A-30[b] A-0	A-30
Machinery spaces and main galleys (12)	A-60	A-60	A-60	A-60	A-0	A-60	A-60	A-60	A-0	A-0	A-60	A-60	A-60	A-60
Store-rooms, workshops, pantries etc. (13)	A-60	A-60 A-15	A-30 A-0	A-15	A-0	A-15 A-0	A-30 A-0	A-60 A-15	A-0	A-0	A-0	A-30	A-0	A-30
Other spaces in which flammable liquids are stowed (14)	A-60	A-60	A-60	A-60	A-0	A-60	A-60	A-60	A-0	A-0	A-60	A-60	A-60	A-60

See notes under table 26.4.

163

TABLE 26.4 – DECKS NOT FORMING STEPS IN MAIN VERTICAL ZONES NOR BOUNDING HORIZONTAL ZONES

Space below ↓ \ Space above →	(1)	(2)	(3)	(4)	(5)	(6)	(7)	(8)	(9)	(10)	(11)	(12)	(13)	(14)
Control stations (1)	A-30/A-0	A-30/A-0	A-15/A-0	A-0	A-0/B-0	A-0	A-15/A-0	A-30/A-0	A-0	A-0	A-0	A-60	A-0	A-60/A-15
Stairways (2)	A-0	A-0	A-0	A-0	A-0/B-0	A-0	A-0	A-0	A-0	A-0	A-0	A-30	A-0	A-30/A-0
Corridors (3)	A-15/A-0	A-0	A-0a/B-0a	A-0	A-0/B-0	A-0/B-0	A-15/B-0	A-15/B-0	A-0/B-0	A-0	A-0	A-30	A-0	A-30/A-0
Lifeboat and liferaft handling and embarkation stations (4)	A-0	A-0	A-0	A-0	—	A-0	A-0/B-0	A-0/B-0	A-0/B-0	A-0	A-0	A-0	A-0	A-0
Open deck spaces (5)	A-0	A-0	A-0/B-0	A-0	—	A-0/B-0	A-0/B-0	A-0/B-0	A-0/B-0	A-0	A-0	A-0	A-0/B-0	A-0
Accommodation spaces of minor fire risk (6)	A-60	A-15/A-0	A-0	A-0	A-0/B-0	A-0/B-0	A-0/B-0	A-30/B-0	A-0/B-0	A-0	A-0	A-15/A-0	A-0	A-15/A-0
Accommodation spaces of moderate fire risk (7)	A-60	A-30/A-0	A-15/A-0	A-15/A-0	A-0/B-0	A-0/B-0	A-15/B-0	A-60/B-0	A-0/B-0	A-0	A-15/A-0	A-30/A-0	A-0	A-30/A-0
Accommodation spaces of greater fire risk (8)	A-60	A-60/A-15	A-60/A-0	A-30/A-0	A-0/B-0	A-15/B-0	A-30/B-0	A-0/B-0	A-0/B-0	A-0	A-30/A-0	A-30/A-0	A-0	A-30/A-0
Sanitary spaces and similar spaces (9)	A-0	A-0	A-0/B-0	A-0	A-0/B-0	A-0/B-0	A-0/B-0	A-0/B-0	A-0/B-0	A-0	A-0	A-0	A-0	A-0
Tanks, voids and auxiliary machinery spaces having little or no fire risk (10)	A-0	A-0	A-0	A-0	A-0	A-0	A-0	A-0	A-0	A-0a	A-0	A-0	A-0	A-0
Auxiliary machinery spaces, cargo spaces, cargo and other oil tanks and other similar spaces of moderate fire risk (11)	A-60	A-60/A-15	A-60/A-15	A-30/A-0	A-0	A-0	A-0	A-30/A-0	A-0	A-0	A-0a	A-0	A-0	A-30b/A-15
Machinery spaces and main galleys (12)	A-60	A-60	A-60	A-60	A-0	A-60	A-60	A-60	A-0	A-0	A-30	A-30a	A-0	A-60
Store-rooms, workshops, pantries etc. (13)	A-60	A-30/A-0	A-15/A-0	A-15/A-0	A-0/B-0	A-15/A-0	A-30/A-0	A-30/A-0	A-0/B-0	A-0	A-0	A-0	A-0	A-15b/A-0
Other spaces in which flammable liquids are stowed (14)	A-60	A-60/A-30	A-60/A-30	A-60	A-0	A-30/A-0	A-60/A-15	A-60/A-15	A-0	A-0	A-30b/A-0	A-30b/A-0	A-0	A-30b/A-0

Notes: To be applied to tables 26.1 to 26.4, as appropriate.

a Where adjacent spaces are in the same numerical category and superscript a appears, a bulkhead or deck between such spaces need not be fitted if deemed unnecessary by the Administration. For example, in category (12) a bulkhead need not be required between a galley and its annexed pantries provided the pantry bulkheads and decks maintain the integrity of the galley boundaries. A bulkhead is, however, required between a galley and a machinery space even though both spaces are in category (12).

b Where superscript b appears the lesser insulation value may be permitted only if at least one of the adjoining spaces is protected by an automatic sprinkler system complying with the provisions of regulation 12.

.4 In determining the applicable fire integrity standard of a boundary between two spaces within a main vertical zone or horizontal zone which is not protected by an automatic sprinkler system complying with the provisions of regulation 12 or between such zones neither of which is so protected, the higher of the two values given in the tables shall apply.

.5 In determining the applicable fire integrity standard of a boundary between two spaces within a main vertical zone or horizontal zone which is protected by an automatic sprinkler system complying with the provisions of regulation 12 or between such zones both of which are so protected, the lesser of the two values given in the tables shall apply. Where a sprinklered zone and a non-sprinklered zone meet within accommodation and service spaces, the higher of the two values given in the tables shall apply to the division between the zones.

.6 Notwithstanding the provisions of regulation 25 there are no special requirements for material or integrity of boundaries where only a dash appears in the tables.

.7 The Administration shall determine in respect of category (5) spaces whether the insulation values in table 26.1 or 26.2 shall apply to ends of deckhouses and superstructures, and whether the insulation values in table 26.3 or 26.4 shall apply to weather decks. In no case shall the requirements of category (5) of tables 26.1 to 26.4 necessitate enclosure of spaces which in the opinion of the Administration need not be enclosed.

3 Continuous "B" class ceilings or linings, in association with the relevant decks or bulkheads, may be accepted as contributing wholly or in part, to the required insulation and integrity of a division.

4 In approving structural fire protection details, the Administration shall have regard to the risk of heat transmission at intersections and terminal points of required thermal barriers.

Regulation 27

Fire integrity of bulkheads and decks in ship carrying not more than 36 passengers

1 In addition to complying with the specific provisions for fire integrity of bulkheads and decks mentioned elsewhere in this part, the minimum fire integrity of bulkheads and decks shall be as prescribed in table 27.1 and table 27.2.

TABLE 27.1 – FIRE INTEGRITY OF BULKHEADS SEPARATING ADJACENT SPACES

Spaces		(1)	(2)	(3)	(4)	(5)	(6)	(7)	(8)	(9)	(10)	(11)
Control stations	(1)	A-0^c	A-0	A-60	A-0	A-15	A-60	A-15	A-60	A-60	*	A-60
Corridors	(2)		C^c	B-0^c	A-0^a B-0^e	B-0^e	A-60	A-0	A-0	A-15 A-0^d	*	A-15
Accommodation spaces	(3)			C^c	A-0^a B-0^e	B-0^e	A-60	A-0	A-0	A-15 A-0^d	*	A-30 A-0^d
Stairways	(4)				A-0^a B-0^e	A-0^a B-0^e	A-60	A-0	A-0	A-15 A-0^d	* *	A-15
Service spaces (low risk)	(5)					C^c	A-60	A-0	A-0	A-0	*	A-0
Machinery spaces of category A	(6)						*	A-0	A-0	A-60	*	A-60
Other machinery spaces	(7)							A-0^b	A-0	A-0	*	A-0
Cargo spaces	(8)								*	A-0	*	A-0
Service spaces (high risk)	(9)									A-0^b	*	A-30
Open decks	(10)											A-0
Special category spaces	(11)											A-0

Notes: To be applied to both tables 27.1 and 27.2, as appropriate.

^{a} For clarification as to which applies see regulations 25 and 29.

^{b} Where spaces are of the same numerical category and superscript ^{b} appears, a bulkhead or deck of the ratings shown in the tables is only required when the adjacent spaces are for a different purpose, e.g. in category (9). A galley next to a galley does not require a bulkhead but a galley next to a paint room requires an "A-0" bulkhead.

^{c} Bulkheads separating the wheelhouse and chartroom from each other may be "B-0" rating.

^{d} See 2.3 and 2.4 of this regulation.

^{e} For the application of regulation 24.1.2, "B-0" and "C", where appearing in table 27.1, shall be read as "A-0".

^{f} Fire insulation need not be fitted if the machinery space of category (7), in the opinion of the Administration, has little or no fire risk.

* Where an asterisk appears in the tables, the division is required to be of steel or other equivalent material but is not required to be of "A" class standard.
For the application of regulation 24.1.2 an asterisk, where appearing in table 27.2, except for categories (8) and (10), shall be read as "A-0".

2   The following requirements shall govern application of the tables:

.1   Tables 27.1 and 27.2 shall apply respectively to the bulkheads and decks separating adjacent spaces.

.2   For determining the appropriate fire integrity standards to be applied to divisions between adjacent spaces, such spaces are classified according to their fire risk as shown in categories (1) to (11) below. The title of each category is intended to be typical rather than restrictive. The number in parentheses preceding each category refers to the applicable column or row in the tables.

166

TABLE 27.2 – FIRE INTEGRITY OF DECKS SEPARATING ADJACENT SPACES

Space below ↓ / Space above →		(1)	(2)	(3)	(4)	(5)	(6)	(7)	(8)	(9)	(10)	(11)
Control stations	(1)	A-0	A-0	A-0	A-0	A-0	A-60	A-0	A-0	A-0	*	A-30
Corridors	(2)	A-0	*	*	A-0	*	A-60	A-0	A-0	A-0	*	A-0
Accommodation spaces	(3)	A-60	A-0	*	A-0	*	A-60	A-0	A-0	A-0	*	A-30 / A-0^d
Stairways	(4)	A-0	A-0	A-0	*	A-0	A-60	A-0	A-0	A-0	*	A-0
Service spaces (low risk)	(5)	A-15	A-0	A-0	A-0	*	A-60	A-0	A-0	A-0	*	A-0
Machinery spaces of category A	(6)	A-60	A-60	A-60	A-60	A-60	*	A-60^f	A-30	A-60	*	A-60
Other machinery spaces	(7)	A-15	A-0	A-0	A-0	A-0	A-0	*	A-0	A-0	*	A-0
Cargo spaces	(8)	A-60	A-0	A-0	A-0	A-0	A-0	A-0	*	A-0	*	A-0
Service spaces (high risk)	(9)	A-60	A-30 / A-0^d	A-30 / A-0^d	A-30 / A-0^d	A-0	A-60	A-0	A-0	A-0	*	A-30
Open decks	(10)	*	*	*	*	*	*	*	*	*	—	A-0
Special category spaces	(11)	A-60	A-15	A-30 / A-0^d	A-15	A-0	A-30	A-0	A-0	A-30	A-0	A-0

(1) *Control stations*

Spaces containing emergency sources of power and lighting.

Wheelhouse and chartroom.

Spaces containing the ship's radio equipment.

Fire-extinguishing rooms, fire control rooms and fire-recording stations.

Control room for propulsion machinery when located outside the machinery space.

Spaces containing centralized fire alarm equipment.

(2) *Corridors*

Passenger and crew corridors and lobbies.

(3) *Accommodation spaces*

Spaces as defined in regulation 3.10 excluding corridors.

(4) *Stairways*

Interior stairways, lifts and escalators (other than those wholly contained within the machinery spaces) and enclosures thereto.

In this connection, a stairway which is enclosed only at one level shall be regarded as part of the space from which it is not separated by a fire door.

(5) *Service spaces (low risk)*

Lockers and store-rooms having areas of less than 2 m², drying rooms and laundries.

(6) *Machinery spaces of category A*

Spaces as defined in regulation 3.19.

(7) *Other machinery spaces*

Spaces as defined in regulation 3.20 excluding machinery spaces of category A.

(8) *Cargo spaces*

All spaces used for cargo (including cargo oil tanks) and trunkways and hatchways to such spaces, other than special category spaces.

(9) *Service spaces (high risk)*

Galleys, pantries containing cooking appliances, paint and lamp rooms, lockers and store-rooms having areas of 2 m² or more and workshops other than those forming part of the machinery spaces.

(10) *Open decks*

Open deck spaces and enclosed promenades having no fire risk. Air spaces (the space outside superstructures and deckhouses).

(11) *Special category spaces*

Spaces as defined in regulation 3.18.

.3 In determining the applicable fire integrity standard of a boundary between two spaces within a main vertical zone or horizontal zone which is not protected by an automatic sprinkler system complying with the provisions of regulation 12 or between such zones neither of which is so protected, the higher of the two values given in the tables shall apply.

.4 In determining the applicable fire integrity standard of a boundary between two spaces within a main vertical zone or horizontal zone which is protected by an automatic sprinkler system complying with the provisions of regulation 12 or between such zones both of which are so protected, the lesser of the two values given in the tables shall apply. Where a sprinklered zone and a non-sprinklered zone meet within accommodation and service spaces, the higher of the two values given in the tables shall apply to the division between the zones.

3   Continuous "B" class ceilings or linings, in association with the relevant decks or bulkheads, may be accepted as contributing, wholly or in part, to the required insulation and integrity of a division.

4   External boundaries which are required in regulation 23.1 to be of steel

168

or other equivalent material may be pierced for the fitting of windows and sidescuttles provided that there is no requirement for such boundaries to have "A" class integrity elsewhere in this part. Similarly, in such boundaries which are not required to have "A" class integrity, doors may be of materials to the satisfaction of the Administration.

Regulation 28

Means of escape

1   Stairways and ladders shall be arranged to provide ready means of escape to the lifeboat and liferaft embarkation deck from all passenger and crew spaces and from spaces in which the crew is normally employed, other than machinery spaces. In particular, the following provisions shall be complied with:

.1   Below the bulkhead deck two means of escape, at least one of which shall be independent of watertight doors, shall be provided from each watertight compartment or similarly restricted space or group of spaces. Exceptionally, the Administration may dispense with one of the means of escape, due regard being paid to the nature and location of spaces and to the number of persons who might normally be accommodated or employed there.

.2   Above the bulkhead deck there shall be at least two means of escape from each main vertical zone or similarly restricted space or group of spaces at least one of which shall give access to a stairway forming a vertical escape.

.3   If a radiotelegraph station has no direct access to the open deck, two means of escape from or access to such station shall be provided, one of which may be a porthole or window of sufficient size or another means to the satisfaction of the Administration.

.4   A corridor or part of a corridor from which there is only one route of escape shall not exceed:

13 m in length for ships carrying more than 36 passengers, and
7 m in length for ships carrying not more than 36 passengers.

.5   At least one of the means of escape required by paragraphs 1.1 and 1.2 shall consist of a readily accessible enclosed stairway, which shall provide continuous fire shelter from the level of its origin to the appropriate lifeboat and liferaft embarkation decks or the highest level served by the stairway, whichever level is the highest. However, where the Administration has granted dispensation under the provisions of paragraph 1.1 the sole means of escape shall provide safe escape to the satisfaction of the Administration. The width, number and continuity of the stairways shall be to the satisfaction of the Administration.

.6   Protection of access from the stairway enclosures to the lifeboat and liferaft embarkation areas shall be to the satisfaction of the Administration.

.7   Stairways serving only a space and a balcony in that space shall not be considered as forming one of the required means of escape.

2.1   In special category spaces the number and disposition of the means of escape both below and above the bulkhead deck shall be to the satisfaction of the Administration and in general the safety of access to the embarkation deck shall be at least equivalent to that provided for under paragraphs 1.1, 1.2, 1.5 and 1.6.

2.2   One of the escape routes from the machinery spaces where the crew is normally employed shall avoid direct access to any special category space.

3.1   Two means of escape shall be provided from each machinery space. In particular, the following provisions shall be complied with:

.1   Where the space is below the bulkhead deck the two means of escape shall consist of either:

.1.1   two sets of steel ladders as widely separated as possible, leading to doors in the upper part of the space similarly separated and from which access is provided to the appropriate lifeboat and liferaft embarkation decks. One of these ladders shall provide continuous fire shelter from the lower part of the space to a safe position outside the space; or

.1.2   one steel ladder leading to a door in the upper part of the space from which access is provided to the embarkation deck and additionally, in the lower part of the space and in a position well separated from the ladder referred to, a steel door capable of being operated from each side and which provides access to a safe escape route from the lower part of the space to the embarkation deck.

.2   Where the space is above the bulkhead deck, the two means of escape shall be as widely separated as possible and the doors leading from such means of escape shall be in a position from which access is provided to the appropriate lifeboat and liferaft embarkation decks. Where such means of escape require the use of ladders, these shall be of steel.

3.2   In a ship of less than 1,000 tons gross tonnage, the Administration may dispense with one of the means of escape, due regard being paid to the width and disposition of the upper part of the space; and in a ship of 1,000 tons gross tonnage and above, the Administration may dispense with one means of escape from any such space so long as either a door or a steel ladder provides a safe escape route to the embarkation deck, due regard being paid to the nature and location of the space and whether persons are normally employed in that space.

4   In no case shall lifts be considered as forming one of the required means of escape.

Regulation 29

Protection of stairways and lifts in accommodation and service spaces

1   All stairways shall be of steel frame construction except where the Administration sanctions the use of other equivalent material, and shall be within enclosures formed of "A" class divisions, with positive means of closure at all openings, except that:

.1   a stairway connecting only two decks need not be enclosed, provided the integrity of the deck is maintained by proper bulkheads or doors in one 'tweendeck space. When a stairway is closed in one 'tween-deck space, the stairway enclosure shall be protected in accordance with the tables for decks in regulations 26 or 27;

.2   stairways may be fitted in the open in a public space, provided they lie wholly within such public space.

2   Stairway enclosures shall have direct communication with the corridors and be of sufficient area to prevent congestion, having in view the number of persons likely to use them in an emergency. In so far as is practicable, stairway enclosures shall not give direct access to cabins, service lockers, or other enclosed spaces containing combustibles in which a fire is likely to originate.

3   Lift trunks shall be so fitted as to prevent the passage of smoke and flame from one 'tweendeck to another and shall be provided with means of closing so as to permit the control of draught and smoke.

Regulation 30

Openings in "A" class divisions

1   Except for hatches between cargo, special category, store, and baggage spaces, and between such spaces and the weather decks, all openings shall be provided with permanently attached means of closing which shall be at least as effective for resisting fires as the divisions in which they are fitted.

2   The construction of all doors and door frames in "A" class divisions, with the means of securing them when closed, shall provide resistance to fire as well as to the passage of smoke and flame, as far as practicable,

equivalent to that of the bulkheads in which the doors are situated. Such doors and door frames shall be constructed of steel or other equivalent material. Watertight doors need not be insulated.

3 It shall be possible for each door to be opened and closed from each side of the bulkhead by one person only.

4 Fire doors in main vertical zone bulkheads and stairway enclosures, other than power-operated watertight doors and those which are normally locked, shall be of the self-closing type capable of closing against an inclination of 3.5° opposing closure. The speed of door closure shall, if necessary, be controlled so as to prevent undue danger to persons. All such doors, except those that are normally closed, shall be capable of release from a control station, either simultaneously or in groups, and also individually from a position at the door. The release mechanism shall be so designed that the door will automatically close in the event of disruption of the control system; however, approved power-operated watertight doors will be considered acceptable for this purpose. Hold-back hooks not subject to control station release will not be permitted. When double swing doors are permitted, they shall have a latch arrangement which is automatically engaged by the operation of the door release system.

5 Where a space is protected by an automatic sprinkler system complying with the provisions of regulation 12 or fitted with a continuous "B" class ceiling, openings in decks not forming steps in main vertical zones nor bounding horizontal zones shall be closed reasonably tight and such decks shall meet the "A" class integrity requirements in so far as is reasonable and practicable in the opinion of the Administration.

6 The requirements for "A" class integrity of the outer boundaries of a ship shall not apply to glass partitions, windows and sidescuttles. Similarly, the requirements for "A" class integrity shall not apply to exterior doors in superstructures and deckhouses.

Regulation 31

Openings in "B" class divisions

1 Doors and door frames in "B" class divisions and means of securing them shall provide a method of closure which shall have resistance to fire as far as practicable equivalent to that of the divisions except that ventilation openings may be permitted in the lower portion of such doors. Where such opening is in or under a door the total net area of any such opening or openings shall not exceed 0.05 m². When such opening is cut in a door it shall be fitted with a grill made of non-combustible material. Doors shall be non-combustible.

2   The requirements for "B" class integrity of the outer boundaries of a ship shall not apply to glass partitions, windows and sidescuttles. Similarly, the requirements for "B" class integrity shall not apply to exterior doors in superstructures and deckhouses. For ships carrying not more than 36 passengers, the Administration may permit the use of combustible materials in doors separating cabins from the individual interior sanitary spaces such as showers.

3   Where an automatic sprinkler system complying with the provisions of regulation 12 is fitted:

.1   openings in decks not forming steps in main vertical zones nor bounding horizontal zones shall be closed reasonably tight and such decks shall meet the "B" class integrity requirements in so far as is reasonable and practicable in the opinion of the Administration; and

.2   openings in corridor bulkheads of "B" class materials shall be protected in accordance with the provisions of regulation 25.

Regulation 32

Ventilation systems

1   *Passenger ships carrying more than 36 passengers*

1.1   The ventilation system of a passenger ship carrying more than 36 passengers shall, in addition to this part of this regulation, also be in compliance with the requirements of regulation 16.2 to 16.9.

1.2   In general, the ventilation fans shall be so disposed that the ducts reaching the various spaces remain within the main vertical zone.

1.3   Where ventilation systems penetrate decks, precautions shall be taken, in addition to those relating to the fire integrity of the deck required by regulations 18.1.1 and 30.5, to reduce the likelihood of smoke and hot gases passing from one 'tweendeck space to another through the system. In addition to insulation requirements contained in this regulation, vertical ducts shall, if necessary, be insulated as required by the appropriate tables in regulation 26.

1.4   Except in cargo spaces, ventilation ducts shall be constructed of the following materials:

.1   ducts not less than $0.075\,m^2$ in sectional area and all vertical ducts serving more than a single 'tweendeck space shall be constructed of steel or other equivalent material;

.2   ducts less than $0.075\,m^2$ in sectional area other than the vertical ducts referred to in paragraph 1.4.1, shall be constructed of non-combustible materials. Where such ducts penetrate "A" or "B" class divisions due regard shall be given to ensuring the fire integrity of the division;

.3 short lengths of duct, not in general exceeding $0.02 \, m^2$ in sectional area nor 2 m in length, need not be non-combustible provided that all of the following conditions are met:

.3.1 the duct is constructed of a material of low fire risk to the satisfaction of the Administration;

.3.2 the duct is used only at the terminal end of the ventilation system; and

.3.3 the duct is not located closer than 600 mm measured along its length to a penetration of an "A" or "B" class division, including continuous "B" class ceilings.

1.5 Where a stairway enclosure is ventilated, the duct or ducts shall be taken from the fan room independently of other ducts in the ventilation system and shall not serve any other space.

1.6 All power ventilation, except machinery space and cargo space ventilation and any alternative system which may be required under regulation 16.6, shall be fitted with controls so grouped that all fans may be stopped from either of two separate positions which shall be situated as far apart as practicable. Controls provided for the power ventilation serving machinery spaces shall also be grouped so as to be operable from two positions, one of which shall be outside such spaces. Fans serving power ventilation systems to cargo spaces shall be capable of being stopped from a safe position outside such spaces.

2 *Passenger ships carrying not more than 36 passengers*

2.1 The ventilation system of passenger ships carrying not more than 36 passengers shall be in compliance with regulation 16.

Regulation 33

Windows and sidescuttles

1 All windows and sidescuttles in bulkheads within accommodation and service spaces and control stations other than those to which the provisions of regulation 30.6 and of regulation 31.2 apply, shall be so constructed as to preserve the integrity requirements of the type of bulkheads in which they are fitted.

2   Notwithstanding the requirements of the tables in regulations 26 and 27:

.1   all windows and sidescuttles in bulkheads separating accommodation and service spaces and control stations from weather shall be constructed with frames of steel or other suitable material. The glass shall be retained by a metal glazing bead or angle;

.2   special attention shall be given to the fire integrity of windows facing open or enclosed lifeboat and liferaft embarkation areas and to the fire integrity of windows situated below such areas in such a position that their failure during a fire would impede the launching of, or embarkation into, lifeboats or liferafts.

Regulation 34

Restricted use of combustible materials

1   Except in cargo spaces, mail rooms, baggage rooms, or refrigerated compartments of service spaces, all linings, grounds, ceilings and insulations shall be of non-combustible materials. Partial bulkheads or decks used to subdivide a space for utility or artistic treatment shall also be of non-combustible material.

2   Vapour barriers and adhesives used in conjunction with insulation, as well as insulation of pipe fittings, for cold service systems need not be non-combustible, but they shall be kept to the minimum quantity practicable and their exposed surfaces shall have qualities of resistance to the propagation of flame to the satisfaction of the Administration.

3   The following surfaces shall have low flame-spread characteristics:*

.1   exposed surfaces in corridors and stairway enclosures, and of bulkheads, wall and ceiling linings in all accommodation and service spaces and control stations;

.2   concealed or inaccessible spaces in accommodation, service spaces and control stations.

4   The total volume of combustible facings, mouldings, decorations and veneers in any accommodation and service space shall not exceed a volume equivalent to 2.5 mm veneer on the combined area of the walls and ceilings. In the case of ships fitted with an automatic sprinkler system complying with

---

* Reference is made to Guidelines on the Evaluation of Fire Hazard Properties of Materials, adopted by the Organization by resolution A.166(ES.IV) and to the Recommendation on Fire Test Procedures for Surface Flammability of Bulkhead and Deck Finish Materials adopted by the Organization by resolution A.516(13).

the provisions of regulation 12, the above volume may include some combustible material used for erection of "C" class divisions.

5   Veneers used on surfaces and linings covered by the requirements of paragraph 3 shall have a calorific value not exceeding $45\,MJ/m^2$ of the area for the thickness used.

6   Furniture in the corridors and stairway enclosures shall be kept to a minimum.

7   Paints, varnishes and other finishes used on exposed interior surfaces shall not be capable of producing excessive quantities of smoke and toxic products.

8   Primary deck coverings, if applied within accommodation and service spaces and control stations, shall be of approved material which will not readily ignite, or give rise to toxic or explosive hazards at elevated temperatures.*

Regulation 35

Details of construction

1   In accommodation and service spaces, control stations, corridors and stairways:

.1   air spaces enclosed behind ceilings, panelling or linings shall be suitably divided by close-fitting draught stops not more than 14 m apart;

.2   in the vertical direction, such enclosed air spaces, including those behind linings of stairways, trunks, etc. shall be closed at each deck.

2   The construction of ceiling and bulkheading shall be such that it will be possible, without impairing the efficiency of the fire protection, for the fire patrols to detect any smoke originating in concealed and inaccessible places, except where in the opinion of the Administration there is no risk of fire originating in such places.

Regulation 36

Fixed fire detection and fire alarm systems
Automatic sprinkler, fire detection and fire alarm systems

In any ship to which this part applies there shall be installed throughout each separate zone, whether vertical or horizontal, in all accommodation and

---

* Reference is made to Improved Provisional Guidelines on Test Procedures for Primary Deck Coverings, adopted by the Organization by resolution A.214(VII).

service spaces and, where it is considered necessary by the Administration, in control stations, except spaces which afford no substantial fire risk such as void spaces, sanitary spaces, etc., either:

.1 a fixed fire detection and fire alarm system of an approved type and complying with the requirements of regulation 13 and so installed and arranged as to detect the presence of fire in such spaces; or

.2 an automatic sprinkler, fire detection and fire alarm system of an approved type and complying with the requirements of regulation 12 and so installed and arranged as to protect such spaces and in addition a fixed fire detection and fire alarm system of an approved type complying with the requirements of regulation 13 so installed and arranged as to provide smoke detection in corridors, stairways and escape routes within accommodation spaces.

Regulation 37

Protection of special category spaces

1 *Provisions applicable to special category spaces whether above or below the bulkhead deck*

1.1 General

1.1.1 The basic principle underlying the provisions of this regulation is that as normal main vertical zoning may not be practicable in special category spaces, equivalent protection must be obtained in such spaces on the basis of a horizontal zone concept and by the provision of an efficient fixed fire-extinguishing system. Under this concept a horizontal zone for the purpose of this regulation may include special category spaces on more than one deck provided that the total overall clear height for vehicles does not exceed 10 m.

1.1.2 The requirements of regulations 16, 18, 30 and 32 for maintaining the integrity of vertical zones shall be applied equally to decks and bulkheads forming the boundaries separating horizontal zones from each other and from the remainder of the ship.

1.2 Structural protection

1.2.1 Boundary bulkheads of special category spaces shall be insulated as required for category (11) spaces in table 26.1 or in table 27.1 and the horizontal boundaries as required for category (11) spaces in table 26.3 or in table 27.2.

1.2.2 Indicators shall be provided on the navigating bridge which shall indicate when any fire door leading to or from the special category spaces is closed.

1.3 Fixed fire-extinguishing system*

Each special category space shall be fitted with an approved fixed pressure water-spraying system for manual operation which shall protect all parts of any deck and vehicle platform in such space, provided that the Administration may permit the use of any other fixed fire-extinguishing system that has been shown by full-scale test in conditions simulating a flowing petrol fire in a special category space to be not less effective in controlling fires likely to occur in such a space.

1.4 Patrols and detection

1.4.1 An efficient patrol system shall be maintained in special category spaces. In any such space in which the patrol is not maintained by a continuous fire watch at all times during the voyage there shall be provided a fixed fire detection and fire alarm system of an approved type complying with the requirements of regulation 13. The fixed fire detection system shall be capable of rapidly detecting the onset of fire. The spacing and location of detectors shall be tested to the satisfaction of the Administration taking into account the effects of ventilation and other relevant factors.

1.4.2 Manually operated call points shall be provided as necessary throughout the special category spaces and one shall be placed close to each exit from such spaces.

1.5 Fire-extinguishing equipment

There shall be provided in each special category space:

.1 at least three water fog applicators;

.2 one portable foam applicator unit complying with the provisions of regulation 6.4, provided that at least two such units are available in the ship for use in such spaces; and

.3 such number of portable fire extinguishers as the Administration may deem sufficient, provided that at least one portable extinguisher is located at each access to such spaces.

1.6 Ventilation system

1.6.1 There shall be provided an effective power ventilation system for the special category spaces sufficient to give at least 10 air changes per hour. The system for such spaces shall be entirely separated from other ventilation systems and shall be operating at all times when vehicles are in such spaces.

---

* Reference is made to Recommendation on Fixed Fire-Extinguishing Systems for Special Category Spaces, adopted by the Organization by resolution A.123(V).

The Administration may require an increased number of air changes when vehicles are being loaded and unloaded. Ventilation ducts serving special category spaces capable of being effectively sealed shall be separated for each such space. The system shall be capable of being controlled from a position outside such spaces.

1.6.2   The ventilation shall be such as to prevent air stratification and the formation of air pockets.

1.6.3   Means shall be provided to indicate on the navigating bridge any loss or reduction of the required ventilating capacity.

1.6.4   Arrangements shall be provided to permit a rapid shutdown and effective closure of the ventilation system in case of fire, taking into account the weather and sea conditions.

1.6.5   Ventilation ducts, including dampers, shall be made of steel and their arrangement shall be to the satisfaction of the Administration.

2   *Additional provisions applicable only to special category spaces above the bulkhead deck*

2.1   Scuppers

In view of the serious loss of stability which could arise due to large quantities of water accumulating on the deck or decks consequent on the operation of the fixed pressure water-spraying system, scuppers shall be fitted so as to ensure that such water is rapidly discharged directly overboard.

2.2   Precautions against ignition of flammable vapours

2.2.1   On any deck or platform, if fitted, on which vehicles are carried and on which explosive vapours might be expected to accumulate, except platforms with openings of sufficient size permitting penetration of petrol gases downwards, equipment which may constitute a source of ignition of flammable vapours and, in particular, electrical equipment and wiring, shall be installed at least 450 mm above the deck or platform. Electrical equipment installed at more than 450 mm above the deck or platform shall be of a type so enclosed and protected as to prevent the escape of sparks. However, if the Administration is satisfied that the installation of electrical equipment and wiring at less than 450 mm above the deck or platform is necessary for the safe operation of the ship, such electrical equipment and wiring may be installed provided that it is of a type approved for use in an explosive petrol and air mixture.

2.2.2   Electrical equipment and wiring, if installed in an exhaust ventilation duct, shall be of a type approved for use in explosive petrol and air mixtures and the outlet from any exhaust duct shall be sited in a safe position, having regard to other possible sources of ignition.

3 Additional provisions applicable only to special category spaces below the bulkhead deck

3.1 Bilge pumping and drainage

In view of the serious loss of stability which could arise due to large quantities of water accumulating on the deck or tank top consequent on the operation of the fixed pressure water-spraying system, the Administration may require pumping and drainage facilities to be provided additional to the requirements of regulation II-1/21.

3.2 Precautions against ignition of flammable vapours

3.2.1 Electrical equipment and wiring, if fitted, shall be of a type suitable for use in explosive petrol and air mixtures. Other equipment which may constitute a source of ignition of flammable vapours shall not be permitted.

3.2.2 Electrical equipment and wiring, if installed in an exhaust ventilation duct, shall be of a type approved for use in explosive petrol and air mixtures and the outlet from any exhaust duct shall be sited in a safe position, having regard to other possible sources of ignition.

Regulation 38

Protection of cargo spaces, other than special category spaces,
intended for the carriage of motor vehicles with
fuel in their tanks for their own propulsion

In any cargo space (other than special category spaces) containing motor vehicles with fuel in their tanks for their own propulsion, the following provisions shall be complied with.

[F] 1 *Fire detection*

There shall be provided an approved automatic fire detection and fire alarm system. The design and arrangements of this system shall be considered in conjunction with the ventilation requirements referred to in paragraph 3.

2 *Fire-extinguishing arrangements*

2.1 There shall be fitted a fixed fire-extinguishing system which shall comply with the provisions of regulation 5, except that, if a carbon dioxide system is fitted, the quantity of gas available shall be at least sufficient to give a minimum volume of free gas equal to 45 per cent of the gross volume of

---

[F] See Annex 2.

180

the largest such cargo space which is capable of being sealed, and the arrangements shall be such as to ensure that at least two thirds of the gas required for the relevant space shall be introduced during 10 minutes. Any other fixed gas fire-extinguishing system or fixed high expansion foam fire-extinguishing system may be fitted provided it gives equivalent protection. Furthermore, any cargo space designated only for vehicles which are not carrying any cargo may be fitted with fixed halogenated hydrocarbon fire-extinguishing systems which shall comply with the provisions of regulation 5.

2.2   As an alternative, a system meeting the requirements of regulation 37.1.3 may be fitted, provided that regulation 37.2.1 or 37.3.1, as appropriate, is also complied with.

2.3   There shall be provided for use in any such space such number of portable fire extinguishers as the Administration may deem sufficient. At least one portable extinguisher shall be located at each access to such spaces.

3   *Ventilation system*

3.1   There shall be provided an effective power ventilation system sufficient to give at least 10 air changes per hour for ships carrying more than 36 passengers, and 6 air changes per hour for ships carrying not more than 36 passengers. The system for such cargo spaces shall be entirely separate from other ventilation systems and shall be operating at all times when vehicles are in such spaces. Ventilation ducts serving such cargo spaces capable of being effectively sealed shall be separated for each such space. The system shall be capable of being controlled from a position outside such spaces.

3.2   The ventilation shall be such as to prevent air stratification and the formation of air pockets.

3.3   Means shall be provided to indicate on the navigating bridge any loss or reduction of the required ventilating capacity.

3.4   Arrangements shall be provided to permit a rapid shutdown and effective closure of the ventilation system in case of fire, taking into account the weather and sea conditions.

3.5   Ventilation ducts, including dampers, shall be made of steel and their arrangement shall be to the satisfaction of the Administration.

4   *Precautions against ignition of flammable vapours*

4.1   Electrical equipment and wiring, if fitted, shall be of a type suitable for use in explosive petrol and air mixtures. Other equipment which may constitute a source of ignition of flammable vapours shall not be permitted.

4.2   Electrical equipment and wiring, if installed in an exhaust ventilation duct, shall be of a type approved for use in explosive petrol and air mixtures and the outlet from any exhaust duct shall be sited in a safe position, having regard to other possible sources of ignition.

4.3   Scuppers shall not be led to machinery or other spaces where sources of ignition may be present.

Regulation 39

Fixed fire-extinguishing arrangements in cargo spaces

1   Except as provided for in paragraph 3, the cargo spaces of ships of 1,000 tons gross tonnage and upwards shall be protected by a fixed gas fire-extinguishing system complying with the provisions of regulation 5, or by a fixed high expansion foam fire-extinguishing system which gives equivalent protection.

2   Where it is shown to the satisfaction of the Administration that a ship is engaged on voyages of such short duration that it would be unreasonable to apply the requirements of paragraph 1 and also in ships of less than 1,000 tons gross tonnage, the arrangements in cargo spaces shall be to the satisfaction of the Administration.

3   A ship engaged in the carriage of dangerous goods shall be provided in any cargo spaces with a fixed gas fire-extinguishing system complying with the provisions of regulation 5 or with a fire-extinguishing system which in the opinion of the Administration gives equivalent protection for the cargoes carried.

Regulation 40

Fire patrols, detection, alarms and public address systems

1   Manually operated call points complying with the requirements of regulation 13 shall be installed.

$\boxed{F}$ 2   A fixed fire detection and fire alarm system of an approved type shall be provided.

3   All ships shall at all times when at sea, or in port (except when out of service), be so manned or equipped as to ensure that any initial fire alarm is immediately received by a responsible member of the crew.

4   A special alarm, operated from the navigating bridge or fire control station, shall be fitted to summon the crew. This alarm may be part of the

---

$\boxed{F}$ See Annex 2.

ship's general alarm system but it shall be capable of being sounded independently of the alarm to the passenger spaces.

5   A public address system or other effective means of communication shall be available throughout the accommodation and service spaces and control stations.

6   For ships carrying more than 36 passengers an efficient patrol system shall be maintained so that an outbreak of fire may be promptly detected. Each member of the fire patrol shall be trained to be familiar with the arrangements of the ship as well as the location and operation of any equipment he may be called upon to use.

Regulation 41

Special requirements for ships carrying dangerous goods

The requirements of regulation 54 shall apply, as appropriate, to passenger ships carrying dangerous goods.

PART C – FIRE SAFETY MEASURES FOR CARGO SHIPS

(Regulation 54 of this part also applies to passenger ships as appropriate).

Regulation 42

Structure

1   Subject to the provisions of paragraph 4, the hull, superstructure, structural bulkheads, decks and deckhouses shall be constructed of steel or other equivalent material.

2   The insulation of aluminium alloy components of "A" or "B" class divisions, except structure which in the opinion of the Administration is non-load-bearing, shall be such that the temperature of the structural core does not rise more than 200°C above the ambient temperature at any time during the applicable exposure to the standard fire test.

3   Special attention shall be given to the insulation of aluminium alloy components of columns, stanchions and other structural members required to support lifeboat and liferaft stowage, launching and embarkation areas, and "A" and "B" class divisions, to ensure:

.1 that for such members supporting lifeboat and liferaft areas and "A" class divisions, the temperature rise limitation specified in paragraph 2 shall apply at the end of one hour;

and

.2 that for such members required to support "B" class divisions, the temperature rise limitation specified in paragraph 2 shall apply at the end of half an hour.

4   Crowns and casings of machinery spaces of category A shall be of steel construction adequately insulated and openings therein, if any, shall be suitably arranged and protected to prevent the spread of fire.

5   One of the following methods of protection shall be adopted in accommodation and service areas:

.1 *Method IC* – The construction of all internal divisional bulkheading of non-combustible "B" or "C" class divisions generally without the installation of an automatic sprinkler, fire detection and fire alarm system in the accommodation and service spaces, except as required by regulation 52.1; or

.2 *Method IIC* – The fitting of an automatic sprinkler, fire detection and fire alarm system as required by regulation 52.2 for the detection and extinction of fire in all spaces in which fire might be expected to originate, generally with no restriction on the type of internal divisional bulkheading; or

.3 *Method IIIC* – The fitting of a fixed fire detection and fire alarm system, as required by regulation 52.3, in all spaces in which a fire might be expected to originate, generally with no restriction on the type of internal divisional bulkheading, except that in no case must the area of any accommodation space or spaces bounded by an "A" or "B" class division exceed $50\,m^2$. Consideration may be given by the Administration to increasing this area for public spaces.

6   The requirements for the use of non-combustible materials in construction and insulation of the boundary bulkheads of machinery spaces, control stations, service spaces, etc., and the protection of stairway enclosures and corridors will be common to all three methods outlined in paragraph 5.

Regulation 43

Bulkheads within the accommodation and service spaces

1   All bulkheads required to be "B" class divisions shall extend from deck to deck and to the shell or other boundaries, unless continuous "B" class

ceilings or linings are fitted on both sides of the bulkhead in which case the bulkhead may terminate at the continuous ceiling or lining.

2   *Method IC* – All bulkheads not required by this or other regulations of this part to be "A" or "B" class divisions, shall be of at least "C" class construction.

3   *Method IIC* – There shall be no restriction on the construction of bulkheads not required by this or other regulations of this part to be "A" or "B" class divisions except in individual cases where "C" class bulkheads are required in accordance with table 44.1.

4   *Method IIIC* – There shall be no restriction on the construction of bulkheads not required by this part to be "A" or "B" class divisions except that the area of any accommodation space or spaces bounded by a continuous "A" or "B" class division must in no case exceed $50\,m^2$ except in individual cases where "C" class bulkheads are required in accordance with table 44.1. Consideration may be given by the Administration to increasing this area for public space.

Regulation 44

Fire integrity of bulkheads and decks

1   In addition to complying with the specific provisions for fire integrity of bulkheads and decks mentioned elsewhere in this part, the minimum fire integrity of bulkheads and decks shall be as prescribed in tables 44.1 and 44.2.

2   The following requirements shall govern application of the tables:

.1   Tables 44.1 and 44.2 shall apply respectively to the bulkheads and decks separating adjacent spaces.

.2   For determining the appropriate fire integrity standards to be applied to divisions between adjacent spaces, such spaces are classified according to their fire risk as shown in categories (1) to (11) below. The title of each category is intended to be typical rather than restrictive. The number in parentheses preceding each category refers to the applicable column or row in the tables.

(1)   *Control stations*

Spaces containing emergency sources of power and lighting.

Wheelhouse and chartroom.

Spaces containing the ship's radio equipment.

185

TABLE 44.1 – FIRE INTEGRITY OF BULKHEADS SEPARATING ADJACENT SPACES

Spaces		(1)	(2)	(3)	(4)	(5)	(6)	(7)	(8)	(9)	(10)	(11)
Control stations	(1)	A-0^e	A-0	A-60	A-0	A-15	A-60	A-15	A-60	A-60	*	A-60
Corridors	(2)		C	B-0	B-0 A-0$_c$	B-0	A-60	A-0	A-0	A-0	*	A-30
Accommodation spaces	(3)			C^{a,b}	B-0 A-0$_c$	B-0	A-60	A-0	A-0	A-0	*	A-30
Stairways	(4)				B-0 A-0$_c$	B-0 A-0$_c$	A-60	A-0	A-0	A-0	* *	A-30
Service spaces (low risk)	(5)					C	A-60	A-0	A-0	A-0	*	A-0
Machinery spaces of category A	(6)						*	A-0	A-0^g	A-60	*	A-60^i
Other machinery spaces	(7)							A-0^d	A-0	A-0	*	A-0
Cargo spaces	(8)								*	A-0	*	A-0
Service spaces (high risk)	(9)									A-0^d	*	A-30
Open decks	(10)										—	A-0
Ro–ro cargo spaces	(11)											*h

Notes: To be applied to tables 44.1 and 44.2, as appropriate.

a No special requirements are imposed upon bulkheads in methods IIC and IIIC fire protection.

b In case of method IIIC, "B" class bulkheads of "B-0" rating shall be provided between spaces or groups of spaces of 50 m^2 and over in area.

c For clarification as to which applies, see regulations 43 and 46.

d Where spaces are of the same numerical category and superscript ^{d} appears, a bulkhead or deck of the rating shown in the tables is only required when the adjacent spaces are for a different purpose e.g. in category (9). A galley next to a galley does not require a bulkhead but a galley next to a paint room requires an "A-0" bulkhead.

e Bulkheads separating the wheelhouse, chartroom and radio room from each other may be "B-0" rating.

f A-0 rating may be used if no dangerous goods are intended to be carried or if such goods are stowed not less than 3 m horizontally from such bulkhead.

g For cargo spaces in which dangerous goods are intended to be carried, regulation 54.2.8 applies.

h Bulkheads and decks separating ro–ro cargo spaces shall be capable of being closed reasonably gastight and such divisions shall have "A" class integrity in so far as is reasonable and practicable in the opinion of the Administration.

i Fire insulation need not be fitted if the machinery space in category (7), in the opinion of the Administration, has little or no fire risk.

* Where an asterisk appears in the tables, the division is required to be of steel or other equivalent material but is not required to be of "A" class standard.

TABLE 44.2 – FIRE INTEGRITY OF DECKS SEPARATING ADJACENT SPACES

Space below ↓ Space above →		(1)	(2)	(3)	(4)	(5)	(6)	(7)	(8)	(9)	(10)	(11)
Control stations	(1)	A-0	A-0	A-0	A-0	A-0	A-60	A-0	A-0	A-0	*	A-60
Corridors	(2)	A-0	*	*	A-0	*	A-60	A-0	A-0	A-0	*	A-30
Accommodation spaces	(3)	A-60	A-0	*	A-0	*	A-60	A-0	A-0	A-0	*	A-30
Stairways	(4)	A-0	A-0	A-0	*	A-0	A-60	A-0	A-0	A-0	*	A-30
Service spaces (low risk)	(5)	A-15	A-0	A-0	A-0	*	A-60	A-0	A-0	A-0	*	A-0
Machinery spaces of category A	(6)	A-60	A-60	A-60	A-60	A-60	*	A-60ⁱ	A-30	A-60	*	A-60
Other machinery spaces	(7)	A-15	A-0	A-0	A-0	A-0	A-0	*	A-0	A-0	*	A-0
Cargo spaces	(8)	A-60	A-0	A-0	A-0	A-0	A-0	A-0	*	A-0	*	A-0
Service spaces (high risk)	(9)	A-60	A-0	A-0	A-0	A-0	A-60	A-0	A-0	A-0ᵈ	*	A-30
Open decks	(10)	*	*	*	*	*	*	*	*	*	—	*
Ro-ro cargo spaces	(11)	A-60	A-30	A-30	A-30	A-0	A-60	A-0	A-0	A-30	*	*ʰ

Fire-extinguishing rooms, fire control rooms and fire-recording stations.

Control room for propulsion machinery when located outside the machinery space.

Spaces containing centralized fire alarm equipment.

(2) *Corridors*

Corridors and lobbies.

(3) *Accommodation spaces*

Spaces as defined in regulation 3.10, excluding corridors.

(4) *Stairways*

Interior stairways, lifts and escalators (other than those wholly contained within the machinery spaces) and enclosures thereto.

In this connection, a stairway which is enclosed only at one level shall be regarded as part of the space from which it is not separated by a fire door.

(5) *Service spaces (low risk)*

Lockers and store-rooms having an area of less than 2 m², drying rooms and laundries.

187

(6) *Machinery spaces of category A*

Spaces as defined in regulation 3.19.

(7) *Other machinery spaces*

Spaces as defined in regulation 3.20 excluding machinery spaces of category A.

(8) *Cargo spaces*

All spaces used for cargo (including cargo oil tanks) and trunkways and hatchways to such spaces.

(9) *Service spaces (high risk)*

Galleys, pantries containing cooking appliances, paint and lamp rooms, lockers and store-rooms having an area of $2\,m^2$ or more, workshops other than those forming part of the machinery spaces.

(10) *Open decks*

Open deck spaces and enclosed promenades having no fire risk. Air spaces (the space outside superstructures and deckhouses).

(11) *Ro–ro cargo spaces*

Spaces as defined in regulation 3.14. Cargo spaces intended for the carriage of motor vehicles with fuel in their tanks for their own propulsion.

3   Continuous "B" class ceilings or linings, in association with the relevant decks or bulkheads, may be accepted as contributing, wholly or in part, to the required insulation and integrity of a division.

4   External boundaries which are required in regulation 42.1 to be of steel or other equivalent material may be pierced for the fitting of windows and sidescuttles provided that there is no requirement for such boundaries to have "A" class integrity elsewhere in this part. Similarly, in such boundaries which are not required to have "A" class integrity, doors may be of materials to the satisfaction of the Administration.

Regulation 45

Means of escape

1   Stairways and ladders shall be so arranged as to provide, from all accommodation spaces and from spaces in which the crew is normally employed, other than machinery spaces, ready means of escape to the open deck and thence to the lifeboats and liferafts. In particular the following general provisions shall be complied with:

.1 At all levels of accommodation there shall be provided at least two widely separated means of escape from each restricted space or group of spaces.

.2.1 Below the lowest open deck the main means of escape shall be a stairway and the second escape may be a trunk or a stairway.

.2.2 Above the lowest open deck the means of escape shall be stairways or doors to an open deck or a combination thereof.

.3 Exceptionally the Administration may dispense with one of the means of escape, due regard being paid to the nature and location of spaces and to the numbers of persons who normally might be quartered or employed there.

.4 No dead-end corridors having a length of more than 7 m shall be accepted. A dead-end corridor is a corridor or part of a corridor from which there is only one escape route.

.5 The width and continuity of the means of escape shall be to the satisfaction of the Administration.

.6 If a radiotelegraph station has no direct access to the open deck, two means of access to or egress from such station shall be provided, one of which may be a porthole or window of sufficient size or other means to the satisfaction of the Administration, to provide an emergency escape.

2 In all ro–ro cargo spaces where the crew is normally employed the number and locations of escape routes to the open deck shall be to the satisfaction of the Administration, but shall in no case be less than two and shall be widely separated.

3 Except as provided in paragraph 4, two means of escape shall be provided from each machinery space of category A. In particular, one of the following provisions shall be complied with:

.1 two sets of steel ladders as widely separated as possible leading to doors in the upper part of the space similarly separated and from which access is provided to the open deck. In general, one of these ladders shall provide continuous fire shelter from the lower part of the space to a safe position outside the space. However, the Administration may not require the shelter if, due to the special arrangement or dimensions of the machinery space, a safe escape route from the lower part of this space is provided. This shelter shall be of steel, insulated, where necessary, to the satisfaction of the Administration and be provided with a self-closing steel door at the lower end; or

.2 one steel ladder leading to a door in the upper part of the space from which access is provided to the open deck and additionally, in the lower part of the space and in a position well separated from the ladder referred to, a steel door capable of being operated from each side and which provides access to a safe escape route from the lower part of the space to the open deck.

4   In a ship of less than 1,000 tons gross tonnage, the Administration may dispense with one of the means of escape required under paragraph 3, due regard being paid to the dimension and disposition of the upper part of the space.

5   From machinery spaces other than those of category A, escape routes shall be provided to the satisfaction of the Administration having regard to the nature and location of the space and whether persons are normally employed in that space.

6   Lifts shall not be considered as forming one of the required means of escape as required by this regulation.

Regulation 46

Protection of stairways and lift trunks in accommodation spaces, service spaces and control stations

1   Stairways which penetrate only a single deck shall be protected at least at one level by at least "B-0" class divisions and self-closing doors. Lifts which penetrate only a single deck shall be surrounded by "A-0" class divisions with steel doors at both levels. Stairways and lift trunks which penetrate more than a single deck shall be surrounded by at least "A-0" class divisions and be protected by self-closing doors at all levels.

2   On ships having accommodation for 12 persons or less, where stairways penetrate more than a single deck and where there are at least two escape routes direct to the open deck at every accommodation level, consideration may be given by the Administration to reducing the "A-0" requirements of paragraph 1 to "B-0".

3   All stairways shall be of steel frame construction except where the Administration sanctions the use of other equivalent material.

Regulation 47

Doors in fire resisting divisions

1   The fire resistance of doors shall, as far as practicable, be equivalent to that of the division in which they are fitted. Doors and door frames in

"A" class divisions shall be constructed of steel. Doors in "B" class divisions shall be non-combustible. Doors fitted in boundary bulkheads of machinery spaces of category A shall be reasonably gastight and self-closing. In ships constructed according to method IC, an Administration may permit the use of combustible materials in doors separating cabins from individual interior sanitary accommodation such as showers.

2　Doors required to be self-closing shall not be fitted with hold-back hooks. However, hold-back arrangements fitted with remote release devices of the fail-safe type may be utilized.

3　In corridor bulkheads ventilation openings may be permitted only in and under the doors of cabins and public spaces. The openings shall be provided only in the lower half of a door. Where such opening is in or under a door the total net area of any such opening or openings shall not exceed $0.05\,m^2$. When such opening is cut in a door it shall be fitted with a grille made of non-combustible material.

4　Watertight doors need not be insulated.

Regulation 48

Ventilation systems

The ventilation systems of cargo ships shall be in compliance with the provisions of regulation 16, except paragraph 8.

Regulation 49

Restricted use of combustible materials

1　All exposed surfaces in corridors and stairway enclosures and surfaces including grounds in concealed or inaccessible spaces in accommodation and service spaces and control stations shall have low flame-spread characteristics.* Exposed surfaces of ceilings in accommodation and service spaces and control stations shall have low flame-spread characteristics.

2　Paints, varnishes and other finishes used on exposed interior surfaces shall not offer an undue fire hazard in the judgement of the Administration and shall not be capable of producing excessive quantities of smoke.

---

* Reference is made to Guidelines on the Evaluation of Fire Hazard Properties of Materials, adopted by the Organization by resolution A.166(ES.IV) and to the Recommendation on Fire Test Procedures for Surface Flammmability of Bulkhead and Deck Finish Materials adopted by the Organization by resolution A.516(13).

3   Primary deck coverings, if applied within accommodation and service spaces and control stations, shall be of approved material which will not readily ignite, or give rise to toxic or explosive hazards at elevated temperatures.*

Regulation 50

Details of construction

1   *Method IC* – In accommodation and service spaces and control stations all linings, draught stops, ceilings and their associated grounds shall be of non-combustible materials.

2   *Methods IIC and IIIC* – In corridors and stairway enclosures serving accommodation and service spaces and control stations, ceilings, linings, draught stops and their associated grounds shall be of non-combustible materials.

3   *Methods IC, IIC and IIIC*

3.1   Except in cargo spaces or refrigerated compartments of service spaces, insulating materials shall be non-combustible. Vapour barriers and adhesives used in conjunction with insulation, as well as the insulation of pipe fittings, for cold service systems, need not be of non-combustible materials, but they shall be kept to the minimum quantity practicable and their exposed surfaces shall have qualities of resistance to the propagation of flame to the satisfaction of the Administration.

3.2   Where non-combustible bulkheads, linings and ceilings are fitted in accommodation and service spaces they may have a combustible veneer not exceeding 2.0 mm in thickness within any such space except corridors, stairway enclosures and control stations, where the veneer shall not exceed 1.5 mm in thickness.

3.3   Air spaces enclosed behind ceilings, panellings, or linings, shall be divided by close-fitting draught stops spaced not more than 14 m apart. In the vertical direction, such air spaces, including those behind linings of stairways, trunks, etc., shall be closed at each deck.

Regulation 51

Arrangements for gaseous fuel for domestic purposes

Where gaseous fuel is used for domestic purposes the arrangements for the storage, distribution and utilization of the fuel shall be such that, having

---

* Reference is made to Improved Provisional Guidelines on Test Procedures for Primary Deck Coverings, adopted by the Organization by resolution A.214(VII).

regard to the hazards of fire and explosion which the use of such fuel may entail, the safety of the ship and the persons on board is preserved.

Regulation 52

Fixed fire detection and fire alarm systems
Automatic sprinkler, fire detection and fire alarm systems

1   In ships in which method IC is adopted, a fixed fire detection and fire alarm system of an approved type complying with the requirements of regulation 13 shall be so installed and arranged as to provide smoke detection and manually operated call points in all corridors, stairways and escape routes within accommodation spaces.

2   In ships in which method IIC is adopted, an automatic sprinkler, fire detection and fire alarm system of an approved type complying with the relevant requirements of regulation 12 shall be so installed and arranged as to protect accommodation spaces, galleys and other service spaces, except spaces which afford no substantial fire risk such as void spaces, sanitary spaces, etc. In addition, a fixed detection and fire alarm system of an approved type complying with the requirements of regulation 13 shall be so installed and arranged as to provide smoke detection and manually operated call points in all corridors, stairways and escape routes within accommodation spaces.

3   In ships in which method IIIC is adopted, a fixed fire detection and fire alarm system of an approved type complying with the requirements of regulation 13 shall be so installed and arranged as to detect the presence of fire in all accommodation spaces and service spaces, except spaces which afford no substantial fire risk such as void spaces, sanitary spaces, etc.

Regulation 53

Fire protection arrangements in cargo spaces

1   *General*

1.1   Except for cargo spaces covered in paragraphs 2 and 3, cargo spaces of ships of 2,000 tons gross tonnage and upwards shall be protected by a fixed gas fire-extinguishing system complying with the provisions of regulation 5 or by a fire-extinguishing system which gives equivalent protection.

1.2   The Administration may exempt from the requirements of paragraph 1.1 cargo spaces of any ship if constructed and solely intended for carrying ore, coal, grain, unseasoned timber and non-combustible cargoes or cargoes which, in the opinion of the Administration, constitute a low fire risk. Such exemptions may be granted only if the ship is fitted with steel hatch covers and effective means of closing all ventilators and other openings leading to the cargo spaces.

1.3 Notwithstanding the provisions of paragraph 1.1, any ship engaged in the carriage of dangerous goods shall be provided in any cargo spaces with a fixed gas fire-extinguishing system complying with the provisions of regulation 5 or with a fire-extinguishing system which in the opinion of the Administration give equivalent protection for the cargoes carried.

2   Ro–ro cargo spaces

F 2.1   Fire detection

There shall be provided a fixed fire detection and fire alarm system of an approved type. The design and arrangements of this system shall be considered in conjunction with the ventilation requirements referred to in 2.3.

2.2   Fire-extinguishing arrangements

2.2.1   Ro–ro cargo spaces capable of being sealed shall be fitted with a fixed gas fire-extinguishing system which shall comply with the provisions of regulation 5, except that:

.1   if a carbon dioxide system is fitted, the quantity of gas available shall be at least sufficient to give a minimum volume of free gas equal to 45 per cent of the gross volume of the largest such cargo space which is capable of being sealed, and the arrangements shall be such as to ensure that at least two thirds of the gas required for the relevant space shall be introduced during 10 minutes;

.2   a halogenated hydrocarbon system may be used only for spaces designated only for vehicles which are not carrying any cargo;

.3   any other fixed gas fire-extinguishing system or fixed high expansion foam fire-extinguishing system may be fitted provided the Administration is satisfied that an equivalent protection is achieved;

.4   as an alternative, a system meeting the requirements of regulation 37.1.3 may be fitted. However, the drainage and pumping arrangements shall be such as to prevent the build-up of free surfaces. If this is not possible the adverse effect upon stability of the added weight and free surface of water shall be taken into account to the extent deemed necessary by the Administration in its approval of the stability information.* Such information shall be included in the

---

F See Annex 2.

* Reference is made to Recommendation on Fixed Fire-Extinguishing Systems for Special Category Spaces, adopted by the Organization by resolution A.123(V).

stability information supplied to the master as required by regulation II-1/22.

2.2.2   Ro–ro cargo spaces not capable of being sealed shall be fitted with a system meeting the requirements of regulation 37.1.3. However, the drainage and pumping arrangements shall be such as to prevent the build-up of free surfaces. If this is not possible the adverse effect upon stability of the added weight and free surface of water shall be taken into account to the extent deemed necessary by the Administration in its approval of the stability information.* Such information shall be included in the stability information supplied to the master as required by regulation II-1/22.

2.2.3   There shall be provided for use in any ro–ro cargo space such number of portable fire extinguishers as the Administration may deem sufficient. At least one portable extinguisher shall be located at each access to such a cargo space.

2.2.4   Each ro–ro cargo space intended for the carriage of motor vehicles with fuel in their tanks for their own propulsion shall be provided with:

.1   at least three water fog applicators;

.2   one portable foam applicator unit complying with the provisions of regulation 6.4 provided that at least two such units are available in the ship for use in such ro–ro cargo spaces.

2.3   Ventilation system

2.3.1   Closed ro–ro cargo sapces shall be provided with an effective power ventilation system sufficient to provide at least six air changes per hour based on an empty hold. Ventilation fans shall normally be run continuously whenever vehicles are on board. Where this is impracticable, they shall be operated for a limited period daily as weather permits and in any case for a reasonable period prior to discharge, after which period the ro–ro cargo space shall be proved gas-free. One or more portable combustible gas detecting instruments shall be carried for this purpose. The system shall be entirely separate from other ventilating systems. Ventilation ducts serving ro–ro cargo spaces capable of being effectively sealed shall be separated for each cargo space. The Administration may require an increased number of air changes when vehicles are being loaded or unloaded. The system shall be capable of being controlled from a position outside such spaces.

2.3.2   The ventilation shall be so arranged as to prevent air stratification and the formation of air pockets.

---

* Reference is made to Recommendation on Fixed Fire-Extinguishing Systems for Special Category Spaces, adopted by the Organization by resolution A.123(V).

2.3.3   Means shall be provided to indicate any loss of the required ventilating capacity on the navigating bridge.

2.3.4   Arrangements shall be provided to permit a rapid shutdown and effective closure of the ventilation system in case of fire, taking into account the weather and sea conditions.

2.3.5   Ventilation ducts, including dampers, shall be made of steel and their arrangement shall be to the satisfaction of the Administration.

2.4   Precautions against ignition of flammable vapours

Closed ro–ro cargo spaces carrying motor vehicles with fuel in their tanks for their own propulsion shall comply with the following additional provisions:

.1   Except as provided in paragraph 2.4.2, electrical equipment and wiring shall be of a type suitable for use in explosive petrol and air mixtures.

.2   Above a height of 450 mm from the deck and from each platform for vehicles, if fitted, except platforms with openings of sufficient size permitting penetration of petrol gases downwards, electrical equipment of a type so enclosed and protected as to prevent the escape of sparks shall be permitted as an alternative on condition that the ventilating system is so designed and operated as to provide continuous ventilation of the cargo spaces at the rate of at least ten air changes per hour whenever vehicles are on board.

.3   Other equipment which may constitute a source of ignition of flammable vapours shall not be permitted.

.4   Electrical equipment and wiring in an exhaust ventilation duct shall be of a type approved for use in explosive petrol and air mixtures and the outlet from any exhaust duct shall be sited in a safe position, having regard to other possible sources of ignition.

.5   Scuppers shall not be led to machinery or other spaces where sources of ignition may be present.

$\boxed{F}$ 3   *Cargo spaces, other than ro–ro cargo spaces, intended for the carriage of motor vehicles with fuel in their tanks for their own propulsion*

Spaces intended for the carriage of motor vehicles with fuel in their tanks for their own propulsion shall comply with requirements of paragraph 2, except that paragraph 2.2.4 need not be complied with.

$\boxed{F}$ See Annex 2.

Regulation 54

Special requirements for ships carrying dangerous goods

1 *General*

1.1 In addition to complying with the requirements of regulation 53 for cargo ships and with the requirements of regulations 38 and 39 for passenger ships as appropriate, ship types and cargo spaces, referred to in paragraph 1.2, intended for the carriage of dangerous goods shall comply with the requirements of this regulation, as appropriate, except when carrying dangerous goods in limited quantities* unless such requirements have already been met by compliance with the requirements elsewhere in this chapter. The types of ships and modes of carriage of dangerous goods are referred to in paragraph 1.2 and in table 54.1, where the numbers appearing in paragraph 1.2 are referred to in the top line.

1.2 The following ship types and cargo spaces shall govern the application of tables 54.1 and 54.2:

.1 Ships and cargo spaces not specifically designed for the carriage of freight containers but intended for the carriage of dangerous goods in packaged form including goods in freight containers and portable tanks.

.2 Purpose built container ships and cargo spaces intended for the carriage of dangerous goods in freight containers and portable tanks.

.3 Ro–ro ships and ro–ro cargo spaces intended for the carriage of dangerous goods.

.4 Ships and cargo spaces intended for the carriage of solid dangerous goods in bulk.

.5 Ships and cargo spaces intended for carriage of dangerous goods other than liquids and gases in bulk in shipborne barges.

2 *Special requirements*

Unless otherwise specified the following requirements shall govern the application of tables 54.1, 54.2 and 54.3 to both "on-deck" and "under-deck" stowage of dangerous goods where the numbers of the following paragraphs are indicated in the first column.

---

* Reference is made to section 18 of the General Introduction to the International Maritime Dangerous Goods Code (the IMDG Code) for a definition of the term "limited quantities".

Wherever "x" appears in table 54.1 it means that this requirement is applicable to all classes of dangerous goods as given in the appropriate line of table 54.3, except as indicated by the notes.

Regulation 54.1.2 → Regulation 54.2 ↓	.1 Not specifically designed	.2 Container cargo spaces	.3 Closed ro–ro cargo spaces	.3 Open ro–ro cargo spaces	.3 Weather decks	.4 Solid dangerous goods in bulk	.5 Shipborne barges
.1.1	x	x	x	x	x		x
.1.2	x	x	x	x	x		—
.1.3	x	x	x	x	—	For application of requirements of regulation 54 to different classes of dangerous goods – see table 54.2	x
.1.4	x	x	x	x	—		x
.2	x	x	x	x	—		x^d
.3	x	x	x	—	—		x^d
.4.1	x	x^a	x	—	—		x^d
.4.2	x	x^a	x	—	—		x^d
.5	x	x	x	—	—		—
.6.1	x	x	x	x	x		—
.6.2	x	x	x	x	x		—
.7	x	—	—	x	x		—
.8	x	x^b	x	x	x		—
.9	—	—	x^c	x	—		—

Notes

^{a} For classes 4 and 5.1 not applicable to closed freight containers.
For classes 2, 3, 6.1 and 8 when carried in closed freight containers the ventilation rate may be reduced to not less than two air changes. For the purpose of this requirement a portable tank is a closed freight container.

^{b} Applicable to decks only.

^{c} Applies only to closed ro–ro cargo spaces, not capable of being sealed.

^{d} In the special case where the barges are capable of containing flammable vapours or alternatively if they are capable of discharging flammable vapours to a safe space outside the barge carrier compartment by means of ventilation ducts connected to the barges, these requirements may be reduced or waived to the satisfaction of the Administration.

TABLE 54.2 – APPLICATION OF THE REQUIREMENTS TO DIFFERENT CLASSES OF DANGEROUS GOODS FOR SHIPS AND CARGO SPACES CARRYING SOLID DANGEROUS GOODS IN BULK

Class – chapter VII / Regulation 54.2	4.1	4.2	4.3^f	5.1	6.1	8	9
.1.1	x	x	—	x	x^g	x^g	x
.1.2^c	x	x	—	x	—	—	x
.2	x	x^g	x	x^g	—	—	x^g
.4.1^h	x^g	x^g	x	x^g	—	—	x^g
.4.2^h	x	x^g	x	x^g	—	—	x^g
.6	x	x	x	x	x	x	x
.8	x	x	x	x^g	x^g	x^g	x

Notes

^{c} This requirement is applicable when the characteristics of the substance call for large quantities of water for fire fighting.

^{f} The hazards of substances in this class which may be carried in bulk are such that special consideration must be given by the Administration to the construction and equipment of the ships involved in addition to meeting the requirements enumerated in this table.

^{g} Reference is made to the International Maritime Dangerous Goods Code (resolution A.81(IV) as amended) or the Code of Safe Practice for Solid Bulk Cargoes (resolution A.434(XI) as amended), as appropriate.

^{h} At least natural ventilation is required in enclosed cargo spaces intended for carriage of solid dangerous goods in bulk. In cases where power ventilation is required in the Code of Safe Practice for Solid Bulk Cargoes (resolution A.434(XI) as amended), the use of portable ventilation units (equipment) to the satisfaction of the Administration may suffice.

2.1 Water supplies

2.1.1 Arrangements shall be made to ensure immediate availability of a supply of water from the fire main at the required pressure either by permanent pressurization or by suitably placed remote starting arrangements for the fire pumps.

2.1.2 The quantity of water delivered shall be capable of supplying four nozzles of a size and at pressures as specified in regulation 4, capable of being trained on any part of the cargo space when empty. This amount of water may by applied by equivalent means to the satisfaction of the Administration.

2.1.3 Means of effectively cooling the designated under-deck cargo space by copious quantities of water, either by a fixed arrangement of spraying nozzles, or flooding the cargo space with water, shall be provided. Hoses may be used for this purpose in small cargo spaces and in small areas of larger cargo spaces at the discretion of the Administration. In any event the

TABLE 54.3 – APPLICATION OF THE REQUIREMENTS TO DIFFERENT CLASSES OF DANGEROUS GOODS EXCEPT SOLID DANGEROUS GOODS IN BULK

Class – chapter VII — Regulation 54.2	1	2	3	4	5.1	5.2	6.1	8
.1.1	x	x	x	x^p	x	x^p	x	x
.1.2^i	x	x	x	x^p	x	x^p	—	—
.1.3	x^k	—	—	—	—	—	—	—
.1.4	x^k	—	—	—	—	—	—	—
.2	x^k	x^l	x^m	—	—	—	$x^{m.p}$	$x^{m.p}$
.3	x	x	x	x	x	—	x	x
.4.1	—	x^j	x^m	x^p	x^p	—	$x^{m.p}$	$x^{m.p}$
.4.2	—	x^l	x^m	—	—	—	$x^{m.p}$	$x^{m.p}$
.5	—	—	x^m	—	—	—	x^n	x^m
.6	—	x	x	x	x	x^p	x	x
.7	—	—	x	x	x	x^p	x^p	x^p
.8	$x^{k.o}$	x	x	x	x^p	—	x^p	x^p
.9	x	x	x^m	x^p	x	—	x^m	x^m

Notes

^{i} This requirement is applicable when the characteristics of the substance call for large quantities of water for fire fighting.

^{j} Applicable to flammable or poisonous gases.

^{k} Except goods of class 1 in division 1.4, compatibility group S.

^{l} All flammable gases.

^{m} All liquids having a flashpoint below 23°C (closed cup test).

^{n} Liquids only.

^{o} Goods of class 1 shall be stowed 3 m horizontally away from the machinery space boundaries in all cases.

^{p} Reference is made to the International Maritime Dangerous Goods Code (resolution A.81(IV) as amended) or the Code of Safe Practice for Solid Bulk Cargoes (resolution A.434(XI) as amended), as appropriate.

drainage and pumping arrangements shall be such as to prevent the build-up of free surfaces. If this is not possible the adverse effect upon stability of the added weight and free surface of water shall be taken into account to the extent deemed necessary by the Administration in its approval of the stability information.*

---

* Reference is made to Recommendation on Fixed Fire-Extinguishing Systems for Special Category Spaces, adopted by the Organization by resolution A.123(V).

2.1.4 Provision to flood a designated under-deck cargo space with suitable specified media may be substituted for the requirements in paragraph 2.1.3.

2.2 Sources of ignition

Electrical equipment and wiring shall not be fitted in enclosed cargo spaces, closed vehicle deck spaces, or open vehicle deck spaces unless it is essential for operational purposes in the opinion of the Administration. However, if electrical equipment is fitted in such spaces, it shall be of a certified safe type* for use in the dangerous environments to which it may be exposed unless it is possible to completely isolate the electrical system (by removal of links in the system, other than fuses). Cable penetrations of the decks and bulkheads shall be sealed against the passage of gas or vapour. Through runs of cables and cables within the cargo spaces shall be protected against damage from impact. Any other equipment which may constitute a source of ignition of flammable vapour shall not be permitted.

[F] 2.3 Detection system

A fixed fire detection and fire alarm system of an approved type shall be fitted to all enclosed cargo spaces including closed vehicle deck spaces. Where the detection system utilizes samples of atmosphere drawn from such cargo spaces provision shall be made to prevent, in the event of cargo leakage, the discharge of contaminated atmosphere through the sampling system into the space in which the detection apparatus is situated. A notice stating that the samples shall be discharged to the open air when cargoes giving off toxic fumes are being carried shall be permanently exhibited at the equipment.

2.4 Ventilation

2.4.1 Adequate power ventilation shall be provided in enclosed cargo spaces. The arrangement shall be such as to provide for at least six air changes per hour in the cargo space based on an empty cargo space and for removal of vapours from the upper or lower parts of the cargo space, as appropriate.

2.4.2 The fans shall be such as to avoid the possibility of ignition of flammable gas air mixtures. Suitable wire mesh guards shall be fitted over inlet and outlet ventilation openings.

2.5 Bilge pumping

Where it is intended to carry flammable or toxic liquids in enclosed cargo spaces the bilge pumping system shall be designed to ensure against inadvertent pumping of such liquids through machinery space piping or pumps.

---

* Reference is made to Recommendations published by the International Electrotechnical Commission and, in particular, publication 92 – Electrical Installations in Ships.
[F] See Annex 2.

Where large quantities of such liquids are carried, consideration shall be given to the provision of additional means of draining those cargo spaces. These means shall be to the satisfaction of the Administration.

2.6 Personnel protection

2.6.1 Four sets of full protective clothing resistant to chemical attack shall be provided in addition to the fireman's outfits required by regulation 17. The protective clothing shall cover all skin, so that no part of the body is unprotected.

2.6.2 At least two self-contained breathing apparatuses additional to those required by regulation 17 shall be provided.

2.7 Portable fire extinguishers

Portable fire extinguishers with a total capacity of at least 12 kg of dry powder or equivalent shall be provided for the cargo spaces. These extinguishers shall be in addition to any portable fire extinguishers required elsewhere in this chapter.

2.8 Insulation of machinery space boundaries

Bulkheads forming boundaries between cargo spaces and machinery spaces of category A shall be insulated to "A-60" standard, unless the dangerous goods are stowed at least 3 m horizontally away from such bulkheads. Other boundaries between such spaces shall be insulated to "A-60" standard.

2.9 Water spray system

Each open ro–ro cargo space having a deck above it and each space deemed to be a closed ro–ro cargo space not capable of being sealed shall be fitted with an approved fixed pressure water-spraying system for manual operation which shall protect all parts of any deck and vehicle platform in such space, except that the Administration may permit the use of any other fixed fire-extinguishing system that has been shown by full-scale test to be no less effective. In any event the drainage and pumping arrangements shall be such as to prevent the build-up of free surfaces. If this is not possible the adverse effect upon stability of the added weight and free surface of water shall be taken into account to the extent deemed necessary by the Administration in its approval of the stability information.*

3   Document of compliance

The Administration shall provide the ship with an appropriate document as evidence of compliance of construction and equipment with the requirements of this regulation.

---

* Reference is made to Recommendation on Fixed Fire-Extinguishing Systems for Special Category Spaces, adopted by the Organization by resolution A.123(V).

PART D – FIRE SAFETY MEASURES FOR TANKERS

(The requirements of this part are additional to those of part C except for regulations 53 and 54 which do not apply to tankers and except as provided otherwise in regulations 57 and 58)

Regulation 55

Application

1   Unless expressly provided otherwise, this part shall apply to tankers carrying crude oil and petroleum products having a flashpoint not exceeding 60°C (closed cup test), as determined by an approved flashpoint apparatus, and a Reid vapour pressure which is below atmospheric pressure and other liquid products having a similar fire hazard.

2   Where liquid cargoes other than those referred to in paragraph 1 or liquefied gases which introduce additional fire hazards are intended to be carried, additional safety measures shall be required to the satisfaction of the Administration, having due regard to the provisions of the International Bulk Chemical Code, the Bulk Chemical Code, the International Gas Carrier Code and the Gas Carrier Code, as appropriate.

3   This paragraph applies to all ships which are combination carriers. Such ships shall not carry solid cargoes unless all cargo tanks are empty of oil and gas-freed or unless the arrangements provided in each case are to the satisfaction of the Administration and in accordance with the relevant operational requirements contained in the Guidelines for Inert Gas Systems.*

4   Tankers carrying petroleum products having a flashpoint exceeding 60°C (closed up test) as determined by an approved flashpoint apparatus shall comply with the provisions of part C, except that in lieu of the fixed fire-extinguishing system required in regulation 53 they shall be fitted with a fixed deck foam system which shall comply with the provisions of regulation 61.

5   The requirements for inert gas systems of regulation 60 need not be applied to all chemical tankers or gas carriers when carrying cargoes described in paragraph 1, provided that alternative arrangements, to be developed by the Organization, are fitted.**

---

 * Reference is made to Revised Guidelines for Inert Gas Systems, adopted by the Maritime Safety Committee at its forty-eighth session in June 1983 (MSC/Circ.353).
 ** Reference is made to Interim Regulation for Inert Gas Systems on Chemical Tankers Carrying Petroleum Products, adopted by the Organization by resolution A.473(XII).

6   Chemical tankers and gas carriers shall comply with the requirements of this part, except where alternative and supplementary arrangements are provided to the satisfaction of the Administration, having due regard to the provisions of the International Bulk Chemical Code, the Bulk Chemical Code, the International Gas Carrier Code and the Gas Carrier Code, as appropriate.

Regulation 56

Location and separation of spaces

1   Machinery spaces shall be positioned aft of cargo tanks and slop tanks; they shall also be situated aft of cargo pump-rooms and cofferdams, but not necessarily aft of the oil fuel bunker tanks. Any machinery space shall be isolated from cargo tanks and slop tanks by cofferdams, cargo pump-rooms, oil fuel bunker tanks or permanent ballast tanks. Pump-rooms containing pumps and their accessories for ballasting those spaces situated adjacent to cargo tanks and slop tanks and pumps for oil fuel transfer shall be considered as equivalent to a cargo pump-room within the context of this regulation, provided that such pump-rooms have the same safety standard as that required for cargo pump-rooms. However, the lower portion of the pump-room may be recessed into machinery spaces of category A to accommodate pumps, provided that the deck head of the recess is in general not more than one third of the moulded depth above the keel, except that in the case of ships of not more than 25,000 tonnes deadweight, where it can be demonstrated that for reasons of access and satisfactory piping arrangements this is impracticable, the Administration may permit a recess in excess of such height, but not exceeding one half of the moulded depth above the keel.

2   Accommodation spaces, main cargo control stations, control stations and service spaces (excluding isolated cargo handling gear lockers) shall be positioned aft of all cargo tanks, slop tanks, cargo pump-rooms and cofferdams which isolate cargo or slop tanks from machinery spaces but not necessarily aft of the oil fuel bunker tanks. A recess provided in accordance with paragraph 1 need not be taken into account when the position of these spaces is being determined.

3   However, where deemed necessary, accommodation spaces, control stations, machinery spaces other than those of category A, and service spaces may be permitted forward of the cargo area, provided they are isolated from the cargo tanks and slop tanks by cofferdams, cargo pump-rooms, oil fuel bunker tanks or permanent ballast tanks and subject to an equivalent standard of safety and appropriate availability of fire-extinguishing arrangements being provided to the satisfaction of the Administration. In addition, where deemed necessary for the safety or navigation of the ship, the Administration may permit machinery spaces containing internal combustion machinery not being main propulsion machinery having an output greater than 375 kW to be located

forward of the cargo area provided the arrangements are in accordance with the provisions of this paragraph.

4   In combination carriers only:

.1   The slop tanks are to be surrounded by cofferdams except where the boundaries of the slop tanks where slop may be carried on dry cargo voyages are the hull, main cargo deck, cargo pump-room bulkhead or oil fuel bunker tank. These cofferdams shall not be open to a double bottom, pipe tunnel, pump-room or other enclosed space. Means shall be provided for filling the cofferdams with water and for draining them. Where the boundary of a slop tank is the cargo pump-room bulkhead the pump-room shall not be open to the double bottom, pipe tunnel or other enclosed space; however, openings provided with gastight bolted covers may be permitted.

.2   Means shall be provided for isolating the piping connecting the pump-room with the slop tanks referred to in paragraph 4.1. The means of isolation shall consist of a valve followed by a spectacle flange or a spool piece with appropriate blank flanges. This arrangement shall be located adjacent to the slop tanks, but where this is unreasonable or impracticable, it may be located within the pump-room directly after the piping penetrates the bulkhead. A separate pumping and piping arrangement shall be provided for discharging the contents of the slop tanks directly over the open deck when the ship is in the dry cargo mode.

.3   Hatches and tank cleaning openings to slop tanks shall only be permitted on the open deck and shall be fitted with closing arrangements. Except where they consist of bolted plates with bolts at watertight spacing, these closing arrangements shall be provided with locking arrangements which shall be under the control of the responsible ship's officer.

.4   Where cargo wing tanks are provided, cargo oil lines below deck shall be installed inside these tanks. However, the Administration may permit cargo oil lines to be placed in special ducts which shall be capable of being adequately cleaned and ventilated and be to the satisfaction of the Administration. Where cargo wing tanks are not provided cargo oil lines below deck shall be placed in special ducts.

5   Where the fitting of a navigation position above the cargo area is shown to be necessary, it shall be for navigation purposes only and it shall be separated from the cargo tank deck by means of an open space with a height of at least 2 m. The fire protection of such a navigation position shall in addition be as required for control spaces in regulation 58.1 and 58.2 and other provisions, as applicable, of this part.

6   Means shall be provided to keep deck spills away from the accommodation and service areas. This may be accomplished by provision of a permanent

continuous coaming of a suitable height extending from side to side. Special consideration shall be given to the arrangements associated with stern loading.

7   Exterior boundaries of superstructures and deckhouses enclosing accommodation and including any overhanging decks which support such accommodation, shall be insulated to "A-60" standard for the whole of the portions which face the cargo area and for 3 m aft of the front boundary. In the case of the sides of those superstructures and deckhouses, such insulation shall be carried as high as is deemed necessary by the Administration.

8.1   Entrances, air inlets and openings to accommodation spaces, service spaces and control stations shall not face the cargo area. They shall be located on the transverse bulkhead not facing the cargo area or on the outboard side of the superstructure or deckhouse at a distance of at least 4 per cent of the length of the ship but not less than 3 m from the end of the superstructure or deckhouse facing the cargo area. This distance, however, need not exceed 5 m.

8.2   No doors shall be fitted within the limits specified in paragraph 8.1 except that doors to spaces not having access to accommodation spaces, service spaces and control stations may be permitted by the Administration. Such spaces may be cargo control stations, provision rooms and store-rooms. Where such doors are fitted to spaces located aft of the cargo area, the boundaries of the space shall be insulated to "A-60"standard, with the exception of the boundary facing the cargo area. Bolted plates for removal of machinery may be fitted within the limits specified in paragraph 8.1. Wheelhouse doors and wheelhouse windows may be located within the limits specified in paragraph 8.1 so long as they are designed to ensure that the wheelhouse can be made rapidly and efficiently gas and vapour tight.

8.3   Windows and sidescuttles facing the cargo area and on the sides of the superstructures and deckhouses within the limits specified in paragraph 8.1 shall be of the fixed (non-opening) type. Such windows and sidescuttles in the first tier on the main deck shall be fitted with inside covers of steel or other equivalent material.

Regulation 57

Structure, bulkheads within accommodation and service spaces and details of construction

1   For the application of the requirements of regulations 42, 43 and 50 to tankers, only method IC as defined in regulation 42.5.1 shall be used.

2   Skylights to cargo pump-rooms shall be of steel, shall not contain any glass and shall be capable of being closed from outside the pump-room.

Fire integrity of bulkheads and decks

1   In lieu of regulation 44 and in addition to complying with the specific provisions for fire integrity of bulkheads and decks mentioned elsewhere in this part the minimum fire integrity of bulkheads and decks shall be as prescribed in tables 58.1 and 58.2

TABLE 58.1 – FIRE INTEGRITY OF BULKHEADS SEPARATING ADJACENT SPACES

Spaces		(1)	(2)	(3)	(4)	(5)	(6)	(7)	(8)	(9)	(10)
Control stations	(1)	A-0^c	A-0	A-60	A-0	A-15	A-60	A-15	A-60	A-60	*
Corridors	(2)		C	B-0	B-0 A-0$_a$	B-0	A-60	A-0	A-60	A-0	*
Accommodation spaces	(3)			C	B-0 A-0$_a$	B-0	A-60	A-0	A-60	A-0	*
Stairways	(4)				B-0 A-0$_a$	B-0 A-0$_a$	A-60	A-0	A-60	A-0	*
Service spaces (low risk)	(5)					C	A-60	A-0	A-60	A-0	*
Machinery spaces of category A	(6)						*	A-0	A-0^d	A-60	*
Other machinery spaces	(7)							A-0^b	A-0	A-0	*
Cargo pump-rooms	(8)								*	A-60	*
Service spaces (high risk)	(9)									A-0^b	*
Open decks	(10)										—

Notes: To be applied to tables 58.1 and 58.2, as appropriate.

^{a} For clarification as to which applies, see regulations 43 and 46 of this chapter.

^{b} Where spaces are of the same numerical category and superscript ^{b} appears, a bulkhead or deck of the rating shown in the tables is only required when the adjacent spaces are for a different purpose, e.g. in category (9). A galley next to a galley does not require a bulkhead but a galley next to a paint room requires an "A-0" bulkhead.

^{c} Bulkheads separating the wheelhouse, chartroom and radio room from each other may be "B-0" rating.

^{d} Bulkheads and decks between cargo pump-rooms and machinery spaces of category A may be penetrated by cargo pump shaft glands and similar glanded penetrations, provided that gastight seals with efficient lubrication or other means of ensuring the permanence of the gas seal are fitted in way of the bulkhead or deck.

^{e} Fire insulation need not be fitted if the machinery space in category (7), in the opinion of the Administration, has little or no fire risk.

* Where an asterisk appears in the tables, the division is required to be of steel or other equivalent material but is not required to be of "A" class standard.

TABLE 58.2 – FIRE INTEGRITY OF DECKS SEPARATING ADJACENT SPACES

Space below ↓ Space above →		(1)	(2)	(3)	(4)	(5)	(6)	(7)	(8)	(9)	(10)
Control stations	(1)	A-0	A-0	A-0	A-0	A-0	A-60	A-0	—	A-0	*
Corridors	(2)	A-0	*	*	A-0	*	A-60	A-0	—	A-0	*
Accommodation spaces	(3)	A-60	A-0	*	A-0	*	A-60	A-0	—	A-0	*
Stairways	(4)	A-0	A-0	A-0	*	A-0	A-60	A-0	—	A-0	*
Service spaces (low risk)	(5)	A-15	A-0	A-0	A-0	*	A-60	A-0	—	A-0	*
Machinery spaces of category A	(6)	A-60	A-60	A-60	A-60	A-60	*	A-60^e	A-0	A-60	*
Other machinery spaces	(7)	A-15	A-0	A-0	A-0	A-0	A-0	*	A-0	A-0	*
Cargo pump-rooms	(8)	—	—	—	—	—	A-0^d	A-0	*	—	*
Service spaces (high risk)	(9)	A-60	A-0	A-0	A-0	A-0	A-60	A-0	—	A-0^b	*
Open decks	(10)	*	*	*	*	*	*	*	*	*	—

2   The following requirements shall govern application of the tables:

  .1   Tables 58.1 and 58.2 shall apply respectively to the bulkhead and decks separating adjacent spaces.

  .2   For determining the appropriate fire integrity standards to be applied to divisions between adjacent spaces, such spaces are classified according to their fire risk as shown in categories (1) to (10) below. The title of each category is intended to be typical rather than restrictive. The number in parentheses preceding each category refers to the applicable column or row in the tables.

    (1)   *Control stations*

        Spaces containing emergency sources of power and lighting.

        Wheelhouse and chartroom.

        Spaces containing the ship's radio equipment.

        Fire-extinguishing rooms, fire control rooms and fire-recording stations.

        Control room for propulsion machinery when located outside the machinery space.

        Spaces containing centralized fire alarm equipment.

    (2)   *Corridors*

        Corridors and lobbies.

    (3)   *Accommodation spaces*

        Spaces as defined in regulation 3.10, excluding corridors.

(4) *Stairways*

Interior stairways, lifts and escalators (other than those wholly contained within the machinery spaces) and enclosures thereto.

In this connection, a stairway which is enclosed only at one level shall be regarded as part of the space from which it is not separated by a fire door.

(5) *Service spaces (low risk)*

Lockers and store-rooms having areas of less than $2\,m^2$, drying rooms and laundries.

(6) *Machinery spaces of category A*

Spaces as defined in regulation 3.19.

(7) *Other machinery spaces*

Spaces as defined in regulation 3.20 excluding machinery spaces of category A.

(8) *Cargo pump-rooms*

Spaces containing cargo pumps and entrances and trunks to such spaces.

(9) *Service spaces (high risk)*

Galleys, pantries containing cooking appliances, paint and lamp rooms, lockers and store-rooms having an area of $2\,m^2$ or more, workshops other than those forming part of the machinery spaces.

(10) *Open decks*

Open deck spaces and enclosed promenades having no fire risk. Air spaces (the space outside superstructures and deck-houses).

3   Continuous "B" class ceilings or linings, in association with the relevant decks or bulkheads, may be accepted as contributing, wholly or in part, to the required insulation and integrity of a division.

4   External boundaries which are required in regulation 57.1 to be of steel or other equivalent material may be pierced for the fitting of windows and sidescuttles provided that there is no requirement for such boundaries to have "A" class integrity elsewhere in this part. Similarly, in such boundaries which are not required to have "A" class integrity, doors may be of materials to the satisfaction of the Administration.

5   Permanent approved gastight lighting enclosures for illuminating cargo pump-rooms may be permitted in bulkheads and decks separating cargo pump-rooms and other spaces provided they are of adequate strength and the integrity and gastightness of the bulkhead or deck is maintained.

Regulation 59

Venting, purging, gas-freeing and ventilation

1 Cargo tank venting

1.1 The venting systems of cargo tanks are to be entirely distinct from the air pipes of the other compartments of the ship. The arrangements and position of openings in the cargo tank deck from which emission of flammable vapours can occur shall be such as to minimize the possibility of flammable vapours being admitted to enclosed spaces containing a source of ignition, or collecting in the vicinity of deck machinery and equipment which may constitute an ignition hazard. In accordance with this general principle the criteria in paragraphs 1.2 to 1.10 will apply.

1.2 The venting arrangements shall be so designed and operated as to ensure that neither pressure nor vacuum in cargo tanks shall exceed design parameters and be such as to provide for:

 .1 the flow of the small volumes of vapour, air or inert gas mixtures caused by thermal variations in a cargo tank in all cases through pressure/vacuum valves; and

 .2 the passage of large volumes of vapour, air or inert gas mixtures during cargo loading and ballasting, or during discharging.

1.3.1 The venting arrangements in each cargo tank may be independent or combined with other cargo tanks and may be incorporated into the inert gas piping.

1.3.2 Where the arrangements are combined with other cargo tanks either stop valves or other acceptable means shall be provided to isolate each cargo tank. Where stop valves are fitted, they shall be provided with locking arrangements which shall be under the control of the responsible ship's officer. Any isolation must continue to permit the flow caused by thermal variations in a cargo tank in accordance with paragraph 1.2.1.

1.4 The venting arrangements shall be connected to the top of each cargo tank and shall be self-draining to the cargo tanks under all normal conditions of trim and list of the ship. Where it may not be possible to provide self-draining lines permanent arrangements shall be provided to drain the vent lines to a cargo tank.

1.5 The venting system shall be provided with devices to prevent the passage of flame into the cargo tanks. The design, testing and locating of these devices shall comply with the requirements established by the Administration which shall contain at least the standards adopted by the Organization.*

---

 * Reference is made to Standards for the Design, Testing and Locating of Devices to Prevent the Passage of Flame into Cargo Tanks in Oil Tankers adopted by the Maritime Safety Committee at its forty-ninth session in April 1984 (MSC/Circ.373).

210

1.6 Provision shall be made to guard against liquid rising in the venting system to a height which would exceed the design head of cargo tanks. This shall be accomplished by high-level alarms or overflow control systems or other equivalent means, together with gauging devices and cargo tank filling procedures.

1.7 Openings for pressure release required by paragraph 1.2.1 shall:

.1 have as great a height as is practicable above the cargo tank deck to obtain maximum dispersal of flammable vapours but in no case less than 2 m above the cargo tank deck;

.2 be arranged at the furthest distance practicable but not less than 5 m from the nearest air intakes and openings to enclosed spaces containing a source of ignition and from deck machinery and equipment which may constitute an ignition hazard.

1.8 Pressure/vacuum valves required by paragraph 1.2.1 may be provided with a by-pass arrangement when they are located in a vent main or masthead riser. Where such an arrangement is provided there shall be suitable indicators to show whether the by-pass is open or closed.

1.9 Vent outlets for cargo loading, discharging and ballasting required by paragraph 1.2.2 shall:

.1.1 permit the free flow of vapour mixtures; or

.1.2 permit the throttling of the discharge of the vapour mixtures to achieve a velocity of not less than 30 m/sec;

.2 be so arranged that the vapour mixture is discharged vertically upwards;

.3 where the method is by free flow of vapour mixtures, be such that the outlet shall be not less than 6 m above the cargo tank deck or fore and aft gangway if situated within 4 m of the gangway and located not less than 10 m measured horizontally from the nearest air intakes and openings to enclosed spaces containing a source of ignition and from deck machinery and equipment which may constitute an ignition hazard;

.4 where the method is by high velocity discharge, be located at a height not less than 2 m above the cargo tank deck and not less than 10 m measured horizontally from the nearest air intakes and openings to enclosed spaces containing a source of ignition and from deck machinery and equipment which may constitute an ignition hazard. These outlets shall be provided with high velocity devices of an approved type;

.5 be designed on the basis of the maximum designed loading rate multiplied by a factor of at least 1.25 to take account of gas evolution, in order to prevent the pressure in any cargo tank from exceeding the design pressure. The master shall be provided with information regarding the maximum permissible loading rate for each cargo tank and in the case of combined venting systems, for each group of cargo tanks.

1.10 In combination carriers, the arrangement to isolate slop tanks containing oil or oil residues from other cargo tanks shall consist of blank flanges which will remain in position at all times when cargoes other than liquid cargoes referred to in regulation 55.1 are carried.

2   *Cargo tank purging and/or gas-freeing*

Arrangements for purging and/or gas-freeing shall be such as to minimize the hazards due to the dispersal of flammable vapours in the atmosphere and to flammable mixtures in a cargo tank. Accordingly:

.1   When the ship is provided with an inert gas system the cargo tanks shall first be purged in accordance with the provisions of regulation 62.13 until the concentration of hydrocarbon vapours in the cargo tanks has been reduced to less than 2 per cent by volume. Thereafter, venting may be at the cargo tank deck level.

.2   When the ship is not provided with an inert gas system, the operation shall be such that the flammable vapour is initially discharged:

.2.1   through the vent outlets as specified in paragraph 1.9; or

.2.2   with a vertical exit velocity of at least 20 m/sec through outlets at least 2 m above the cargo tank deck level and which are protected by suitable devices to prevent the passage of flame.

When the flammable vapour concentration in the outlet has been reduced to 30 per cent of the lower flammable limit the discharge of the vapour mixture may be at the cargo tank deck level.

3   *Ventilation*

3.1   Cargo pump-rooms shall be mechanically ventilated and discharges from the exhaust fans shall be led to a safe place on the open deck. The ventilation of these rooms shall have sufficient capacity to minimize the possibility of accumulation of flammable vapours. The number of changes of air shall be at least 20 per hour, based upon the gross volume of the space. The air ducts shall be arranged so that all of the space is effectively ventilated. The ventilation shall be of the suction type using fans of the non-sparking type.

3.2   The arrangement of ventilation inlets and outlets and other deckhouse and superstructure boundary space openings shall be such as to complement the provisions of paragraph 1. Such vents especially for machinery spaces shall be situated as far aft as practicable. Due consideration in this regard should be given when the ship is equipped to load or discharge at the stern. Sources of ignition such as electrical equipment shall be so arranged as to avoid an explosion hazard.

3.3   In combination carriers all cargo spaces and any enclosed spaces adjacent to cargo spaces shall be capable of being mechanically ventilated. The mechanical ventilation may be provided by portable fans. An approved fixed gas warning system capable of monitoring flammable vapours shall be provided in cargo pump-rooms and pipe ducts and cofferdams referred to in regulation 56.4 adjacent to slop tanks. Suitable arrangements shall be made to facilitate measurement of flammable vapours in all other spaces within the cargo area. Such measurements shall be made possible from open deck or easily accessible positions.

Regulation 60

Cargo tank protection

1   For tankers of 20,000 tonnes deadweight and upwards the protection of the cargo tanks deck area and cargo tanks shall be achieved by a fixed deck foam system and a fixed inert gas system in accordance with the requirements of regulations 61 and 62, except that, in lieu of the above installations, the Administration, after having given consideration to the ship's arrangement and equipment, may accept other combinations of fixed installations if they afford protection equivalent to the above, in accordance with regulation I/5.

2   To be considered equivalent, the system proposed in lieu of the deck foam system shall:

.1   be capable of extinguishing spill fires and also preclude ignition of spilled oil not yet ignited; and

.2   be capable of combating fires in ruptured tanks.

3   To be considered equivalent, the system proposed in lieu of the fixed inert gas system shall:

.1   be capable of preventing dangerous accumulations of explosive mixtures in intact cargo tanks during normal service throughout the ballast voyage and necessary in-tank operations; and

.2   be so designed as to minimize the risk of ignition from the generation of static electricity by the system itself.

4   Tankers of 20,000 tonnes deadweight and upwards constructed before 1 September 1984 which are engaged in the trade of carrying crude oil shall be fitted with an inert gas system, complying with the requirements of paragraph 1, not later than:

.1   for a tanker of 70,000 tonnes deadweight and upwards 1 September 1984 or the date of delivery of the ship, whichever occurs later; and

.2 for a tanker of less than 70,000 tonnes deadweight 1 May 1985 or the date of delivery of the ship, whichever occurs later except that for tankers of less than 40,000 tonnes deadweight not fitted with tank washing machines having an individual throughput of greater than 60 m³/hour the Administration may exempt such tankers from the requirements of this paragraph, if it would be unreasonable and impracticable to apply these requirements, taking into account the ship's design characteristics.

5   Tankers of 40,000 tonnes deadweight and upwards constructed before 1 September 1984 which are engaged in the trade of carrying oil other than crude oil and any such tanker of 20,000 tonnes deadweight and upwards engaged in the trade of carrying oil other than crude oil fitted with tank washing machines having an individual throughput of greater than 60 m³/hour shall be fitted with an inert gas system, complying with the requirements of paragraph 1, not later than:

.1 for a tanker of 70,000 tonnes deadweight and upwards 1 September 1984 or the date of delivery of the ship, whichever occurs later; and

.2 for a tanker of less than 70,000 tonnes deadweight 1 May 1985 or the date of delivery of the ship, whichever occurs later.

6   All tankers operating with a cargo tank cleaning procedure using crude oil washing shall be fitted with an inert gas system complying with the requirements of regulation 62 and with fixed tank washing machines.

7   All tankers fitted with a fixed inert gas system shall be provided with a closed ullage system.

8   Tankers of less than 20,000 tonnes deadweight shall be provided with a deck foam system complying with the requirements of regulation 61.

Regulation 61

Fixed deck foam systems

1   The arrangements for providing foam shall be capable of delivering foam to the entire cargo tanks deck area as well as into any cargo tank the deck of which has been ruptured.

2   The deck foam system shall be capable of simple and rapid operation. The main control station for the system shall be suitably located outside the cargo area, adjacent to the accommodation spaces and readily accessible and operable in the event of fire in the areas protected.

3   The rate of supply of foam solution shall be not less than the greatest of the following:

.1   0.6 ℓ/minute per square metre of cargo tanks deck area, where cargo tanks deck area means the maximum breadth of the ship multiplied by the total longitudinal extent of the cargo tank spaces;

.2   6 ℓ/minute per square metre of the horizontal sectional area of the single tank having the largest such area; or

.3   3 ℓ/minute per square metre of the area protected by the largest monitor, such area being entirely forward of the monitor, but not less than 1,250 ℓ/minute.

4   Sufficient foam concentrate shall be supplied to ensure at least 20 minutes of foam generation in tankers fitted with an inert gas installation or 30 minutes of foam generation in tankers not fitted with an inert gas installation when using solution rates stipulated in paragraphs 3.1, 3.2 or 3.3, whichever is the greatest. The foam expansion ratio (i.e. the ratio of the volume of foam produced to the volume of the mixture of water and foam-making concentrate supplied) shall not generally exceed 12 to 1. Where systems essentially produce low-expansion foam but at an expansion ratio slightly in excess of 12 to 1 the quantity of foam solution available shall be calculated as for 12 to 1 expansion ratio systems. When medium-expansion ratio foam (between 50 to 1 and 150 to 1 expansion ratio) is employed the application rate of the foam and the capacity of a monitor installation shall be to the satisfaction of the Administration.

5   Foam from the fixed foam system shall be supplied by means of monitors and foam applicators. At least 50 per cent of the foam solution supply rate required in paragraphs 3.1 and 3.2 shall be delivered from each monitor. On tankers of less than 4,000 tonnes deadweight the Administration may not require installation of monitors but only applicators. However, in such a case the capacity of each applicator shall be at least 25 per cent of the foam solution supply rate required in paragraphs 3.1 or 3.2.

6.1   The number and position of monitors shall be such as to comply with paragraph 1. The capacity of any monitor shall be at least 3 ℓ/minute of foam solution per square metre of deck area protected by that monitor, such area being entirely forward of the monitor. Such capacity shall be not less than 1,250 ℓ/minute.

6.2   The distance from the monitor to the farthest extremity of the protected area forward of that monitor shall not be more than 75 per cent of the monitor throw in still air conditions.

7   A monitor and hose connection for a foam applicator shall be situated both port and starboard at the front of the poop or accommodation spaces facing the cargo tanks deck. On tankers of less than 4,000 tonnes deadweight a hose connection for a foam applicator shall be situated both port and

starboard at the front of the poop or accommodation spaces facing the cargo tanks deck.

8   Applicators shall be provided to ensure flexibility of action during fire-fighting operations and to cover areas screened from the monitors. The capacity of any applicator shall be not less than 400 ℓ/minute and the applicator throw in still air conditions shall be not less than 15 m. The number of foam applicators provided shall be not less than four. The number and disposition of foam main outlets shall be such that foam from at least two applicators can be directed on to any part of the cargo tanks deck area.

9   Valves shall be provided in the foam main, and in the fire main when this is an integral part of the deck foam system, immediately forward of any monitor position to isolate damaged sections of those mains.

10   Operation of a deck foam system at its required output shall permit the simultaneous use of the minimum required number of jets of water at the required pressure from the fire main.

Regulation 62

Inert gas systems

1   The inert gas system referred to in regulation 60 shall be designed, constructed and tested to the satisfaction of the Administration. It shall be so designed and operated as to render and maintain the atmosphere of the cargo tanks* non-flammable at all times, except when such tanks are required to be gas-free. In the event that the inert gas system is unable to meet the operational requirement set out above and it has been assessed that it is impractical to effect a repair, then cargo discharge, deballasting and necessary tank cleaning shall only be resumed when the "emergency conditions" laid down in the Guidelines on Inert Gas Systems** are complied with.

2   The system shall be capable of:

.1   inerting empty cargo tanks by reducing the oxygen content of the atmosphere in each tank to a level at which combustion cannot be supported;

.2   maintaining the atmosphere in any part of any cargo tank with an oxygen content not exceeding 8 per cent by volume and at a positive

---

* Throughout this regulation the term "cargo tank" includes also "slop tanks".

** Reference is made to Revised Guidelines for Inert Gas Systems, adopted by the Maritime Safety Committee at its forty-eighth session in June 1983 (MSC/Circ.353).

pressure at all times in port and at sea except when it is necessary for such a tank to be gas-free;

.3 eliminating the need for air to enter a tank during normal operations except when it is necessary for such a tank to be gas-free;

.4 purging empty cargo tanks of hydrocarbon gas, so that subsequent gas-freeing operations will at no time create a flammable atmosphere within the tank.

3.1 The system shall be capable of delivering inert gas to the cargo tanks at a rate of at least 125 per cent of the maximum rate of discharge capacity of the ship expressed as a volume.

3.2 The system shall be capable of delivering inert gas with an oxygen content of not more than 5 per cent by volume in the inert gas supply main to the cargo tanks at any required rate of flow.

4 The inert gas supply may be treated flue gas from main or auxiliary boilers. The Administration may accept systems using flue gases from one or more separate gas generators or other sources or any combination thereof, provided that an equivalent standard of safety is achieved. Such systems should, as far as practicable, comply with the requirements of this regulation. Systems using stored carbon dioxide shall not be permitted unless the Administration is satisfied that the risk of ignition from generation of static electricity by the system itself is minimized.

5 Flue gas isolating valves shall be fitted in the inert gas supply mains between the boiler uptakes and the flue gas scrubber. These valves shall be provided with indicators to show whether they are open or shut, and precautions shall be taken to maintain them gastight and keep the seatings clear of soot. Arrangements shall be made to ensure that boiler soot blowers cannot be operated when the corresponding flue gas valve is open.

6.1 A flue gas scrubber shall be fitted which will effectively cool the volume of gas specified in paragraph 3 and remove solids and sulphur combustion products. The cooling water arrangements shall be such that an adequate supply of water will always be available without interfering with any essential services on the ship. Provision shall also be made for an alternative supply of cooling water.

6.2 Filters or equivalent devices shall be fitted to minimize the amount of water carried over to the inert gas blowers.

6.3 The scrubber shall be located aft of all cargo tanks, cargo pump-rooms and cofferdams separating these spaces from machinery spaces of category A.

7.1 At least two blowers shall be fitted which together shall be capable of delivering to the cargo tanks at least the volume of gas required by paragraph 3. In the system with gas generator the Administration may permit only one blower if that system is capable of delivering the total volume of gas required by paragraph 3 to the protected cargo tanks, provided that sufficient spares for the blower and its prime mover are carried on board to enable any failure of the blower and its prime mover to be rectified by the ship's crew.

7.2   Two fuel oil pumps shall be fitted to the inert gas generator. The Administration may permit only one fuel oil pump on condition that sufficient spares for the fuel oil pump and its prime mover are carried on board to enable any failure of the fuel oil pump and its prime mover to be rectified by the ship's crew.

7.3   The inert gas system shall be so designed that the maximum pressure which it can exert on any cargo tank will not exceed the test pressure of any cargo tank. Suitable shutoff arrangements shall be provided on the suction and discharge connections of each blower. Arrangements shall be provided to enable the functioning of the inert gas plant to be stabilized before commencing cargo discharge. If the blowers are to be used for gas-freeing, their air inlets shall be provided with blanking arrangements.

7.4   The blowers shall be located aft of all cargo tanks, cargo pump-rooms and cofferdams separating these spaces from machinery spaces of category A.

8.1   Special consideration shall be given to the design and location of scrubber and blowers with relevant piping and fittings in order to prevent flue gas leakages into enclosed spaces.

8.2   To permit safe maintenance, an additional water seal or other effective means of preventing flue gas leakage shall be fitted between the flue gas isolating valves and scrubber or incorporated in the gas entry to the scrubber.

9.1   A gas regulating valve shall be fitted in the inert gas supply main. This valve shall be automatically controlled to close as required in paragraphs 19.3 and 19.4. It shall also be capable of automatically regulating the flow of inert gas to the cargo tanks unless means are provided to automatically control the speed of the inert gas blowers required in paragraph 7.

9.2   The valve referred to in paragraph 9.1 shall be located at the forward bulkhead of the forwardmost gas-safe space* through which the inert gas supply main passes.

10.1   At least two nonreturn devices, one of which shall be a water seal, shall be fitted in the inert gas supply main, in order to prevent the return of hydrocarbon vapour to the machinery space uptakes or to any gas-safe

---

* Gas-safe space is a space in which the entry of hydrocarbon gases would produce hazards with regard to flammability or toxicity.

spaces under all normal conditions of trim, list and motion of the ship. They shall be located between the automatic valve required by paragraph 9.1 and the aftermost connection to any cargo tank or cargo pipeline.

10.2 The devices referred to in paragraph 10.1 shall be located in the cargo area on deck.

10.3 The water seal referred to in paragraph 10.1 shall be capable of being supplied by two separate pumps, each of which shall be capable of maintaining an adequate supply at all times.

10.4 The arrangement of the seal and its associated fittings shall be such that it will prevent backflow of hydrocarbon vapours and will ensure the proper functioning of the seal under operating conditions.

10.5 Provision shall be made to ensure that the water seal is protected against freezing, in such a way that the integrity of seal is not impaired by overheating.

10.6 A water loop or other approved arrangement shall also be fitted to each associated water supply and drain pipe and each venting or pressure-sensing pipe leading to gas-safe spaces. Means shall be provided to prevent such loops from being emptied by vacuum.

10.7 The deck water seal and all loop arrangements shall be capable of preventing return of hydrocarbon vapours at a pressure equal to the test pressure of the cargo tanks.

10.8 The second device shall be a nonreturn valve or equivalent capable of preventing the return of vapours or liquids and fitted forward of the deck water seal required in paragraph 10.1. It shall be provided with positive means of closure. As an alternative to positive means of closure, an additional valve having such means of closure may be provided forward of the nonreturn valve to isolate the deck water seal from the inert gas main to the cargo tanks.

10.9 As an additional safeguard against the possible leakage of hydrocarbon liquids or vapours back from the deck main, means shall be provided to permit this section of the line between the valve having positive means of closure referred to in paragraph 10.8 and the valve referred to in paragraph 9 to be vented in a safe manner when the first of these valves is closed.

11.1 The inert gas main may be divided into two or more branches forward of the nonreturn devices required by paragraph 10.

11.2.1 The inert gas supply mains shall be fitted with branch piping leading to each cargo tank. Branch piping for inert gas shall be fitted with either stop valves or equivalent means of control for isolating each tank. Where stop valves are fitted, they shall be provided with locking arrangements, which shall be under the control of a responsible ship's officer.

11.2.2 In combination carriers, the arrangement to isolate the slop tanks containing oil or oil residues from other tanks shall consist of blank flanges which will remain in position at all times when cargoes other than oil are being carried except as provided for in the relevant section of the Guidelines on Inert Gas Systems.

11.3 Means shall be provided to protect cargo tanks against the effect of overpressure or vacuum caused by thermal variations when the cargo tanks are isolated from the inert gas mains.

11.4 Piping systems shall be so designed as to prevent the accumulation of cargo or water in the pipelines under all normal conditions.

11.5 Suitable arrangements shall be provided to enable the inert gas main to be connected to an external supply of inert gas.

12   The arrangements for the venting of all vapours displaced from the cargo tanks during loading and ballasting shall comply with regulation 59.1 and shall consist of either one or more mast risers, or a number of high-velocity vents. The inert gas supply mains may be used for such venting.

13   The arrangements for inerting, purging or gas-freeing of empty tanks as required in paragraph 2 shall be to the satisfaction of the Administration and shall be such that the accumulation of hydrocarbon vapours in pockets formed by the internal structural members in a tank is minimized and that:

.1   on individual cargo tanks the gas outlet pipe, if fitted, shall be positioned as far as practicable from the inert gas/air inlet and in accordance with regulation 59.1. The inlet of such outlet pipes may be located either at deck level or at not more than 1 m above the bottom of the tank;

.2   the cross-sectional area of such gas outlet pipe referred to in paragraph 13.1 shall be such that an exit velocity of at least 20 m/sec can be maintained when any three tanks are being simultaneously supplied with inert gas. Their outlets shall extend not less than 2 m above deck level;

.3   each gas outlet referred to in paragraph 13.2 shall be fitted with suitable blanking arrangements;

.4.1   if a connection is fitted between the inert gas supply mains and the cargo piping system, arrangements shall be made to ensure an effective isolation having regard to the large pressure difference which may exist between the systems. This shall consist of two shutoff valves with an arrangement to vent the space between the valves in a safe manner or an arrangement consisting of a spool-piece with associated blanks;

.4.2   the valve separating the inert gas supply main from the cargo main and which is on the cargo main side shall be a nonreturn valve with a positive means of closure.

220

14.1 One or more pressure/vacuum-breaking devices shall be provided to prevent the cargo tanks from being subject to:

.1 a positive pressure in excess of the test pressure of the cargo tank if the cargo were to be loaded at the maximum rated capacity and all other outlets are left shut; and

.2 a negative pressure in excess of 700 mm water gauge if cargo were to be discharged at the maximum rated capacity of the cargo pumps and the inert gas blowers were to fail.

Such devices shall be installed on the inert gas main unless they are installed in the venting system required by regulation 59.1.1 or on individual cargo tanks.

14.2 The location and design of the devices referred to in paragraph 14.1 shall be in accordance with regulation 59.1.

15 Means shall be provided for continuously indicating the temperature and pressure of the inert gas at the discharge side of the gas blowers, whenever the gas blowers are operating.

16.1 Instrumentation shall be fitted for continuously indicating and permanently recording, when the inert gas is being supplied:

.1 the pressure of the inert gas supply mains forward of the nonreturn devices required by paragraph 10.1; and

.2 the oxygen content of the inert gas in the inert gas supply mains on the discharge side of the gas blowers.

16.2 The devices referred to in paragraph 16.1 shall be placed in the cargo control room where provided. But where no cargo control room is provided, they shall be placed in a position easily accessible to the officer in charge of cargo operations.

16.3 In addition, meters shall be fitted:

.1 in the navigating bridge to indicate at all times the pressure referred to in paragraph 16.1.1 and the pressure in the slop tanks of combination carriers, whenever those tanks are isolated from the inert gas supply main; and

.2 in the machinery control room or in the machinery space to indicate the oxygen content referred to in paragraph 16.1.2.

17 Portable instruments for measuring oxygen and flammable vapour concentration shall be provided. In addition, suitable arrangement shall be made on each cargo tank such that the condition of the tank atmosphere can be determined using these portable instruments.

18 Suitable means shall be provided for the zero and span calibration of

both fixed and portable gas concentration measurement instruments, referred to in paragraphs 16 and 17.

19.1 Audible and visual alarms shall be provided to indicate:

.1 low water pressure or low water flow rate to the flue gas scrubber as referred to in paragraph 6.1;

.2 high water level in the flue gas scrubber as referred to in paragraph 6.1;

.3 high gas temperature as referred to in paragraph 15;

.4 failure of the inert gas blowers referred to in paragraph 7;

.5 oxygen content in excess of 8 per cent by volume as referred to in paragraph 16.1.2;

.6 failure of the power supply to the automatic control system for the gas regulating valve and to the indicating devices as referred to in paragraphs 9 and 16.1;

.7 low water level in the water seal as referred to in paragraph 10.1;

.8 gas pressure less than 100 mm water gauge as referred to in paragraph 16.1.1. The alarm arrangement shall be such as to ensure that the pressure in slop tanks in combination carriers can be monitored at all times; and

.9 high gas pressure as referred to in paragraph 16.1.1.

19.2 In the system with gas generators audible and visual alarms shall be provided in accordance with 19.1.1, 19.1.3, 19.1.5 to 19.1.9 and additional alarms to indicate:

.1 insufficient fuel oil supply;

.2 failure of the power supply to the generator;

.3 failure of the power supply to the automatic control system for the generator.

19.3 Automatic shutdown of the inert gas blowers and gas regulating valve shall be arranged on predetermined limits being reached in respect of paragraphs 19.1.1, 19.1.2 and 19.1.3.

19.4 Automatic shutdown of the gas regulating valve shall be arranged in respect of paragraph 19.1.4.

19.5 In respect of paragraph 19.1.5, when the oxygen content of the inert gas exceeds 8 per cent by volume, immediate action shall be taken to improve the gas quality. Unless the quality of the gas improves, all cargo tank operations shall be suspended so as to avoid air being drawn into the tanks and the isolation valve referred to in paragraph 10.8 shall be closed.

19.6 The alarms required in paragraphs 19.1.5, 19.1.6 and 19.1.8 shall be fitted in the machinery space and cargo control room, where provided, but in each case in such a position that they are immediately received by responsible members of the crew.

19.7 In respect of paragraph 19.1.7 the Administration shall be satisfied as to the maintenance of an adequate reserve of water at all times and the integrity of the arrangements to permit the automatic formation of the water seal when the gas flow ceases. The audible and visual alarm on the low level of water in the water seal shall operate when the inert gas is not being supplied.

19.8 An audible alarm system independent of that required in paragraph 19.1.8 or automatic shutdown of cargo pumps shall be provided to operate on predetermined limits of low pressure in the inert gas mains being reached.

20 Tankers constructed before 1 September 1984 which are required to have an inert gas system shall at least comply with the requirements of regulation 62 of chapter II-2 of the International Convention for the Safety of Life at Sea, 1974.* In addition they shall comply with the requirements of this regulation, except that:

.1 inert gas systems fitted on board such tankers before 1 June 1981 need not comply with the following paragraphs: 3.2, 6.3, 7.4, 8, 9.2, 10.2, 10.7, 10.9, 11.3, 11.4, 12, 13.1, 13.2, 13.4.2, 14.2 and 19.8;

.2 inert gas systems fitted on board such tankers on or after 1 June 1981 need not comply with the following paragraphs: 3.2, 6.3, 7.4, 12, 13.1, 13.2 and 14.2.

21 Detailed instruction manuals shall be provided on board, covering the operations, safety and maintenance requirements and occupational health hazards relevant to the inert gas system and its application to the cargo tank system.** The manuals shall include guidance on procedures to be followed in the event of a fault or failure of the inert gas system.

Regulation 63

Cargo pump-rooms

1 Each cargo pump-room shall be provided with one of the following fixed fire-extinguishing systems operated from a readily accessible position outside the pump-room. Cargo pump-rooms should be provided with a system suitable for machinery spaces of category A.

---

* The text as adopted by the International Conference on Safety of Life at Sea, 1974.
** Reference is made to Revised Guidelines for Inert Gas Systems, adopted by the Maritime Safety Committee at its forty-eighth session in June 1983 (MSC/Circ.353).

1.1   Either a carbon dioxide or a halogenated hydrocarbon system complying with the provisions of regulation 5 and with the following:

.1   the alarms referred to in regulation 5.1.6 shall be safe for use in a flammable cargo vapour/air mixture;

.2   a notice shall be exhibited at the controls stating that due to the electrostatic ignition hazard, the system is to be used only for fire extinguishing and not for inerting purposes.

1.2   A high-expansion foam system complying with the provisions of regulation 9, provided that the foam concentrate supply is suitable for extinguishing fires involving the cargoes carried.

1.3   A fixed pressure water-spraying system complying with the provisions of regulation 10.

2   Where the extinguishing medium used in the cargo pump-room system is also used in systems serving other spaces, the quantity of medium provided or its delivery rate need not be more than the maximum required for the largest compartment.

Chapter III

LIFE-SAVING APPLIANCES AND ARRANGEMENTS

PART A – GENERAL

Page

1 Application 228
2 Exemptions 229
3 Definitions 230
4 Evaluation, testing and approval of life-saving appliances and
   arrangements 232
5 Production tests 233

PART B – SHIP REQUIREMENTS

SECTION I – PASSENGER SHIPS AND CARGO SHIPS

6 Communications 233
7 Personal life-saving appliances 235
8 Muster list and emergency instructions 236
9 Operating instructions 236
10 Manning of survival craft and supervision 237
11 Survival craft muster and embarkation arrangements 238
12 Launching stations 238
13 Stowage of survival craft 239
14 Stowage of rescue boats 240
15 Survival craft launching and recovery arrangements 240
16 Rescue boat embarkation, launching and recovery arrangements . 241
17 Line-throwing appliances 242
18 Abandon ship training and drills 242
19 Operational readiness, maintenance and inspections 244

SECTION II – PASSENGER SHIPS
(ADDITIONAL REQUIREMENTS)

20 Survival craft and rescue boats 246

225

21	Personal life-saving appliances	249
22	Survival craft and rescue boat embarkation arrangements	250
23	Stowage of liferafts	250
24	Muster stations	251
25	Drills	251

SECTION III – CARGO SHIPS

(ADDITIONAL REQUIREMENTS)

26	Survival craft and rescue boats	251
27	Personal life-saving appliances	254
28	Survival craft embarkation and launching arrangements	255
29	Stowage of liferafts	256

PART C – LIFE-SAVING APPLIANCE REQUIREMENTS

SECTION I – GENERAL

30	General requirements for life-saving appliances	256

SECTION II – PERSONAL LIFE-SAVING APPLIANCES

31	Lifebuoys	257
32	Lifejackets	259
33	Immersion suits	260
34	Thermal protective aids	262

SECTION III – VISUAL SIGNALS

35	Rocket parachute flares	262
36	Hand flares	263
37	Buoyant smoke signals	264

SECTION IV – SURVIVAL CRAFT

38	General requirements for liferafts	264
39	Inflatable liferafts	269
40	Rigid liferafts	273
41	General requirements for lifeboats	275
42	Partially enclosed lifeboats	283

43 Self-righting partially enclosed lifeboats 284
44 Totally enclosed lifeboats................................. 286
45 Lifeboats with a self-contained air support system 288
46 Fire-protected lifeboats 289

SECTION V – RESCUE BOATS

47 Rescue boats 289

SECTION VI – LAUNCHING AND EMBARKATION
APPLIANCES

48 Launching and embarkation appliances...................... 293

SECTION VII – OTHER LIFE-SAVING APPLIANCES

49 Line-throwing appliances................................. 297
50 General emergency alarm system 297

SECTION VIII – MISCELLANEOUS

51 Training manual 298
52 Instructions for on-board maintenance 299
53 Muster list and emergency instructions 299

PART A – GENERAL

Regulation 1

Application

1   Unless expressly provided otherwise, this chapter shall apply to ships the keels of which are laid or which are at a similar stage of construction on or after 1 July 1986.

2   For the purpose of this chapter the term "a similar stage of construction" means the stage at which:

.1   construction identifiable with a specific ship begins; and

.2   assembly of that ship has commenced comprising at least 50 tonnes or 1% of the estimated mass of all structural material, whichever is less.

3   For the purpose of this chapter:

.1   the expression "ships constructed" means "ships the keels of which are laid or which are at a similar stage of construction";

.2   the expression "all ships" means "ships constructed before, on or after 1 July 1986"; the expressions "all passenger ships" and "all cargo ships" shall be construed accordingly;

.3   a cargo ship, whenever built, which is converted to a passenger ship shall be treated as a passenger ship constructed on the date on which such a conversion commences.

4   For ships constructed before 1 July 1986, the Administration shall:

.1   ensure that, subject to the provisions of paragraph 4.2 and 4.3, the requirements which are applicable under chapter III of the International Convention for the Safety of Life at Sea, 1974, in force prior to 1 July 1986 to new or existing ships as prescribed by that chapter are complied with;

.2   consider the life-saving appliances and arrangements in ships which do not comply with the requirements referred to in paragraph 4.1, with a view to securing, so far as this is reasonable and practicable and as early as possible, substantial compliance with those requirements;

.3   ensure that when life-saving appliances or arrangements on such ships are replaced or such ships undergo repairs, alterations or modifications of a major character which involve replacement of, or any addition to, their existing life-saving appliances or arrangements, such life-saving appliances or arrangements, in so far as is reasonable and practicable, comply with the requirements of this chapter. However, if a survival craft is replaced without replacing its launching appliance, or vice versa, the survival craft or launching appliance may be of the same type as that replaced;

.4 approve the life-saving appliances to be provided in compliance with paragraph 6. The Administration may permit those life-saving appliances provided on board ships prior to 1 July 1991 not to comply fully with the requirements of this chapter as long as they remain in a satisfactory condition;

.5 except as provided for survival craft and launching appliances referred to in paragraph 4.3, ensure that life-saving appliances replaced or installed on or after 1 July 1991 are evaluated, tested and approved in accordance with the requirements of regulations 4 and 5.

5   With respect to ships constructed before 1 July 1986 the requirements of regulations 8, 9, 10, 18 and 25 and, to the extent prescribed therein, regulation 19 shall apply.

6   With respect to ships constructed before 1 July 1986 the requirements of regulations 6.2.3, 6.2.4, 21.3, 21.4, 26.3, 27.2, 27.3 and 30.2.7 shall apply not later than 1 July 1991.

Regulation 2

Exemptions

1   The Administration may, if it considers that the sheltered nature and conditions of the voyage are such as to render the application of any specific requirements of this chapter unreasonable or unnecessary, exempt from those requirements individual ships or classes of ships which, in the course of their voyage, do not proceed more than 20 miles from the nearest land.

2   In the case of passenger ships which are employed in special trades for the carriage of large numbers of special trade passengers, such as the pilgrim trade, the Administration, if satisfied that it is impracticable to enforce compliance with the requirements of this chapter, may exempt such ships from those requirements, provided that such ships comply fully with the provisions of:

.1 the rules annexed to the Special Trade Passenger Ships Agreement, 1971; and

.2 the rules annexed to the Protocol on Space Requirements for Special Trade Passenger Ships, 1973.

Regulation 3

Definitions

For the purpose of this chapter, unless expressly provided otherwise:

1 *Certificated person* is a person who holds a certificate of proficiency in survival craft issued under the authority of, or recognized as valid by, the Administration in accordance with the requirements of the International Convention on Standards of Training, Certification and Watchkeeping for Seafarers, in force; or a person who holds a certificate issued or recognized by the Administration of a State not a Party to that Convention for the same purpose as the convention certificate.

2 *Detection* is the determination of the location of survivors or survival craft.

3 *Embarkation ladder* is the ladder provided at survival craft embarkation stations to permit safe access to survival craft after launching.

4 *Float-free launching* is that method of launching a survival craft whereby the craft is automatically released from a sinking ship and is ready for use.

5 *Free-fall launching* is that method of launching a survival craft whereby the craft with its complement of persons and equipment on board is released and allowed to fall into the sea without any restraining apparatus.

6 *Immersion suit* is a protective suit which reduces the body heat-loss of a person wearing it in cold water.

7 *Inflatable appliance* is an appliance which depends upon non-rigid, gas-filled chambers for buoyancy and which is normally kept uninflated until ready for use.

8 *Inflated appliance* is an appliance which depends upon non-rigid, gas-filled chambers for buoyancy and which is kept inflated and ready for use at all times.

9 *Launching appliance or arrangement* is a means of transferring a survival craft or rescue boat from its stowed position safely to the water.

10 *Length* is 96% of the total length on a waterline at 85% of the least moulded depth measured from the top of the keel, or the length from the fore-side of the stem to the axis of the rudder stock on that waterline, if that be greater. In ships designed with a rake of keel the waterline on which this is measured shall be parallel to the designed waterline.

11   *Moulded depth*

  .1   The moulded depth is the vertical distance measured from the top
        of the keel to the top of the freeboard deck beam at side. In wood
        and composite ships the distance is measured from the lower edge
        of the keel rabbet. Where the form at the lower part of the midship
        section is of a hollow character, or where thick garboards are fitted,
        the distance is measured from the point where the line of the flat
        of the bottom continued inwards cuts the side of the keel.

  .2   In ships having rounded gunwales, the moulded depth shall be
        measured to the point of intersection of the moulded lines of the
        deck and side shell plating, the lines extending as though the gunwale
        were of angular design.

  .3   Where the freeboard deck is stepped and the raised part of the
        deck extends over the point at which the moulded depth is to be
        determined, the moulded depth shall be measured to a line of refer-
        ence extending from the lower part of the deck along a line parallel
        with the raised part.

12   *Novel life-saving appliance or arrangement* is a life-saving appliance or
arrangement which embodies new features not fully covered by the provisions
of this chapter but which provides an equal or higher standard of safety.

13   *Rescue boat* is a boat designed to rescue persons in distress and to marshal
survival craft.

14   *Retrieval* is the safe recovery of survivors.

15   *Retro-reflective material* is a material which reflects in the opposite direction a beam of light directed on it.

16   *Short international voyage* is an international voyage in the course of
which a ship is not more than 200 miles from a port or place in which the
passengers and crew could be placed in safety. Neither the distance between
the last port of call in the country in which the voyage begins and the final
port of destination nor the return voyage shall exceed 600 miles. The final
port of destination is the last port of call in the scheduled voyage at which
the ship commences its return voyage to the country in which the voyage
began.

17   *Survival craft* is a craft capable of sustaining the lives of persons in distress
from the time of abandoning the ship.

18   *Thermal protective aid* is a bag or suit made of waterproof material with
low thermal conductivity.

Regulation 4

Evaluation, testing and approval of
life-saving appliances and arrangements

1   Except as provided in paragraphs 5 and 6, life-saving appliances and arrangements required by this chapter shall be approved by the Administration.

2   Before giving approval to life-saving appliances and arrangements, the Administration shall ensure that such life-saving appliances and arrangements:

.1   are tested, to confirm that they comply with the requirements of this chapter, in accordance with the recommendations of the Organization;* or

.2   have successfully undergone, to the satisfaction of the Administration, tests which are substantially equivalent to those specified in those recommendations.

3   Before giving approval to novel life-saving appliances or arrangements, the Administration shall ensure that such appliances or arrangements:

.1   provide safety standards at least equivalent to the requirements of this chapter and have been evaluated and tested in accordance with the recommendations of the Organization;** or

.2   have successfully undergone, to the satisfaction of the Administration, evaluation and tests which are substantially equivalent to those recommendations.

4   Procedures adopted by the Administration for approval shall also include the conditions whereby approval would continue or would be withdrawn.

5   Before accepting life-saving appliances and arrangements that have not been previously approved by the Administration, the Administration shall be satisfied that life-saving appliances and arrangements comply with the requirements of this chapter.

6   Life-saving appliances required by this chapter for which detailed specifications are not included in part C shall be to the satisfaction of the Administration.

---

* Reference is made to the Recommendation on Testing of Life-Saving Appliances adopted by the Organization by resolution A.521(13).

** Reference is made to the Code of Practice for the Evaluation, Testing and Acceptance of Prototype Novel Life-Saving Appliances and Arrangements adopted by the Organization by resolution A.520(13).

Regulation 5

Production tests

The Administration shall require life-saving appliances to be subjected to such production tests as are necessary to ensure that the life-saving appliances are manufactured to the same standard as the approved prototype.

PART B – SHIP REQUIREMENTS

SECTION I – PASSENGER SHIPS AND CARGO SHIPS

Regulation 6

Communications

1 Paragraphs 2.3 and 2.4 apply to all ships. With respect to ships constructed before 1 July 1986, paragraphs 2.3 and 2.4 shall apply not later than 1 July 1991.

2 *Radio life-saving appliances*

2.1 *Portable radio apparatus for survival craft*

2.1.1 A portable radio apparatus for survival craft complying with the requirements of regulation IV/14 shall be provided. The portable radio apparatus shall be stowed in a protected and easily accessible position ready to be moved to any survival craft in an emergency, except that in the case of a ship with lifeboats stowed in widely separated positions fore and aft, the portable radio apparatus shall be stowed in the vicinity of the lifeboats which are furthest away from the ship's main transmitter.

2.1.2 The requirements of paragraph 2.1.1 need not be complied with if a radio installation complying with the requirements of regulation IV/13 is fitted in a lifeboat on each side of the ship or in the stern-launched lifeboat referred to in regulation 26.1.2.1.

2.1.3 On ships engaged on voyages of such duration that in the opinion of the Administration portable radio apparatus for survival craft is unnecessary, the Administration may allow such equipment to be dispensed with.

2.2 Radiotelegraph installation for lifeboats

On passenger ships engaged on international voyages which are not short international voyages:

.1 where the total number of persons on board is more than 199 but less than 1,500, a radiotelegraph installation complying with the requirements of regulation IV/13 shall be fitted in at least one of the lifeboats required by regulation 20.1.1.1;

.2 where the total number of persons on board is 1,500 or more, at least one lifeboat on each side shall be so fitted.

2.3 Survival craft emergency position-indicating radio beacons

One manually activated emergency position-indicating radio beacon complying with the requirements of regulation IV/14-1 shall be carried on each side of the ship. They shall be so stowed that they can be rapidly placed in any survival craft other than the liferaft or liferafts required by regulation 26.1.4.

2.4 Two-way radiotelephone apparatus

2.4.1 Two-way radiotelephone apparatus complying with the requirements of regulation IV/14-3 shall be provided for communication between survival craft, between survival craft and ship and between ship and rescue boat. An apparatus need not be provided for every survival craft; however, at least three apparatus shall be provided on each ship. This requirement may be complied with by other apparatus used on board provided such apparatus is not incompatible with the appropriate requirements of regulation IV/14-3.

2.4.2 For ships constructed before 1 July 1986 such apparatus need only comply with the frequency requirements of regulation IV/14-3.

3 Distress flares

Not less than 12 rocket parachute flares, complying with the requirements of regulation 35, shall be carried and be stowed on or near the navigating bridge.

4 On-board communications and alarm systems

4.1 An emergency means comprised of either fixed or portable equipment or both shall be provided for two-way communications between emergency control stations, muster and embarkation stations and strategic positions on board.

4.2 A general emergency alarm system complying with the requirements of regulation 50 shall be provided and shall be used for summoning passengers and crew to muster stations and to initiate the actions included in the muster list. The system shall be supplemented by either a public address system or other suitable means of communication.

Regulation 7

Personal life-saving appliances

1 Lifebuoys

1.1   Lifebuoys complying with the requirements of regulation 31.1 shall be:

  .1   so distributed as to be readily available on both sides of the ship and as far as practicable on all open decks extending to the ship's side; at least one shall be placed in the vicinity of the stern;

  .2   so stowed as to be capable of being rapidly cast loose, and not permanently secured in any way.

1.2   At least one lifebuoy on each side of the ship shall be fitted with a buoyant lifeline complying with the requirements of regulation 31.4 equal in length to not less than twice the height at which it is stowed above the waterline in the lightest seagoing condition, or 30 m, whichever is the greater.

1.3   Not less than one half of the total number of lifebuoys shall be provided with self-igniting lights complying with the requirements of regulation 31.2; not less than two of these shall also be provided with self-activating smoke signals complying with the requirements of regulation 31.3 and be capable of quick release from the navigating bridge; lifebuoys with lights and those with lights and smoke signals shall be equally distributed on both sides of the ship and shall not be the lifebuoys provided with lifelines in compliance with the requirements of paragraph 1.2.

1.4   Each lifebuoy shall be marked in block capitals of the Roman alphabet with the name and port of registry of the ship on which it is carried.

2 Lifejackets

2.1   A lifejacket complying with the requirements of regulation 32.1 or 32.2 shall be provided for every person on board the ship and, in addition:

  .1   a number of lifejackets suitable for children equal to at least 10% of the number of passengers on board shall be provided or such greater number as may be required to provide a lifejacket for each child;

  .2   a sufficient number of lifejackets shall be carried for persons on watch and for use at remotely located survival craft stations.

2.2   Lifejackets shall be so placed as to be readily accessible and their position shall be plainly indicated. Where, due to the particular arrangements of the ship, the lifejackets provided in compliance with the requirements of paragraph 2.1 may become inaccessible, alternative provisions shall be made to the satisfaction of the Administration which may include an increase in the number of lifejackets to be carried.

3   *Immersion suits*

3.1   An immersion suit, of an appropriate size, complying with the requirements of regulation 33 shall be provided for every person assigned to crew the rescue boat.

Regulation 8

Muster list and emergency instructions

1   This regulation applies to all ships.

2   Clear instructions to be followed in the event of an emergency shall be provided for every person on board.

3   Muster lists complying with the requirements of regulation 53 shall be exhibited in conspicuous places throughout the ship including the navigating bridge, engine-room and crew accommodation spaces.

4   Illustrations and instructions in appropriate languages shall be posted in passenger cabins and be conspicuously displayed at muster stations and other passenger spaces to inform passengers of:

   .1   their muster station;

   .2   the essential actions they must take in an emergency;

   .3   the method of donning lifejackets.

Regulation 9

Operating instructions

1   This regulation applies to all ships.

2   Posters or signs shall be provided on or in the vicinity of survival craft and their launching controls and shall:

   .1   illustrate the purpose of controls and the procedures for operating the appliance and give relevant instructions or warnings;

   .2   be easily seen under emergency lighting conditions;

   .3   use symbols in accordance with the recommendations of the Organization.

Regulation 10

Manning of survival craft and supervision

1   This regulation applies to all ships.

2   There shall be a sufficient number of trained persons on board for mustering and assisting untrained persons.

3   There shall be a sufficient number of crew members, who may be deck officers or certificated persons, on board for operating the survival craft and launching arrangements required for abandonment by the total number of persons on board.

4   A deck officer or certificated person shall be placed in charge of each survival craft to be used. However, the Administration, having due regard to the nature of the voyage, the number of persons on board and the characteristics of the ship, may permit persons practised in the handling and operation of liferafts to be placed in charge of liferafts in lieu of persons qualified as above. A second-in-command shall also be nominated in the case of lifeboats.

5   The person in charge of the survival craft shall have a list of the survival craft crew and shall see that the crew under his command are acquainted with their duties. In lifeboats the second-in-command shall also have a list of the lifeboat crew.

6   Every lifeboat required to carry a radiotelegraph installation complying with the requirements of regulation 6.2.2 shall have a person assigned who is capable of operating the equipment.

7   Every motorized survival craft shall have a person assigned who is capable of operating the engine and carrying out minor adjustments.

8   The master shall ensure the equitable distribution of persons referred to in paragraphs 2, 3 and 4 among the ship's survival craft.

Regulation 11

Survival craft muster and embarkation arrangements

1   Lifeboats and liferafts for which approved launching appliances are required shall be stowed as close to accommodation and service spaces as possible.

2   Muster stations shall be provided close to the embarkation stations. Each muster station shall have sufficient space to accommodate all persons assigned to muster at that station.

3   Muster and embarkation stations shall be readily accessible from accommodation and work areas.

4   Muster and embarkation stations shall be adequately illuminated by lighting supplied from the emergency source of electrical power required by regulation II-1/42 or II-1/43, as appropriate.

5   Alleyways, stairways and exits giving access to the muster and embarkation stations shall be lighted. Such lighting shall be capable of being supplied by the emergency source of electrical power required by regulation II-1/42 or II-1/43, as appropriate.

6   Davit-launched survival craft muster and embarkation stations shall be so arranged as to enable stretcher cases to be placed in survival craft.

7   An embarkation ladder complying with the requirements of regulation 48.7 extending, in a single length, from the deck to the waterline in the lightest seagoing condition under unfavourable conditions of trim and with the ship listed not less than 15° either way shall be provided at each launching station or at every two adjacent launching stations. However, the Administration may permit such ladders to be replaced by approved devices to afford access to the survival craft when waterborne, provided that there shall be at least one embarkation ladder on each side of the ship. Other means of embarkation may be permitted for the liferafts required by regulation 26.1.4.

8   Where necessary, means shall be provided for bringing the davit-launched survival craft against the ship's side and holding them alongside so that persons can be safely embarked.

Regulation 12

Launching stations

Launching stations shall be in such positions as to ensure safe launching having particular regard to clearance from the propeller and steeply overhanging portions of the hull and so that, as far as possible, survival craft, except survival craft specially designed for free-fall launching, can be launched down the straight side of the ship. If positioned forward, they shall be located abaft the collision bulkhead in a sheltered position and, in this respect, the Administration shall give special consideration to the strength of the launching appliance.

Regulation 13

Stowage of survival craft

1 Each survival craft shall be stowed:

.1 so that neither the survival craft nor its stowage arrangements will interfere with the operation of any other survival craft or rescue boat at any other launching station;

.2 as near the water surface as is safe and practicable and, in the case of a survival craft other than a liferaft intended for throw-overboard launching, in such a position that the survival craft in the embarkation position is not less than 2 m above the waterline with the ship in the fully loaded condition under unfavourable conditions of trim and listed up to 20° either way, or to the angle at which the ship's weatherdeck edge becomes submerged, whichever is less;

.3 in a state of continuous readiness so that two crew members can carry out preparations for embarkation and launching in less than 5 min;

.4 fully equipped as required by this chapter;

.5 as far as practicable, in a secure and sheltered position and protected from damage by fire and explosion.

2 Lifeboats for lowering down the ship's side shall be stowed as far forward of the propeller as practicable. On cargo ships of 80 m in length and upwards but less than 120 m in length, each lifeboat shall be so stowed that the after end of the lifeboat is not less than the length of the lifeboat forward of the propeller. On cargo ships of 120 m in length and upwards and passenger ships of 80 m in length and upwards, each lifeboat shall be so stowed that the after end of the lifeboat is not less than 1.5 times the length of the lifeboat forward of the propeller. Where appropriate, the ship shall be so arranged that lifeboats, in their stowed positions, are protected from damage by heavy seas.

3 Lifeboats shall be stowed attached to launching appliances.

4 In addition to meeting the requirements of regulations 23 and 29, liferafts shall be so stowed as to permit manual release from their securing arrangements.

5   Davit-launched liferafts shall be stowed within reach of the lifting hooks, unless some means of transfer is provided which is not rendered inoperable within the limits of trim and list prescribed in paragraph 1.2 or by ship motion or power failure.

6   Liferafts intended for throw-overboard launching shall be so stowed as to be readily transferable for launching on either side of the ship unless liferafts, of the aggregate capacity required by regulation 26.1 to be capable of being launched on either side, are stowed on each side of the ship.

Regulation 14

Stowage of rescue boats

Rescue boats shall be stowed:

.1   in a state of continuous readiness for launching in not more than 5 min;

.2   in a position suitable for launching and recovery;

.3   so that neither the rescue boat nor its stowage arrangements will interfere with the operation of any survival craft at any other launching station;

.4   if it is also a lifeboat, in compliance with the requirements of regulation 13.

Regulation 15

Survival craft launching and recovery arrangements

1   Launching appliances complying with the requirements of regulation 48 shall be provided for all survival craft except:

.1   survival craft which are boarded from a position on deck which is less than 4.5 m above the waterline in the lightest seagoing condition and which either:

.1.1   have a mass of not more than 185 kg; or

.1.2   are stowed for launching directly from the stowed position under unfavourable conditions of trim of up to 10° and with the ship listed not less than 20° either way;

.2   survival craft having a mass of not more than 185 kg and which are carried in excess of the survival craft for 200% of the total number of persons on board the ship.

2   Each lifeboat shall be provided with an appliance which is capable of launching and recovering the lifeboat.

3   Launching and recovery arrangements shall be such that the appliance operator on the ship is able to observe the survival craft at all times during launching and for lifeboats during recovery.

4   Only one type of release mechanism shall be used for similar survival craft carried on board the ship.

5   Preparation and handling of survival craft at any one launching station shall not interfere with the prompt preparation and handling of any other survival craft or rescue boat at any other station.

6   Falls, where used, shall be long enough for the survival craft to reach the water with the ship in its lightest seagoing condition, under unfavourable conditions of trim and with the ship listed not less than 20° either way.

7   During preparation and launching, the survival craft, its launching appliance, and the area of water into which it is to be launched shall be adequately illuminated by lighting supplied from the emergency source of electrical power required by regulation II-1/42 or II-1/43, as appropriate.

8   Means shall be available to prevent any discharge of water on to survival craft during abandonment.

9   If there is a danger of the survival craft being damaged by the ship's stabilizer wings, means shall be available, powered by an emergency source of energy, to bring the stabilizer wings inboard; indicators operated by an emergency source of energy shall be available on the navigating bridge to show the position of the stabilizer wings.

10   If lifeboats complying with the requirements of regulation 42 or 43 are carried, a davit span shall be provided, fitted with not less than two lifelines of sufficient length to reach the water with the ship in its lightest seagoing condition, under unfavourable conditions of trim and with the ship listed not less than 20° either way.

Regulation 16

Rescue boat embarkation, launching and
recovery arrangements

1   The rescue boat embarkation and launching arrangements shall be such that the rescue boat can be boarded and launched in the shortest possible time.

2   If the rescue boat is one of the ship's survival craft, the embarkation arrangements and launching station shall comply with the requirements of regulations 11 and 12.

3   Launching arrangements shall comply with the requirements of regulation 15. However, all rescue boats shall be capable of being launched, where necessary utilizing painters, with the ship making headway at speeds up to 5 knots in calm water.

4   Rapid recovery of the rescue boat shall be possible when loaded with its full complement of persons and equipment. If the rescue boat is also a lifeboat, rapid recovery shall be possible when loaded with its lifeboat equipment and the approved rescue boat complement of at least six persons.

Regulation 17

Line-throwing appliances

A line-throwing appliance complying with the requirements of regulation 49 shall be provided.

Regulation 18

Abandon ship training and drills

1   This regulation applies to all ships.

2   *Manuals*

A training manual complying with the requirements of regulation 51 shall be provided in each crew messroom and recreation room or in each crew cabin.

3   *Practice musters and drills*

3.1   Each member of the crew shall participate in at least one abandon ship drill and one fire drill every month. The drills of the crew shall take place within 24 h of the ship leaving a port if more than 25% of the crew have not participated in abandon ship and fire drills on board that particular ship in the previous month. The Administration may accept other arrangements that are at least equivalent for those classes of ship for which this is impracticable.

3.2   On a ship engaged on an international voyage which is not a short international voyage, musters of the passengers shall take place within 24 h after their embarkation. Passengers shall be instructed in the use of the lifejackets and the action to take in an emergency. If only a small number of passengers embark at a port after the muster has been held it shall be sufficient, instead of holding another muster, to draw the attention of these passengers to the emergency instructions required by regulations 8.2 and 8.4.

3.3   On a ship engaged on a short international voyage, if a muster of the passengers is not held on departure, the attention of the passengers shall be drawn to the emergency instructions required by regulations 8.2 and 8.4.

3.4   Each abandon ship drill shall include:

.1   summoning of passengers and crew to muster stations with the alarm required by regulation 6.4.2 and ensuring that they are made aware of the order to abandon ship specified in the muster list;

.2   reporting to stations and preparing for the duties described in the muster list;

.3   checking that passengers and crew are suitably dressed;

.4   checking that lifejackets are correctly donned;

.5   lowering of at least one lifeboat after any necessary preparation for launching;

.6   starting and operating the lifeboat engine;

.7   operation of davits used for launching liferafts.

3.5   Different lifeboats shall, as far as practicable, be lowered in compliance with the requirements of paragraph 3.4.5 at successive drills.

3.6   Drills shall, as far as practicable, be conducted as if there were an actual emergency.

3.7   Each lifeboat shall be launched with its assigned operating crew aboard and manoeuvred in the water at least once every 3 months during an abandon ship drill. The Administration may allow ships operating on short international voyages not to launch the lifeboats on one side if their berthing arrangements in port and their trading patterns do not permit launching of lifeboats on that side. However, all such lifeboats shall be lowered at least once every 3 months and launched at least annually.

3.8   As far as is reasonable and practicable, rescue boats other than lifeboats which are also rescue boats, shall be launched each month with their assigned crew aboard and manoeuvred in the water. In all cases this requirement shall be complied with at least once every 3 months.

3.9   If lifeboat and rescue boat launching drills are carried out with the ship making headway, such drills shall, because of the dangers involved, be practised in sheltered waters only and under the supervision of an officer experienced in such drills.

3.10 Emergency lighting for mustering and abandonment shall be tested at each abandon ship drill.

4   On-board training and instructions

4.1 On-board training in the use of the ship's life-saving appliances, including survival craft equipment, shall be given as soon as possible but not later than 2 weeks after a crew member joins the ship. However, if the crew member is on a regularly scheduled rotating assignment to the ship, such training shall be given not later than 2 weeks after the time of first joining the ship.

4.2 Instructions in the use of the ship's life-saving appliances and in survival at sea shall be given at the same interval as the drills. Individual instruction may cover different parts of the ship's life-saving system, but all the ship's life-saving equipment and appliances shall be covered within any period of 2 months. Each member of the crew shall be given instructions which shall include but not necessarily be limited to:

.1   operation and use of the ship's inflatable liferafts;

.2   problems of hypothermia, first-aid treatment of hypothermia and other appropriate first-aid procedures;

.3   special instructions necessary for use of the ship's life-saving appliances in severe weather and severe sea conditions.

4.3 On-board training in the use of davit-launched liferafts shall take place at intervals of not more than 4 months on every ship fitted with such appliances. Whenever practicable this shall include the inflation and lowering of a liferaft. This liferaft may be a special liferaft intended for training purposes only, which is not part of the ship's life-saving equipment; such a special liferaft shall be conspicuously marked.

5   Records

The date when musters are held, details of abandon ship drills and fire drills, drills of other life-saving appliances and on-board training shall be recorded in such log-book as may be prescribed by the Administration. If a full muster, drill or training session is not held at the appointed time, an entry shall be made in the log-book stating the circumstances and the extent of the muster, drill or training session held.

Regulation 19

Operational readiness, maintenance and inspections

1   This regulation applies to all ships. The requirements of paragraphs 3 and 6.2 shall be complied with, as far as is practicable, on ships constructed before 1 July 1986.

2   Operational readiness

Before the ship leaves port and at all times during the voyage, all life-saving appliances shall be in working order and ready for immediate use.

3   Maintenance

3.1   Instructions for on-board maintenance of life-saving appliances complying with the requirements of regulation 52 shall be provided and maintenance shall be carried out accordingly.

3.2   The Administration may accept, in lieu of the instructions required by paragraph 3.1, a shipboard planned maintenance programme which includes the requirements of regulation 52.

4   Maintenance of falls

Falls used in launching shall be turned end for end at intervals of not more than 30 months and be renewed when necessary due to deterioration of the falls or at intervals of not more than 5 years, whichever is the earlier.

5   Spares and repair equipment

Spares and repair equipment shall be provided for life-saving appliances and their components which are subject to excessive wear or consumption and need to be replaced regularly.

6   Weekly inspection

The following tests and inspections shall be carried out weekly:

.1   all survival craft, rescue boats and launching appliances shall be visually inspected to ensure that they are ready for use;

.2   all engines in lifeboats and rescue boats shall be run ahead and astern for a total period of not less than 3 min provided the ambient temperature is above the minimum temperature required for starting the engine. In special cases the Administration may waive this requirement for ships constructed before 1 July 1986;

.3   the general emergency alarm system shall be tested.

7   Monthly inspections

Inspection of the life-saving appliances, including lifeboat equipment, shall be carried out monthly using the checklist required by regulation 52.1 to ensure that they are complete and in good order. A report of the inspection shall be entered in the log-book.

8   *Servicing of inflatable liferafts, inflatable lifejackets and inflated rescue boats*

8.1   Every inflatable liferaft and inflatable lifejacket shall be serviced:

   .1   at intervals not exceeding 12 months. However, in cases where it appears proper and reasonable, the Administration may extend this period to 17 months;

   .2   at an approved servicing station which is competent to service them, maintains proper servicing facilities and uses only properly trained personnel.*

8.2   All repairs and maintenance of inflated rescue boats shall be carried out in accordance with the manufacturer's instructions. Emergency repairs may be carried out on board the ship; however, permanent repairs shall be effected at an approved servicing station.

9   *Periodic servicing of hydrostatic release units*

   Hydrostatic release units shall be serviced:

   .1   at intervals not exceeding 12 months. However, in cases where it appears proper and reasonable, the Administration may extend this period to 17 months;

   .2   at a servicing station which is competent to service them, maintains proper servicing facilities and uses only properly trained personnel.

SECTION II – PASSENGER SHIPS

(Additional requirements)

Regulation 20

Survival craft and rescue boats

1   *Survival craft*

1.1   Passenger ships engaged on international voyages which are not short international voyages shall carry:

   .1   lifeboats complying with the requirements of regulation 42, 43, or 44 on each side of such aggregate capacity as will accommodate

---

* Reference is made to the Recommendation on the Conditions for the Approval of Servicing Stations for Inflatable Liferafts adopted by the Organization by resolution A.333(IX).

not less than 50% of the total number of persons on board. The Administration may permit the substitution of lifeboats by liferafts of equivalent total capacity provided that there shall never be less than sufficient lifeboats on each side of the ship to accommodate 37.5% of the total number of persons on board. The liferafts shall comply with the requirements of regulation 39 or 40 and shall be served by launching appliances equally distributed on each side of the ship; and

.2 in addition, liferafts complying with the requirements of regulation 39 or 40 of such aggregate capacity as will accomodate at least 25% of the total number of persons on board. These liferafts shall be served by at least one launching appliance on each side which may be those provided in compliance with the requirements of paragraph 1.1.1 or equivalent approved appliances capable of being used on both sides. However, stowage of these liferafts need not comply with the requirements of regulation 13.5.

1.2   Passenger ships engaged on short international voyages and complying with the special standards of subdivision prescribed by regulation II-1/6.5 shall carry:

.1 lifeboats complying with the requirements of regulation 42, 43 or 44 equally distributed, as far as practicable, on each side of the ship and of such aggregate capacity as will accommodate at least 30% of the total number of persons on board and liferafts complying with requirements of regulation 39 or 40 of such aggregate capacity that, together with the lifeboat capacity, the survival craft will accommodate the total number of persons on board. The liferafts shall be served by launching appliances equally distributed on each side of the ship; and

.2 in addition, liferafts complying with the requirements of regulation 39 or 40 of such aggregate capacity as will accommodate at least 25% of the total number of persons on board. These liferafts shall be served by at least one launching appliance on each side which may be those provided in compliance with the requirements of paragraph 1.2.1 or equivalent approved appliances capable of being used on both sides. However, stowage of these liferafts need not comply with the requirements of regulation 13.5.

1.3   Passenger ships engaged on short international voyages and not complying with the special standard of subdivision prescribed by regulation II-1/6.5, shall carry survival craft complying with the requirements of paragraph 1.1.

1.4   All survival craft required to provide for abandonment by the total number of persons on board shall be capable of being launched with their full complement of persons and equipment within a period of 30 min from the time the abandon ship signal is given.

1.5   In lieu of meeting the requirements of paragraph 1.1, 1.2 or 1.3, passenger ships of less than 500 tons gross tonnage where the total number of persons on board is less than 200, may comply with the following:

.1   They shall carry on each side of the ship, liferafts complying with the requirements of regulation 39 or 40 and of such aggregate capacity as will accommodate the total number of persons on board.

.2   Unless the liferafts required by paragraph 1.5.1 can be readily transferred for launching on either side of the ship, additional liferafts shall be provided so that the total capacity available on each side will accommodate 150% of the total number of persons on board.

.3   If the rescue boat required by paragraph 2.2. is also a lifeboat complying with the requirements of regulation 42, 43 or 44, it may be included in the aggregate capacity required by paragraph 1.5.1, provided that the total capacity available on either side of the ship is at least 150% of the total number of persons on board.

.4   In the event of any one survival craft being lost or rendered unserviceable, there shall be sufficient survival craft available for use on each side to accommodate the total number of persons on board.

2   *Rescue boats*

2.1   Passenger ships of 500 tons gross tonnage and over shall carry at least one rescue boat complying with the requirements of regulation 47 on each side of the ship.

2.2   Passenger ships of less than 500 tons gross tonnage shall carry at least one rescue boat complying with the requirements of regulation 47.

2.3   A lifeboat may be accepted as a rescue boat provided it also complies with the requirements for a rescue boat.

3   *Marshalling of liferafts*

3.1   The number of lifeboats and rescue boats that are carried on passenger ships shall be sufficient to ensure that in providing for abandonment by the total number of persons on board not more than six liferafts need be marshalled by each lifeboat or rescue boat.

3.2   The number of lifeboats and rescue boats that are carried on passenger ships engaged on short international voyages and complying with the special standards of subdivision prescribed by regulation II-1/6.5 shall be sufficient to ensure that in providing for abandonment by the total number of persons on board not more than nine liferafts need be marshalled by each lifeboat or rescue boat.

Regulation 21

Personal life-saving appliances

1 Lifebuoys

1.1 A passenger ship shall carry not less than the number of lifebuoys complying with the requirements of regulations 7.1 and 31 prescribed in the following table:

Length of ship in metres	Minimum number of lifebuoys
Under 60	8
60 and under 120	12
120 and under 180	18
180 and under 240	24
240 and over	30

1.2 Notwithstanding regulation 7.1.3, passenger ships of under 60 m in length shall carry not less than six lifebuoys provided with self-igniting lights.

2 Lifejackets

In addition to the lifejackets required by regulation 7.2, every passenger ship shall carry lifejackets for not less than 5% of the total number of persons on board. These lifejackets shall be stowed in conspicuous places on deck or at muster stations.

3 Lifejacket lights

3.1 This paragraph applies to all passenger ships. With respect to passenger ships constructed before 1 July 1986, the requirements of this paragraph shall apply not later than 1 July 1991.

3.2 On passenger ships engaged on international voyages which are not short international voyages each lifejacket shall be fitted with a light complying with the requirements of regulation 32.3.

4 Immersion suits and thermal protective aids

4.1 This paragraph applies to all passenger ships. With respect to passenger ships constructed before 1 July 1986, the requirements of this paragraph shall apply not later than 1 July 1991.

4.2 Passenger ships shall carry for each lifeboat on the ship at least three immersion suits complying with the requirements of regulation 33 and, in addition, a thermal protective aid complying with the requirements of regulation 34 for every person to be accommodated in the lifeboat and not provided with an immersion suit. These immersion suits and thermal protective aids need not be carried:

.1 for persons to be accommodated in totally or partially enclosed lifeboats; or

.2 if the ship is constantly engaged on voyages in warm climates where, in the opinion of the Administration, thermal protective aids are unnecessary.

4.3 The provisions of paragraph 4.2.1 also apply to totally or partially enclosed lifeboats not complying with the requirements of regulation 42, 43 or 44, provided they are carried on ships constructed before 1 July 1986.

Regulation 22

Survival craft and rescue boat embarkation arrangements

1 On passenger ships, survival craft embarkation arrangements shall be designed for:

.1 all lifeboats to be boarded and launched either directly from the stowed position or from an embarkation deck but not both;

.2 davit-launched liferafts to be boarded and launched from a position immediately adjacent to the stowed position or from a position to which, in compliance with the requirements of regulation 13.5, the liferaft is transferred prior to launching.

2 Rescue boat arrangements shall be such that the rescue boat can be boarded and launched directly from the stowed position with the number of persons assigned to crew the rescue boat on board. Notwithstanding the requirements of paragraph 1.1, if the rescue boat is also a lifeboat and the other lifeboats are boarded and launched from an embarkation deck, the arrangements shall be such that the rescue boat can also be boarded and launched from the embarkation deck.

Regulation 23

Stowage of liferafts

On passenger ships, every liferaft shall be stowed with its painter permanently attached to the ship and with a float-free arrangement complying with the requirements of regulation 38.6 so that, as far as practicable, the liferaft floats free and, if inflatable, inflates automatically when the ship sinks.

Regulation 24

Muster stations

Every passenger ship shall, in addition to complying with the requirements of regulation 11, have passenger muster stations which shall:

.1 be in the vicinity of, and permit ready access for the passengers to, the embarkation stations unless in the same location;

.2 have ample room for marshalling and instruction of the passengers.

Regulation 25

Drills

1 This regulation applies to all passenger ships.

2 On passenger ships, an abandon ship drill and fire drill shall take place weekly.

SECTION III – CARGO SHIPS

(Additional requirements)

Regulation 26

Survival craft and rescue boats

1 *Survival craft*

1.1 Cargo ships shall carry:

.1 one or more lifeboats complying with the requirements of regulation 44 of such aggregate capacity on each side of the ship as will accommodate the total number of persons on board. The Administration may, however, permit cargo ships (except oil tankers, chemical tankers and gas carriers) operating under favourable climatic conditions and in suitable areas, to carry lifeboats complying with the requirements of regulation 43, provided the limits of the trade area are specified in the Cargo Ship Safety Equipment Certificate; and

.2 in addition, a liferaft or liferafts, complying with the requirements of regulation 39 or 40, capable of being launched on either side of the ship and of such aggregate capacity as will accommodate the total number of persons on board. If the liferaft or liferafts cannot be readily transferred for launching on either side of the ship, the total capacity available on each side shall be sufficient to accommodate the total number of persons on board.

1.2 In lieu of meeting the requirements of paragraph 1.1, cargo ships may carry:

.1 one or more lifeboats, complying with the requirements of regulation 44, capable of being free-fall launched over the stern of the ship of such aggregate capacity as will accommodate the total number of persons on board; and

.2 in addition, one or more liferafts complying with the requirements of regulation 39 or 40, on each side of the ship, of such aggregate capacity as will accommodate the total number of persons on board. The liferafts on at least one side of the ship shall be served by launching appliances.

1.3 In lieu of meeting the requirements of paragraph 1.1 or 1.2, cargo ships of less than 85 m in length other than oil tankers, chemical tankers and gas carriers, may comply with the following:

.1 They shall carry on each side of the ship, one or more liferafts complying with the requirements of regulation 39 or 40 and of such aggregate capacity as will accommodate the total number of persons on board.

.2 Unless the liferafts required by paragraph 1.3.1 can be readily transferred for launching on either side of the ship, additional liferafts shall be provided so that the total capacity available on each side will accommodate 150% of the total number of persons on board.

.3 If the rescue boat required by paragraph 2 is also a lifeboat complying with the requirements of regulation 43 or 44, it may be included in the aggregate capacity required by paragraph 1.3.1, provided that the total capacity available on either side of the ship is at least 150% of the total number of persons on board.

.4 In the event of any one survival craft being lost or rendered unserviceable, there shall be sufficient survival craft available for use on each side to accommodate the total number of persons on board.

1.4 Cargo ships where the survival craft are stowed in a position which is

252

more than 100 m from the stem or stern shall carry, in addition to the liferafts required by paragraphs 1.1.2 and 1.2.2, a liferaft stowed as far forward or aft, or one as far forward and another as far aft, as is reasonable and practicable. Notwithstanding the requirements of regulation 29, such liferaft or liferafts may be securely fastened so as to permit manual release and need not be of the type which can be launched from an approved launching device.

1.5   With the exception of the survival craft referred to in regulation 15.1.1, all survival craft required to provide for abandonment by the total number of persons on board shall be capable of being launched with their full complement of persons and equipment within a period of 10 min from the time the abandon ship signal is given.

1.6   Chemical tankers and gas carriers carrying cargoes emitting toxic vapours or gases* shall carry, in lieu of lifeboats complying with the requirements of regulation 43 or 44, lifeboats complying with the requirements of regulation 45.

1.7   Oil tankers, chemical tankers and gas carriers carrying cargoes having a flashpoint not exceeding 60°C (closed cup test) shall carry, in lieu of lifeboats complying with the requirements of regulation 43 or 44, lifeboats complying with the requirements of regulation 46.

2   *Rescue boats*

Cargo ships shall carry at least one rescue boat complying with the requirements of regulation 47. A lifeboat may be accepted as a rescue boat, provided that it also complies with the requirements for a rescue boat.

3   In addition to their lifeboats, cargo ships constructed before 1 July 1986 shall carry not later than 1 July 1991:

.1   one or more liferafts of such aggregate capacity as will accommodate the total number of persons on board. The liferaft or liferafts shall be equipped with a lashing or an equivalent means of securing the liferaft which will automatically release it from a sinking ship;

.2   where the survival craft are stowed in a position which is more than 100 m from the stem or stern, in addition to the liferafts required by paragraph 3.1, a liferaft stowed as far forward or aft, or one as far forward and another as far aft, as is reasonable and practicable. Notwithstanding the requirements of paragraph 3.1, such liferaft or liferafts may be securely fastened so as to permit manual release.

---

* Reference is made to products for which emergency escape respiratory protection is required in chapter 17 of the International Code for the Construction and Equipment of Ships Carrying Dangerous Chemicals in Bulk (IBC Code) adopted by the Maritime Safety Committee by resolution MSC.4(48) and in chapter 19 of the International Code for the Construction and Equipment of Ships Carrying Liquefied Gases in Bulk (IGC Code) adopted by the Maritime Safety Committee by resolution MSC.5(48).

Regulation 27

Personal life-saving appliances

1   *Lifebuoys*

1.1   Cargo ships shall carry not less than the number of lifebuoys complying with the requirements of regulations 7.1 and 31 prescribed in the following table:

Length of ship in metres	Minimum number of lifebuoys
Under 100	8
100 and under 150	10
150 and under 200	12
200 and over	14

1.2   Self-igniting lights for lifebuoys on tankers required by regulation 7.1.3 shall be of an electric battery type.

2   *Lifejacket lights*

2.1   This paragraph applies to all cargo ships. With respect to cargo ships constructed before 1 July 1986, this paragraph shall apply not later than 1 July 1991.

2.2   On cargo ships each lifejacket shall be fitted with a light complying with the requirements of regulation 32.3.

3   *Immersion suits and thermal protective aids*

3.1   This paragraph applies to all cargo ships. With respect to cargo ships constructed before 1 July 1986, this paragraph shall apply not later than 1 July 1991.

3.2   Cargo ships shall carry for each lifeboat on the ship at least three immersion suits complying with the requirements of regulation 33 or, if the Administration considers it necessary and practicable, one immersion suit complying with the requirements of regulation 33 for every person on board the ship; however, the ship shall carry in addition to the thermal protective aids required by regulations 38.5.1.24, 41.8.31 and 47.2.2.13, thermal protective aids complying with the requirements of regulation 34 for persons on board not provided with immersion suits. These immersion suits and thermal protective aids need not be required if the ship:

.1 has totally enclosed lifeboats on each side of the ship of such aggregate capacity as will accommodate the total number of persons on board; or

.2 has totally enclosed lifeboats capable of being launched by free fall over the stern of the ship of such aggregate capacity as will accommodate the total number of persons on board and which are boarded and launched directly from the stowed position, together with liferafts on each side of the ship of such aggregate capacity as will accommodate the total number of persons on board; or

.3 is constantly engaged on voyages in warm climates where, in the opinion of the Administration, immersion suits are unnecessary.

3.3 Cargo ships complying with the requirements of regulation 26.1.3 shall carry immersion suits complying with the requirements of regulation 33 for every person on board unless the ship:

.1 has davit-launched liferafts; or

.2 has liferafts served by equivalent approved appliances capable of being used on both sides of the ship and which do not require entry into the water to board the liferaft; or

.3 is constantly engaged on voyages in warm climates where, in the opinion of the Administration, immersion suits are unnecessary.

3.4 The immersion suits required by this regulation may be used to comply with the requirements of regulation 7.3.

3.5 The totally enclosed lifeboats referred to in paragraphs 3.2.1 and 3.2.2 carried on cargo ships constructed before 1 July 1986 need not comply with the requirements of regulation 44.

Regulation 28

Survival craft embarkation and launching arrangements

1 Cargo ship survival craft embarkation arrangements shall be so designed that lifeboats can be boarded and launched directly from the stowed position and davit-launched liferafts can be boarded and launched from a position immediately adjacent to the stowed position or from a position to which the liferaft is transferred prior to launching in compliance with the requirements of regulation 13.5.

2 On cargo ships of 20,000 tons gross tonnage and upwards, lifeboats shall be capable of being launched, where necessary utilizing painters, with the ship making headway at speeds up to 5 knots in calm water.

Regulation 29

Stowage of liferafts

On cargo ships, every liferaft, other than those required by regulation 26.1.4, shall be stowed with its painter permanently attached to the ship and with a float-free arrangement complying with the requirements of regulation 38.6 so that the liferaft floats free and, if inflatable, inflates automatically when the ship sinks.

PART C – LIFE-SAVING APPLIANCE REQUIREMENTS

SECTION I – GENERAL

Regulation 30

General requirements for life-saving appliances

1   Paragraph 2.7 applies to all ships. With respect to ships constructed before 1 July 1986, paragraph 2.7 shall apply not later than 1 July 1991.

2   Unless expressly provided otherwise or unless, in the opinion of the Administration having regard to the particular voyages on which the ship is constantly engaged, other requirements are appropriate, all life-saving appliances prescribed in this part shall:

.1   be constructed with proper workmanship and materials;

.2   not be damaged in stowage throughout the air temperature range −30°C to +65°C;

.3   if they are likely to be immersed in seawater during their·use, operate throughout the seawater temperature range −1°C to +30°C;

.4   where applicable, be rot-proof, corrosion-resistant, and not be unduly affected by seawater, oil or fungal attack;

.5   where exposed to sunlight, be resistant to deterioration;

.6   be of a highly visible colour on all parts where this will assist detection;

.7 be fitted with retro-reflective material where it will assist in detection and in accordance with the recommendations of the Organization;*

.8 if they are to be used in a seaway, be capable of satisfactory operation in that environment.

3   The Administration shall determine the period of acceptability of life-saving appliances which are subject to deterioration with age. Such life-saving appliances shall be marked with a means for determining their age or the date by which they must be replaced.

SECTION II – PERSONAL LIFE-SAVING APPLIANCES

Regulation 31

Lifebuoys

1   *Lifebuoy specification*

Every lifebuoy shall:

.1   have an outer diameter of not more than 800 mm and an inner dia-meter of not less than 400 mm;

.2   be constructed of inherently buoyant material; it shall not depend upon rushes, cork shavings or granulated cork, any other loose gran-ulated material or any air compartment which depends on inflation for buoyancy;

.3   be capable of supporting not less than 14.5 kg of iron in fresh water for a period of 24 h;

.4   have a mass of not less than 2.5 kg;

.5   not sustain burning or continue melting after being totally enveloped in a fire for a period of 2 s;

.6   be constructed to withstand a drop into the water from the height at which it is stowed above the waterline in the lightest seagoing condition or 30 m, whichever is the greater, without impairing either its operating capability or that of its attached components;

---

* Reference is made to the Recommendation on Retro-reflective Tapes on Life-Saving Appliances adopted by the Organization by resolution A.274(VIII).

.7 if it is intended to operate the quick-release arrangement provided for the self-activated smoke signals and self-igniting lights, have a mass sufficient to operate the quick-release arrangement or 4 kg, whichever is the greater;

.8 be fitted with a grabline not less than 9.5 mm in diameter and not less than 4 times the outside diameter of the body of the buoy in length. The grabline shall be secured at four equidistant points around the circumference of the buoy to form four equal loops.

2 *Lifebuoy self-igniting lights*

Self-igniting lights required by regulation 7.1.3 shall:

.1 be such that they cannot be extinguished by water;

.2 be capable of either burning continuously with a luminous intensity of not less than 2 cd in all directions of the upper hemisphere or flashing (discharge flashing) at a rate of not less than 50 flashes per minute with at least the corresponding effective luminous intensity;

.3 be provided with a source of energy capable of meeting the requirement of paragraph 2.2 for a period of at least 2 h;

.4 be capable of withstanding the drop test required by paragraph 1.6.

3 *Lifebuoy self-activating smoke signals*

Self-activating smoke signals required by regulation 7.1.3 shall:

.1 emit smoke of a highly visible colour at a uniform rate for a period of at least 15 min when floating in calm water;

.2 not ignite explosively or emit any flame during the entire smoke emission time of the signal;

.3 not be swamped in a seaway;

.4 continue to emit smoke when fully submerged in water for a period of at least 10 s;

.5 be capable of withstanding the drop test required by paragraph 1.6.

4 *Buoyant lifelines*

Buoyant lifelines required by regulation 7.1.2 shall:

.1 be non-kinking;

.2 have a diameter of not less than 8 mm;

.3 have a breaking strength of not less than 5 kN.

Regulation 32

Lifejackets

1 *General requirements for lifejackets*

1.1 A lifejacket shall not sustain burning or continue melting after being totally enveloped in a fire for a period of 2 s.

1.2 A lifejacket shall be so constructed that:

.1 after demonstration, a person can correctly don it within a period of 1 min without assistance;

.2 it is capable of being worn inside-out or is clearly capable of being worn in only one way and, as far as possible, cannot be donned incorrectly;

.3 it is comfortable to wear;

.4 it allows the wearer to jump from a height of at least 4.5 m into the water without injury and without dislodging or damaging the lifejacket.

1.3 A lifejacket shall have sufficient buoyancy and stability in calm fresh water to:

.1 lift the mouth of an exhaused or unconscious person not less than 120 mm clear of the water with the body inclined backwards at an angle of not less than 20° and not more than 50° from the vertical position;

.2 turn the body of an unconscious person in the water from any position to one where the mouth is clear of the water in not more than 5 s.

1.4 A lifejacket shall have buoyancy which is not reduced by more than 5% after 24 h submersion in fresh water.

1.5 A lifejacket shall allow the person wearing it to swim a short distance and to board a survival craft.

1.6 Each lifejacket shall be fitted with a whistle firmly secured by a cord.

2 *Inflatable lifejackets*

A lifejacket which depends on inflation for buoyancy shall have not less than two separate compartments and comply with the requirements of paragraph 1 and shall:

.1 inflate automatically on immersion, be provided with a device to permit inflation by a single manual motion and be capable of being inflated by mouth;

.2 in the event of loss of buoyancy in any one compartment be capable of complying with the requirements of paragraphs 1.2, 1.3 and 1.5;

.3 comply with the requirements of paragraph 1.4 after inflation by means of the automatic mechanism.

3   *Lifejacket lights*

3.1 Each lifejacket light shall:

.1 have a luminous intensity of not less than 0.75 cd;

.2 have a source of energy capable of providing a luminous intensity of 0.75 cd for a period of at least 8 h;

.3 be visible over as great a segment of the upper hemisphere as is practicable when attached to a lifejacket.

3.2 If the light referred to in paragraph 3.1 is a flashing light it shall, in addition:

.1 be provided with a manually operated switch;

.2 not be fitted with a lens or curved reflector to concentrate the beam;

.3 flash at a rate of not less than 50 flashes per minute with an effective luminous intensity of at least 0.75 cd.

Regulation 33

Immersion suits

1   *General requirements for immersion suits*

1.1 The immersion suit shall be constructed with waterproof materials such that:

.1 it can be unpacked and donned without assistance within 2 min, taking into account any associated clothing*, and a lifejacket if the immersion suit is to be worn in conjunction with a lifejacket;

.2 it will not sustain burning or continue melting after being totally enveloped in a fire for a period of 2 s;

.3 it will cover the whole body with the exception of the face. Hands shall also be covered unless permanently attached gloves are provided;

---

* Reference is made to paragraph 3.1.3.1 of the Recommendation on Testing of Life-Saving Appliances adopted by the Organization by resolution A.521(13).

.4   it is provided with arrangements to minimize or reduce free air in the legs of the suit;

.5   following a jump from a height of not less than 4.5 m into the water there is no undue ingress of water into the suit.

1.2   An immersion suit which also complies with the requirements of regulation 32 may be classified as a lifejacket.

1.3   An immersion suit shall permit the person wearing it, and also wearing a lifejacket if the immersion suit is to be worn in conjunction with a lifejacket, to:

.1   climb up and down a vertical ladder at least 5 m in length;

.2   perform normal duties during abandonment;

.3   jump from a height of not less than 4.5 m into the water without damaging or dislodging the immersion suit, or being injured; and

.4   swim a short distance through the water and board a survival craft.

1.4   An immersion suit which has buoyancy and is designed to be worn without a lifejacket shall be fitted with a light complying with the requirements of regulation 32.3 and the whistle prescribed by regulation 32.1.6.

1.5   If the immersion suit is to be worn in conjunction with a lifejacket, the lifejacket shall be worn over the immersion suit. A person wearing such an immersion suit shall be able to don a lifejacket without assistance.

2   *Thermal performance requirements for immersion suits*

2.1   An immersion suit made of material which has no inherent insulation shall be:

.1   marked with instructions that it must be worn in conjunction with warm clothing;

.2   so constructed that, when worn in conjunction with warm clothing, and with a lifejacket if the immersion suit is to be worn with a lifejacket, the immersion suit continues to provide sufficient thermal protection, following one jump by the wearer into the water from a height of 4.5 m, to ensure that when it is worn for a period of 1 h in calm circulating water at a temperature of 5°C, the wearer's body core temperature does not fall more than 2°C.

2.2   An immersion suit made of material with inherent insulation, when worn either on its own or with a lifejacket, if the immersion suit is to be worn in conjunction with a lifejacket, shall provide the wearer with sufficient thermal insulation, following one jump into the water from a height of 4.5 m, to ensure that the wearer's body core temperature does not fall more than 2°C after a period of 6 h immersion in calm circulating water at a temperature of between 0°C and 2°C.

261

2.3   The immersion suit shall permit the person wearing it with hands covered to pick up a pencil and write after being immersed in water at 5°C for a period of 1 h.

3   *Buoyancy requirements*

A person in fresh water wearing either an immersion suit complying with the requirements of regulation 32, or an immersion suit with a lifejacket, shall be able to turn from a face-down to a face-up position in not more than 5 s.

Regulation 34

Thermal protective aids

1   A thermal protective aid shall be made of waterproof material having a thermal conductivity of not more than $0.25\,W/(m\cdot K)$ and shall be so constructed that, when used to enclose a person, it shall reduce both the convective and evaporative heat loss from the wearer's body.

2   The thermal protective aid shall:

.1   cover the whole body of a person wearing a lifejacket with the exception of the face. Hands shall also be covered unless permanently attached gloves are provided;

.2   be capable of being unpacked and easily donned without assistance in a survival craft or rescue boat;

.3   permit the wearer to remove it in the water in not more than 2 min, if it impairs ability to swim.

3   The thermal protective aid shall function properly throughout an air temperature range −30°C to +20°C.

SECTION III – VISUAL SIGNALS

Regulation 35

Rocket parachute flares

1   The rocket parachute flare shall:

.1   be contained in a water-resistant casing;

262

.2 have brief instructions or diagrams clearly illustrating the use of the rocket parachute flare printed on its casing;

.3 have integral means of ignition;

.4 be so designed as not to cause discomfort to the person holding the casing when used in accordance with the manufacturer's operating instructions.

2   The rocket shall, when fired vertically, reach an altitude of not less than 300 m. At or near the top of its trajectory, the rocket shall eject a parachute flare, which shall:

.1 burn with a bright red colour;

.2 burn uniformly with an average luminous intensity of not less than 30,000 cd;

.3 have a burning period of not less than 40 s;

.4 have a rate of descent of not more than 5 m/s;

.5 not damage its parachute or attachments while burning.

Regulation 36

Hand flares

1   The hand flare shall:

.1 be contained in a water-resistant casing;

.2 have brief instructions or diagrams clearly illustrating the use of the hand flare printed on its casing;

.3 have a self-contained means of ignition;

.4 be so designed as not to cause discomfort to the person holding the casing and not endanger the survival craft by burning or glowing residues when used in accordance with the manufacturer's operating instructions.

2   The hand flare shall:

.1 burn with a bright red colour;

.2 burn uniformly with an average luminous intensity of not less than 15,000 cd;

.3 have a burning period of not less than 1 min;

.4 continue to burn after having been immersed for a period of 10 s under 100 mm of water.

Regulation 37

Buoyant smoke signals

1 The buoyant smoke signal shall:

.1 be contained in a water-resistant casing;

.2 not ignite explosively when used in accordance with the manufacturer's operating instructions;

.3 have brief instructions or diagrams clearly illustrating the use of the buoyant smoke signal printed on its casing.

2 The buoyant smoke signal shall:

.1 emit smoke of a highly visible colour at a uniform rate for a period of not less than 3 min when floating in calm water;

.2 not emit any flame during the entire smoke emission time;

.3 not be swamped in a seaway;

.4 continue to emit smoke when submerged in water for a period of 10 s under 100 mm of water.

SECTION IV – SURVIVAL CRAFT

Regulation 38

General requirements for liferafts

1 *Construction of liferafts*

1.1 Every liferaft shall be so constructed as to be capable of withstanding exposure for 30 days afloat in all sea conditions.

1.2 The liferaft shall be so constructed that when it is dropped into the water from a height of 18 m, the liferaft and its equipment will operate satisfactorily. If the liferaft is to be stowed at a height of more than 18 m above the waterline in the lightest seagoing condition, it shall be of a type which has been satisfactorily drop-tested from at least that height.

1.3 The floating liferaft shall be capable of withstanding repeated jumps on to it from a height of at least 4.5 m above its floor both with and without the canopy erected.

1.4   The liferaft and its fittings shall be so constructed as to enable it to be towed at a speed of 3 knots in calm water when loaded with its full complement of persons and equipment and with one of its sea-anchors streamed.

1.5   The liferaft shall have a canopy to protect the occupants from exposure which is automatically set in place when the liferaft is launched and waterborne. The canopy shall comply with the following:

.1   it shall provide insulation against heat and cold by means of either two layers of material separated by an air gap or other equally efficient means. Means shall be provided to prevent accumulation of water in the air gap;

.2   its interior shall be of a colour that does not cause discomfort to the occupants;

.3   each entrance shall be clearly indicated and be provided with efficient adjustable closing arrangements which can be easily and quickly opened from inside and outside the liferaft so as to permit ventilation but exclude seawater, wind and cold. Liferafts accommodating more than eight persons shall have at least two diametrically opposite entrances;

.4   it shall admit sufficient air for the occupants at all times, even with the entrances closed;

.5   it shall be provided with at least one viewing port;

.6   it shall be provided with means for collecting rain water;

.7   it shall have sufficient headroom for sitting occupants under all parts of the canopy.

2   Minimum carrying capacity and mass of liferafts

2.1   No liferaft shall be approved which has a carrying capacity of less than six persons calculated in accordance with the requirements of regulation 39.3 or 40.3, as appropriate.

2.2   Unless the liferaft is to be launched by an approved launching appliance complying with the requirements of regulation 48 and is not required to be portable, the total mass of the liferaft, its container and its equipment shall not be more than 185 kg.

3   Liferaft fittings

3.1   Lifelines shall be securely becketed around the inside and outside of the liferaft.

3.2   The liferaft shall be provided with arrangements for adequately siting and securing in the operating position the antenna provided with the portable radio apparatus required by regulation 6.2.1.

3.3   The liferaft shall be fitted with an efficient painter of length equal to not less than twice the distance from the stowed position to the waterline in the lightest seagoing condition or 15 m whichever is the greater.

4   *Davit-launched liferafts*

4.1   In addition to the above requirements, a liferaft for use with an approved launching appliance shall:

   .1   when the liferaft is loaded with its full complement of persons and equipment, be capable of withstanding a lateral impact against the ship's side at an impact velocity of not less than 3.5 m/s and also a drop into the water from a height of not less than 3 m without damage that will affect its function;

   .2   be provided with means for bringing the liferaft alongside the embarkation deck and holding it securely during embarkation.

4.2   Every passenger ship davit-launched liferaft shall be so arranged that it can be rapidly boarded by its full complement of persons.

4.3   Every cargo ship davit-launched liferaft shall be so arranged that it can be boarded by its full complement of persons in not more than 3 min from the time the instruction to board is given.

5   *Equipment*

5.1   The normal equipment of every liferaft shall consist of:

   .1   one buoyant rescue quoit, attached to not less than 30 m of buoyant line;

   .2   one knife of the non-folding type having a buoyant handle and lanyard attached and stowed in a pocket on the exterior of the canopy near the point at which the painter is attached to the liferaft. In addition, a liferaft which is permitted to accommodate 13 persons or more shall be provided with a second knife which need not be of the non-folding type;

   .3   for a liferaft which is permitted to accommodate not more than 12 persons, one buoyant bailer. For a liferaft which is permitted to accommodate 13 persons or more, two buoyant bailers;

   .4   two sponges;

   .5   two sea-anchors each with a shock-resistant hawser and tripping line, one being spare and the other permanently attached to the liferaft in such a way that when the liferaft inflates or is waterborne it will cause the liferaft to lie oriented to the wind in the most stable manner. The strength of each sea-anchor and its hawser and tripping line shall be adequate for all sea conditions. The sea-anchors shall be fitted with a swivel at each end of the line and shall be of a type which is unlikely to turn inside-out between its shroud lines;

.6 two buoyant paddles;

.7 three tin-openers, safety knives containing special tin-opener blades are satisfactory for this requirement;

.8 one first-aid outfit in a waterproof case capable of being closed tightly after use;

.9 one whistle or equivalent sound signal;

.10 four rocket parachute flares complying with the requirements of regulation 35;

.11 six hand flares complying with the requirements of regulation 36;

.12 two buoyant smoke signals complying with the requirements of regulation 37;

.13 one waterproof electric torch suitable for Morse signalling together with one spare set of batteries and one spare bulb in a waterproof container;

.14 an efficient radar reflector;

.15 one daylight signalling mirror with instructions on its use for signalling to ships and aircraft;

.16 one copy of the life-saving signals referred to in regulation V/16 on a waterproof card or in a waterproof container;

.17 one set of fishing tackle;

.18 a food ration totalling not less than 10,000 kJ for each person the liferaft is permitted to accommodate; these rations shall be kept in airtight packaging and be stowed in a watertight container;

.19 watertight receptacles containing a total of 1.5 ℓ of fresh water for each person the liferaft is permitted to accommodate, of which 0.5 ℓ per person may be replaced by a de-salting apparatus capable of producing an equal amount of fresh water in 2 days;

.20 one rustproof graduated drinking vessel;

.21 six doses of anti-seasickness medicine and one seasickness bag for each person the liferaft is permitted to accommodate;

.22 instructions on how to survive;

.23 instructions for immediate action;

.24 thermal protective aids complying with the requirements of regulation 34 sufficient for 10% of the number of persons the liferaft is permitted to accommodate or two, whichever is the greater.

5.2 The marking required by regulations 39.7.3.5 and 40.7.7 on liferafts equipped in accordance with paragraph 5.1 shall be "SOLAS A PACK" in block capitals of the Roman alphabet.

5.3 In the case of passenger ships engaged on short international voyages of such a nature and duration that, in the opinion of the Administration, not all the items specified in paragraph 5.1 are necessary, the Administration may allow the liferafts carried on any such ships to be provided with the equipment specified in paragraphs 5.1.1 to 5.1.6 inclusive, 5.1.8, 5.1.9, 5.1.13 to 5.1.16 inclusive and 5.1.21 to 5.1.24 inclusive and one half of the equipment specified in paragraphs 5.1.10 to 5.1.12 inclusive. The marking required by regulations 39.7.3.5 and 40.7.7 on such liferaft shall be "SOLAS B PACK" in block capitals of the Roman alphabet.

5.4   Where appropriate the equipment shall be stowed in a container which, if it is not an integral part of, or permanently attached to, the liferaft, shall be stowed and secured inside the liferaft and be capable of floating in water for at least 30 min without damage to its contents.

6   *Float-free arrangements for liferafts*

6.1   *Painter system*

The liferaft painter system shall provide a connection between the ship and the liferaft and shall be so arranged as to ensure that the liferaft when released and, in the case of an inflatable liferaft, inflated is not dragged under by the sinking ship.

6.2   *Weak link*

If a weak link is used in the float-free arrangement, it shall:

.1   not be broken by the force required to pull the painter from the liferaft container;

.2   if applicable, be of sufficient strength to permit the inflation of the liferaft;

.3   break under a strain of 2.2 ± 0.4 kN.

6.3   *Hydrostatic release units*

If a hydrostatic release unit is used in the float-free arrangements, it shall:

.1   be constructed of compatible materials so as to prevent malfunction of the unit. Galvanizing or other forms of metallic coating on parts of the hydrostatic release unit shall not be accepted;

.2   automatically release the liferaft at a depth of not more than 4 m;

.3   have drains to prevent the accumulation of water in the hydrostatic chamber when the unit is in its normal position;

.4   be so constructed as to prevent release when seas wash over the unit;

.5   be permanently marked on its exterior with its type and serial number;

.6 be provided with a document or identification plate stating the date of manufacture, type and serial number;

.7 be such that each part connected to the painter system has a strength of not less than that required for the painter.

Regulation 39

Inflatable liferafts

1 Inflatable liferafts shall comply with the requirements of regulation 38 and, in addition, shall comply with the requirements of this regulation.

2 *Construction of inflatable liferafts*

2.1 The main buoyancy chamber shall be divided into not less than two separate compartments, each inflated through a nonreturn inflation valve on each compartment. The buoyancy chambers shall be so arranged that, in the event of any one of the compartments being damaged or failing to inflate, the intact compartments shall be able to support, with positive freeboard over the liferaft's entire periphery, the number of persons which the liferaft is permitted to accommodate, each having a mass of 75 kg and seated in their normal positions.

2.2 The floor of the liferaft shall be waterproof and shall be capable of being sufficiently insulated against cold either:

.1 by means of one or more compartments that the occupants can inflate, or which inflate automatically and can be deflated and reinflated by the occupants; or

.2 by other equally efficient means not dependent on inflation.

2.3 The liferaft shall be inflated with a non-toxic gas. Inflation shall be completed within a period of 1 min at an ambient temperature of between 18°C and 20°C and within a period of 3 min at an ambient temperature of −30°C. After inflation the liferaft shall maintain its form when loaded with its full complement of persons and equipment.

2.4 Each inflatable compartment shall be capable of withstanding a pressure equal to at least 3 times the working pressure and shall be prevented from reaching a pressure exceeding twice the working pressure either by means of relief valves or by a limited gas supply. Means shall be provided for fitting the topping-up pump or bellows required by paragraph 10.1.2 so that the working pressure can be maintained.

269

3   Carrying capacity of inflatable liferafts

The number of persons which a liferaft shall be permitted to accommodate shall be equal to the lesser of:

.1   the greatest whole number obtained by dividing by 0.096 the volume, measured in cubic metres of the main buoyancy tubes (which for this purpose shall include neither the arches nor the thwarts if fitted) when inflated; or

.2   the greatest whole number obtained by dividing by 0.372 the inner horizontal cross-sectional area of the liferaft measured in square metres (which for this purpose may include the thwart or thwarts, if fitted) measured to the innermost edge of the buoyancy tubes; or

.3   the number of persons having an average mass of 75 kg, all wearing lifejackets, that can be seated with sufficient comfort and headroom without interfering with the operation of any of the liferaft's equipment.

4   Access into inflatable liferafts

4.1   At least one entrance shall be fitted with a semi-rigid boarding ramp to enable persons to board the liferaft from the sea so arranged as to prevent significant deflation of the liferaft if the ramp is damaged. In the case of a davit-launched liferaft having more than one entrance, the boarding ramp shall be fitted at the entrance opposite the bowsing lines and embarkation facilities.

4.2   Entrances not provided with a boarding ramp shall have a boarding ladder, the lowest step of which shall be situated not less than 0.4 m below the liferaft's light waterline.

4.3   There shall be means inside the liferaft to assist persons to pull themselves into the liferaft from the ladder.

5   Stability of inflatable liferafts

5.1   Every inflatable liferaft shall be so constructed that, when fully inflated and floating with the canopy uppermost, it is stable in a seaway.

5.2   The stability of the liferaft when in the inverted position shall be such that it can be righted in a seaway and in calm water by one person.

5.3   The stability of the liferaft when loaded with its full complement of persons and equipment shall be such that it can be towed at speeds of up to 3 knots in calm water.

6 Inflatable liferaft fittings

6.1 The breaking strength of the painter system including its means of attachment to the liferaft, except the weak link required by regulation 38.6, shall be not less than 10.0 kN for a liferaft permitted to accommodate nine persons or more, and not less than 7.5 kN for any other liferaft. The liferaft shall be capable of being inflated by one person.

6.2 A manually controlled lamp visible on a dark night with a clear atmosphere at a distance of at least 2 miles for a period of not less than 12 h shall be fitted to the top of the liferaft canopy. If the light is a flashing light it shall flash at a rate of not less than 50 flashes per minute for the first 2 h of operation of the 12 h operating period. The lamp shall be powered by a sea-activated cell or a dry chemical cell and shall light automatically when the liferaft inflates. The cell shall be of a type that does not deteriorate due to damp or humidity in the stowed liferaft.

6.3 A manually controlled lamp shall be fitted inside the liferaft capable of continuous operation for a period of at least 12 h. It shall light automatically when the liferaft inflates and be of sufficient intensity to enable reading of survival and equipment instructions.

7 Containers for inflatable liferafts

7.1 The liferaft shall be packed in a container that is:

.1 so constructed as to withstand hard wear under conditions encountered at sea;

.2 of sufficient inherent buoyancy, when packed with the liferaft and its equipment, to pull the painter from within and to operate the inflation mechanism should the ship sink;

.3 as far as practicable watertight, except for drain holes in the container bottom.

7.2 The liferaft shall be packed in its container in such a way as to ensure, as far as possible, that the waterborne liferaft inflates in an upright position on breaking free from its container.

7.3 The container shall be marked with:

.1 maker's name or trade mark;

.2 serial number;

.3 name of approved authority and the number of persons it is permitted to carry;

.4 SOLAS;

.5 type of emergency pack enclosed;

.6 date when last serviced;

.7 length of painter;

.8 maximum permitted height of stowage above waterline (depending on drop-test height and length of painter);

.9 launching instructions.

8 *Markings on inflatable liferafts*

The liferaft shall be marked with:

.1 maker's name or trade mark;

.2 serial number;

.3 date of manufacture (month and year);

.4 name of approving authority;

.5 name and place of servicing station where it was last serviced;

.6 number of persons it is permitted to accommodate over each entrance in characters not less than 100 mm in height of a colour contrasting with that of the liferaft.

9 *Davit-launched inflatable liferafts*

9.1 In addition to complying with the above requirements, a liferaft for use with an approved launching appliance shall, when suspended from its lifting hook or bridle, withstand a load of:

.1 4 times the mass of its full complement of persons and equipment, at an ambient temperature and a stabilized liferaft temperature of $20 \pm 3°C$ with all relief valves inoperative; and

.2 1.1 times the mass of its full complement of persons and equipment at an ambient temperature and a stabilized liferaft temperature of $-30°C$ with all relief valves operative.

9.2 Rigid containers for liferafts to be launched by a launching appliance shall be so secured that the container or parts of it are prevented from falling into the sea during and after inflation and launching of the contained liferaft.

10 *Additional equipment for inflatable liferafts*

10.1 In addition to the equipment required by regulation 38.5, every inflatable liferaft shall be provided with:

.1 one repair outfit for repairing punctures in buoyancy compartments;

.2 one topping-up pump or bellows.

10.2 The knives required by regulation 38.5.1.2 shall be safety knives.

Regulation 40

Rigid liferafts

1   Rigid liferafts shall comply with the requirements of regulation 38 and, in addition, shall comply with the requirements of this regulation.

2   *Construction of rigid liferafts*

2.1   The buoyancy of the liferaft shall be provided by approved inherently buoyant material placed as near as possible to the periphery of the liferaft. The buoyant material shall be fire-retardant or be protected by a fire-retardant covering.

2.2   The floor of the liferaft shall prevent the ingress of water and shall effectively support the occupants out of the water and insulate them from cold.

3   *Carrying capacity of rigid liferafts*

The number of persons which a liferaft shall be permitted to accommodate shall be equal to the lesser of:

.1   the greatest whole number obtained by dividing by 0.096 the volume, measured in cubic metres of the buoyancy material multiplied by a factor of 1 minus the specific gravity of that material; or

.2   the greatest whole number obtained by dividing by 0.372 the horizontal cross-sectional area of the floor of the liferaft measured in square metres; or

.3   the number of persons having an average mass of 75 kg, all wearing lifejackets, that can be seated with sufficient comfort and headroom without interfering with the operation of any of the liferaft's equipment.

4   *Access into rigid liferafts*

4.1   At least one entrance shall be fitted with a rigid boarding ramp to enable persons to board the liferaft from the sea. In the case of a davit-launched liferaft having more than one entrance, the boarding ramp shall be fitted at the entrance opposite to the bowsing and embarkation facilities.

4.2   Entrances not provided with a boarding ramp shall have a boarding ladder, the lowest step of which shall be situated not less than 0.4 m below the liferaft's light waterline.

4.3   There shall be means inside the liferaft to assist persons to pull themselves into the liferaft from the ladder.

5 Stability of rigid liferafts

5.1 Unless the liferaft is capable of operating safely whichever way up it is floating, its strength and stability shall be such that it is either self-righting or can be readily righted in a seaway and in calm water by one person.

5.2 The stability of a liferaft when loaded with its full complement of persons and equipment shall be such that it can be towed at speeds of up to 3 knots in calm water.

6 Rigid liferaft fittings

6.1 The liferaft shall be fitted with an efficient painter. The breaking strength of the painter system, including its means of attachment to the liferaft, except the weak link required by regulation 38.6, shall be not less than 10.0 kN for liferafts permitted to accommodate nine persons or more, and not less than 7.5 kN for any other liferaft.

6.2 A manually controlled lamp visible on a dark night with a clear atmosphere at a distance of at least 2 miles for a period of not less than 12 h shall be fitted to the top of the liferaft canopy. If the light is a flashing light it shall flash at a rate of not less than 50 flashes per minute for the first 2 h of operation of the 12 h operating period. The lamp shall be powered by a sea-activated cell or a dry chemical cell and shall light automatically when the liferaft canopy is set in place. The cell shall be of a type that does not deteriorate due to damp or humidity in the stowed liferaft.

6.3 A manually controlled lamp shall be fitted inside the liferaft, capable of continuous operation for a period of at least 12 h. It shall light automatically when the canopy is set in place and be of sufficient intensity to enable reading of survival and equipment instructions.

7 Markings on rigid liferafts

The liferaft shall be marked with:

.1 name and port of registry of the ship to which it belongs;

.2 maker's name or trade mark;

.3 serial number;

.4 name of approving authority;

.5 number of persons it is permitted to accommodate over each entrance in characters not less than 100 mm in height of a colour contrasting with that of the liferaft;

.6 SOLAS;

.7 type of emergency pack enclosed;

.8 length of painter;

.9 maximum permitted height of stowage above waterline (drop-test height);

.10 launching instructions.

8   *Davit-launched rigid liferafts*

In addition to the above requirements, a rigid liferaft for use with an approved launching appliance shall, when suspended from its lifting hook or bridle, withstand a load of 4 times the mass of its full complement of persons and equipment.

Regulation 41

General requirements for lifeboats

1   *Construction of lifeboats*

1.1   All lifeboats shall be properly constructed and shall be of such form and proportions that they have ample stability in a seaway and sufficient freeboard when loaded with their full complement of persons and equipment. All lifeboats shall have rigid hulls and shall be capable of maintaining positive stability when in an upright position in calm water and loaded with their full complement of persons and equipment and holed in any one location below the waterline, assuming no loss of buoyancy material and no other damage.

1.2   All lifeboats shall be of sufficient strength to:

.1   enable them to be safely lowered into the water when loaded with their full complement of persons and equipment; and

.2   be capable of being launched and towed when the ship is making headway at a speed of 5 knots in calm water.

1.3   Hulls and rigid covers shall be fire-retardant or non-combustible.

1.4   Seating shall be provided on thwarts, benches or fixed chairs fitted as low as practicable in the lifeboat and constructed so as to be capable of supporting the number of persons each weighing 100 kg for which spaces are provided in compliance with the requirements of paragraph 2.2.2.

1.5   Each lifeboat shall be of sufficient strength to withstand a load, without residual deflection on removal of that load:

.1   in the case of boats with metal hulls, 1.25 times the total mass of the lifeboat when loaded with its full complement of persons and equipment; or

.2 in the case of other boats, twice the total mass of the lifeboat when loaded with its full complement of persons and equipment.

1.6 Each lifeboat shall be of sufficient strength to withstand, when loaded with its full complement of persons and equipment and with, where applicable, skates or fenders in position, a lateral impact against the ship's side at an impact velocity of at least 3.5 m/s and also a drop into the water from a height of at least 3 m.

1.7 The vertical distance between the floor surface and the interior of the enclosure or canopy over 50% of the floor area shall be:

.1 not less than 1.3 m for a lifeboat permitted to accommodate nine persons or less;

.2 not less than 1.7 m for a lifeboat permitted to accommodate 24 persons or more;

.3 not less than the distance as determined by linear interpolation between 1.3 m and 1.7 m for a lifeboat permitted to accommodate between nine and 24 persons.

2   *Carrying capacity of lifeboats*

2.1 No lifeboat shall be approved to accommodate more than 150 persons.

2.2 The number of persons which a lifeboat shall be permitted to accommodate shall be equal to the lesser of:

.1 the number of persons having an average mass of 75 kg, all wearing lifejackets, that can be seated in a normal position without interfering with the means of propulsion or the operation of any of the lifeboat's equipment; or

.2 the number of spaces that can be provided on the seating arrangements in accordance with figure 1. The shapes may be overlapped as shown, provided footrests are fitted and there is sufficient room for legs and the vertical separation between the upper and lower seat is not less than 350 mm.

2.3 Each seating position shall be clearly indicated in the lifeboat.

3   *Access into lifeboats*

3.1 Every passenger ship lifeboat shall be so arranged that it can be rapidly boarded by its full complement of persons. Rapid disembarkation shall also be possible.

3.2 Every cargo ship lifeboat shall be so arranged that it can be boarded

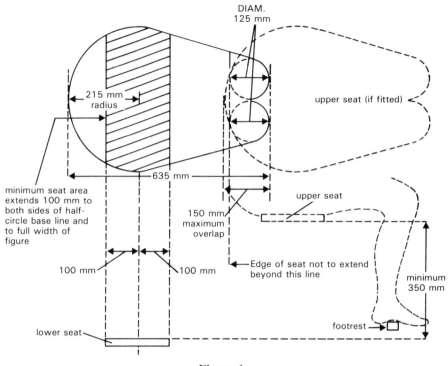

Figure 1

by its full complement of persons in not more than 3 min from the time the instruction to board is given. Rapid disembarkation shall also be possible.

3.3   Lifeboats shall have a boarding ladder that can be used on either side of the lifeboat to enable persons in the water to board the lifeboat. The lowest step of the ladder shall be not less than 0.4 m below the lifeboat's light waterline.

3.4   The lifeboat shall be so arranged that helpless people can be brought on board either from the sea or on stretchers.

3.5   All surfaces on which persons might walk shall have a non-skid finish.

4   *Lifeboat buoyancy*

All lifeboats shall have inherent buoyancy or shall be fitted with inherently buoyant material which shall not be adversely affected by seawater, oil or oil products, sufficient to float the lifeboat with all its equipment on board when flooded and open to the sea. Additional inherently buoyant material, equal to 280 N of buoyant force per person shall be provided for the number of persons the lifeboat is permitted to accommodate. Buoyant material, unless in addition to that required above, shall not be installed external to the hull of the lifeboat.

5 Lifeboat freeboard and stability

All lifeboats, when loaded with 50% of the number of persons the lifeboat is permitted to accommodate seated in their normal positions to one side of the centreline, shall have a freeboard, measured from the waterline to the lowest opening through which the lifeboat may become flooded, of at least 1.5% of the lifeboat's length or 100 mm, whichever is the greater.

6 Lifeboat propulsion

6.1 Every lifeboat shall be powered by a compression ignition engine. No engine shall be used for any lifeboat if its fuel has a flashpoint of 43°C or less (closed cup test).

6.2 The engine shall be provided with either a manual starting system, or a power starting system with two independent rechargeable energy sources. Any necessary starting aids shall also be provided. The engine starting systems and starting aids shall start the engine at an ambient temperature of −15°C within 2 min of commencing the start procedure unless, in the opinion of the Administration having regard to the particular voyages in which the ship carrying the lifeboat is constantly engaged, a different temperature is appropriate. The starting systems shall not be impeded by the engine casing, thwarts or other obstructions.

6.3 The engine shall be capable of operating for not less than 5 min after starting from cold with the lifeboat out of the water.

6.4 The engine shall be capable of operating when the lifeboat is flooded up to the centreline of the crankshaft.

6.5 The propeller shafting shall be so arranged that the propeller can be disengaged from the engine. Provision shall be made for ahead and astern propulsion of the lifeboat.

6.6 The exhaust pipe shall be so arranged as to prevent water from entering the engine in normal operation.

6.7 All lifeboats shall be designed with due regard to the safety of persons in the water and to the possibility of damage to the propulsion system by floating debris.

6.8 The speed of a lifeboat when proceeding ahead in calm water, when loaded with its full complement of persons and equipment and with all engine-powered auxiliary equipment in operation, shall be at least 6 knots and at least 2 knots when towing a 25-person liferaft loaded with its full complement of persons and equipment or its equivalent. Sufficient fuel, suitable for use throughout the temperature range expected in the area in which the ship operates, shall be provided to run the fully loaded lifeboat at 6 knots for a period of not less than 24 h.

6.9   The lifeboat engine, transmission and engine accessories shall be enclosed in a fire-retardant casing or other suitable arrangements providing similar protection. Such arrangements shall also protect persons from coming into accidental contact with hot or moving parts and protect the engine from exposure to weather and sea. Adequate means shall be provided to reduce the engine noise. Starter batteries shall be provided with casings which form a watertight enclosure around the bottom and sides of the batteries. The battery casings shall have a tight fitting top which provides for necessary gas venting.

6.10   The lifeboat engine and accessories shall be designed to limit electromagnetic emissions so that engine operation does not interfere with the operation of radio life-saving appliances used in the lifeboat.

6.11   Means shall be provided for recharging all enging-starting, radio and searchlight batteries. Radio batteries shall not be used to provide power for engine starting. Means shall be provided for recharging lifeboat batteries from the ship's power supply at a supply voltage not exceeding 55 V which can be disconnected at the lifeboat embarkation station.

6.12   Water-resistant instructions for starting and operating the engine shall be provided and mounted in a conspicuous place near the engine starting controls.

7   *Lifeboat fittings*

7.1   All lifeboats shall be provided with at least one drain valve fitted near the lowest point in the hull, which shall automatically open to drain water from the hull when the lifeboat is not waterborne and shall automatically close to prevent entry of water when the lifeboat is waterborne. Each drain valve shall be provided with a cap or plug to close the valve, which shall be attached to the lifeboat by a lanyard, a chain, or other suitable means. Drain valves shall be readily accessible from inside the lifeboat and their position shall be clearly indicated.

7.2   All lifeboats shall be provided with a rudder and tiller. When a wheel or other remote steering mechanism is also provided the tiller shall be capable of controlling the rudder in case of failure of the steering mechanism. The rudder shall be permanently attached to the lifeboat. The tiller shall be permanently installed on, or linked to, the rudder stock; however, if the lifeboat has a remote steering mechanism, the tiller may be removable and securely stowed near the rudder stock. The rudder and tiller shall be so arranged as not to be damaged by operation of the release mechanism or the propeller.

7.3 Except in the vicinity of the rudder and propeller, a buoyant lifeline shall be becketed around the outside of the lifeboat.

7.4 Lifeboats which are not self-righting when capsized shall have suitable handholds on the underside of the hull to enable persons to cling to the lifeboat. The handholds shall be fastened to the lifeboat in such a way that, when subjected to an impact sufficient to cause them to break away from the lifeboat, they break away without damaging the lifeboat.

7.5 All lifeboats shall be fitted with sufficient watertight lockers or compartments to provide for the storage of the small items of equipment, water and provisions required by paragraph 8. Means shall be provided for the storage of collected rainwater.

7.6 Every lifeboat to be launched by a fall or falls shall be fitted with a release mechanism complying with the following requirements:

.1 The mechanism shall be so arranged that all hooks are released simultaneously.

.2 The mechanism shall have two release capabilities as follows:

.2.1 a normal release capability which will release the lifeboat when it is waterborne or when there is no load on the hooks;

.2.2 an on-load release capability which will release the lifeboat with a load on the hooks. This release shall be so arranged as to release the lifeboat under any conditions of loading from no-load with the lifeboat waterborne to a load of 1.1 times the total mass of the lifeboat when loaded with its full complement of persons and equipment. This release capability shall be adequately protected against accidental or premature use.

.3 The release control shall be clearly marked in a colour that contrasts with its surroundings.

.4 The mechanism shall be designed with a factor of safety of 6 based on the ultimate strength of the materials used, assuming the mass of the lifeboat is equally distributed between the falls.

7.7 Every lifeboat shall be fitted with a release device to enable the forward painter to be released when under tension.

7.8 Every lifeboat shall be provided with a permanently installed earth connection and arrangements for adequately siting and securing in the operating position the antenna provided with the portable radio apparatus required by regulation 6.2.1.

7.9 Lifeboats intended for launching down the side of a ship shall have skates and fenders as necessary to facilitate launching and prevent damage to the lifeboat.

7.10 A manually controlled lamp visible on a dark night with a clear atmosphere at a distance of at least 2 miles for a period of not less than 12 h shall be fitted to the top of the cover or enclosure. If the light is a flashing light, it shall initially flash at a rate of not less than 50 flashes per minute over the first 2 h of operation of the 12 h operating period.

7.11 A lamp or source of light shall be fitted inside the lifeboat to provide illumination for not less than 12 h to enable reading of survival and equipment instructions; however, oil lamps shall not be permitted for this purpose.

7.12 Unless expressly provided otherwise, every lifeboat shall be provided with effective means of bailing or be automatically self-bailing.

7.13 Every lifeboat shall be so arranged that an adequate view forward, aft and to both sides is provided from the control and steering position for safe launching and manoeuvring.

8   *Lifeboat equipment*

All items of lifeboat equipment, whether required by this paragraph or elsewhere in this chapter, with the exception of boat-hooks which shall be kept free for fending off purposes, shall be secured within the lifeboat by lashings, storage in lockers or compartments, storage in brackets or similar mounting arrangements or other suitable means. The equipment shall be secured in such a manner as not to interfere with any abandonment procedures. All items of lifeboat equipment shall be as small and of as little mass as possible and shall be packed in a suitable and compact form. Except where otherwise stated, the normal equipment of every lifeboat shall consist of:

.1   sufficient buoyant oars to make headway in calm seas. Thole pins, crutches or equivalent arrangements shall be provided for each oar provided. Thole pins or crutches shall be attached to the boat by lanyards or chains;

.2   two boat-hooks;

.3   a buoyant bailer and two buckets;

.4   a survival manual;

.5   a binnacle containing an efficient compass which is luminous or provided with suitable means of illumination. In a totally enclosed lifeboat, the binnacle shall be permanently fitted at the steering position; in any other lifeboat, it shall be provided with suitable mounting arrangements;

.6   a sea-anchor of adequate size fitted with a shock-resistant hawser and a tripping line which provides a firm hand grip when wet. The strength of the sea-anchor, hawser and tripping line shall be adequate for all sea conditions;

.7   two efficient painters of a length equal to not less than twice the distance from the stowage position of the lifeboat to the waterline in the lightest seagoing condition or 15 m, whichever is the greater. One painter attached to the release device required by regulation 41.7.7 shall be placed at the forward end of the lifeboat and the other shall be firmly secured at or near the bow of the lifeboat ready for use;

.8 two hatchets, one at each end of the lifeboat;

.9 watertight receptacles containing a total of 3 *ℓ* of fresh water for each person the lifeboat is permitted to accommodate, of which 1 *ℓ* per person may be replaced by a de-salting apparatus capable of producing an equal amount of fresh water in 2 days;

.10 a rustproof dipper with lanyard;

.11 a rustproof graduated drinking vessel;

.12 a food ration totalling not less than 10,000 kJ for each person the lifeboat is permitted to accommodate; these rations shall be kept in airtight packaging and be stowed in a watertight container;

.13 four rocket parachute flares complying with the requirements of regulation 35;

.14 six hand flares complying with the requirements of regulation 36;

.15 two buoyant smoke signals complying with the requirements of regulation 37;

.16 one waterproof electric torch suitable for Morse signalling together with one spare set of batteries and one spare bulb in a waterproof container;

.17 one daylight signalling mirror with instructions for its use for signalling to ships and aircraft;

.18 one copy of the life-saving signals prescribed by regulation V/16 on a waterproof card or in a waterproof container;

.19 one whistle or equivalent sound signal;

.20 a first-aid outfit in a waterproof case capable of being closed tightly after use;

.21 six doses of anti-seasickness medicine and one seasickness bag for each person;

.22 a jack-knife to be kept attached to the boat by a lanyard;

.23 three tin-openers;

.24 two buoyant rescue quoits, attached to not less than 30 m of buoyant line;

.25 a manual pump;

.26 one set of fishing tackle;

.27 sufficient tools for minor adjustments to the engine and its accessories;

.28 portable fire-extinguishing equipment suitable for extinguishing oil fires;

.29 a searchlight capable of effectively illuminating a light-coloured object at night having a width of 18 m at a distance of 180 m for a total period of 6 h and of working for not less than 3 h continuously;

.30 an efficient radar reflector;

.31 thermal protective aids complying with the requirements of regulation 34 sufficient for 10% of the number of persons the lifeboat is permitted to accommodate or two, whichever is the greater.

.32 In the case of ships engaged on voyages of such a nature and duration that, in the opinion of the Administration, the items specified in paragraphs 8.12 and 8.26 are unnecessary, the Administration may allow these items to be dispensed with.

9   Lifeboat markings

9.1   The dimensions of the lifeboat and the number of persons which it is permitted to accommodate shall be marked on it in clear permanent characters.

9.2   The name and port of registry of the ship to which the lifeboat belongs shall be marked on each side of the lifeboat's bow in block capitals of the Roman alphabet.

9.3   Means of identifying the ship to which the lifeboat belongs and the number of the lifeboat shall be marked in such a way that they are visible from above.

Regulation 42

Partially enclosed lifeboats

1   Partially enclosed lifeboats shall comply with the requirements of regulation 41 and in addition shall comply with the requirements of this regulation.

2   Every partially enclosed lifeboat shall be provided with effective means of bailing or be automatically self-bailing.

3   Partially enclosed lifeboats shall be provided with permanently attached rigid covers extending over not less than 20% of the length of the lifeboat from the stem and not less than 20% of the length of the lifeboat from the aftermost part of the lifeboat. The lifeboat shall be fitted with a permanently attached foldable canopy which together with the rigid covers completely

encloses the occupants of the lifeboat in a weatherproof shelter and protects them from exposure. The canopy shall be so arranged that:

.1 it is provided with adequate rigid sections or battens to permit erection of the canopy;

.2 it can be easily erected by not more than two persons;

.3 it is insulated to protect the occupants against heat and cold by means of not less than two layers of material separated by an air gap or other equally efficient means; means shall be provided to prevent accumulation of water in their air gap;

.4 its exterior is of a highly visible colour and its interior is of a colour which does not cause discomfort to the occupants;

.5 it has entrances at both ends and on each side, provided with efficient adjustable closing arrangements which can be easily and quickly opened and closed from inside or outside so as to permit ventilation but exclude seawater, wind and cold; means shall be provided for holding the entrances securely in the open and closed position;

.6 with the entrances closed, it admits sufficient air for the occupants at all times;

.7 it has means for collecting rainwater;

.8 the occupants can escape in the event of the lifeboat capsizing.

4   The interior of the lifeboat shall be of a highly visible colour.

5   The radiotelegraph installation required by regulation 6.2.2 shall be installed in a cabin large enough to accommodate both the equipment and the person using it. No separate cabin is required if the construction of the lifeboat provides a sheltered space to the satisfaction of the Administration.

Regulation 43

Self-righting partially enclosed lifeboats

1   Self-righting partially enclosed lifeboats shall comply with the requirements of regulation 41 and in addition shall comply with the requirements of this regulation.

2   *Enclosure*

2.1   Permanently attached rigid covers shall be provided extending over not less than 20% of the length of the lifeboat from the stem and not less than 20% of the length of the lifeboat from the aftermost part of the lifeboat.

2.2   The rigid covers shall form two shelters. If the shelters have bulkheads they shall have openings of sufficient size to permit easy access by persons each wearing an immersion suit or warm clothes and a lifejacket. The interior height of the shelters shall be sufficient to permit persons easy access to their seats in the bow and stern of the lifeboat.

2.3   The rigid covers shall be so arranged that they include windows or translucent panels to admit sufficient daylight to the inside of the lifeboat with the openings or canopies closed so as to make artificial light unnecessary.

2.4   The rigid covers shall have railings to provide a secure handhold for persons moving about the exterior of the lifeboat.

2.5   Open parts of the lifeboat shall be fitted with a permanently attached foldable canopy so arranged that:

   .1   it can be easily erected by not more than two persons in not more than 2 min;

   .2   it is insulated to protect the occupants against cold by means of not less than two layers of material separated by an air gap or other equally efficient means.

2.6   The enclosure formed by the rigid covers and canopy shall be so arranged:

   .1   as to allow launching and recovery operations to be performed without any occupant having to leave the enclosure;

   .2   that it has entrances at both ends and on each side, provided with efficient adjustable closing arrangements which can be easily and quickly opened and closed from inside or outside so as to permit ventilation but exclude seawater, wind and cold; means shall be provided for holding the entrances securely in the open and in the closed position;

   .3   that with the canopy erected and all entrances closed, sufficient air is admitted for the occupants at all times;

   .4   that it has means for collecting rainwater;

   .5   that the exterior of the rigid covers and canopy and the interior of that part of the lifeboat covered by the canopy is of a highly visible colour. The interior of the shelters shall be of a colour which does not cause discomfort to the occupants;

   .6   that it is possible to row the lifeboat.

3   *Capsizing and re-righting*

3.1   A safety belt shall be fitted at each indicated seating position. The safety belt shall be so designed as to hold a person of a mass of 100 kg securely in place when the lifeboat is in a capsized position.

3.2   The stability of the lifeboat shall be such that it is inherently or automatically self-righting when loaded with its full or a partial complement of persons and equipment and the persons are secured with safety belts.

4   *Propulsion*

4.1   The engine and transmission shall be controlled from the helmsman's position.

4.2   The engine and engine installation shall be capable of running in any position during capsize and continue to run after the lifeboat returns to the upright or shall automatically stop on capsizing and be easily restarted after the lifeboat returns to the upright and the water has been drained from the lifeboat. The design of the fuel and lubricating systems shall prevent the loss of fuel and the loss of more than 250 ml of lubricating oil from the engine during capsize.

4.3   Air-cooled engines shall have a duct system to take in cooling air from, and exhaust it to, the outside of the lifeboat. Manually operated dampers shall be provided to enable cooling air to be taken in from, and exhausted to, the interior of the lifeboat.

5   *Construction and fendering*

5.1   Notwithstanding regulation 41.1.6, a self-righting partially enclosed lifeboat shall be so constructed and fendered as to ensure that the lifeboat renders protection against harmful accelerations resulting from an impact of the lifeboat, when loaded with its full complement of persons and equipment, against the ship's side at an impact velocity of not less than 3.5 m/s.

5.2   The lifeboat shall be automatically self-bailing.

Regulation 44

Totally enclosed lifeboats

1   Totally enclosed lifeboats shall comply with the requirements of regulation 41 and in addition shall comply with the requirements of this regulation.

2   *Enclosure*

Every totally enclosed lifeboat shall be provided with a rigid watertight enclosure which completely encloses the lifeboat. The enclosure shall be so arranged that:
   .1   it protects the occupants against heat and cold;

.2 access to the lifeboat is provided by hatches which can be closed to make the lifeboat watertight;

.3 hatches are positioned so as to allow launching and recovery operations to be performed without any occupant having to leave the enclosure;

.4 access hatches are capable of being opened and closed from both inside and outside and are equipped with means to hold them securely in open positions;

.5 it is possible to row the lifeboat;

.6 it is capable, when the lifeboat is in the capsized position with the hatches closed and without significant leakage, of supporting the entire mass of the lifeboat, including all equipment, machinery and its full complement of persons;

.7 it includes windows or translucent panels on both sides which admit sufficient daylight to the inside of the lifeboat with the hatches closed to make artificial light unnecessary;

.8 its exterior is of a highly visible colour and its interior of a colour which does not cause discomfort to the occupants;

.9 handrails provide a secure handhold for persons moving about the exterior of the lifeboat, and aid embarkation and disembarkation;

.10 persons have access to their seats from an entrance without having to climb over thwarts or other obstructions;

.11 the occupants are protected from the effects of dangerous subatmospheric pressures which might be created by the lifeboat's engine.

3   *Capsizing and re-righting*

3.1   A safety belt shall be fitted at each indicated seating position. The safety belt shall be designed to hold a person of a mass of 100 kg securely in place when the lifeboat is in a capsized position.

3.2   The stability of the lifeboat shall be such that it is inherently or automatically self-righting when loaded with its full or a partial complement of persons and equipment and all entrances and openings are closed watertight and the persons are secured with safety belts.

3.3   The lifeboat shall be capable of supporting its full complement of persons and equipment when the lifeboat is in the damaged condition prescribed in regulation 41.1.1 and its stability shall be such that in the event of capsizing, it will automatically attain a position that will provide an above-water escape for its occupants.

3.4   The design of all engine exhaust pipes, air ducts and other openings shall be such that water is excluded from the engine when the lifeboat capsizes and re-rights.

4 *Propulsion*

4.1 The engine and transmission shall be controlled from the helmsman's position.

4.2 The engine and engine installation shall be capable of running in any position during capsize and continue to run after the lifeboat returns to the upright or shall automatically stop on capsizing and be easily restarted after the lifeboat returns to the upright. The design of the fuel and lubricating systems shall prevent the loss of fuel and the loss of more than 250 ml of lubricating oil from the engine during capsize.

4.3 Air cooled engines shall have a duct system to take in cooling air from, and exhaust it to, the outside of the lifeboat. Manually operated dampers shall be provided to enable cooling air to be taken in from, and exhausted to, the interior of the lifeboat.

5 *Construction and fendering*

Notwithstanding regulation 41.1.6, a totally enclosed lifeboat shall be so constructed and fendered as to ensure that the lifeboat renders protection against harmful accelerations resulting from an impact of the lifeboat, when loaded with its full complement of persons and equipment, against the ship's side at an impact velocity of not less than 3.5 m/s.

6 *Free-fall lifeboats*

A lifeboat arranged for free-fall launching shall be so constructed that it is capable of rendering protection against harmful accelerations resulting from being launched, when loaded with its full complement of persons and equipment, from at least the maximum height at which it is designed to be stowed above the waterline with the ship in its lightest seagoing condition, under unfavourable conditions of trim of up to 10° and with the ship listed not less than 20° either way.

Regulation 45

Lifeboats with a self-contained air support system

In addition to complying with the requirements of regulations 41 and 44, a lifeboat with a self-contained air support system shall be so arranged that, when proceeding with all entrances and openings closed, the air in the lifeboat remains safe and breathable and the engine runs normally for a period of not less than 10 min. During this period the atmospheric pressure inside the lifeboat shall never fall below the outside atmospheric pressure nor shall it exceed it by more than 20 mbar. The system shall have visual indicators to indicate the pressure of the air supply at all times.

Regulation 46

Fire-protected lifeboats

1   In addition to complying with the requirements of regulations 41, 44 and 45, a fire-protected lifeboat when waterborne shall be capable of protecting the number of persons it is permitted to accommodate when subjected to a continuous oil fire that envelops the lifeboat for a period of not less than 8 min.

2   *Water spray system*

A lifeboat which has a water spray fire-protection system shall comply with the following:

.1   water for the system shall be drawn from the sea by a self-priming motor pump. It shall be possible to turn "on" and turn "off" the flow of water over the exterior of the lifeboat;

.2   the seawater intake shall be so arranged as to prevent the intake of flammable liquids from the sea surface;

.3   the system shall be arranged for flushing with fresh water and allowing complete drainage.

SECTION V – RESCUE BOATS

Regulation 47

Rescue boats

1   *General requirements*

1.1   Except as provided by this regulation, all rescue boats shall comply with the requirements of regulations 41.1 to 41.7.4 inclusive and 41.7.6, 41.7.7, 41.7.9, 41.7.12 and 41.9.

1.2   Rescue boats may be either of rigid or inflated construction or a combination of both and shall:

.1   be not less than 3.8 m and not more than 8.5 m in length;

.2   be capable of carrying at least five seated persons and a person lying down.

289

1.3 Rescue boats which are a combination of rigid and inflated construction shall comply with the appropriate requirements of this regulation to the satisfaction of the Administration.

1.4 Unless the rescue boat has adequate sheer, it shall be provided with a bow cover extending for not less than 15% of its length.

1.5 Rescue boats shall be capable of manoeuvring at speeds up to 6 knots and maintaining that speed for a period of at least 4 h.

1.6 Rescue boats shall have sufficient mobility and manoeuvrability in a seaway to enable persons to be retrieved from the water, marshal liferafts and tow the largest liferaft carried on the ship when loaded with its full complement of persons and equipment or its equivalent at a speed of at least 2 knots.

1.7 A rescue boat shall be fitted with an inboard engine or outboard motor. If it is fitted with an outboard motor, the rudder and tiller may form part of the engine. Notwithstanding the requirements of regulation 41.6.1, petrol-driven outboard engines with an approved fuel system may be fitted in rescue boats provided the fuel tanks are specially protected against fire and explosion.

1.8 Arrangements for towing shall be permanently fitted in rescue boats and shall be sufficiently strong to marshal or tow liferafts as required by paragraph 1.6.

1.9 Rescue boats shall be fitted with weathertight stowage for small items of equipment.

2 *Rescue boat equipment*

2.1 All items of rescue boat equipment, with the exception of boat-hooks which shall be kept free for fending off purposes, shall be secured within the rescue boat by lashings, storage in lockers or compartments, storage in brackets or similar mounting arrangements, or other suitable means. The equipment shall be secured in such a manner as not to interfere with any launching or recovery procedures. All items of rescue boat equipment shall be as small and of as little mass as possible and shall be packed in suitable and compact form.

2.2 The normal equipment of every rescue boat shall consist of:

.1 sufficient buoyant oars or paddles to make headway in calm seas. Thole pins, crutches or equivalent arrangements shall be provided for each oar. Thole pins or crutches shall be attached to the boat by lanyards or chains;

.2 a buoyant bailer;

.3 a binnacle containing an efficient compass which is luminous or provided with suitable means of illumination;

.4 a sea-anchor and tripping line with a hawser of adequate strength not less than 10 m in length;

.5 a painter of sufficient length and strength, attached to the release device complying with the requirements of regulation 41.7.7 and placed at the forward end of the rescue boat;

.6 one buoyant line, not less than 50 m in length, of sufficient strength to tow a liferaft as required by paragraph 1.6;

.7 one waterproof electric torch suitable for Morse signalling, together with one spare set of batteries and one spare bulb in a waterproof container;

.8 one whistle or equivalent sound signal;

.9 a first-aid outfit in a waterproof case capable of being closed tightly after use;

.10 two buoyant rescue quoits, attached to not less than 30 m of buoyant line;

.11 a searchlight capable of effectively illuminating a light-coloured object at night having a width of 18 m at a distance of 180 m for a total period of 6 h and of working for at least 3 h continuously;

.12 an efficient radar reflector;

.13 thermal protective aids complying with the requirements of regulation 34 sufficient for 10% of the number of persons the rescue boat is permitted to accommodate or two, whichever is the greater.

2.3   In addition to the equipment required by paragraph 2.2, the normal equipment of every rigid rescue boat shall include:

.1 a boat-hook;

.2 a bucket;

.3 a knife or hatchet.

2.4   In addition to the equipment required by paragraph 2.2 the normal equipment of every inflated rescue boat shall consist of:

.1 a buoyant safety knife;

.2 two sponges;

.3 an efficient manually operated bellows or pump;

.4 a repair kit in a suitable container for repairing punctures;

.5 a safety boat-hook.

3   *Additional requirements for inflated rescue boats*

3.1   The requirements of regulations 41.1.3 and 41.1.5 do not apply to inflated rescue boats.

3.2   An inflated rescue boat shall be constructed in such a way that, when suspended by its bridle or lifting hook:

.1   it is of sufficient strength and rigidity to enable it to be lowered and recovered with its full complement of persons and equipment;

.2   it is of sufficient strength to withstand a load of 4 times the mass of its full complement of persons and equipment at an ambient temperature of $20 \pm 3°C$ with all relief valves inoperative;

.3   it is of sufficient strength to withstand a load of 1.1 times the mass of its full complement of persons and equipment at an ambient temperature of $-30°C$, with all relief valves operative.

3.3   Inflated rescue boats shall be so constructed as to be capable of withstanding exposure:

.1   when stowed on an open deck on a ship at sea;

.2   for 30 days afloat in all sea conditions.

3.4   In addition to complying with the requirements of regulation 41.9, inflated rescue boats shall be marked with a serial number, the maker's name or trade mark and the date of manufacture.

3.5   The buoyancy of an inflated rescue boat shall be provided by either a single tube subdivided into at least five separate compartments of approximately equal volume or two separate tubes neither exceeding 60% of the total volume. The buoyancy tubes shall be so arranged that, in the event of any one of the compartments being damaged, the intact compartments shall be able to support the number of persons which the rescue boat is permitted to accommodate, each having a mass of 75 kg, when seated in their normal positions with positive freeboard over the rescue boat's entire periphery.

3.6   The buoyancy tubes forming the boundary of the inflated rescue boat shall on inflation provide a volume of not less than $0.17 \, m^3$ for each person the rescue boat is permitted to accommodate.

3.7   Each buoyancy compartment shall be fitted with a nonreturn valve for manual inflation and means for deflation. A safety relief valve shall also be fitted unless the Administration is satisfied that such an appliance is unnecessary.

3.8   Underneath the bottom and on vulnerable places on the outside of the inflated rescue boat, rubbing strips shall be provided to the satisfaction of the Administration.

3.9   Where a transom is fitted it shall not be inset by more than 20% of the overall length of the rescue boat.

3.10 Suitable patches shall be provided for securing the painters fore and aft and the becketed lifelines inside and outside the boat.

3.11 The inflated rescue boat shall be maintained at all times in a fully inflated condition.

SECTION VI – LAUNCHING AND EMBARKATION APPLIANCES

Regulation 48

Launching and embarkation appliances

1 *General requirements*

1.1 Each launching appliance together with all its lowering and recovery gear shall be so arranged that the fully equipped survival craft or rescue boat it serves can be safely lowered against a trim of up to 10° and a list of up to 20° either way:

.1 when boarded, as required by regulation 22 or 28, by its full complement of persons;

.2 without persons in the survival craft or rescue boat.

1.2 Notwithstanding the requirements of paragraph 1.1, lifeboat launching appliances for oil tankers, chemical tankers and gas carriers with a final angle of heel greater than 20° calculated in accordance with the International Convention for the Prevention of Pollution from Ships, 1973, as modified by the 1978 Protocol related thereto and the recommendations of the Organization*, as applicable, shall be capable of operating at the final angle of heel on the lower side of the ship.

1.3 A launching appliance shall not depend on any means other than gravity or stored mechanical power which is independent of the ship's power supplies to launch the survival craft or rescue boat it serves in the fully loaded and equipped condition and also in the light condition.

1.4 A launching mechanism shall be so arranged that it may be actuated by one person from a position on the ship's deck, and from a position within the survival craft or rescue boat; the survival craft shall be visible to the person on deck operating the launching mechanism.

---

* Reference is made to the damage stability requirements of the International Code for the Construction and Equipment of Ships Carrying Dangerous Chemicals in Bulk (IBC Code) adopted by the Maritime Safety Committee by resolution MSC.4(48) and the International Code for the Construction and Equipment of Ships carrying Liquefied Gases in Bulk (IGC Code) adopted by the Maritime Safety Committee by resolution MSC.5(48).

1.5 Each launching appliance shall be so constructed that a minimum amount of routine maintenance is necessary. All parts requiring regular maintenance by the ship's crew shall be readily accessible and easily maintained.

1.6 The winch brakes of a launching appliance shall be of sufficient strength to withstand:

    .1 a static test with a proof load of not less than 1.5 times the maximum working load; and

    .2 a dynamic test with a proof load of not less than 1.1 times the maximum working load at maximum lowering speed.

1.7 The launching appliance and its attachments other than winch brakes shall be of sufficient strength to withstand a static proof load on test of not less than 2.2 times the maximum working load.

1.8 Structural members and all blocks, falls, padeyes, links, fastenings and all other fittings used in connection with launching equipment shall be designed with not less than a minimum factor of safety on the basis of the maximum working load assigned and the ultimate strength of the material used for construction. A minimum factor of safety of 4.5 shall be applied to all davit and winch structural members, and a minimum factor of safety of 6 shall be applied to falls, suspension chains, links and blocks.

1.9 Each launching appliance shall, as far as practicable, remain effective under conditions of icing.

1.10 A lifeboat launching appliance shall be capable of recovering the lifeboat with its crew.

1.11 The arrangements of the launching appliance shall be such as to enable safe boarding of the survival craft in accordance with the requirements of regulations 38.4.2, 38.4.3, 41.3.1 and 41.3.2.

2 *Launching appliances using falls and a winch*

2.1 Falls shall be of rotation-resistant and corrosion-resistant steel wire rope.

2.2 In the case of a multiple drum winch, unless an efficient compensatory device is fitted, the falls shall be so arranged as to wind off the drums at the same rate when lowering, and to wind on to the drums evenly at the same rate when hoisting.

2.3 Every rescue boat launching appliance shall be fitted with a powered winch motor of such capacity that the rescue boat can be raised from the water with its full complement of persons and equipment.

2.4 An efficient hand gear shall be provided for recovery of each survival craft and rescue boat. Hand gear handles or wheels shall not be rotated by moving parts of the winch when the survival craft or rescue boat is being lowered or when it is being hoisted by power.

2.5 Where davit arms are recovered by power, safety devices shall be fitted which will automatically cut off the power before the davit arms reach the stops in order to avoid overstressing the falls or davits, unless the motor is designed to prevent such overstressing.

2.6 The speed at which the survival craft or rescue boat is lowered into the water shall be not less than that obtained from the formula:

$$S = 0.4 + (0.02 \times H)$$

where S = speed of lowering in metres per second

and H = height in metres from davit head to the waterline at the lightest seagoing condition.

2.7 The maximum lowering speed shall be established by the Administration having regard to the design of the survival craft or rescue boat, the protection of its occupants from excessive forces, and the strength of the launching arrangements taking into account inertia forces during an emergency stop. Means shall be incorporated in the appliance to ensure that this speed is not exceeded.

2.8 Every rescue boat launching appliance shall be capable of hoisting the rescue boat when loaded with its full rescue boat complement of persons and equipment at a rate of not less than 0.3 m/s.

2.9 Every launching appliance shall be fitted with brakes capable of stopping the descent of the survival craft or rescue boat and holding it securely when loaded with its full complement of persons and equipment; brake pads shall, where necessary, be protected from water and oil.

2.10 Manual brakes shall be so arranged that the brake is always applied unless the operator, or a mechanism activated by the operator, holds the brake control in the "off" position.

3   *Float-free launching*

Where a survival craft requires a launching appliance and is also designed to float free, the float-free release of the survival craft from its stowed position shall be automatic.

4   *Free-fall launching*

Every free-fall launching appliance using an inclined plane shall, in addition to complying with the applicable requirements of paragraph 1, also comply with the following requirements:

.1 The launching appliance shall be so arranged that excessive forces are not experienced by the occupants of the survival craft during launching.

.2 The launching appliance shall be a rigid structure with a ramp angle and length sufficient to ensure that the survival craft effectively clears the ship.

.3 The launching appliance shall be efficiently protected against corrosion and be so constructed as to prevent incendive friction or impact sparking during the launching of the survival craft.

5 Evacuation-slide launching and embarkation

Every evacuation-slide launching appliance shall, in addition to complying with the applicable requirements of paragraph 1, also comply with the following requirements:

.1 The evacuation slide shall be capable of being deployed by one person at the embarkation station.

.2 The evacuation slide shall be capable of being used in high winds and in a seaway.

6 Liferaft launching appliances

Every liferaft launching appliance shall comply with the requirements of paragraphs 1 and 2, except with regard to use of gravity for turning out the appliance, embarkation in the stowed position and recovery of the loaded liferaft. The launching appliance shall be so arranged as to prevent premature release during lowering and shall release the liferaft when waterborne.

7 Embarkation ladders

7.1 Handholds shall be provided to ensure a safe passage from the deck to the head of the ladder and vice versa.

7.2 The steps of the ladder shall be:

.1 made of hardwood, free from knots or other irregularities, smoothly machined and free from sharp edges and splinters, or of suitable material of equivalent properties;

.2 provided with an efficient non-slip surface either by longitudinal grooving or by the application of an approved non-slip coating;

.3 not less than 480 mm long, 115 mm wide and 25 mm in depth, excluding any non-slip surface or coating;

.4 equally spaced not less than 300 mm or more than 380 mm apart and secured in such a manner that they will remain horizontal.

7.3 The side ropes of the ladder shall consist of two uncovered manila ropes not less than 65 mm in circumference on each side. Each rope shall be continuous with no joints below the top step. Other materials may be used provided the dimensions, breaking strain, weathering, stretching and gripping properties are at least equivalent to those of manila rope. All rope ends shall be secured to prevent unravelling.

SECTION VII – OTHER LIFE-SAVING APPLIANCES

Regulation 49

Line-throwing appliances

1   Every line-throwing appliance shall:

.1   be capable of throwing a line with reasonable accuracy;

.2   include not less than four projectiles each capable of carrying the line at least 230 m in calm weather;

.3   include not less than four lines each having a breaking strength of not less than 2 kN;

.4   have brief instructions or diagrams clearly illustrating the use of the line-throwing appliance.

2   The rocket, in the case of a pistol-fired rocket, or the assembly, in the case of an integral rocket and line, shall be contained in a water-resistant casing. In addition, in the case of a pistol-fired rocket, the line and rockets together with the means of ignition shall be stowed in a container which provides protection from the weather.

Regulation 50

General emergency alarm system

The general emergency alarm system shall be capable of sounding the general emergency alarm signal consisting of seven or more short blasts followed by one long blast on the ship's whistle or siren and additionally on an electrically operated bell or klaxon or other equivalent warning system, which shall be powered from the ship's main supply and the emergency source of electrical power required by regulation II-1/42 or II-1/43, as appropriate.

The system shall be capable of operation from the navigating bridge and, except for the ship's whistle, also from other strategic points. The system shall be audible throughout all the accommodation and normal crew working spaces.

SECTION VIII – MISCELLANEOUS

Regulation 51

Training manual

The training manual, which may comprise several volumes, shall contain instructions and information, in easily understood terms illustrated wherever possible, on the life-saving appliances provided in the ship and on the best methods of survival. Any part of such information may be provided in the form of audio-visual aids in lieu of the manual. The following shall be explained in detail:

.1 donning of lifejackets and immersion suits, as appropriate;

.2 muster at the assigned stations;

.3 boarding, launching, and clearing the survival craft and rescue boats;

.4 method of launching from within the survival craft;

.5 release from launching appliances;

.6 methods and use of devices for protection in launching areas, where appropriate;

.7 illumination in launching areas;

.8 use of all survival equipment;

.9 use of all detection equipment;

.10 with the assistance of illustrations, the use of radio life-saving appliances;

.11 use of drogues;

.12 use of engine and accessories;

.13 recovery of survival craft and rescue boats including stowage and securing;

.14 hazards of exposure and the need for warm clothing;

.15 best use of the survival craft facilities in order to survive;

298

.16 methods of retrieval, including the use of helicopter rescue gear (slings, baskets, stretchers), breeches-buoy and shore life-saving apparatus and ship's line-throwing apparatus;

.17 all other functions contained in the muster list and emergency instructions;

.18 instructions for emergency repair of the life-saving appliances.

Regulation 52

Instructions for on-board maintenance

Instructions for on-board maintenance of life-saving appliances shall be easily understood, illustrated wherever possible, and, as appropriate, shall include the following for each appliance:

.1 a checklist for use when carrying out the inspections required by regulation 19.7;

.2 maintenance and repair instructions;

.3 schedule of periodic maintenance;

.4 diagram of lubrication points with the recommended lubricants;

.5 list of replaceable parts;

.6 list of sources of spare parts;

.7 log for records of inspections and maintenance.

Regulation 53

Muster list and emergency instructions

1   The muster list shall specify details of the general emergency alarm signal prescribed by regulation 50 and also action to be taken by crew and passengers when this alarm is sounded. The muster list shall also specify how the order to abandon ship will be given.

2   The muster list shall show the duties assigned to the different members of the crew including:

.1 closing of the watertight doors, fire doors, valves, scuppers, sidescuttles, skylights, portholes and other similar openings in the ship;

.2 equipping of the survival craft and other life-saving appliances;

.3   preparation and launching of survival craft;

.4   general preparations of other life-saving appliances;

.5   muster of passengers;

.6   use of communication equipment;

.7   manning of fire parties assigned to deal with fires;

.8   special duties assigned in respect of the use of fire-fighting equipment and installations.

3   The muster list shall specify which officers are assigned to ensure that life-saving and fire appliances are maintained in good condition and are ready for immediate use.

4   The muster list shall specify substitutes for key persons who may become disabled, taking into account that different emergencies may call for different actions.

5   The muster list shall show the duties assigned to members of the crew in relation to passengers in case of emergency. These duties shall include:

.1   warning the passengers;

.2   seeing that they are suitably clad and have donned their lifejackets correctly;

.3   assembling passengers at muster stations;

.4   keeping order in the passageways and on the stairways and generally controlling the movements of the passengers;

.5   ensuring that a supply of blankets is taken to the survival craft.

6   The muster list shall be prepared before the ship proceeds to sea. After the muster list has been prepared, if any change takes place in the crew which necessitates an alteration in the muster list, the master shall either revise the list or prepare a new list.

7   The format of the muster list used on passenger ships shall be approved.

Chapter IV

RADIOTELEGRAPHY AND RADIOTELEPHONY

Page

PART A – APPLICATION AND DEFINITIONS

1   Application 302
2   Terms and definitions 302
3   Radiotelegraph station 303
4   Radiotelephone station 303
4–1 VHF radiotelephone station 304
5   Exemptions from regulations 3 and 4 304

PART B — WATCHES

6   Watches – radiotelegraph 305
7   Watches – radiotelephone 307
8   Watches – VHF radiotelephone 307

PART C – TECHNICAL REQUIREMENTS

9   Radiotelegraph stations 308
10 Radiotelegraph installations 309
11 Radiotelegraph auto alarms............................. 315
12 Direction-finders..................................... 316
13 Radiotelegraph installation for lifeboats 318
14 Portable radio apparatus for survival craft........... 319
14–1 Survival craft emergency position-indicating radio beacons 320
14–2 Periodic inspection and testing of emergency position-indicating
      radio beacons.. 321
14–3 Two-way radiotelephone apparatus for survival craft 321
15 Radiotelephone stations............................... 322
16 Radiotelephone installations 322
17 VHF radiotelephone installation 325
18 Radiotelephone auto alarms 326

PART D – RADIO LOGS

19 Radio logs 327

PART A – APPLICATION AND DEFINITIONS

Regulation 1

Application

(a)   Unless expressly provided otherwise, this chapter applies to all ships to which the present regulations apply.

(b)   This chapter does not apply to ships to which present regulations would otherwise apply while such ships are being navigated within the Great Lakes of North America and their connecting and tributary waters as far east as the lower exit of the St. Lambert Lock at Montreal in the Province of Quebec, Canada.*

(c)   No provision in this chapter shall prevent the use by a ship or survival craft in distress of any means at its disposal to attract attention, make known its position and obtain help.

Regulation 2

Terms and definitions

For the purpose of this chapter the following terms shall have the meanings defined below. All other terms which are used in this chapter and which are also defined in the Radio Regulations shall have the same meanings as defined in those regulations:

(a)   *Radio regulations* means the Radio Regulations annexed to, or regarded as being annexed to, the most recent International Telecommunication Convention which may be in force at any time.

(b)   *Radiotelegraph auto alarm* means an automatic alarm receiving apparatus which responds to the radiotelegraph alarm signal and has been approved.

(c)   *Radiotelephone auto alarm* means an automatic alarm receiving apparatus which responds to the radiotelephone alarm signal and has been approved.

(d)   *Radiotelephone station*, *radiotelephone installation* and *watches – radio-*

---

* Such ships are subject to special requirements relative to radio for safety purposes, as contained in the relevant agreement between Canada and the United States of America.

302

telephone shall be considered as relating to the medium frequency band, unless expressly provided otherwise.

(e) *Radio officer* means a person holding at least a first or second class radiotelegraph operator's certificate, or a radiocommunication operator's general certificate for the maritime mobile service, complying with the provisions of the Radio Regulations, who is employed in the radiotelegraph station of a ship which is provided with such a station in compliance with the provisions of regulation 3 or regulation 4 of this chapter.

(f) *Radiotelephone operator* means a person holding an appropriate certificate complying with the provisions of the Radio Regulations.

(g) *Existing installation* means:

(i) an installation wholly installed on board a ship before the date on which the present convention enters into force irrespective of the date on which acceptance by the respective Administration takes effect; and

(ii) an installation part of which was installed on board a ship before the date of entry into force of the present convention and the rest of which consists either of parts installed in replacement of identical parts, or parts which comply with the requirements of this chapter.

(h) *New installation* means any installation which is not an existing installation.

(i) *Emergency position-indicating radio beacon* means a station in the mobile service the emissions of which are intended to facilitate search and rescue operations.

Regulation 3

Radiotelegraph station

Passenger ships irrespective of size and cargo ships of 1,600 tons gross tonnage and upwards, unless exempted under regulation 5 of this chapter, shall be fitted with a radiotelegraph station complying with the provisions of regulations 9 and 10 of this chapter.

Regulation 4

Radiotelephone station

Cargo ships of 300 tons gross tonnage and upwards but less than 1,600 tons gross tonnage, unless fitted with a radiotelegraph station complying with the provisions of regulations 9 and 10 of this chapter shall, provided they are not exempted under regulation 5 of this chapter, be fitted with a radiotelephone station complying with the provisions of regulations 15 and 16 of this chapter.

Regulation 4-1

VHF radiotelephone installation

(a)   Passenger ships irrespective of size and cargo ships of 300 tons gross tonnage and upwards shall be fitted with a VHF radiotelephone installation complying with the provisions of regulation 17.

(b)   The provisions of regulation 17 shall also apply for VHF radiotelephone installations required by a Contracting Government for all ships to which chapter V applies navigating in an area under its jurisdiction and for which a VHF radiotelephone installation is not made compulsory by paragraph (a).

Regulation 5

Exemptions from regulations 3 and 4

(a)   The Contracting Governments consider it highly desirable not to deviate from the application of regulations 3 and 4 of this chapter; nevertheless the Administration may grant to individual passenger or cargo ships exemptions of a partial or conditional nature, or complete exemption from the requirements of regulation 3 or regulation 4.

(b)   The exemptions permitted under paragraph (a) of this regulation shall be granted only to a ship engaged on a voyage where the maximum distance of the ship from the shore, the length of the voyage, the absence of general navigational hazards, and other conditions affecting safety are such as to render the full application of regulation 3 or regulation 4 of this chapter unreasonable or unnecessary. When deciding whether or not to grant exemptions to individual ships, Administrations shall have regard to the effect that exemptions may have upon the general efficiency of the distress service for the safety of all ships. Administrations should bear in mind the desirability of requiring ships which are exempted from the requirement of regulation 3 of this chapter to be fitted with a radiotelephone station which complies with the provisions of regulations 15 and 16 of this chapter as a condition of exemption.

(c)   Each Administration shall submit to the Organization as soon as possible after the first of January in each year a report showing all exemptions granted under paragraphs (a) and (b) of this regulation during the previous calendar year and giving the reasons for granting such exemptions.

PART B – WATCHES

Regulation 6

Watches – radiotelegraph

(a)   Each ship which in accordance with regulation 3 or regulation 4 of this chapter is fitted with a radiotelegraph station shall, while at sea, carry at least one radio officer and, if not fitted with a radiotelegraph auto alarm, shall, subject to the provisions of paragraph (d) of this regulation, listen continuously on the radiotelegraph distress frequency by means of a radio officer using headphones or a loudspeaker.

(b)   Each passenger ship which in accordance with regulation 3 of this chapter is fitted with a radiotelegraph station, if fitted with a radiotelegraph auto alarm, shall, subject to the provisions of paragraph (d) of this regulation, and while at sea, listen on the radiotelegraph distress frequency by means of a radio officer using headphones or a loudspeaker, as follows:

(i)   if carrying or certificated to carry 250 passengers or less, at least 8 hours' listening a day in the aggregate;

(ii)   if carrying or certificated to carry more than 250 passengers and engaged on a voyage exceeding 16 hours' duration between two consecutive ports, at least 16 hours' listening a day in the aggregate. In this case the ship shall carry at least two radio officers;

(iii)   if carrying or certificated to carry more than 250 passengers and engaged on a voyage of less than 16 hours' duration between two consecutive ports, at least 8 hours' listening a day in the aggregate.

(c)   (i)   Each cargo ship which in accordance with regulation 3 of this chapter is fitted with a radiotelegraph station, if fitted with a radiotelegraph auto alarm, shall, subject to the provisions of paragraph (d) of this regulation, and while at sea, listen on the radiotelegraph distress frequency by means of a radio officer using headphones or a loudspeaker, for at least 8 hours a day in the aggregate.

(ii)   Each cargo ship of 300 tons gross tonnage and upwards but less than 1,600 tons gross tonnage which is fitted with a radiotelegraph station as a consequence of regulation 4 of this chapter, if fitted with a radiotelegraph auto alarm shall, subject to the provisions of paragraph (d) of this regulation, and while at sea, listen on the radiotelegraph distress frequency by means of a radio officer using headphones or a loudspeaker, during such periods as may be determined by the Administration. Administrations shall, however, have regard to the desirability of requiring, whenever practicable, a listening watch of at least 8 hours a day in the aggregate.

(d) (i) During the period when a radio officer is required by this regulation to listen on the radiotelegraph distress frequency, the radio officer may discontinue such listening during the time when he is handling traffic on other frequencies, or performing other essential radio duties, but only if it is impracticable to listen by split headphones or loudspeaker. The listening watch shall always be maintained by a radio officer using headphones or a loudspeaker during the silence periods provided for by the Radio Regulations.

The term "essential radio duties" in this paragraph includes urgent repairs of:

(1) equipment for radiocommunication used for safety;

(2) radio navigational equipment by order of the master.

(ii) In addition to the provisions of subparagraph (i) of this paragraph, on ships other than multi-radio officer passenger ships, the radio officer may, in exceptional cases, i.e. when it is impractical to listen by split headphones or loudspeaker, discontinue listening by order of the master in order to carry out maintenance required to prevent imminent malfunction of:

– equipment for radiocommunication used for safety;
– radio navigational equipment;
– other electronic navigational equipment including its repair;

provided that:

(1) the radio officer, at the discretion of the Administration concerned, is appropriately qualified to perform these duties; and

(2) the ship is fitted with a receiving selector which meets the requirements of the Radio Regulations;

(3) the listening watch is always maintained by a radio officer using headphones or loudspeaker during the silence periods provided for by the Radio Regulations.

(e) In all ships fitted with a radiotelegraph auto alarm this radiotelegraph auto alarm shall, while the ship is at sea, be in operation whenever there is no listening being kept under paragraphs (b), (c) or (d) of this regulation and whenever practicable, during direction-finding operations.

(f) The listening periods provided for by this regulation, including those which are determined by the Administration, should be maintained preferably during periods prescribed for the radiotelegraph service by the Radio Regulations.

Regulation 7

Watches – radiotelephone

(a) Each ship which is fitted with a radiotelephone station in accordance with regulation 4 shall, for safety purposes while at sea, maintain continuous watch on the radiotelephone distress frequency in the place on board from which the ship is usually navigated, by use of a radiotelephone distress frequency watch receiver*, using a loudspeaker, a filtered loudspeaker or radiotelephone auto alarm.

(b) Each ship referred to in paragraph (a) shall carry qualified radiotelephone operators (who may be the master, an officer or a member of the crew) as follows:

(i) if of 300 tons gross tonnage and upwards but less than 500 tons gross tonnage, at least one operator;

(ii) if of 500 tons gross tonnage and upwards but less than 1,600 tons gross tonnage, at least two operators. If such a ship carries one radiotelephone operator exclusively employed for duties related to radiotelephony, a second operator is not obligatory.

(c) Each ship which in accordance with regulation 3 or regulation 4 is fitted with a radiotelegraph station shall, while at sea, maintain continuous watch on the radiotelephone distress frequency in a place to be determined by the Administration, by use of a radiotelephone distress frequency watch receiver, using a loudspeaker, a filtered loudspeaker or radiotelephone auto alarm.

Regulation 8

Watches – VHF radiotelephone

Each ship which is fitted with a VHF radiotelephone installation in accordance with regulation 4–1 shall at sea maintain a continuous listening watch on the navigating bridge:

(i) on 156.8 MHz (channel 16) when practicable;** or

(ii) for such periods and on such channels as may be required by the Contracting Government referred to in regulation 4–1(b).**

---

* Reference is made to the Recommendation on Operational Standards for Radiotelephone Watch Receivers adopted by the Organization by resolution A.383(X).

** Reference is made to the Performance Standards for VHF Multiple Watch Facilities adopted by the Organization by resolution A.524(13).

PART C – TECHNICAL REQUIREMENTS

Regulation 9

Radiotelegraph stations

(a)   The radiotelegraph station shall be so located that no harmful interference from extraneous mechanical or other noise will be caused to the proper reception of radio signals. The station shall be placed as high in the ship as is practicable, so that the greatest possible degree of safety may be secured.

(b)   The radiotelegraph operating room shall be of sufficient size and of adequate ventilation to enable the main and reserve radiotelegraph installations to be operated efficiently, and shall not be used for any purpose which will interfere with the operation of the radiotelegraph station.

(c)   The sleeping accommodation of at least one radio officer shall be situated as near as practicable to the radiotelegraph operating room. In new ships, this sleeping accommodation shall not be within the radiotelegraph operating room.

(d)   There shall be provided between the radiotelegraph operating room and the bridge and one other place, if any, from which the ship is navigated, an efficient two-way system for calling and voice communication which shall be independent of the main communication system on the ship.

(e)   The radiotelegraph installation shall be installed in such a position that it will be protected against the harmful effects of water or extremes of temperature. It shall be readily accessible both for immediate use in case of distress and for repair.

(f)   A reliable clock with a dial not less than 12.5 centimetres (5 inches) in diameter and a concentric seconds hand, the face of which is marked to indicate the silence periods prescribed for the radiotelegraph service by the Radio Regulations, shall be provided. It shall be securely mounted in the radiotelegraph operating room in such a position that the entire dial can be easily and accurately observed by the radio officer from the radiotelegraph operating position and from the position for testing the radiotelegraph auto alarm receiver.

(g)   A reliable emergency light shall be provided in the radiotelegraph operating room, consisting of an electric lamp permanently arranged so as to provide satisfactory illumination of the operating controls of the main and reserve radiotelegraph installations and of the clock required by paragraph (f) of this regulation. In new installations, this lamp shall, if supplied from the reserve source of energy required by subparagraph (a)(iii) of regulation 10

308

of this chapter, be controlled by two-way switches placed near the main entrance to the radiotelegraph operating room and at the radiotelegraph operating position, unless the layout of the radiotelegraph operating room does not warrant it. These switches shall be clearly labelled to indicate their purpose.

(h) Either an electric inspection lamp, operated from the reserve source of energy required by subparagraph (a)(iii) of regulation 10 of this chapter and provided with a flexible lead of adequate length, or a flashlight shall be provided and kept in the radiotelegraph operating room.

(i) The radiotelegraph station shall be provided with such spare parts, tools and testing equipment as will enable the radiotelegraph installation to be maintained in efficient working condition while at sea. The testing equipment shall include an instrument or instruments for measuring A.C. volts, D.C. volts and ohms.

(j) If a separate emergency radiotelegraph operating room is provided the requirements of paragraphs (d), (e), (f), (g) and (h) of this regulation shall apply to it.

Regulation 10

Radiotelegraph installations

(a) Except as otherwise expressly provided in this regulation:

(i) The radiotelegraph station shall include a main installation and reserve installation, electrically separate and electrically independent of each other.

(ii) The main installation shall include a main transmitter, main receiver, radiotelephone distress frequency watch receiver,* and main source of energy.

(iii) The reserve installation shall include a reserve transmitter, reserve receiver and reserve source of energy.

(iv) A main and a reserve antenna shall be provided and installed, provided that the Administration may except any ship from the provision of a reserve antenna if it is satisfied that the fitting of such an antenna is impracticable or unreasonable, but in such case a suitable spare antenna completely assembled for immediate installation shall be carried. In addition, sufficient antenna wire and insulators shall in all cases be provided to enable a suitable antenna to be erected. The main antenna, if suspended between supports liable to whipping, shall be suitably protected against breakage.

---

* Reference is made to the Recommendation on Operational Standards for Radiotelephone Watch Receivers adopted by the Organization by resolution A.383(X).

(b)   In installations on cargo ships (except those on cargo ships of 1,600 tons gross tonnage and upwards installed on or after 19 November 1952), if the main transmitter complies with all the requirements for the reserve transmitter, the latter is not obligatory.

(c)   (i)   The main and reserve transmitters shall be capable of being quickly connected with and tuned to the main antenna, and the reserve antenna if one is fitted.

(ii)   The main and reserve receivers shall be capable of being quickly connected with any antenna with which they are required to be used.

(d)   All parts of the reserve installation shall be placed as high in the ship as is practicable, so that the greatest possible degree of safety may be secured.

(e)   The main and reserve transmitters shall be capable of transmitting on the radiotelegraph distress frequency using a class of emission assigned by the Radio Regulations for that frequency. In addition, the main transmitter shall be capable of transmitting on at least two working frequencies in the authorized bands between 405 kHz and 535 kHz, using classes of emission assigned by the Radio Regulations for these frequencies. The reserve transmitter may consist of a ship's emergency transmitter, as defined in and limited in use by the Radio Regulations.

(f)   The main and reserve transmitters shall, if modulated emission is prescribed by the Radio Regulations, have a depth of modulation of not less than 70 per cent and a note frequency between 450 and 1,350 Hz.

(g–1) The main and reserve transmitters shall, when connected to the main antenna, have a minimum normal range as specified below, that is to say, they must be capable of transmitting clearly perceptible signals from ship to ship by day and under normal conditions and circumstances over the specified ranges.* (Clearly perceptible signals will normally be received if the R.M.S. value of the field strength at the receiver is at least 50 microvolts per metre.)

---

* In the absence of a direct measurement of the field strength the following data may be used as a guide for approximately determining the normal range:

A. In the case of antennae other than self-supporting types:

Normal range in miles	Metre-amperes[1]
200	128
175	102
150	76
125	58
100	45
75	34

[1] The product of the distance (in metres) from the highest part of the antenna to the deepest load waterline and the antenna current (in amperes).

	Minimum normal range in miles	
	Main transmitter	Reserve transmitter
All passenger ships and cargo ships of 1,600 tons gross tonnage and upwards	150	100
Cargo ships below 1,600 tons gross tonnage	100	75

(g–2) The radiotelegraph installation shall include facilities for radiotelephone transmission and reception on the radiotelephone distress frequency. This requirement may be fulfilled by including such facilities in the main or reserve installation or other installed equipment. The transmitter power and receiver sensitivity of the radiotelephony part of the installation shall comply with regulation 16(c)(i) and (f) respectively if that part is fitted after 1 September 1986. For installations fitted prior to that date, such transmitter power and receiver sensitivity shall be as determined by the Administration. The location and other conditions of the radiotelephony facilities required by this regulation shall be as determined by the Administration, except when they form part of the main or reserve radiotelegraph installation.

(h) (i) The main and reserve receivers shall be capable of receiving the radiotelegraph distress frequency and the classes of emission assigned by the Radio Regulations for that frequency.

The values given in the second column of the table correspond to an average value of the ratio

$$\frac{\text{effective antenna height}}{\text{maximum antenna height}} = 0.47$$

This ratio varies with local conditions of the antenna and may vary between about 0.3 and 0.7.

B. In the case of self-supporting transmitting antennae:

Normal range in miles	Metre-amperes[2]
200	305
175	215
150	150
125	110
100	85
75	55

[2] The product of the distance (in metres) from the highest part of the antenna to the deepest load waterline and the current (in amperes) measured at the base of the radiating portion of the antenna. The values given in the second column are based on the propagation curves given in CCIR Recommendation 368–2 and also the method, experimental results and calculations in CCIR Report 502–1 and Opinion 43–1. The necessary value of metre-amperes varies considerably with local conditions of the antenna.

311

(ii) In addition, the main receiver shall permit the reception of such of the frequencies and classes of emission used for the transmission of time signals, meteorological messages and such other communications relating to safety of navigation as may be considered necessary by the Administration.

(iii) The radiotelephone distress frequency watch receiver shall be preset to this frequency. It shall be provided with a filtering unit or a device to silence the loudspeaker if on the bridge in the absence of a radiotelephone alarm signal. The device shall be capable of being easily switched in and out and may be used when, in the opinion of the master, conditions are such that maintenance of the listening watch would interfere with the safe navigation of the ship.

(iv) (1) The radiotelephone transmitting facility required by paragraph (g–2) shall be fitted with an automatic device for generating the radiotelephone alarm signal,* so designed as to prevent actuation by mistake, and complying with the requirements of regulation 16(e). The device shall be capable of being taken out of operation at any time in order to permit the immediate transmission of a distress message. For installations fitted prior to 1 September 1986, the fitting of automatic devices for generating the radiotelephone alarm signal shall be as determined by the Administration.

(2) Arrangements shall be made to check periodically the proper functioning of the automatic device for generating the radiotelephone alarm signal on frequencies other than the radiotelephone distress frequency using a suitable artificial antenna. An exception shall be made for radiotelephone emergency equipment having only the radiotelephone distress frequency in which case a suitable artificial antenna shall be employed.

Note: While all reasonable steps shall be taken to maintain the apparatus in an efficient condition, malfunction of the radiotelephone transmitting facilities required by this regulation shall not be considered as making the ship unseaworthy or as a reason for delaying the ship in ports where repair facilities are not readily available.

(i) The main receiver shall have sufficient sensitivity to produce signals in headphones or by means of a loudspeaker when the receiver input is as low as 50 microvolts. The reserve receiver shall have sufficient sensitivity to produce such signals when the receiver input is as low as 100 microvolts.

---

* Reference is made to the Operational Standards for Radiotelephone Alarm Signal Generators adopted by the Organization by resolution A.421(XI).

(j)   There shall be available at all times, while the ship is at sea, a supply of electrical energy sufficient to operate the main installation over the normal range required by paragraph (g) of this regulation as well as for the purpose of charging any batteries forming part of the radiotelegraph station. The voltage of the supply for the main installation shall, in the case of new ships, be maintained within ±10 per cent of the rated voltage. In the case of existing ships, it shall be maintained as near the rated voltage as possible and, if practicable, within ±10 per cent.

(k)   The reserve installation shall be provided with a source of energy independent of the propelling power of the ship and of the ship's electrical system.

(l)   The reserve source of energy shall preferably consist of accumulator batteries, which may be charged from the ship's electrical system, and shall under all circumstances be capable of being put into operation rapidly and of operating the reserve transmitter and receiver for at least six hours continuously under normal working conditions besides any of the additional loads mentioned in paragraphs (m) and (n) of this regulation.*

(m)   The reserve source of energy shall be used to supply the reserve installation and the automatic alarm signal keying device specified in paragraph (r) of this regulation if it is electrically operated.

The reserve source of energy may also be used to supply:

(i)   the radiotelegraph auto alarm;

(ii)   the emergency light specified in paragraph (g) of regulation 9 of this chapter;

(iii)   the direction-finder;

(iv)   the VHF installation in accordance with the provisions of regulation 17(c);

(v)   the device for generating the radiotelephone alarm signal, if provided;

(vi)   any device, prescribed by the Radio Regulations, to permit changeover from transmission to reception and vice versa.

Subject to the provisions of paragraph (n) of this regulation, the reserve source of energy shall not be used other than for the purposes specified in this paragraph.

(n)   Notwithstanding the provisions of paragraph (m) of this regulation, the Administration may authorize the use in cargo ships of the reserve source

---

* For the purpose of determining the electrical load to be supplied by the reserve source of energy, the following formula is recommended as a guide:

½ of the transmitter current consumption with the key down (mark)
+ ½ of the transmitter current consumption with the key up (space)
+ current consumption of receiver and additional circuits connected to the reserve source of energy.

of energy for a small number of low-power emergency circuits which are wholly confined to the upper part of the ship, such as emergency lighting on the boat deck, on condition that these can be readily disconnected if necessary, and that the source of energy is of sufficient capacity to carry the additional load or loads.

(o)   The reserve source of energy and its switchboard shall be as high as practicable in the ship and readily accessible to the radio officer. The switchboard shall, wherever possible, be situated in a radio room; if it is not, it shall be capable of being illuminated.

(p)   While the ship is at sea, accumulator batteries, whether forming part of the main installation or reserve installation, shall be brought up to the normal fully-charged condition daily.

(q)   All steps shall be taken to eliminate so far as is possible the causes of, and to suppress, radio interference from electrical and other apparatus on board. If necessary, steps shall be taken to ensure that the antennae attached to broadcast receivers do not cause interference to the efficient or correct working of the radiotelegraph installation. Particular attention shall be paid to this requirement in the design of new ships.

(r)   In addition to a means for manually transmitting the radiotelegraph alarm signal, an automatic radiotelegraph alarm signal keying device shall be provided, capable of keying the main and the reserve transmitters so as to transmit the radiotelegraph alarm signal. The device shall be capable of being taken out of operation at any time in order to permit immediate manual operation of the transmitter. If electrically operated, this keying device shall be capable of operation from the reserve source of energy.

(s)   At sea, the reserve transmitter, if not used for communications, shall be tested daily using a suitable artificial antenna, and at least once during each voyage using the reserve antenna if installed. The reserve source of energy shall also be tested daily.

(t)   All equipment forming part of the radiotelegraph installation shall be reliable, and shall be so constructed that it is readily accessible for maintenance purposes.

(u)   Notwithstanding the provision of regulation 4 of this chapter, the Administration may, in the case of cargo ships of less than 1,600 tons gross tonnage, relax the full requirements of regulation 9 of this chapter and the present regulation, provided that the standard of the radiotelegraph station shall in no case fall below the equivalent of that prescribed under regulation 15 and regulation 16 of this chapter for radiotelephone stations, so far as applicable. In particular, in the case of cargo ships of 300 tons gross tonnage and upwards but less than 500 tons gross tonnage, the Administration need not require:

(i)   a reserve receiver;

314

(ii)   a reserve source of energy in existing installations;

(iii) protection of the main antenna against breakage by whipping;

(iv)   the means of communication between the radiotelegraph station and the bridge to be independent of the main communication system;

(v)   the range of the transmitter to be greater than 75 miles.

Regulation 11

Radiotelegraph auto alarms

(a)   Any radiotelegraph auto alarm installed after 26 May 1965 shall comply with the following minimum requirements:

(i)   In the absence of interference of any kind it shall be capable of being actuated, without manual adjustment, by any radiotelegraph alarm signal transmitted on the radiotelegraph distress frequency by any coast station, ship's emergency or survival craft transmitter operating in accordance with the Radio Regulations, provided that the strength of the signal at the receiver input is greater than 100 microvolts and less than 1 volt.

(ii)   In the absence of interference of any kind, it shall be actuated by either three or four consecutive dashes when the dashes vary in length from 3.5 to as near 6 seconds as possible and the spaces vary in length between 1.5 seconds and the lowest practicable value, preferably not greater than 10 milliseconds.

(iii) It shall not be actuated by atmospherics or by any signal other than the radiotelegraph alarm signal, provided that the received signals do not in fact constitute a signal falling within the tolerance limits indicated in subparagraph (ii) above.

(iv)   The selectivity of the radiotelegraph auto alarm shall be such as to provide a practically uniform sensitivity over a band extending not less than 4 kHz and not more than 8 kHz on each side of the radiotelegraph distress frequency and to provide outside this band a sensitivity which decreases as rapidly as possible in conformity with the best engineering practice.

(v)   If practicable, the radiotelegraph auto alarm shall, in the presence of atmospherics or interfering signals, automatically adjust itself so that within a reasonably short time it approaches the condition in which it can most readily distinguish the radiotelegraph alarm signal.

(vi)   When actuated by a radiotelegraph alarm signal, or in the event of failure of the apparatus, the radiotelegraph auto alarm shall

315

cause a continuous audible warning to be given in the radiotelegraph operating room, in the radio officer's sleeping accommodation and on the bridge. If practicable, warning shall also be given in the case of failure of any part of the whole alarm-receiving system. Only one switch for stopping the warning shall be provided and this shall be situated in the radiotelegraph operating room.

(vii) For the purpose of regularly testing the radiotelegraph auto alarm, the apparatus shall include a generator pre-tuned to the radiotelegraph distress frequency and a keying device by means of which a radiotelegraph alarm signal of the minimum strength indicated in subparagraph (i) above is produced. A means shall also be provided for attaching headphones for the purpose of listening to signals received on the radiotelegraph auto alarm.

(viii) The radiotelegraph auto alarm shall be capable of withstanding vibration, humidity and changes of temperature, equivalent to severe conditions experienced on board ships at sea, and shall continue to operate under such conditions.

(b) Before a new type of radiotelegraph auto alarm is approved, the Administration concerned shall be satisfied, by practical tests made under operating conditions equivalent to those obtaining in practice, that the apparatus complies with paragraph (a) of this regulation.

(c) In ships fitted with a radiotelegraph auto alarm, its efficiency shall be tested by a radio officer at least once every 24 hours while at sea. If it is not in working order, the radio officer shall report that fact to the master or officer on watch on the bridge.

(d) A radio officer shall periodically check the proper functioning of the radiotelegraph auto alarm receiver, with its normal antenna connected, by listening to signals and by comparing them with similar signals received on the radiotelegraph distress frequency on the main installation.

(e) As far as practicable, the radiotelegraph auto alarm, when connected to an antenna shall not affect the accuracy of the direction-finder.

Regulation 12

Direction-finders

(a)   (i)   The direction-finding apparatus required by regulation 12* of

_____

* Reference is made to the Recommendation on Performance Standards for Radio Direction-Finding Systems adopted by the Organization by resolution A.223(VII).

chapter V shall be efficient and capable of receiving signals with the minimum of receiver noise and of taking bearings from which the true bearing and direction may be determined.

(ii)   It shall be capable of receiving signals on the radiotelegraph frequencies assigned by the Radio Regulations for the purposes of distress and direction-finding and for maritime radio beacons.

(iii) In the absence of interference the direction-finding apparatus shall have a sensitivity sufficient to permit accurate bearings being taken on a signal having a field strength as low as 50 microvolts per metre.

(iv)   As far as is practicable, the direction-finding apparatus shall be so located that as little interference as possible from mechanical or other noise will be caused to the efficient determination of bearings.

(v)   As far as is practicable, the direction-finding antenna system shall be erected in such a manner that the efficient determination of bearings will be hindered as little as possible by the close proximity of other antennae, derricks, wire halyards or other large metal objects.

(vi)   An efficient two-way means of calling and voice communication shall be provided between the direction-finder and the bridge.

(vii) All direction-finders shall be calibrated to the satisfaction of the Administration on first installation. The calibration shall be verified by check bearings or by a further calibration whenever any changes are made in the position of any antennae or of any structures on deck which might affect appreciably the accuracy of the direction-finder. The calibration particulars shall be checked at yearly intervals, or as near thereto as possible. A record shall be kept of the calibrations and of any checks made of their accuracy.

(b)   (i)   Radio equipment for homing on the radiotelephone distress frequency shall be capable of taking direction-finding bearings on that frequency without ambiguity of sense within an arc of 30 degrees on either side of the bow.

(ii)   When installing and testing the equipment referred to in this paragraph due regard should be given to the relevant recommendation of the International Radio Consultative Committee (CCIR).

(iii) All reasonable steps shall be taken to ensure the homing capability required by this paragraph. In cases where due to technical difficulties the homing capability cannot be achieved, Administrations may grant to individual ships exemptions from the requirements of this paragraph.

317

Regulation 13

Radiotelegraph installation for lifeboats

(a)   The radiotelegraph installation required by regulation III/6.2.2 shall include a transmitter, a receiver and a source of energy. It shall be so designed that it can be used in an emergency by an unskilled person.

(b)   The transmitter shall be capable of transmitting on the radiotelegraph distress frequency using a class of emission assigned by the Radio Regulations for that frequency. The transmitter shall also be capable of transmitting on the frequency, and of using a class of emission, assigned by the Radio Regulations for use by survival craft in the bands between 4,000 kHz and 27,500 kHz.

(c)   The transmitter shall, if modulated emission is prescribed by the Radio Regulations, have a depth of modulation of not less than 70 per cent and a note frequency between 450 and 1,350 Hz.

(d)   In addition to a key for manual transmissions, the transmitter shall be fitted with an automatic keying device for the transmission of the radiotelegraph alarm and distress signals.

(e)   On the radiotelegraph distress frequency the transmitter shall have a minimum normal range (as specified in paragraph (g) of regulation 10 of this chapter) of 25 miles using the fixed antenna.*

(f)   The receiver shall be capable of receiving the radiotelegraph distress frequency and the classes of emission assigned by the Radio Regulations for that frequency.

(g)   The source of energy shall consist of an accumulator battery with sufficient capacity to supply the transmitter for four hours continuously under normal working conditions. If the battery is of a type that requires charging, means shall be available for charging it from the ship's power supply. In addition there shall be a means for charging it after the lifeboat has been launched.

(h)   When the power for the radiotelegraph installation and the searchlight required by regulation III/41.8.29 are drawn from the same battery, it shall have sufficient capacity to provide for the additional load of the searchlight.

(i)   A fixed-type antenna will be provided together with means for supporting it at the maximum practicable height. In addition an antenna supported by a kite or balloon shall be provided if practicable.

---

* In the absence of a measurement of the field strength, it may be assumed that this range will be obtained if the product of the height of the antenna above the waterline and the antenna current (R.M.S. value) is 10 metre amperes.

318

(j)   At sea a radio officer shall at weekly intervals test the transmitter using a suitable artificial antenna, and shall bring the battery up to full charge if it is of a type which requires charging.

Regulation 14

Portable radio apparatus for survival craft

(a)   The apparatus required by regulation III/6.2.1 shall include a transmitter, a receiver, an antenna and a source of energy. It shall be so designed that it can be used in an emergency by an unskilled person.

(b)   The apparatus shall be readily portable, watertight, capable of floating in seawater and capable of being dropped into the sea without damage. New equipment shall be as light-weight and compact as practicable and shall preferably be capable of use in both lifeboats and liferafts.

(c)   The transmitter shall be capable of transmitting on the radiotelegraph distress frequency using a class of emission assigned by the Radio Regulations for that frequency, and, in the bands between 4,000 kHz and 27,500 kHz, of transmitting on the radiotelegraph frequency, and of using a class of emission assigned by the Radio Regulations for survival craft. However, the Administration may permit the transmitter to be capable of transmitting on the radiotelephone distress frequency, and of using a class of emission assigned by the Radio Regulations for that frequency, as an alternative or in addition to transmission on the radiotelegraph frequency assigned by the Radio Regulations for survival craft in the bands between 4,000 kHz and 27,500 kHz.

(d)   The transmitter shall, if modulated emission is prescribed by the Radio Regulations, have a depth of modulation of not less than 70 per cent and in the case of radiotelegraph emission have a note frequency between 450 and 1,350 Hz.

(e)   In addition to a key for manual transmissions, the transmitter shall be fitted with an automatic keying device for the transmission of the radiotelegraph alarm and distress signals. If the transmitter is capable of transmitting on the radiotelephone distress frequency, it shall be fitted with an automatic device, complying with the requirements of paragraph (e) of regulation 16 of this chapter, for transmitting the radiotelephone alarm signal.

(f)   The receiver shall be capable of receiving the radiotelegraph distress frequency and the classes of emission assigned by the Radio Regulations for that frequency. If the transmitter is capable of transmitting on the radiotelephone distress frequency the receiver shall also be capable of receiving that frequency and a class of emission assigned by the Radio Regulations for that frequency.

(g)   The antenna shall be either self-supporting or capable of being supported by the mast of a lifeboat at the maximum practicable height. In addition it is desirable that an antenna supported by a kite or balloon shall be provided if practicable.

(h)   The transmitter shall supply an adequate radio frequency power* to the antenna required by paragraph (a) of this regulation and shall preferably derive its supply from a hand generator. If operated from a battery, the battery shall comply with conditions laid down by the Administration to ensure that it is of a durable type and is of adequate capacity.

(i)   At sea a radio officer or a radiotelephone operator, as appropriate, shall at weekly intervals test the transmitter, using a suitable artificial antenna and shall bring the battery up to full charge if it is of a type which requires charging.

(j)   For the purpose of this regulation, new equipment means equipment supplied to a ship after the date of entry into force of the present Convention.

Regulation 14-1

Survival craft emergency position-indicating radio beacons

(a)   Survival craft emergency position-indicating radio beacons required by regulation III/6.2.3 to be carried in survival craft shall provide transmissions to enable aircraft to locate the survival craft and may also provide transmissions for alerting purposes.

(b)   Survival craft emergency position-indicating radio beacons shall, at least, be capable of transmitting alternately or simultaneously signals complying with the relevant standards and recommended practices of the International Civil Aviation Organization (ICAO) on the frequencies 121.5 MHz and 243.0 MHz.

(c)   Survival craft emergency position-indicating radio beacons shall:

    (i)   be of a highly visible colour, so designed that they can be used by an unskilled person and so constructed that they may be easily tested and maintained. Batteries shall not require replacement at intervals of less than 12 months, taking into account testing arrangements;

---

* It may be assumed that the purposes of this regulation will be satisfied by the following performance:

At least 10 watts input to the anode of the final stage or a radio-frequency output of at least 2.0 watts (A2 emission) at 500 kHz into an artificial antenna having an effective resistance of 15 ohms and 100×10^{-12} farads capacitance in series. The depth of modulation shall be at least 70 per cent.

(ii) be watertight, capable of floating and being dropped into the water without damage from a height of at least 20 m;

(iii) be capable only of manual activation and de-activation;

(iv) be portable, lightweight, and compact;

(v) be provided with an indication that signals are being emitted;

(vi) derive their energy supply from a battery forming an integral part of the device and having sufficient capacity to operate the apparatus for a period of 48 h. The transmission may be intermittent. Determination of the duty cycle should take into account the probability of homing being properly carried out, the need to avoid congestion on the frequencies and the need to comply with the requirements of the International Civil Aviation Organization (ICAO); and

(vii) be tested and, if necessary, have their source of energy replaced at intervals not exceeding 12 months.

Regulation 14–2

Periodic inspection and testing of emergency position-indicating radio beacons

Emergency position-indicating radio beacons provided in accordance with regulation III/6.2.3 shall at intervals not exceeding 12 months be inspected, tested and, if necessary, have their source of energy replaced. However, in cases where it appears proper and reasonable, the Administration may extend this period to 17 months.

Regulation 14–3

Two-way radiotelephone apparatus for survival craft

(a) The apparatus required by regulation III/6.2.4 shall be so designed that it can be used in an emergency by an unskilled person.

(b) The apparatus shall be portable and capable of being used for on-board communications.

(c) The appparatus shall conform to the requirements laid down in the relevant Radio Regulations for equipment used in the maritime mobile service for on-board communications and shall be capable of operation on those channels specified by the Radio Regulations and as required by the Administration.

If the apparatus is operating in the VHF band, precautions shall be taken to prevent the inadvertent selection of VHF channel 16 on equipment capable of being operated on that frequency.

(d)   The apparatus shall be operated from a battery of adequate capacity to ensure 4 h operation with a duty cycle of 1:9.

(e)   While at sea, the equipment shall be maintained in satisfactory condition, and, whenever necessary, the battery shall be brought to the fully charged condition or replaced.

Regulation 15

Radiotelephone stations

(a)   The radiotelephone station shall be in the upper part of the ship and so located that it is sheltered to the greatest possible extent from noise which might impair the correct reception of messages and signals.

(b)   There shall be efficient communication between the radiotelephone station and the bridge.

(c)   A reliable clock shall be securely mounted in such a position that the entire dial can be easily observed from the radiotelephone operating position.

(d)   A reliable emergency light shall be provided, independent of the system which supplies the normal lighting of the radiotelephone installation, and permanently arranged so as to be capable of providing adequate illumination of the operating controls of the radiotelephone installation, of the clock required by paragraph (c) of this regulation and of the card of instructions required by paragraph (f).

(e)   Where a source of energy consists of a battery or batteries, the radiotele-phone station shall be provided with a means of assessing the charge condition.

(f)   A card of instructions giving a clear summary of the radiotelephone distress procedure shall be displayed in full view of the radiotelephone operating position.

Regulation 16

Radiotelephone installations

(a)   The radiotelephone installation shall include transmitting and receiving equipment, and appropriate sources of energy (referred to in the following paragraphs as "the transmitter", "the receiver", "the radiotelephone distress frequency watch receiver",* and "the source of energy" respectively).

(b)   The transmitter shall be capable of transmitting on the radiotelephone distress frequency and on at least one other frequency in the bands between 1,605 kHz and 2,850 kHz, using the classes of emission assigned by the Radio Regulations for these frequencies. In normal operation a double sideband transmission or a single sideband transmission with full carrier shall have a depth of modulation of at least 70 per cent at peak intensity. Modulation of a single sideband transmission with reduced or suppressed carrier shall be such that the intermodulation products shall not exceed the values given in the Radio Regulations.

(c)   (i)   In the case of cargo ships of 300 tons gross tonnage and upwards but less than 1,600 tons gross tonnage the transmitter shall have a minimum normal range of 150 miles, i.e. it shall be capable of transmitting clearly perceptible signals from ship to ship by day and under normal conditions and circumstances over this range.** (Clearly perceptible signals will normally be received if the R.M.S. value of the field strength produced at the receiver by an unmodulated carrier is at least 25 microvolts per metre for double sideband and single sideband full carrier emissions.)

(ii)   In the case of existing installations using double sideband emissions on cargo ships of 300 tons gross tonnage and upwards but less than 500 tons gross tonnage, the transmitter shall have a minimum normal range of at least 75 miles.

(d)   The transmitter shall be fitted with a device for generating the radiotelephone alarm signal by automatic means so designed as to prevent actuation by mistake. The device shall be capable of being taken out of operation at any time in order to permit the immediate transmission of a distress message. Arrangements shall be made to check periodically the proper functioning of the device on frequencies other than the radiotelephone distress frequency using a suitable artificial antenna.

(e)   The device required by paragraph (d) of this regulation shall comply with the following requirements.***

(i)   The tolerance of the frequency of each tone shall be ±1.5 per cent.

---

* Reference is made to the Recommendation on Operational Standards for Radiotelephone Watch Receivers adopted by the Organization by resolution A.383(X).

** In the absence of field strength measurements, it may be assumed that this range will be obtained by a power in the antenna of 15 watts (unmodulated carrier) with an antenna efficiency of 27 per cent for double sideband emissions or 60 watts peak envelope power for single sideband full carrier emissions when 100 per cent modulated by a single sinusoidal oscillation.

*** Reference is made to the Operational Standards for Radiotelephone Alarm signal Generators adopted by the Organization by resolution A.421(XI).

(ii)   The tolerance on the duration of each tone shall be ±50 milliseconds.

(iii)   The interval between successive tones shall not exceed 50 milliseconds.

(iv)   The ratio of the amplitude of the stronger tone to that of the weaker shall be within the range 1 to 1.2.

(f)   The receiver required by paragraph (a) of this regulation shall be capable of receiving the radiotelephone distress frequency and at least one other frequency available for maritime radiotelephone stations in the bands between 1,605 kHz and 2,850 kHz, using the classes of emission assigned by the Radio Regulations for these frequencies. In addition the receiver shall permit the reception of such other frequencies, using the classes of emission assigned by the Radio Regulations, as are used for the transmission by radiotelephony of meteorological messages and such other communications relating to the safety of navigation as may be considered necessary by the Administration. The receiver shall have sufficient sensitivity to produce signals by means of a loudspeaker when the receiver input is as low as 50 microvolts.

(g)   The radiotelephone distress frequency watch receiver shall be preset to this frequency. It shall be provided with a filtering unit or a device to silence the loudspeaker in the absence of a radiotelephone alarm signal. The device shall be capable of being easily switched in and out and may be used when, in the opinion of the master, conditions are such that maintenance of the listening watch would interfere with the safe navigation of the ship.

(h)   To permit rapid change-over from transmission to reception when manual switching is used, the control for the switching device shall, where practicable, be located on the microphone or the telephone handset.

(i)   While the ship is at sea, there shall be available at all times a main source of energy sufficient to operate the installation over the normal range required by paragraph (c) of this regulation. If batteries are provided they shall under all circumstances have sufficient capacity to operate the transmitter and receiver for at least six hours continuously under normal working conditions.* In installations in cargo ships of 500 tons gross tonnage and upwards but less than 1,600 tons gross tonnage made on or after 19 November 1952, a reserve source of energy shall be provided in the upper part of the ship unless the main source of energy is so situated.

---

* For the purpose of determining the electrical load to be supplied by batteries required to have six hours reserve capacity, the following formula is recommended as a guide:

$\frac{1}{2}$ of the current consumption necessary for speech transmission
+ current consumption of receiver
+ current consumption of all additional loads to which the batteries may supply energy in time of distress or emergency.

(j)   The reserve source of energy, if provided, may be used only to supply:

(i)   the radiotelephone installation;

(ii)   the emergency light required by paragraph (d) of regulation 15 of this chapter;

(iii)   the device required by paragraph (d) of this regulation, for generating the radiotelephone alarm signal; and

(iv)   the VHF installation in accordance with the provisions of regulation 17(c).

(k)   Notwithstanding the provisions of paragraph (j) of this regulation, the Administration may authorize the use of the reserve source of energy, if provided, for a direction-finder, if fitted, and for a number of low-power emergency circuits which are wholly confined to the upper part of the ship, such as emergency lighting on the boat deck, on condition that the additional loads can be readily disconnected, and that the source of energy is of sufficient capacity to carry them.

(l)   While at sea, any battery provided shall be kept charged so as to meet the requirements of paragraph (i) of this regulation.

(m)   An antenna shall be provided and installed and, if suspended between supports liable to whipping, shall in the case of cargo ships of 500 tons gross tonnage and upwards but less than 1,600 tons gross tonnage be protected against breakage. In addition, there shall be a spare antenna completely assembled for immediate replacement or, where this is not practicable, sufficient antenna wire and insulators to enable a spare antenna to be erected. The necessary tools to erect an antenna shall also be provided.

Regulation 17

VHF radiotelephone installation

(a)   The VHF radiotelephone installation shall be in the upper part of the ship complying with the provisions of this regulation and comprising a transmitter and receiver, a source of energy capable of actuating them at their rated power levels, and an antenna suitable for efficient radiating and receiving signals at the operating frequencies.

(b)   On board passenger ships irrespective of size and cargo ships of 500 tons gross tonnage and upwards it shall be possible to operate the VHF radiotelephone installation from a source of energy which is situated in the upper part of the ship and has sufficient capacity for at least six hours of operation.

(c)   The Administration may authorize the use of the reserve source of energy of the radiotelegraph installation or the radiotelephone installation respectively referred to in regulation 10(m) and regulation 16(j) to supply the VHF radiotelephone installation. In this case the reserve source of energy is required to be of a capacity sufficient to operate simultaneously the VHF radiotelephone installation and:

(i)   the reserve radiotelegraph transmitter and receiver for at least six hours unless a switching device is fitted to ensure alternate operation only; or

(ii)   the radiotelephone transmitter and receiver for at least six hours unless a switching device is fitted to ensure alternate operation only.

(d)   The VHF radiotelephone installation shall conform to the requirements laid down in the Radio Regulations for equipment used in the VHF maritime mobile radiotelephone service and shall be capable of operation on those channels specified by the Radio Regulations and as may be required by the Contracting Government referred to in regulation 4–1(b).*

(e)   The Contracting Government referred to in regulation 4–1(b) shall not require the transmitter R.F. carrier power output to be greater than 10 watts. The antenna shall, in so far as is practicable, have an unobstructed view in all directions.**

(f)   Control of the channels required for navigational safety shall be immediately available on the navigating bridge convenient to the conning position and, where necessary, facilities should be available to permit radiocommunications from the wings of the navigating bridge.

Regulation 18

Radiotelephone auto alarms

(a)   The radiotelephone auto alarm shall comply with the following minimum requirements:

(i)   the frequencies of maximum response of the tuned circuits, and other tone selecting devices, shall be subject to a tolerance of

---

* Reference is made to the Recommendation on Operational Standards for VHF Radiotelephone Installations adopted by the Organization by resolution A.385(X).

** For guidance purposes, it is assumed that each ship is fitted with a vertically polarized unity gain antenna at a nominal height of 9.15 m above water, a transmitter R.F. power output of 10 W and a receiver sensitivity of 2 μV across the input terminals for 20 dB signal-to-noise ratio.

±1.5 per cent in each instance; and the response shall not fall below 50 per cent of the maximum response for frequencies within 3 per cent of the frequency of maximum response;

(ii)　in the absence of noise and interference, the automatic receiving equipment shall be capable of operating from the alarm signal in a period of not less than four and not more than six seconds;

(iii)　the automatic receiving equipment shall respond to the alarm signal, under conditions of intermittent interference caused by atmospherics and powerful signals other than the alarm signal, preferably without any manual adjustment being required during any period of watch maintained by the equipment;

(iv)　the automatic receiving equipment shall not be actuated by atmospherics or by strong signals other than the alarm signal;

(v)　the automatic receiving equipment shall be effective beyond the range at which speech transmission is satisfactory;

(vi)　the automatic receiving equipment shall be capable of withstanding vibration, humidity, changes of temperature and variations in power supply voltage equivalent to the severe conditions experienced on board ships at sea, and shall continue to operate under such conditions;

(vii)　the automatic receiving equipment should, as far as practicable, give warning of faults that would prevent the apparatus from performing its normal functions during watch hours.

(b)　Before a new type of radiotelephone auto alarm is approved, the Administration concerned shall be satisfied by practical tests, made under operating conditions equivalent to those obtained in practice, that the apparatus complies with paragraph (a) of this regulation.

PART D – RADIO LOGS

Regulation 19

Radio logs

(a)　The radio log (diary of the radio service) required by the Radio Regulations for a ship which is fitted with a radiotelegraph station in accordance with regulation 3 or regulation 4 of this chapter shall be kept in the radiotelegraph operating room during the voyage. Every radio officer shall enter in

327

the log his name, the times at which he goes on and off watch, and all incidents connected with the radio service which occur during his watch which may appear to be of importance to safety of life at sea. In addition, there shall be entered in the log:

(i) the entries required by the Radio Regulations;

(ii) details of the maintenance, including a record of the charging of the batteries, in such forms as may be prescribed by the Administration;

(iii) a daily statement that the requirement of paragraph (p) of regulation 10 of this chapter has been fulfilled;

(iv) details of the tests of the reserve transmitter and reserve source of energy made under paragraph (s) of regulation 10 of this chapter;

(v) in ships fitted with a radiotelegraph auto alarm details of tests made under paragraph (c) of regulation 11 of this chapter;

(vi) details of the maintenance of the batteries, including a record of the charging (if applicable) required by paragraph (j) of regulation 13 of this chapter, and details of the tests required by that paragraph in respect of the transmitters fitted in lifeboats;

(vii) details of the maintenance of the batteries, including a record of the charging (if applicable) required by paragraph (i) of regulation 14 of this chapter, and details of the tests required by that paragraph in respect of portable radio apparatus for survival craft;

(viii) the time at which the listening watch was discontinued in accordance with paragraph (d) of regulation 6 of this chapter, together with the reason and the time at which the listening watch was resumed.

(b)   The radio log (diary of the radio service) required by the Radio Regulations for a ship which is fitted with a radiotelephone station in accordance with regulation 4 of this chapter shall be kept at the place where listening watch is maintained. Every qualified operator, and every master, officer or crew member carrying out a listening watch in accordance with regulation 7 of this chapter, shall enter in the log, with his name, the details of all incidents connected with the radio service which occur during his watch which may appear to be of importance to safety of life at sea. In addition, there shall be entered in the log:

(i) the details required by the Radio Regulations;

(ii) the time at which listening watch begins when the ship leaves port, and the time at which it ends when the ship reaches port;

(iii) the time at which listening watch is for any reason discontinued, together with the reason, and the time at which listening watch is resumed;

(iv)   details of the maintenance of the batteries (if provided), including a record of the charging required by paragraph (l) of regulation 16 of this chapter;

(v)   details of the maintenance of the batteries, including a record of the charging (if applicable) required by paragraph (i) of regulation 14 of this chapter, and details of the tests required by that paragraph in respect of portable radio apparatus for survival craft.

(c)   On each ship fitted with a VHF radiotelephone installation in accordance with regulation 4–1:

(i)   the entries required by the Radio Regulations shall be recorded in the radio log in accordance with the requirements of the Administration;

(ii)   a summary of all communications relating to distress, urgency and safety traffic shall be recorded in the ship's log.

(d)   Radio logs shall be available for inspection by the officers authorized by the Administration to make such inspection.

Chapter V

SAFETY OF NAVIGATION

		Page
1	Application	332
2	Danger messages	332
3	Information required in danger messages	332
4	Meteorological services	334
5	Ice patrol service	336
6	Ice patrol – management and cost	336
7	Speed near ice	337
8	Routeing	338
9	Misuse of distress signals	338
10	Distress messages – obligations and procedures	339
11	Signalling lamps	339
12	Shipborne navigational equipment	340
13	Manning	344
14	Aids to navigation	344
15	Search and rescue	344
16	Life-saving signals	345
17	Pilot ladders and mechanical pilot hoists	348
18	VHF radiotelephones	351
19	Use of the automatic pilot	351
19–1	Operation of steering gear	351
19–2	Steering gear – testing and drills	351
20	Nautical publications	353
21	International Code of Signals	353

Regulation 1

Application

This chapter, unless otherwise expressly provided in this chapter, applies to all ships on all voyages, except ships of war and ships solely navigating the Great Lakes of North America and their connecting and tributary waters as far east as the lower exit of the St. Lambert Lock at Montreal in the Province of Quebec, Canada.

Regulation 2

Danger messages

(a)   The master of every ship which meets with dangerous ice, a dangerous derelict, or any other direct danger to navigation, or a tropical storm, or encounters sub-freezing air temperatures associated with gale force winds causing severe ice accretion on superstructures, or winds of force 10 or above on the Beaufort scale for which no storm warning has been received, is bound to communicate the information by all the means at his disposal to ships in the vicinity, and also to the competent authorities at the first point on the coast with which he can communicate. The form in which the information is sent is not obligatory. It may be transmitted either in plain language (preferably English) or by means of the International Code of Signals. It should be broadcast to all ships in the vicinity and sent to the first point on the coast to which communication can be made, with a request that it be transmitted to the appropriate authorities.

(b)   Each Contracting Government will take all steps necessary to ensure that when intelligence of any of the dangers specified in paragraph (a) of this regulation is received, it will be promptly brought to the knowledge of those concerned and communicated to other interested Governments.

(c)   The transmission of messages respecting the dangers specified is free of cost to the ships concerned.

(d)   All radio messages issued under paragraph (a) of this regulation shall be preceded by the safety signal, using the procedure as prescribed by the Radio Regulations as defined in regulation 2 of chapter IV.

Regulation 3

Information required in danger messages

The following information is required in danger messages:

(a)   *Ice, derelicts and other direct dangers to navigation*

   (i)   The kind of ice, derelict or danger observed.

(ii)　The position of the ice, derelict or danger when last observed.

(iii)　The time and date (Greenwich Mean Time) when danger last observed.

(b)　*Tropical storms* (hurricanes in the West Indies, typhoons in the China Sea, cyclones in Indian waters, and storms of a similar nature in other regions)

(i)　A statement that a tropical storm has been encountered. This obligation should be interpreted in a broad spirit, and information transmitted whenever the master has good reason to believe that a tropical storm is developing or exists in his neighbourhood.

(ii)　Time, date (Greenwich Mean Time) and position of ship when the observation was taken.

(iii)　As much of the following information as is practicable should be included in the message:

– barometric pressure, preferably corrected (stating millibars, millimetres, or inches, and whether corrected or uncorrected);

– barometric tendency (the change in barometric pressure during the past three hours);

– true wind direction;

– wind force (Beaufort scale);

– state of the sea (smooth, moderate, rough, high);

– swell (slight, moderate, heavy) and the true direction from which it comes. Period or length of swell (short, average, long) would also be of value;

– true course and speed of ship.

(c)　*Subsequent observations*

When a master has reported a tropical or other dangerous storm, it is desirable but not obligatory, that further observations be made and transmitted hourly, if practicable, but in any case at intervals of not more than three hours, so long as the ship remains under the influence of the storm.

(d)　*Winds of force 10 or above on the Beaufort scale for which no storm warning has been received*

This is intended to deal with storms other than the tropical storms referred to in paragraph (b) of this regulation; when such a storm is encountered, the message should contain similar information to that listed under the paragraph but excluding the details concerning sea and swell.

(e)　*Sub-freezing air temperatures associated with gale force winds causing severe ice accretion on superstructures*

(i)　Time and date (Greenwich Mean Time).

(ii)　Air temperature.

(iii)   Sea temperature (if practicable).

(iv)   Wind force and direction.

Examples

Ice

TTT Ice. Large berg sighted in 4605 N., 4410 W., at 0800 GMT. May 15.

Derelicts

TTT Derelict. Observed derelict almost submerged in 4006 N., 1243 W., at 1630 GMT. April 21.

Danger to Navigation

TTT Navigation. Alpha lightship not on station. 1800 GMT. January 3.

Tropical Storm

TTT Storm. 0030 GMT. August 18. 2004 N., 11354 E. Barometer corrected 994 millibars, tendency down 6 millibars. Wind NW., force 9, heavy squalls. Heavy easterly swell. Course 067, 5 knots.

TTT Storm. Appearances indicate approach of hurricane. 1300 GMT. September 14. 2200 N., 7236 W. Barometer corrected 29.64 inches, tendency down .015 inches. Wind NE., force 8, frequent rain squalls. Course 035, 9 knots.

TTT Storm. Conditions indicate intense cyclone has formed. 0200 GMT. May 4. 1620 N., 9203 E. Barometer uncorrected 753 millimetres, tendency down 5 millimetres. Wind S. by W., force 5. Course 300, 8 knots.

TTT Storm. Typhoon to southeast. 0300 GMT. June 12. 1812 N., 12605 E. Barometer falling rapidly. Wind increasing from N.

TTT Storm. Wind force 11, no storm warning received. 0300 GMT. May 4. 4830 N., 30 W. Barometer corrected 983 millibars, tendency down 4 millibars. Wind SW., force 11 veering. Course 260, 6 knots.

Icing

TTT experiencing severe icing. 1400 GMT. March 2. 69 N., 10 W. Air temperature 18. Sea temperature 29. Wind NE., force 8.

Regulation 4

Meteorological services

(a)   The Contracting Governments undertake to encourage the collection of meteorological data by ships at sea and to arrange for their examination, dissemination and exchange in the manner most suitable for the purpose of aiding navigation. Administrations shall encourage the use of instruments of a high degree of accuracy, and shall facilitate the checking of such instruments upon request.

(b)   In particular, the Contracting Governments undertake to co-operate in carrying out, as far as practicable, the following meteorological arrangements:

(i)   To warn ships of gales, storms and tropical storms, both by the issue of radio messages and by the display of appropriate signals at coastal points.

(ii)   To issue daily, by radio, weather bulletins suitable for shipping, containing data of existing weather, waves and ice, forecasts and, when practicable, sufficient additional information to enable simple weather charts to be prepared at sea and also to encourage the transmission of suitable facsimile weather charts.

(iii)   To prepare and issue such publications as may be necessary for the efficient conduct of meteorological work at sea and to arrange, if practicable, for the publication and making available of daily weather charts for the information of departing ships.

(iv)   To arrange for selected ships to be equipped with tested instruments (such as a barometer, a barograph, a psychrometer, and suitable apparatus for measuring sea temperature) for use in this service, and to take meteorological observations at main standard times for surface synoptic observations (at least four times daily, whenever circumstances permit) and to encourage other ships to take observations in a modified form, particularly when in areas where shipping is sparse; these ships to transmit their observations by radio for the benefit of the various official meteorological services, repeating the information for the benefit of ships in the vicinity. When in the vicinity of a tropical storm, or of a suspected tropical storm, ships should be encouraged to take and transmit their observations at more frequent intervals whenever practicable, bearing in mind navigational preoccupations of ships' officers during storm conditions.

(v)   To arrange for the reception and transmission by coast radio stations of weather messages from and to ships. Ships which are unable to communicate direct with shore shall be encouraged to relay their weather messages through ocean weather ships or through other ships which are in contact with shore.

(vi)   To encourage all masters to inform ships in the vicinity and also shore stations whenever they experience a wind speed of 50 knots or more (force 10 on the Beaufort scale).

(vii)   To endeavour to obtain a uniform procedure in regard to the international meteorological services already specified, and, as far as is practicable, to conform to the technical regulations and recommendations made by the World Meteorological Organization, to which the Contracting Governments may refer for study and advice any meteorological question which may arise in carrying out the present Convention.

(c)   The information provided for in this regulation shall be furnished in form for transmission and transmitted in the order of priority prescribed by the Radio Regulations, and during transmission "to all stations" of meteorological information, forecasts and warnings, all ship stations must conform to the provisions of the Radio Regulations.

(d)   Forecasts, warnings, synoptic and other meteorological reports intended for ships shall be issued and disseminated by the national service in the best position to serve various zones and areas, in accordance with mutual arrangements made by the Contracting Governments concerned.

Regulation 5

Ice patrol service

(a)   The Contracting Governments undertake to continue an ice patrol and a service for study and observation of ice conditions in the North Atlantic. During the whole of the ice season the south-eastern, southern and south-western limits of the regions of icebergs in the vicinity of the Grand Banks of Newfoundland shall be guarded for the purpose of informing passing ships of the extent of this dangerous region; for the study of ice conditions in general; and for the purpose of affording assistance to ships and crews requiring aid within the limits of operation of the patrol ships. During the rest of the year the study and observation of ice conditions shall be maintained as advisable.

(b)   Ships and aircraft used for the ice patrol service and the study and observation of ice conditions may be assigned other duties by the managing Government, provided that such other duties do not interfere with their primary purpose or increase the cost of this service.

Regulation 6

Ice patrol — management and cost

(a)   The Government of the United States of America agrees to continue the management of the ice patrol service and the study and observation of ice conditions, including the dissemination of information received therefrom. The Contracting Governments specially interested in these services undertake to contribute to the expense of maintaining and operating these services; each contribution to be based upon the total gross tonnage of the vessels of each contributing Government passing through the regions of icebergs guarded by the ice patrol; in particular, each Contracting Government specially interested undertakes to contribute annually to the expense of maintaining and operating these services a sum determined by the ratio which the total gross tonnage of that Contracting Government's vessels passing during the ice season through the regions of icebergs guarded by the ice patrol bears to the combined total gross tonnage of the vessels of all contributing Governments passing during the ice season through the regions of icebergs guarded by the ice patrol. Non-contracting Governments specially interested may contribute to the expense of maintaining and operating these services on the same basis. The managing Government will furnish annually to each contributing Government a statement of the total cost of maintaining and operating the ice patrol and of the proportionate share of each contributing Government.

(b)   Each of the contributing Governments has the right to alter or discontinue its contribution, and other interested Governments may undertake to contribute to the expense. The contributing Government which avails itself of this right will continue responsible for its current contribution up to 1 September following the date of giving notice of intention to alter or discontinue its contribution. To take advantage of the said right it must give notice to the managing Government at least six months before the said 1 September.

(c)   If, at any time, the United States Government should desire to discontinue these services, or if one of the contributing Governments should express a wish to relinquish responsibility for its pecuniary contribution, or to have its contribution altered, or another Contracting Government should desire to undertake to contribute to the expense, the contributing Governments shall settle the question in accordance with their mutual interests.

(d)   The contributing Governments shall have the right by common consent to make from time to time such alterations in the provisions of this regulation and of regulation 5 of this chapter as appear desirable.

(e)   Where this regulation provides that a measure may be taken after agreement among the contributing Governments, proposals made by any Contracting Government for effecting such a measure shall be communicated to the managing Government which shall approach the other contributing Governments with a view to ascertaining whether they accept such proposals, and the results of the enquiries thus made shall be sent to the other contributing Governments and the Contracting Government making the proposals. In particular, the arrangements relating to contributions to the cost of the services shall be reviewed by the contributing Governments at intervals not exceeding three years. The managing Government shall initiate the action necessary to this end.

Regulation 7

Speed near ice

When ice is reported on or near his course the master of every ship at night is bound to proceed at a moderate speed or to alter his course so as to go well clear of the danger zone.

Regulation 8

Routeing

(a)   The practice of following, particularly in converging areas, routes adopted for the purpose of separation of traffic including avoidance of passage through areas designated as areas to be avoided by ships or certain classes of ships, or for the purpose of avoiding unsafe conditions, has contributed to the safety of navigation and is recommended for use by all ships concerned.

(b)   The Organization is recognized as the only international body for establishing and adopting measures on an international level concerning routeing and areas to be avoided by ships or certain classes of ships. It will collate and disseminate to Contracting Governments all relevant information.*

(c)   The selection of the routes and the initiation of action with regard to them, and the delineation of what constitutes converging areas, will be primarily the responsibility of the Governments concerned. In the development of routeing schemes which impinge upon international waters, or such other schemes they may wish adopted by the Organization, they will give due consideration to relevant information published by the Organization.

(d)   Contracting Governments will use their influence to secure the appropriate use of adopted routes and will do everything in their power to ensure adherence to the measures adopted by the Organization in connection with routeing of ships.

(e)   Contracting Governments will also induce all ships proceeding on voyages in the vicinity of the Grand Banks of Newfoundland to avoid, as far as practicable, the fishing banks of Newfoundland north of latitude 43° N and to pass outside regions known or believed to be endangered by ice.

Regulation 9

Misuse of distress signals

The use of an international distress signal, except for the purpose of indicating that a ship or aircraft is in distress, and the use of any signal which may be confused with an international distress signal, are prohibited on every ship or aircraft.

---

* Reference is made to the current edition of Ships' Routeing published by the Organization.

Regulation 10

Distress messages – obligations and procedures

(a)   The master of a ship at sea, on receiving a signal from any source that a ship or aircraft or survival craft thereof is in distress, is bound to proceed with all speed to the assistance of the persons in distress informing them if possible that he is doing so. If he is unable or, in the special circumstances of the case, considers it unreasonable or unnecessary to proceed to their assistance, he must enter in the log-book the reason for failing to proceed to the assistance of the persons in distress.

(b)   The master of a ship in distress, after consultation, so far as may be possible, with the masters of the ships which answer his call for assistance, has the right to requisition such one or more of those ships as he considers best able to render assistance, and it shall be the duty of the master or masters of the ship or ships requisitioned to comply with the requisition by continuing to proceed with all speed to the assistance of persons in distress.

(c)   The master of a ship shall be released from the obligation imposed by paragraph (a) of this regulation when he learns that one or more ships other than his own have been requisitioned and are complying with the requisition.

(d)   The master of a ship shall be released from the obligation imposed by paragraph (a) of this regulation, and, if his ship has been requisitioned, from the obligation imposed by paragraph (b) of this regulation, if he is informed by the persons in distress or by the master of another ship which has reached such persons that assistance is no longer necessary.

(e)   The provisions of this regulation do not prejudice the Convention for the unification of certain rules of law relating to Assistance and Salvage at Sea, signed at Brussels on 23 September 1910, particularly the obligation to render assistance imposed by article 11 of that Convention.

Regulation 11

Signalling lamps

All ships of over 150 tons gross tonnage, when engaged on international voyages, shall have on board an efficient daylight signalling lamp which shall not be solely dependent upon the ship's main source of electrical power.

Regulation 12

Shipborne navigational equipment

(a)   For the purpose of this regulation "constructed" in respect of a ship means a stage of construction where:

   (i)   the keel is laid; or

   (ii)   construction identifiable with a specific ship begins; or

   (iii)   assembly of that ship has commenced comprising at least 50 tonnes or 1 per cent of the estimated mass of all structural material, whichever is less.

(b)   (i)   Ships of 150 tons gross tonnage and upwards shall be fitted with:

      (1)   a standard magnetic compass, except as provided in subparagraph (iv);

      (2)   a steering magnetic compass, unless heading information provided by the standard compass required under (1) is made available and is clearly readable by the helmsman at the main steering position;

      (3)   adequate means of communication between the standard compass position and the normal navigation control position to the satisfaction of the Administration; and

      (4)   means for taking bearings as nearly as practicable over an arc of the horizon of 360°.

   (ii)   Each magnetic compass referred to in subparagraph (i) shall be properly adjusted and its table or curve of residual deviations shall be available at all times.

   (iii)   A spare magnetic compass, interchangeable with the standard compass, shall be carried, unless the steering compass mentioned in subparagraph (i)(2) or a gyro-compass is fitted.

   (iv)   The Administration, if it considers it unreasonable or unnecessary to require a standard magnetic compass, may exempt individual ships or classes of ships from these requirements if the nature of the voyage, the ship's proximity to land or the type of ship does not warrant a standard compass, provided that a suitable steering compass is in all cases carried.

(c)   Ships of less than 150 tons gross tonnage shall, as far as the Administration considers it reasonable and practicable, be fitted with a steering compass and have means for taking bearings.

(d)   Ships of 500 tons gross tonnage and upwards constructed on or after 1 September 1984 shall be fitted with a gyro-compass complying with the following requirements:

(i)   the master gyro-compass or a gyro repeater shall be clearly readable by the helmsman at the main steering position;

(ii) on ships of 1,600 tons gross tonnage and upwards a gyro repeater or gyro repeaters shall be provided and shall be suitably placed for taking bearings as nearly as practicable over an arc of the horizon of 360°.

(e)   Ships of 1,600 tons gross tonnage and upwards, constructed before 1 September 1984 when engaged on international voyages, shall be fitted with a gyro-compass complying with the requirements of paragraph (d).

(f)   On ships provided with emergency steering positions, arrangements shall be made to supply heading information to such positions.

(g)   Ships of 500 tons gross tonnage and upwards constructed on or after 1 September 1984 and ships of 1,600 tons gross tonnage and upwards constructed before 1 September 1984 shall be fitted with a radar installation.

(h)   Ships of 10,000 tons gross tonnage and upwards shall be fitted with two radar installations, each capable of being operated independently* of the other.

(i)   Facilities for plotting radar readings shall be provided on the navigating bridge of ships required by paragraph (g) or (h) to be fitted with a radar installation. In ships of 1,600 tons gross tonnage and upwards constructed on or after 1 September 1984 the plotting facilities shall be at least as effective as a reflection plotter.

(j)   (i)   An automatic radar plotting aid shall be fitted on:

(1)   ships of 10,000 tons gross tonnage and upwards, constructed on or after 1 September 1984;

(2)   tankers constructed before 1 September 1984 as follows:

(aa) if of 40,000 tons gross tonnage and upwards by 1 January 1985;

(bb) if of 10,000 tons gross tonnage and upwards but less than 40,000 tons gross tonnage, by 1 January 1986;

(3)   ships constructed before 1 September 1984, that are not tankers, as follows:

(aa) if of 40,000 tons gross tonnage and upwards by 1 September 1986;

(bb) if of 20,000 tons gross tonnage and upwards, but less than 40,000 tons gross tonnage, by 1 September 1987;

---

* Reference is made to section 4 of the Recommendation on Performance Standards for Radar Equipment, adopted by the Organization by resolution A.477(XII).

341

(cc) if of 15,000 tons gross tonnage and upwards, but less than 20,000 tons gross tonnage, by 1 September 1988.

(ii) Automatic radar plotting aids fitted prior to 1 September 1984 which do not fully conform to the performance standards adopted by the Organization* may, at the discretion of the Administration, be retained until 1 January 1991.

(iii) The Administration may exempt ships from the requirements of this paragraph, in cases where it considers it unreasonable or unnecessary for such equipment to be carried, or when the ships will be taken permanently out of service within two years of the appropriate implementation date.

(k)   When engaged on international voyages ships of 1,600 tons gross tonnage and upwards constructed before 25 May 1980 and ships of 500 tons gross tonnage and upwards constructed on or after 25 May 1980 shall be fitted with an echo-sounding device.

(l)   When engaged on international voyages ships of 500 tons gross tonnage and upwards constructed on or after 1 September 1984 shall be fitted with a device to indicate speed and distance. Ships required by paragraph (j) to be fitted with an automatic radar plotting aid shall be fitted with a device to indicate speed and distance through the water.

(m) Ships of 1,600 tons gross tonnage and upwards constructed before 1 September 1984 and all ships of 500 tons gross tonnage and upwards constructed on or after 1 September 1984 shall be fitted with indicators showing the rudder angle, the rate of revolution of each propeller and in addition, if fitted with variable pitch propellers or lateral thrust propellers, the pitch and operational mode of such propellers. All these indicators shall be readable from the conning position.

(n)   Ships of 100,000 tons gross tonnage and upwards constructed on or after 1 September 1984 shall be fitted with a rate-of-turn indicator.

(o)   Except as provided in regulations I/7(b)(ii), I/8 and I/9, while all reasonable steps shall be taken to maintain the apparatus referred to in paragraphs (d) to (n) in efficient working order, malfunctions of the equipment shall not be considered as making a ship unseaworthy or as a reason for delaying the ship in ports where repair facilities are not readily available.

(p)   When engaged on international voyages ships of 1,600 tons gross tonnage and upwards shall be fitted with a radio direction-finding apparatus complying with the provisions of regulation IV/12(a). The Administration may, in areas where it considers it unreasonable or unnecessary for such apparatus to be

---

* Reference is made to the Performance Standards for Automatic Radar Plotting Aids (ARPA) adopted by the Organization by resolution A.422(XI).

carried, exempt any ship of less than 5,000 tons gross tonnage from this requirement, due regard being had to the fact that radio direction-finding apparatus is of value both as a navigational instrument and as an aid to locating ships, aircraft or survival craft.

(q)   When engaged on international voyages ships of 1,600 tons gross tonnage and upwards constructed on or after 25 May 1980 shall be fitted with radio equipment for homing on the radiotelephone distress frequency, complying with the relevant provisions of regulation IV/12(b).

(r)   All equipment fitted in compliance with this regulation shall be of a type approved by the Administration. Equipment installed on board ships on or after 1 September 1984 shall conform to appropriate performance standards not inferior to those adopted by the Organization.* Equipment fitted prior to the adoption of related performance standards may be exempted from full compliance with those standards at the discretion of the Administration, having due regard to the recommended criteria which the Organization might adopt in connection with the standards concerned.

(s)   A rigidly connected composite unit of a pushing vessel and associated pushed vessel, when designed as a dedicated and integrated tug and barge combination, shall be regarded as a single ship for the purpose of this regulation.

(t)   If the application of the requirements of this regulation necessitates structural alterations to a ship constructed before 1 September 1984, the Administration may allow extension of the time limit for fitting the required equipment not later than 1 September 1989, taking into account the first scheduled dry-docking of such a ship required by the present regulations.

(u)   Except as provided elsewhere in this regulation, the Administration may grant to individual ships exemptions of a partial or conditional nature, when any such ship is engaged on a voyage where the maximum distance of the ship from the shore, the length and nature of the voyage, the absence of

---

* Reference is made to the following recommendations adopted by the Organization by the resolutions indicated:

Recommendation on General Requirements for Electronic Navigational Aids (resolution A.281(VIII))

Recommendation on Performance Standards for Magnetic Compasses (resolution A.382(X))

Recommendation on Performance Standards for Gyro-Compasses (resolution A.424(XI))

Recommendation on Performance Standards for Radar Equipment (resolution A.477(XII))

Performance Standards for Automatic Radar Plotting Aids (ARPA) (resolution A.422(XI))

Recommendation on Performance Standards for Echo-Sounding Equipment (resolution A.224(VII))

Recommendation on Performance Standards for Devices to Indicate Speed and Distance (resolution A.478(XII))

Performance Standards for Rate-of-Turn Indicators (resolution A.526(13))

general navigation hazards, and other conditions affecting safety are such as to render the full application of this regulation unreasonable or unnecessary. When deciding whether or not to grant exemptions to an individual ship, the Administration shall have regard to the effect that an exemption may have upon the safety of all other ships.

Regulation 13

Manning

The Contracting Governments undertake, each for its national ships, to maintain, or, if it is necessary, to adopt, measures for the purpose of ensuring that, from the point of view of safety of life at sea, all ships shall be sufficiently and efficiently manned.*

Regulation 14

Aids to navigation

The Contracting Governments undertake to arrange for the establishment and maintenance of such aids to navigation, including radio beacons and electronic aids as, in their opinion, the volume of traffic justifies and the degree of risk requires, and to arrange for information relating to these aids to be made available to all concerned.**

Regulation 15

Search and rescue

(a) Each Contracting Government undertakes to ensure that any necessary arrangements are made for coast watching and for the rescue of persons in

---

* Reference is made to the Principles of Safe Manning adopted by the Organization by resolution A.481(XII).

** Reference is made to the following recommendations adopted by the Organization by the resolutions indicated:

Accuracy Standards for Navigation (resolution A.529(13))

Radar Beacons and Transponders (resolution A.423 (XI))

Performance Standards for Differential Omega Correction Transmitting Stations (resolution A.425(XI))

distress at sea round its coasts. These arrangements should include the establishment, operation and maintenance of such maritime safety facilities as are deemed practicable and necessary having regard to the density of the seagoing traffic and the navigational dangers and should, so far as possible, afford adequate means of locating and rescuing such persons.*

(b)   Each Contracting Government undertakes to make available information concerning its existing rescue facilities and the plans for changes therein, if any.

Regulation 16

Life-saving signals

The following signals shall be used by life-saving stations and maritime rescue units when communicating with ships or persons in distress and by ships or persons in distress when communicating with life-saving stations and maritime rescue units. The signals used by aircraft engaged in search and rescue operations to direct ships are indicated in paragraph (d) below. An illustrated table describing the signals listed below shall be readily available to the officer of the watch of every ship to which this chapter applies.

(a)   Replies from life-saving stations or maritime rescue units to distress signals made by a ship or person:

Signal	*Signification*
By day – Orange smoke signal or combined light and sound signal (thunderlight) consisting of three single signals which are fired at intervals of approximately one minute. *By night* – White star rocket consisting of three single signals which are fired at intervals of approximately one minute.	"You are seen – assistance will be given as soon as possible." (Repetition of such signals shall have the same meaning.)

If necessary the day signals may be given at night or the night signals by day.

---

* Reference is made to the following recommendations adopted by the Organization by the resolutions indicated:

Homing Capability of Search and Rescue (SAR) Aircraft (resolution A.225(VIII))

IMO Search and Rescue Manual (IMOSAR) (resolution A.439(XI))

Use of Radar Transponders for Search and Rescue Purposes (resolution A.530(13))

(b) Landing signals for the guidance of small boats with crews or persons in distress:

Signal	*Signification*
By day – Vertical motion of a white flag or the arms or firing of a green star-signal or signalling the code letter "K" (—·—) given by light or sound-signal apparatus. *By night* – Vertical motion of a white light or flare, or firing of a green star-signal or signalling the code letter "K" (—·—) given by light or sound-signal apparatus. A range (indication of direction) may be given by placing a steady white light or flare at a lower level and in line with the observer.	"This is the best place to land."
By day – Horizontal motion of a white flag or arms extended horizontally or firing of a red star-signal or signalling the code letter "S" (···) given by light or sound-signal apparatus. *By night* – Horizontal motion of a white light or flare or firing of a red star-signal or signalling the code letter "S" (···) given by light or sound-signal apparatus.	"Landing here highly dangerous."
By day – Horizontal motion of a white flag, followed by the placing of the white flag in the ground and the carrying of another white flag in the direction to be indicated or firing of a red star-signal vertically and a white star-signal in the direction towards the better landing place or signalling the code letter "S" (···) followed by the code letter "R" (·—·) if a better landing place for the craft in distress is located more to the right in the direction of approach or the code letter "L" (·—··) if a better landing place for the craft in distress is located more to the left in the direction of approach.	"Landing here highly dangerous. A more favourable location for landing is in the direction indicated."

By night – Horizontal motion of a white light or flare, followed by the placing of the white light or flare on the ground and the carrying of another white light or flare in the direction to be indicated or firing of a red star-signal vertically and a white star-signal in the direction towards the better landing place or signalling the code letter "S" (· · ·) followed by code letter "R" (·—·) if a better landing place for the craft in distress is located more to the right in the direction of approach or the code letter "L" (·—· ·) if a better landing place for the craft in distress is located more to the left in the direction,of approach.

"Landing here highly dangerous. A more favourable location for landing is in the direction indicated."

(c) Signals to be employed in connection with the use of shore life-saving apparatus:

Signal	Signification
By day – Vertical motion of a white flag or the arms or firing of a green star-signal. *By night* – Vertical motion of a white light or flare or firing of a green star-signal.	In general – "Affirmative." Specifically: "Rocket line is held." "Tail block is made fast." "Hawser is made fast." "Man is in the breeches buoy." "Haul away."
By day – Horizontal motion of a white flag or arms extended horizontally or firing of a red star-signal. *By night* – Horizontal motion of a white light or flare or firing of a red star-signal.	In general – "Negative." Specifically: "Slack away." "Avast hauling."

(d) Signals used by aircraft engaged on search and rescue operations to direct ships towards an aircraft, ship or person in distress:

(i) The following manoeuvres performed in sequence by an aircraft mean that the aircraft wishes to direct a surface craft towards an aircraft or a surface craft in distress:

(1) circling the surface craft at least once;

(2) crossing the projected course of the surface craft close ahead at low altitude, and:

– rocking the wings; or

– opening and closing the throttle; or

– changing the propeller pitch;

(Due to high noise level on board surface craft, the sound signals may be less effective than the visual signal and are regarded as alternative means of attracting attention.)

(3)   heading in the direction in which the surface craft is to be directed.

Repetition of such manoeuvres has the same meaning.

(ii)   The following manoeuvre by an aircraft means that the assistance of the surface craft to which the signal is directed is no longer required:

crossing the wake of the surface craft close astern at a low altitude, and:

– rocking the wings; or

– opening and closing the throttle; or

– changing the propeller pitch.

(Due to high noise level on board surface craft, the sound signals may be less effective than the visual signal and are regarded as an alternative means of attracting attention.)

Note: Advance notification of changes in these signals will be given by the Organization as necessary. *

Regulation 17

Pilot ladders and mechanical pilot hoists

Ships engaged on voyages in the course of which pilots are likely to be employed shall comply with the following requirements: **

(a)   *Pilot ladders*

(i)   The ladder shall be efficient for the purpose of enabling pilots to embark and disembark safely, kept clean and in good order and may be used by officials and other persons while a ship is arriving at or leaving a port.

---

* Reference is made to the IMO Search and Rescue Manual (IMOSAR), IMO publication 974 80.12, and the Merchant Ship Search and Rescue Manual (MERSAR), IMO publication 963 80.16, adopted by the Organization and subsequently amended as indicated in resolutions A.439(XI) and A.229(VII), respectively.

** Reference is made to the Recommendation on Arrangements for Embarking and Disembarking Pilots in Very Large Ships adopted by the Organization by resolution A.426(XI).

(ii) The ladder shall be secured in a position so that it is clear from any possible discharges from the ship, that each step rests firmly against the ship's side, that it is clear so far as is practicable of the finer lines of the ship and that the pilot can gain safe and convenient access to the ship after climbing not less than 1.5 metres (5 feet) and not more than 9 metres (30 feet). A single length of ladder shall be used capable of reaching the water from the point of access to the ship; in providing for this due allowance shall be made for all conditions of loading and trim of the ship and for an adverse list of 15 degrees. Whenever the distance from sea level to the point of access to the ship is more than 9 metres (30 feet), access from the pilot ladder to the ship shall be by means of an accommodation ladder or other equally safe and convenient means.

(iii) The steps of the pilot ladder shall be:

   (1) of hardwood, or other material of equivalent properties, made in one piece free of knots, having an efficient non-slip surface; the four lowest steps may be made of rubber of sufficient strength and stiffness or of other suitable material of equivalent characteristics;

   (2) not less than 480 millimetres (19 inches) long, 115 millimetres ($4\frac{1}{2}$ inches) wide, and 25 millimetres (1 inch) in depth, excluding any non-slip device;

   (3) equally spaced not less than 300 millimetres (12 inches) nor more than 380 millimetres (15 inches) apart and be secured in such a manner that they will remain horizontal.

(iv) No pilot ladder shall have more than two replacement steps which are secured in position by a method different from that used in the original construction of the ladder and any steps so secured shall be replaced as soon as reasonably practicable by steps secured in position by the method used in the original construction of the ladder. When any replacement step is secured to the side ropes of the ladder by means of grooves in the sides of the step, such grooves shall be in the longer sides of the step.

(v) The side ropes of the ladder shall consist of two uncovered manila ropes not less than 60 millimetres ($2\frac{1}{4}$ inches) in circumference on each side. Each rope shall be continuous with no joints below the top step. Two man-ropes properly secured to the ship and not less than 65 millimetres ($2\frac{1}{2}$ inches) in circumference and a safety line shall be kept at hand ready for use if required.

(vi) Battens made of hardwood, or other material of equivalent properties, in one piece and not less than 1.80 metres (5 feet 10 inches) long shall be provided at such intervals as will prevent the pilot ladder from twisting. The lowest batten shall be on the fifth step

349

from the bottom of the ladder and the interval between any batten and the next shall not exceed 9 steps.

(vii) Means shall be provided to ensure safe and convenient passage on to or into and off the ship between the head of the pilot ladder or of any accommodation ladder or other appliance provided. Where such passage is by means of a gateway in the rails or bulwark, adequate handholds shall be provided. Where such passage is by means of a bulwark ladder, such ladder shall be securely attached to the bulwark rail or platform and two handhold stanchions shall be fitted at the point of boarding or leaving the ship not less than 0.70 metre (2 feet 3 inches) nor more than 0.80 metre (2 feet 7 inches) apart. Each stanchion shall be rigidly secured to the ship's structure at or near its base and also at a higher point, shall be not less than 40 millimetres ($1\frac{1}{2}$ inches) in diameter and shall extend not less than 1.20 metres (3 feet 11 inches) above the top of the bulwark.

(viii) Lighting shall be provided at night such that both the pilot ladder overside and also the position where the pilot boards the ship shall be adequately lit. A lifebuoy equipped with a self-igniting light shall be kept at hand ready for use. A heaving line shall be kept at hand ready for use if required.

(ix) Means shall be provided to enable the pilot ladder to be used on either side of the ship.

(x) The rigging of the ladder and the embarkation and disembarkation of a pilot shall be supervised by a responsible officer of the ship.

(xi) Where on any ship constructional features such as rubbing bands would prevent the implementation of any of these provisions, special arrangements shall be made to the satisfaction of the Administration to ensure that persons are able to embark and disembark safely.

(b) *Mechanical pilot hoists*

(i) A mechanical pilot hoist, if provided, and its ancillary equipment shall be of a type approved by the Administration. It shall be of such design and construction as to ensure that the pilot can be embarked and disembarked in a safe manner including a safe access from the hoist to the deck and *vice versa*.*

(ii) A pilot ladder complying with the provisions of paragraph (a) of this regulation shall be kept on deck adjacent to the hoist and available for immediate use.

---

* Reference is made to the Recommendation on Performance Standards for Mechanical Pilot Hoists adopted by the Organization by resolution A.275(VIII).

350

Regulation 18

VHF radiotelephones

The text of this regulation has been deleted (see regulation IV/4-1(b)).

Regulation 19

Use of the automatic pilot

(a)   In areas of high traffic density, in conditions of restricted visibility and in all other hazardous navigational situations where the automatic pilot is used, it shall be possible to establish human control of the ship's steering immediately.*

(b)   In circumstances as above, it shall be possible for the officer of the watch to have available without delay the services of a qualified helmsman who shall be ready at all times to take over steering control.

(c)   The change-over from automatic to manual steering and *vice versa* shall be made by or under the supervision of a responsible officer.

(d)   The manual steering shall be tested after prolonged use of the automatic pilot, and before entering areas where navigation demands special caution.

Regulation 19-1

Operation of steering gear

In areas where navigation demands special caution, ships shall have more than one steering gear power unit in operation when such units are capable of simultaneous operation.

Regulation 19-2

Steering gear – testing and drills

(a)   Within 12 hours before departure, the ship's steering gear shall be checked and tested by the ship's crew. The test procedure shall include, where applicable, the operation of the following:

---

* Reference is made to the Recommendation of Performance Standards for Automatic Pilots adopted by the Organization by resolution A.342(IX).

(i) the main steering gear;

(ii) the auxiliary steering gear;

(iii) the remote steering gear control systems;

(iv) the steering positions located on the navigating bridge;

(v) the emergency power supply;

(vi) the rudder angle indicators in relation to the actual position of the rudder;

(vii) the remote steering gear control system power failure alarms;

(viii) the steering gear power unit failure alarms; and

(ix) automatic isolating arrangements and other automatic equipment.

(b) The checks and tests shall include:

(i) the full movement of the rudder according to the required capabilities of the steering gear;

(ii) a visual inspection of the steering gear and its connecting linkage; and

(iii) the operation of the means of communication between the navigating bridge and steering gear compartment.

(c) (i) Simple operating instructions with a block diagram showing the change-over procedures for remote steering gear control systems and steering gear power units shall be permanently displayed on the navigating bridge and in the steering gear compartment.

(ii) All ships' officers concerned with the operation or maintenance of steering gear shall be familiar with the operation of the steering systems fitted on the ship and with the procedures for changing from one system to another.

(d) In addition to the routine checks and tests prescribed in paragraphs (a) and (b), emergency steering drills shall take place at least once every three months in order to practise emergency steering procedures. These drills shall include direct control from within the steering gear compartment, the communications procedure with the navigating bridge and, where applicable, the operation of alternative power supplies.

(e) The Administration may waive the requirement to carry out the checks and tests prescribed in paragraphs (a) and (b) for ships which regularly engage on voyages of short duration. Such ships shall carry out these checks and tests at least once every week.

(f)   The date upon which the checks and tests prescribed in paragraphs (a) and (b) are carried out and the date and details of emergency steering drills carried out under paragraph (d), shall be recorded in the log-book as may be prescribed by the Administration.

Regulation 20

Nautical publications

All ships shall carry adequate and up-to-date charts, sailing directions, lists of lights, notices to mariners, tide tables and all other nautical publications necessary for the intended voyage.

Regulation 21

International Code of Signals

All ships which in accordance with the present Convention are required to carry a radiotelegraph or a radiotelephone installation shall carry the International Code of Signals. This publication shall also be carried by any other ship which in the opinion of the Administration has a need to use it.

Chapter VI

CARRIAGE OF GRAIN

Page

PART A – GENERAL PROVISIONS

1 Application 357
2 Definitions 357
3 Trimming of grain 357
4 Intact stability requirements 358
5 Longitudinal divisions and saucers 359
6 Securing 359
7 Feeders and trunks 360
8 Combination arrangements 360
9 Application of parts B and C 360
10 Authorization 361
11 Grain loading information 361
12 Equivalents 362
13 Exemptions for certain voyages 362

PART B – CALCULATION OF ASSUMED HEELING MOMENTS

SECTION I – DESCRIPTION OF THE ASSUMED VOIDS AND METHODS OF
CALCULATING INTACT STABILITY 363

SECTION II – ASSUMED VOLUMETRIC HEELING MOMENT OF A FILLED
COMPARTMENT 366
(A) General 366
(B) Assumptions 366
(C) Compartments loaded in combination 368

SECTION III – ASSUMED VOLUMETRIC HEELING MOMENT OF FEEDERS
AND TRUNKS 369
(A) Suitably placed wing feeders 369
(B) Trunks situated over main hatchways 370

SECTION IV – ASSUMED VOLUMETRIC HEELING MOMENT OF PARTLY
    FILLED COMPARTMENTS 370
(A) General 370
(B) Discontinuous longitudinal divisions 370

SECTION V – ALTERNATIVE LOADING ARRANGEMENTS FOR EXISTING
    SHIPS 371
(A) General 371
(B) Stowage of specially suitable ships 371
(C) Ships without documents of authorization 372

PART C – GRAIN FITTINGS AND SECURING

SECTION I – STRENGTH OF GRAIN FITTINGS 374
(A) General (including working stresses) 374
(B) Divisions loaded on both sides 375
(C) Divisions loaded on one side only.......................... 377
(D) Saucers 380
(E) Bundling of bulk 381
(F) Securing hatch covers of filled compartments 382

SECTION II – SECURING OF PARTLY FILLED COMPARTMENTS 382
(A) Strapping or lashing 382
(B) Overstowing arrangements 383
(C) Bagged grain 383

PART A – GENERAL PROVISIONS

Regulation 1

Application

Unless expressly provided otherwise this chapter applies to the carriage of grain in all ships to which the present regulations apply and in cargo ships of less than 500 tons gross tonnage.

Regulation 2

Definitions

(a)   The term "grain" includes wheat, maize (corn), oats, rye, barley, rice, pulses, seeds and processed forms thereof, whose behaviour is similar to that of grain in its natural state.

(b)   The term "filled compartment" refers to any compartment in which, after loading and trimming as required under regulation 3, the bulk grain is at its highest possible level.

(c)   The term "partly filled compartment" refers to any compartment wherein bulk grain is not loaded in the manner prescribed in paragraph (b) of this regulation.

(d)   The term "angle of flooding" (θ_f) means an angle of heel at which openings in the hull, superstructures or deckhouses, which cannot be closed weathertight, immerse. In applying this definition, small openings through which progressive flooding cannot take place need not be considered as open.

Regulation 3

Trimming of grain

All necessary and reasonable trimming shall be performed to level all free grain surfaces and to minimize the effect of grain shifting.

(a)   In any filled compartment, the bulk grain shall be trimmed so as to fill all the spaces under the decks and hatch covers to the maximum extent possible.

(b)   After loading, all free grain surfaces in partly filled compartments shall be level.

(c)   The Administration issuing the document of authorization may, under regulation 9 of this chapter, grant dispensation from trimming in those cases where the underdeck void geometry resulting from free flowing grain into a compartment, which may be provided with feeding ducts, perforated decks or other similar means, is taken into account to its satisfaction when calculating the void depths.

Regulation 4

Intact stability requirements

(a)   The calculations required by this regulation shall be based upon the stability information provided in accordance with regulation 19 of chapter II–1 of the present Convention, or with the requirements of the Administration issuing the document of authorization under regulation 10 of this chapter.

(b)   The intact stability characteristics of any ship carrying bulk grain shall be shown to meet, throughout the voyage, at least the following criteria after taking into account in the manner described in part B, the heeling moments due to grain shift:

(i)   the angle of heel due to the shift of grain shall be not greater than 12 degrees except that an Administration giving authorization in accordance with regulation 10 of this chapter may require a lesser angle of heel if it considers that experience shows this to be necessary;*

(ii)   in the statical stability diagram, the net or residual area between the heeling arm curve and the righting arm curve up to the angle of heel of maximum difference between the ordinates of the two curves, or 40 degrees or the angle of flooding (θ_f), whichever is the least, shall in all conditions of loading be not less than 0.075 metre-radians; and

(iii)   the initial metacentric height, after correction for the free surface effects of liquids in tanks, shall be not less than 0.30 metre.

(c)   Before loading bulk grain the master shall, if so required by the Contracting Government of the country of the port of loading, demonstrate the ability of the ship at all stages of any voyage to comply with the stability criteria

---

* For example, the permissible angle of heel might be limited to the angle of heel at which the edge of the weather deck would be immersed in still water.

required by paragraph (b) of this regulation using the information approved and issued under regulations 10 and 11 of this chapter.

(d)   After loading, the master shall ensure that the ship shall be upright before proceeding to sea.

Regulation 5

Longitudinal divisions and saucers

(a)   In both filled compartments and partly filled compartments, longitudinal divisions may be provided as a device either to reduce the adverse heeling effect of grain shift or to limit the depth of cargo used for securing the grain surface. Such divisions shall be fitted grain-tight and constructed in accordance with the provisions of section I of part C.

(b)   In a filled compartment, a division, if fitted to reduce the adverse effects of grain shift, shall:

(i)   in a 'tweendeck compartment extend from deck to deck; and

(ii)   in a hold extend downwards from the underside of the deck or hatch covers as described in section II of part B of this chapter.

Except in the case of linseed and other seeds having similar properties, a longitudinal division beneath a hatchway may be replaced by a saucer formed in the manner described in section I of part C of this chapter.

(c)   In a partly filled compartment, a division, if fitted, shall extend from one eighth of the maximum breadth of the compartment above the level of the grain surface and to the same distance below the grain surface. When used to limit the depth of overstowing, the height of the centreline division shall be at least 0.6 metre above the level grain surface.

(d)   Furthermore, the adverse heeling effects of grain shift may be reduced by tightly stowing the wings and ends of a compartment with bagged grain or other suitable cargo adequately restrained from shifting.

Regulation 6

Securing

(a)   Unless account is taken of the adverse heeling effect due to grain shift in accordance with these regulations, the surface of the bulk grain in any partly filled compartment shall be level and topped off with bagged grain tightly stowed and extending to a height of not less than one sixteenth of the maximum breadth of the free grain surface or 1.2 metres, whichever is the greater. Instead of bagged grain, other suitable cargo exerting at least the same pressure may be used.

(b)   The bagged grain or such other suitable cargo shall be supported in the manner described in section II of part C of this chapter. Alternatively, the bulk grain surface may be secured by strapping or lashing as described in that section.

Regulation 7

Feeders and trunks

If feeders or trunks are fitted, proper account shall be taken of the effects thereof when calculating the heeling moments as described in section III of part B of this chapter. The strength of the divisions forming the boundaries of such feeders shall conform with the provisions of section I of part C of this chapter.

Regulation 8

Combination arrangements

Lower holds and 'tweendeck spaces in way thereof may be loaded as one compartment provided that, in calculating transverse heeling moments, proper account is taken of the flow of grain into the lower spaces.

Regulation 9

Application of parts B and C

An Administration or a Contracting Government on behalf of an Administration may authorize departure from the assumptions contained in parts B and C of this chapter in those cases where it considers this to be justified having regard to the provisions for loading or the structural arrangements, provided the stability criteria in paragraph (b) of regulation 4 of this chapter are met. Where such authorization is granted under this regulation, particulars shall be included in the document of authorization or grain loading data.

Regulation 10

Authorization

(a)   A document of authorization shall be issued for every ship loaded in accordance with the regulations of this chapter either by the Administration or an organization recognized by it or by a Contracting Government on behalf of the Administration. It shall be accepted as evidence that the ship is capable of complying with the requirements of these regulations.

(b)   The document shall accompany and refer to the grain loading stability booklet provided to enable the master to meet the requirements of paragraph (c) of regulation 4 of this chapter. This booklet shall meet the requirements of regulation 11 of this chapter.

(c)   Such a document, grain loading stability data and associated plans may be drawn up in the official language or languages of the issuing country. If the language used is neither English nor French, the text shall include a translation into one of these languages.

(d)   A copy of such a document, grain loading stability data and associated plans shall be placed on board in order that the master, if so required, shall produce them for the inspection of the Contracting Government of the country of the port of loading.

(e)   A ship without such a document of authorization shall not load grain until the master demonstrates to the satisfaction of the Administration or the Contracting Government of the port of loading on behalf of the Administration that the ship in its proposed loaded condition will comply with the requirements of these regulations.

Regulation 11

Grain loading information

This information shall be sufficient to allow the master to determine in all reasonable loading conditions the heeling moments due to grain shift calculated in accordance with part B of this chapter. It shall include the following:

(a)   Information which shall be approved by the Administration or by a Contracting Government on behalf of the Administration:

   (i)   curves or tables of grain heeling moments for every compartment, filled or partly filled, or combination thereof, including the effects of temporary fittings;

(ii) tables of maximum permissible heeling moments or other information sufficient to allow the master to demonstrate compliance with the requirements of paragraph (c) of regulation 4 of this chapter;

(iii) details of the scantlings of any temporary fittings and where applicable the provisions necessary to meet the requirements of section I(E) of part C of this chapter;

(iv) typical loaded service departure and arrival conditions and where necessary, intermediate worst service conditions;

(v) a worked example for the guidance of the master;

(vi) loading instructions in the form of notes summarizing the requirements of this chapter.

(b) Information which shall be acceptable to the Administration or to a Contracting Government on behalf of the Administration:

(i) ship's particulars;

(ii) lightship displacement and the vertical distance from the intersection of the moulded base line and midship section to the centre of gravity (KG);

(iii) table of free surface corrections;

(iv) capacities and centres of gravity.

Regulation 12

Equivalents

Where an equivalent accepted by the Administration in accordance with regulation 5 of chapter I of this Convention is applied, particulars shall be included in the document of authorization or grain loading data.

Regulation 13

Exemptions for certain voyages

The Administration, or a Contracting Government on behalf of the Administration may, if it considers that the sheltered nature and conditions of the voyage are such as to render the application of any of the requirements of regulations 3 to 12 of this chapter unreasonable or unnecessary, exempt from those particular requirements individual ships or classes of ships.

PART B – CALCULATION OF ASSUMED HEELING MOMENTS

SECTION I – DESCRIPTION OF THE ASSUMED VOIDS AND
METHOD OF CALCULATING INTACT STABILITY

SECTION II – ASSUMED VOLUMETRIC HEELING MOMENT OF A
FILLED COMPARTMENT

SECTION III – ASSUMED VOLUMETRIC HEELING MOMENT OF
FEEDERS AND TRUNKS

SECTION IV – ASSUMED VOLUMETRIC HEELING MOMENT OF
PARTLY FILLED COMPARTMENTS

SECTION V – ALTERNATIVE LOADING ARRANGEMENTS FOR
EXISTING SHIPS

SECTION I – DESCRIPTION OF THE ASSUMED VOIDS AND METHOD OF CALCULATING INTACT STABILITY

(A) GENERAL

(a) For the purpose of calculating the adverse heeling moment due to a shift of cargo surface in ships carrying bulk grain it shall be assumed that:

(i) In filled compartments which have been trimmed in accordance with regulation 3 of this chapter a void exists under all boundary surfaces having an inclination to the horizontal less than 30 degrees and that the void is parallel to the boundary surface having an average depth calculated according to the formula:

$$Vd = Vd_1 + 0.75(d - 600)\,mm$$

Where:

Vd = average void depth in mm;

Vd_1 = standard void depth from table I below;

d = actual girder depth in mm.

In no case shall Vd be assumed to be less than 100 mm.

TABLE I

Distance from hatch end or hatch side to boundary of compartment	Standard void depth Vd_1
metres	*mm*
0.5	570
1.0	530
1.5	500
2.0	480
2.5	450
3.0	440
3.5	430
4.0	430
4.5	430
5.0	430
5.5	450
6.0	470
6.5	490
7.0	520
7.5	550
8.0	590

Notes on table I:

For distances greater than 8.0 metres the standard void depth Vd_1 shall be linearly extrapolated at 80 mm increase for each 1.0 metre increase in distance. Where there is a difference in depth between the hatch side girder or its continuation and the hatch end beam the greater depth shall be used except that:

(1) when the hatch side girder or its continuation is shallower than the hatch end beam the voids abreast the hatchway may be calculated using the lesser depth; and

(2) when the hatch end beam is shallower than the hatch side girder or its continuation the voids fore and aft of the hatchway inboard of the continuation of the hatch side girder may be calculated using the lesser depth;

(3) where there is a raised deck clear of a hatchway the average void depth measured from the underside of the raised deck shall be calculated using the standard void depth in association with a girder depth of the hatch end beam plus the height of the raised deck.

(ii) In filled compartments which are not trimmed in accordance with regulation 3 of this chapter and where the boundary surface has an inclination to the horizontal which is less than 30 degrees, the cargo surface has an inclination of 30 degrees to the horizontal after loading.

(iii) Within filled hatchways and in addition to any open void within the hatch cover there is a void of average depth of 150 mm measured down to the grain surface from the lowest part of the hatch cover or the top of the hatch side coaming, whichever is the lower.

(b) The description of the pattern of grain surface behaviour to be assumed in partly filled compartments is shown in section IV of this part.

(c) For the purpose of demonstrating compliance with the stability criteria in paragraph (b) of regulation 4 of this chapter (see figure 1), the ship's stability calculations shall be normally based upon the assumption that the centre of gravity of cargo in a filled compartment is at the volumetric centre of the whole cargo space. In those cases where the Administration authorizes account to be taken of the effect of assumed under-deck voids on the vertical position of the centre of gravity of the cargo in filled compartments it will be necessary to compensate for the adverse effect of the vertical shift of grain surfaces by increasing the assumed heeling moment due to the transverse shift of grain as follows:

total heeling moment = 1.06 × calculated transverse heeling moment.

In all cases the weight of cargo in a filled compartment shall be the volume of the whole cargo space divided by the stowage factor.

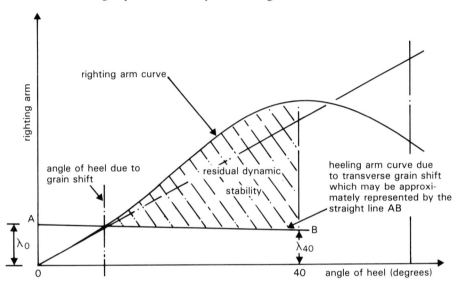

Figure 1

Notes on figure 1:

(1)   Where:

$$\lambda_0 = \frac{\text{assumed volumetric heeling moment due to transverse shift}}{\text{stowage factor} \times \text{displacement}};$$

$\lambda_{40} = 0.8 \times \lambda_0$;

Stowage factor = volume per unit weight of grain cargo;

Displacement = weight of ship, fuel, fresh water, stores etc. and cargo.

(2)   The righting arm curve shall be derived from cross-curves which are sufficient in number to accurately define the curve for the purpose of these requirements and shall include cross-curves at 12 degrees and 40 degrees.

(d)   In partly filled compartments the adverse effect of the vertical shift of grain surfaces shall be taken into account as follows:

total heeling moment = 1.12 × calculated transverse heeling moment.

(e)   Any other equally effective method may be adopted to make the compensation required in paragraphs (c) and (d) above.

SECTION II – ASSUMED VOLUMETRIC HEELING MOMENT OF A FILLED COMPARTMENT

(A)   GENERAL

(a)   The pattern of grain surface movement relates to a transverse section across the portion of the compartment being considered and the resultant heeling moment should be multiplied by the length to obtain the total moment for that portion.

(b)   The assumed transverse heeling moment due to grain shifting is a consequence of final changes of shape and position of voids after grain has moved from the high side to the low side.

(c)   The resulting grain surface after shifting shall be assumed to be at 15 degrees to the horizontal.

(d)   In calculating the maximum void area that can be formed against a longitudinal structural member, the effects of any horizontal surfaces, e.g. flanges or face bars, shall be ignored.

(e)   The total areas of the initial and final voids shall be equal.

(f)   A discontinuous longitudinal division shall be considered effective over its full length.

(B)   ASSUMPTIONS

In the following paragraphs it is assumed that the total heeling moment for a compartment is obtained by adding the results of separate considerations of the following portions:

(a)   *Before and abaft hatchways:*
  (i)   If a compartment has two or more main hatchways through which loading may take place the depth of the under-deck void for the portion(s) between such hatchways shall be determined using the fore and aft distance to the midpoint between the hatchways.

366

(ii) After the assumed shift of grain the final void pattern shall be as shown in figure 2 below:

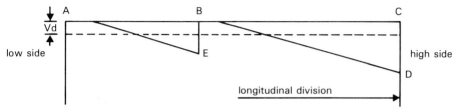

Figure 2

Notes on figure 2:

(1) If the maximum void area which can be formed against the girder at B is less than the initial area of the void under AB, i.e. AB × Vd, the excess area shall be assumed to transfer to the final void on the high side.

(2) If the longitudinal division at C is one which has been provided in accordance with subparagraph (b)(ii) of regulation 5 of this chapter it shall extend to at least 0.6 metre below D or E whichever gives the greater depth.

(b) *In and abreast of hatchways:*

After the assumed shift of grain the final void pattern shall be as shown in the following figure 3 or figure 4.

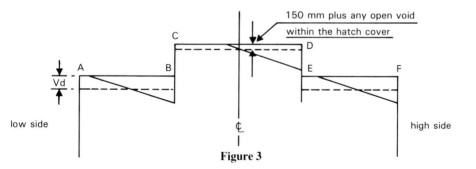

Figure 3

Notes on figure 3:

(1) AB Any area in excess of that which can be formed against the girder at B shall transfer to the final void area in the hatchway.

(2) CD Any area in excess of that which can be formed against the girder at E shall transfer to the final void area on the high side.

367

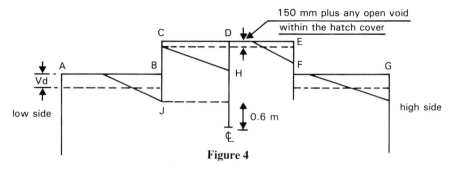

Figure 4

Notes on figure 4:

(1) If the centreline division is one which has been provided in accordance with sub-paragraph (b)(ii) of regulation 5 of this chapter it shall extend to at least 0.6 metre below H or J whichever gives the greater depth.

(2) The excess void area from AB shall transfer to the low side half of the hatchway in which two separate final void areas will be formed viz. one against the centreline division and the other against the hatch side coaming and girder on the high side.

(3) If a bagged saucer or bulk bundle is formed in a hatchway it shall be assumed, for the purpose of calculating transverse heeling moment, that such a device is at least equivalent to the centreline division.

(C) COMPARTMENTS LOADED IN COMBINATION

The following paragraphs describe the pattern of void behaviour which shall be assumed when compartments are loaded in combination:

(a) *Without effective centreline divisions:*

(i) Under the upper deck – as for the single deck arrangement described in section II(B) of this part.

(ii) Under the second deck – the area of void available for transfer from the low side, i.e. original void area less area against the hatch side girder, shall be assumed to transfer as follows:

one half to the upper deck hatchway and one quarter each to the high side under the upper and second deck.

(iii) Under the third and lower decks – the void areas available for transfer from the low side of each of these decks shall be assumed to transfer in equal quantities to all the voids under the decks on the high side and the void in the upper deck hatchway.

(b) *With effective centreline divisions which extend into the upper deck hatchway:*

(i) At all deck levels abreast the division the void areas available for transfer from the low side shall be assumed to transfer to the void under the low side half of the upper deck hatchway.

(ii) At the deck level immediately below the bottom of the division the void area available for transfer from the low side shall be assumed to transfer as follows:

368

one half to the void under the low side half of the upper deck hatchway and the remainder in equal quantities to the voids under the decks on the high side.

(iii) At deck levels lower than those described in subparagraphs (i) and (ii) of this paragraph the void area available for transfer from the low side of each of those decks shall be assumed to transfer in equal quantities to the voids in each of the two halves of the upper deck hatchway on each side of the division and the voids under the decks on the high side.

(c) *With effective centreline divisions which do not extend into the upper deck hatchway:*

Since no horizontal transfer of voids may be assumed to take place at the same deck level as the division the void area available for transfer from the low side at this level shall be assumed to transfer above the division to voids on the high sides in accordance with the principles of paragraphs (a) and (b).

SECTION III – ASSUMED VOLUMETRIC HEELING MOMENT OF FEEDERS AND TRUNKS

(A)   SUITABLY PLACED WING FEEDERS (see figure 5)

It may be assumed that under the influence of ship motion under-deck voids will be substantially filled by the flow of grain from a pair of longitudinal feeders provided that:

(a)   the feeders extend for the full length of the deck and that the perforations therein are adequately spaced;

(b)   the volume of each feeder is equal to the volume of the under-deck void outboard of the hatch side girder and its continuation.

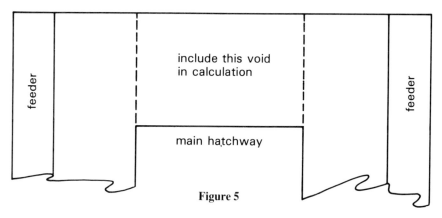

Figure 5

(B) TRUNKS SITUATED OVER MAIN HATCHWAYS

After the assumed shift of grain the final void pattern shall be as shown in figure 6.

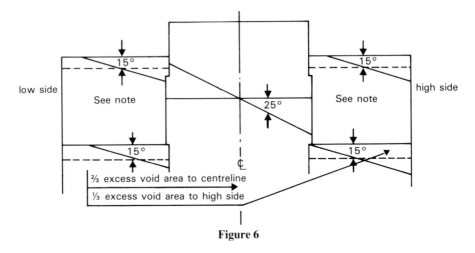

Figure 6

Notes on figure 6:

If the wing spaces in way of the trunk cannot be properly trimmed in accordance with regulation 3 of this chapter it shall be assumed that a 25 degree surface shift takes place.

SECTION IV – ASSUMED VOLUMETRIC HEELING MOMENT OF PARTLY FILLED COMPARTMENTS

(A) GENERAL

When the free surface of the bulk grain has not been secured in accordance with regulation 6 of this chapter it shall be assumed that the grain surface after shifting shall be at 25 degrees to the horizontal.

(B) DISCONTINUOUS LONGITUDINAL DIVISIONS

In a compartment in which the longitudinal divisions are not continuous between the transverse boundaries, the length over which any such divisions are effective as devices to prevent full width shifts of grain surfaces shall be taken to be the actual length of the portion of the division under consideration less two sevenths of the greater of the transverse distances between the division and its adjacent division or ship's side.

This correction does not apply in the lower compartments of any combination loading in which the upper compartment is either a filled compartment or a partly filled compartment.

SECTION V – ALTERNATIVE LOADING ARRANGEMENTS FOR EXISTING SHIPS

(A) GENERAL

A ship loaded in accordance with either subsection (B) or subsection (C) shall be considered to have intact stability characteristics at least equivalent to the requirements of paragraph (b) of regulation 4 of this chapter. Documents of authorization permitting such loadings shall be accepted under the provisions of paragraph (e) of regulation 10 of this chapter.

For the purpose of this part the term "existing ship" means a ship, the keel of which is laid before 25 May 1980.

(B) STOWAGE OF SPECIALLY SUITABLE SHIPS

(a) Notwithstanding anything contained in part B of this chapter, bulk grain may be carried without regard to the requirements specified therein in ships which are constructed with two or more vertical or sloping grain-tight longitudinal divisions suitably disposed to limit the effect of any transverse shift of grain under the following conditions:

(i) as many holds and compartments as possible shall be full and trimmed full;

(ii) for any specified arrangement of stowage the ship will not list to an angle greater than 5 degrees at any stage of the voyage where:

(1) in holds or compartments which have been trimmed full the grain surface settled 2 per cent by volume from the original surface and shifts to an angle of 12 degrees with that surface under all boundaries of these holds and compartments which have an inclination of less than 30 degrees to the horizontal;

(2) in partly filled compartments or holds free grain surfaces settle and shift as in subparagraph (1) or to such larger angle as may be deemed necessary by the Administration, or by a Contracting Government on behalf of the Administration, and grain surfaces, if overstowed, with the bulk grain levelled

and topped off with bagged grain or other suitable cargo tightly stowed and extending to a height of not less than 1.22 m above the top of the bulk grain within spaces divided by a longitudinal bulkhead or shifting board, and not less than 1.52 m within spaces not so divided and the bagged grain or other suitable cargo supported on suitable platforms laid over the whole surface of the bulk grain, such platforms consisting of bearers spaced not more than 1.22 m apart and 25 mm boards laid thereon spaced not more than 0.10 m apart or of strong separation cloths with adequate overlapping, will shift to an angle of 8 degrees with the original levelled surfaces. For the purpose of this paragraph shifting boards, if fitted, will be considered to limit the transverse shift of the surface of the grain;*

(iii)   the master is provided with a grain loading plan covering the stowage arrangements to be adopted and a stability booklet, both approved by the Administration, or by a Contracting Government on behalf of the Administration, showing the stability conditions upon which the calculations given in subparagraph (ii) of this paragraph are based.

(b)   The Administration, or a Contracting Government on behalf of the Administration, shall prescribe the precautions to be taken against shifting in all other conditions of loading of ships designed in accordance with paragraph (B)(a) of this section which meet the requirements of subparagraphs (ii) and (iii) of that paragraph.

(C)   SHIPS WITHOUT DOCUMENTS OF AUTHORIZATION

A ship not having on board documents of authorization issued in accordance with regulations 4 and 10 of this chapter may be permitted to load bulk grain under the requirements of subsection (B) of this section or provided that:

(a)   All filled compartments shall be fitted with centreline divisions extending for the full length of such compartments which extend downwards from the underside of the deck or hatch covers to a distance below the deck line of at least one eighth of the maximum breadth of the compartment or 2.4 metres, whichever is the greater except that saucers constructed in accordance with section II of part C may be accepted in lieu of a centreline division in and beneath a hatchway except in the case of linseed and other seeds having similar properties.

---

* It has consistently been the intention that valid approvals given under resolutions A.184(VI) and A.264(VIII) and regulation 12 of the 1960 Convention should be accepted as being in compliance with or equivalent to the requirements of the 1974 Convention.

(b) All hatches to filled compartments shall be closed and covers secured in place.

(c) All free grain surfaces in partly filled compartments shall be trimmed level and secured in accordance with section II of part C.

(d) Throughout the voyage the metacentric height after correction for the free surface effects of liquids in tanks shall be 0.3 metre or that given by the following formula, whichever is the greater:

$$GM_R = \frac{L\,B\,Vd\,(0.25\,B - 0.645\sqrt{Vd\,B})}{SF \times \Delta \times 0.0875}$$

Where:

L = total combined length of all full compartments;

B = moulded breadth of vessel;

SF = stowage factor;

Vd = calculated average void depth as per paragraph (a)(i) of section I(A) of this part;

Δ = displacement.

PART C — GRAIN FITTINGS AND SECURING

SECTION I – STRENGTH OF GRAIN FITTINGS
- (A) General (including working stresses)
- (B) Divisions loaded on both sides
- (C) Divisions loaded on one side only
- (D) Saucers
- (E) Bundling of bulk
- (F) Securing hatch covers of filled compartments

SECTION II – SECURING OF PARTLY FILLED COMPARTMENTS
- (A) Strapping or lashing
- (B) Overstowing arrangements
- (C) Bagged grain

SECTION I – STRENGTH OF GRAIN FITTINGS

(A) GENERAL

(a) *Timber*

All timber used for grain fittings shall be of good sound quality and of a type and grade which has been proved to be satisfactory for this purpose. The actual finished dimensions of the timber shall be in accordance with the dimensions hereinafter specified in this part. Plywood of an exterior type bonded with waterproof glue and fitted so that the direction of the grain in the face plies is perpendicular to the supporting uprights or binder may be used provided that its strength is equivalent to that of solid timber of the appropriate scantlings.

(b) *Working stresses*

When calculating the dimensions of divisions loaded on one side, using the tables in paragraphs (a) and (b) of subsection (C) of this section, the following working stresses should be adopted:

For divisions of steel	2000 kg per square cm
For divisions of wood	160 kg per square cm

(c) *Other materials*

Materials other than wood or steel may be approved for such divisions provided that proper regard has been paid to their mechanical properties.

(d) *Uprights*

(i) Unless means are provided to prevent the ends of uprights being dislodged from their sockets, the depth of housing at each end of each upright shall be not less than 75 mm. If an upright is not secured at the top, the uppermost shore or stay shall be fitted as near thereto as is practicable.

(ii) The arrangements provided for inserting shifting boards by removing a part of the cross-section of an upright shall be such that the local level of stresses is not unduly high.

(iii) The maximum bending moment imposed upon an upright supporting a division loaded on one side shall normally be calculated assuming that the ends of the uprights are freely supported. However, if an Administration is satisfied that any degree of fixity assumed will be achieved in practice, account may be taken of any reduction in the maximum bending moment arising from any degree of fixity provided at the ends of the upright.

374

(e) *Composite section*

Where uprights, binders or any other strength members are formed by two separate sections, one fitted on each side of a division and interconnected by through bolts at adequate spacing, the effective section modulus shall be taken as the sum of the two moduli of the separate sections.

(f) *Partial division*

Where divisions do not extend to the full depth of the hold such divisions and their uprights shall be supported or stayed so as to be as efficient as those which do extend to the full depth of the hold.

(B) DIVISIONS LOADED ON BOTH SIDES

(a) *Shifting boards*

(i) Shifting boards shall have a thickness of not less than 50 mm and shall be fitted grain-tight and where necessary supported by uprights.

(ii) The maximum unsupported span for shifting boards of various thicknesses shall be as follows:

Thickness	Maximum unsupported span
50 mm	2.5 metres
60 mm	3.0 metres
70 mm	3.5 metres
80 mm	4.0 metres

If thicknesses greater than these are provided the maximum unsupported span will vary directly with the increase in thickness.

(iii) The ends of all shifting boards shall be securely housed with 75 mm minimum bearing length.

(b) *Other materials*

Divisions formed by using materials other than wood shall have a strength equivalent to the shifting boards required in paragraph (a) of this subsection.

(c) *Uprights*

(i) Steel uprights used to support divisions loaded on both sides shall have a section modulus given by

$$W = a \times W_1$$

Where:

W = section modulus in cubic centimetres;
a = horizontal span between uprights in metres.

375

The section modulus per metre span W_1 shall be not less than that given by the formula:

$$W_1 = 14.8\,(h_1 - 1.2)\,\text{cm}^3\text{ per metre};$$

Where:

h_1 is the vertical unsupported span in metres and shall be taken as the maximum value of the distance between any two adjacent stays or between the stay or either end of the upright. Where this distance is less than 2.4 metres the respective modulus shall be calculated as if the actual value was 2.4 metres.

(ii) The moduli of wood uprights shall be determined by multiplying by 12.5 the corresponding moduli for steel uprights. If other materials are used their moduli shall be at least that required for steel increased in proportion to the ratio of the permissible stresses for steel to that of the material used. In such cases attention shall be paid also to the relative rigidity of each upright to ensure that the deflection is not excessive.

(iii) The horizontal distance between uprights shall be such that the unsupported spans of the shifting boards do not exceed the maximum span specified in subparagraph (ii) of paragraph (a) of this subsection.

(d) *Shores*

(i) Wood shores, when used, shall be in a single piece and shall be securely fixed at each end and heeled against the permanent structure of the ship except that they shall not bear directly against the side plating of the ship.

(ii) Subject to the provisions of subparagraphs (iii) and (vi) below, the minimum size of wood shores shall be as follows:

Length of shore in metres	Rectangular section mm	Diameter of circular section mm
Not exceeding 3 m	150 × 100	140
Over 3 m but not exceeding 5 m	150 × 150	165
Over 5 m but not exceeding 6 m	150 × 150	180
Over 6 m but not exceeding 7 m	200 × 150	190
Over 7 m but not exceeding 8 m	200 × 150	200
Exceeding 8 m	200 × 150	215

Shores of 7 metres or more in length shall be securely bridged at approximately mid-length.

(iii) When the horizontal distance between the uprights differs significantly from 4 metres, the moments of inertia of the shores may be changed in direct proportion.

(iv) Where the angle of the shore to the horizontal exceeds 10 degrees the next larger shore to that required by subparagraph (ii) of this paragraph shall be fitted provided that in no case shall the angle between any shore and the horizontal exceed 45 degrees.

(e) *Stays*

Where stays are used to support divisions loaded on both sides, they shall be fitted horizontally or as near thereto as practicable, well secured at each end and formed of steel wire rope. The sizes of the wire rope shall be determined assuming that the divisions and upright which the stay supports are uniformly loaded at $500 \, kg/m^2$. The working load so assumed in the stay shall not exceed one third of its breaking load.

(C) DIVISIONS LOADED ON ONE SIDE ONLY

(a) *Longitudinal divisions*

The load in kg per metre length of the division shall be taken to be as follows:

TABLE I*

B (m)

h (m)	2	3	4	5	6	7	8	10
1.5	850	900	1010	1225	1500	1770	2060	2645
2.0	1390	1505	1710	1985	2295	2605	2930	3590
2.5	1985	2160	2430	2740	3090	3435	3800	4535
3.0	2615	2845	3150	3500	3885	4270	4670	5480
3.5	3245	3525	3870	4255	4680	5100	5540	6425
4.0	3890	4210	4590	5015	5475	5935	6410	7370
4.5	4535	4890	5310	5770	6270	6765	7280	8315
5.0	5185	5570	6030	6530	7065	7600	8150	9260
6.0	6475	6935	7470	8045	8655	9265	9890	11150
7.0	7765	8300	8910	9560	10245	10930	11630	13040
8.0	9055	9665	10350	11075	11835	12595	13370	14930
9.0	10345	11030	11790	12590	13425	14260	15110	16820
10.0	11635	12395	13230	14105	15015	15925	16850	18710

h = height of grain in metres from the bottom of the division**
B = transverse extent of the bulk grain in metres

For other values of h or B the loads shall be determined by linear interpolation or extrapolation as necessary.

* This table is currently under review for bulkheads of extreme height. An explanatory note and a convenient arithmetic device to achieve adequate values is given in MSC/Circ. 363.

** Where the distance from a division to a feeder or hatchway is 1 metre or less, the height – h – shall be taken to the level of the grain within that hatchway or feeder. In all other cases the height shall be taken to the overhead deck in way of the division.

(b)   Transverse divisions

The load in kg per metre length of the division shall be taken to be as follows:

TABLE II*

L (m)

h (m)	2	3	4	5	6	7	8	10	12	14	16
1.5	670	690	730	780	835	890	935	1000	1040	1050	1050
2.0	1040	1100	1170	1245	1325	1400	1470	1575	1640	1660	1660
2.5	1460	1565	1675	1780	1880	1980	2075	2210	2285	2305	2305
3.0	1925	2065	2205	2340	2470	2590	2695	2845	2925	2950	2950
3.5	2425	2605	2770	2930	3075	3205	3320	3480	3570	3595	3595
4.0	2950	3160	3355	3535	3690	3830	3950	4120	4210	4235	4240
4.5	3495	3725	3940	4130	4295	4440	4565	4750	4850	4880	4885
5.0	4050	4305	4535	4735	4910	5060	5190	5385	5490	5525	5530
6.0	5175	5465	5720	5945	6135	6300	6445	6655	6775	6815	6825
7.0	6300	6620	6905	7150	7365	7445	7700	7930	8055	8105	8115
8.0	7425	7780	8090	8360	8590	8685	8950	9200	9340	9395	9410
9.0	8550	8935	9275	9565	9820	9930	10205	10475	10620	10685	10705
10.0	9680	10095	10460	10770	11045	11270	11460	11745	11905	11975	11997

h = height of grain in metres from the bottom of the division**
L = longitudinal extent of the bulk grain in metres

For other values of h or L the loads shall be determined by linear interpolation or extrapolation as necessary.

(c)   Vertical distribution of the loads

The total load per unit length of divisions shown in the tables I and II above may, if considered necessary, be assumed to have a trapezoidal distribution with height. In such cases, the reaction loads at the upper and lower ends of a vertical member or upright are not equal. The reaction loads at the upper end expressed as percentages of the total load supported by the vertical member or upright shall be taken to be those shown in tables III and IV below.

---

* This table is currently under review for bulkheads of extreme height. An explanatory note and a convenient arithmetic device to achieve adequate values is given in MSC/Circ. 363.

** Where the distance from a division to a feeder or hatchway is 1 metre or less, the height – h – shall be taken to the level of the grain within that hatchway or feeder. In all other cases the height shall be taken to the overhead deck in way of the division.

TABLE III*

LONGITUDINAL DIVISIONS LOADED ON ONE SIDE ONLY

Bearing reaction at the upper end of upright as percentage of load (table I)

B (m)

h (m)	2	3	4	5	6	7	8	10
1.5	43.3	45.1	45.9	46.2	46.2	46.2	46.2	46.2
2	44.5	46.7	47.6	47.8	47.8	47.8	47.8	47.8
2.5	45.4	47.6	48.6	48.8	48.8	48.8	48.8	48.8
3	46.0	48.3	49.2	49.4	49.4	49.4	49.4	49.4
3.5	46.5	48.8	49.7	49.8	49.8	49.8	49.8	49.8
4	47.0	49.1	49.9	50.1	50.1	50.1	50.1	50.1
4.5	47.4	49.4	50.1	50.2	50.2	50.2	50.2	50.2
5	47.7	49.4	50.1	50.2	50.2	50.2	50.2	50.2
6	47.9	49.5	50.1	50.2	50.2	50.2	50.2	50.2
7	47.9	49.5	50.1	50.2	50.2	50.2	50.2	50.2
8	47.9	49.5	50.1	50.2	50.2	50.2	50.2	50.2
9	47.9	49.5	50.1	50.2	50.2	50.2	50.2	50.2
10	47.9	49.5	50.1	50.2	50.2	50.2	50.2	50.2

B = transverse extent of the bulk grain in metres

For other values of h or B the reaction loads shall be determined by linear interpolation or extrapolation as necessary.

TABLE IV*

TRANSVERSE DIVISIONS LOADED ON ONE SIDE ONLY

Bearing reaction at the upper end of upright as percentage of load (table II)

L (m)

h (m)	2	3	4	5	6	7	8	10	12	14	16
1.5	37.3	38.7	39.7	40.6	41.4	42.1	42.6	43.6	44.3	44.8	45.0
2	39.6	40.6	41.4	42.1	42.7	43.1	43.6	44.3	44.7	45.0	45.2
2.5	41.0	41.8	42.5	43.0	43.5	43.8	44.2	44.7	45.0	45.2	45.2
3	42.1	42.8	43.3	43.8	44.2	44.5	44.7	45.0	45.2	45.3	45.3
3.5	42.9	43.5	43.9	44.3	44.6	44.8	45.0	45.2	45.3	45.3	45.3
4	43.5	44.0	44.4	44.7	44.9	45.0	45.2	45.4	45.4	45.4	45.4
5	43.9	44.3	44.6	44.8	45.0	45.2	45.3	45.5	45.5	45.5	45.5
6	44.2	44.5	44.8	45.0	45.2	45.3	45.4	45.6	45.6	45.6	45.6
7	44.3	44.6	44.9	45.1	45.3	45.4	45.5	45.6	45.6	45.6	45.6
8	44.3	44.6	44.9	45.1	45.3	45.4	45.5	45.6	45.6	45.6	45.6
9	44.3	44.6	44.9	45.1	45.3	45.4	45.5	45.6	45.6	45.6	45.6
10	44.3	44.6	44.9	45.1	45.3	45.4	45.5	45.6	45.6	45.6	45.6

L = longitudinal extent of the bulk grain in metres

For other values of h or L the reaction loads shall be determined by linear interpolation or extrapolation as necessary.

* This table is currently under review.

379

The strength of the end connections of such vertical members or uprights may be calculated on the basis of the maximum load likely to be imposed at either end. These loads are as follows:

Longitudinal divisions

Maximum load at the top	50% of the appropriate total load from table I
Maximum load at the bottom	55% of the appropriate total load from table I

Transverse divisions

Maximum load at the top	45% of the appropriate total load from table II
Maximum load at the bottom	60% of the appropriate total load from table II

The thickness of horizontal wooden boards may also be determined having regard to the vertical distribution of the loading represented by tables III and IV above and in such cases

$$t = 10a\sqrt{\frac{p \times k}{h \times 213.3}}$$

Where:

t = thickness of board in mm;

a = horizontal span of the board, i.e. distance between uprights in metres;

h = head of grain to the bottom of the division in metres;

p = total load per unit length derived from table I or II in kilogrammes;

k = factor dependent upon vertical distribution of the loading.

When the vertical distribution of the loading is assumed to be uniform, i.e. rectangular, k shall be taken as equal to 1.0. For a trapezoidal distribution

$$k = 1.0 + 0.06(50 - R)$$

Where:

R is the upper end bearing reaction taken from table III or IV.

(d) *Stays or shores*

The sizes of stays and shores shall be so determined that the loads derived from tables I and II in the preceding paragraphs (a) and (b) shall not exceed one third of the breaking loads.

(D) SAUCERS

When a saucer is used to reduce the heeling moments in a filled compartment, its depth, measured from the bottom of the saucer to the deck line, shall be as follows:

For ships with a moulded breadth of up to 9.1 metres, not less than 1.2 metres.

For ships with a moulded breadth of 18.3 metres or more, not less than 1.8 metres.

For ships with a moulded breadth between 9.1 metres and 18.3 metres, the minimum depth of the saucer shall be calculated by interpolation.

The top (mouth) of the saucer shall be formed by the under-deck structure in the way of the hatchway, i.e. hatch side girders or coamings and hatch end beams. The saucer and hatchway above shall be completely filled with bagged grain or other suitable cargo laid down on a separation cloth or its equivalent and stowed tightly against adjacent structures and the portable hatchway beams if the latter are in place.

(E)   BUNDLING OF BULK

As an alternative to filling the saucer with bagged grain or other suitable cargo a bundle of bulk grain may be used provided that:

(a)   The saucer is lined with a material acceptable to the Administration having a tensile strength of not less than 274 kg per 5 cm strip and which is provided with suitable means for securing at the top.

(b)   As an alternative to paragraph (a) above a material acceptable to the Administration having a tensile strength of not less than 137 kg per 5 cm strip may be used if the saucer is constructed as follows:

Athwartship lashings acceptable to the Administration shall be placed inside the saucer formed in the bulk grain at intervals of not more than 2.4 metres. These lashings shall be of sufficient length to permit being drawn up tight and secured at the top of the saucer.

Dunnage not less than 25 mm in thickness or other suitable material of equal strength and between 150 to 300 mm in width shall be placed fore and aft over these lashings to prevent the cutting or chafing of the material which shall be placed thereon to line the saucer.

(c)   The saucer shall be filled with bulk grain and secured at the top except that when using material approved under paragraph (b) further dunnage shall be laid on top after lapping the material before the saucer is secured by setting up the lashings.

(d)   If more than one sheet of material is used to line the saucer they shall be joined at the bottom either by sewing or a double lap.

(e)   The top of the saucer shall be coincidental with the bottom of the beams when these are in place and suitable general cargo or bulk grain may be placed between the beams on top of the saucer.

(F)   SECURING HATCH COVERS OF FILLED COMPARTMENTS

If there is no bulk grain or other cargo above a filled compartment the hatch covers shall be secured in an approved manner having regard to the weight and permanent arrangements provided for securing such covers.

The documents of authorization issued under regulation 10 of this chapter shall include reference to the manner of securing considered necessary by the Administration issuing such documents.

SECTION II – SECURING OF PARTLY FILLED COMPARTMENTS

(A)   STRAPPING OR LASHING

(a)   When, in order to eliminate heeling moments in partly filled compartments, strapping or lashing is utilized, the securing shall be accomplished as follows:

(i)   The grain shall be trimmed and levelled to the extent that it is very slightly crowned and covered with burlap separation cloths, tarpaulins or the equivalent.

(ii)   The separation cloths and/or tarpaulins shall overlap at least 1.8 metres.

(iii)   Two solid floors of rough 25 mm by 150 mm to 300 mm lumber shall be laid with the top floor running longitudinally and nailed to an athwartships bottom floor. Alternatively, one solid floor of 50 mm lumber, running longitudinally and nailed over the top of a 50 mm bottom bearer not less than 150 mm wide, may be used. The bottom bearers shall extend the full breadth of the compartment and shall be spaced not more than 2.4 metres apart. Arrangements utilizing other materials and deemed by an Administration to be equivalent to the foregoing may be accepted.

(iv)   Steel wire rope (19 mm diameter or equivalent), doubled steel strapping (50 mm × 1.3 mm and having a breaking load of at least 5000 kg), or chain of equivalent strength, each of which shall be set tight by means of a 32 mm turnbuckle, may be used for lashings. A winch tightener, used in conjunction with a locking arm, may be substituted for the 32 mm turnbuckle when steel strapping is used, provided suitable wrenches are available for setting up as necessary. When steel strapping is used, not less than three crimp seals shall be used for securing the ends. When wire is used, not less than four clips shall be used for forming eyes in the lashings.

(v) Prior to the completion of loading the lashing shall be positively attached to the framing at a point approximately 450 mm below the anticipated final grain surface by means of either a 25 mm shackle or beam clamp of equivalent strength.

(vi) The lashings shall be spaced not more than 2.4 metres apart and each shall be supported by a bearer nailed over the top of the fore and aft floor. This bearer shall consist of not less than 25 mm by 150 mm lumber or its equivalent and shall extend the full breadth of the compartment.

(vii) During the voyage the strapping shall be regularly inspected and set up where necessary.

(B) OVERSTOWING ARRANGEMENTS

Where bagged grain or other suitable cargo is utilized for the purpose of securing partly filled compartments, the free grain surface shall be covered with a separation cloth or equivalent or by a suitable platform. Such platforms shall consist of bearers spaced not more than 1.2 metres apart and 25 mm boards laid thereon spaced not more than 100 mm apart. Platforms may be constructed of other materials provided they are deemed by an Administration to be equivalent.

(C) BAGGED GRAIN

Bagged grain shall be carried in sound bags which shall be well filled and securely closed.

Chapter VII

CARRIAGE OF DANGEROUS GOODS

Page

PART A – CARRIAGE OF DANGEROUS GOODS IN
PACKAGED FORM OR IN SOLID FORM IN
BULK

1	Application	386
2	Classification	386
3	Packaging	387
4	Marking, labelling and placarding	388
5	Documents	388
6	Stowage requirements	389
7	Explosives in passenger ships	389

PART B – CONSTRUCTION AND EQUIPMENT OF SHIPS
CARRYING DANGEROUS LIQUID CHEMICALS
IN BULK

8	Definitions	390
9	Application to chemical tankers	391
10	Requirements for chemical tankers	391

PART C – CONSTRUCTION AND EQUIPMENT OF SHIPS
CARRYING LIQUEFIED GASES IN BULK

11	Definitions	392
12	Application to gas carriers	392
13	Requirements for gas carriers	393

PART A – CARRIAGE OF DANGEROUS GOODS IN PACKAGED FORM OR IN SOLID FORM IN BULK

Regulation 1

Application

1   Unless expressly provided otherwise, this part applies to dangerous goods classified under regulation 2 which are carried in packaged form or in solid form in bulk (hereinafter referred to as "dangerous goods"), in all ships to which the present regulations apply and in cargo ships of less than 500 tons gross tonnage.

2   The provisions of this part do not apply to ships' stores and equipment.

3   The carriage of dangerous goods is prohibited except in accordance with the provisions of this part.

4   To supplement the provisions of this part, each Contracting Government shall issue, or cause to be issued, detailed instructions on safe packaging and stowage of dangerous goods which shall include the precautions necessary in relation to other cargo.*

Regulation 2

Classification

Dangerous goods shall be divided into the following classes:

Class 1   –   Explosives

Class 2   –   Gases: compressed, liquefied or dissolved under pressure

Class 3   –   Flammable liquids

Class 4.1   –   Flammable solids

Class 4.2   –   Substances liable to spontaneous combustion

Class 4.3   –   Substances which, in contact with water, emit flammable gases

---

* Reference is made to the International Maritime Dangerous Goods Code (IMDG Code) adopted by the Organization by resolution A.81(IV), and to the relevant sections and the related parts of Appendix B of the Code of Safe Practice for Solid Bulk Cargoes (BC Code) adopted by the Organization by resolution A.434(XI), as have been or may be amended by the Maritime Safety Committee.

Class 5.1 – Oxidizing substances

Class 5.2 – Organic peroxides

Class 6.1 – Poisonous (toxic) substances

Class 6.2 – Infectious substances

Class 7 – Radioactive materials

Class 8 – Corrosives

Class 9 – Miscellaneous dangerous substances, that is any other substance which experience has shown, or may show, to be of such a dangerous character that the provisions of this part shall apply to it.

Regulation 3

Packaging

1   The packaging of dangerous goods shall be:

.1   well made and in good condition;

.2   of such a character that any interior surface with which the contents may come in contact is not dangerously affected by the substance being conveyed; and

.3   capable of withstanding the ordinary risks of handling and carriage by sea.

2   Where the use of absorbent or cushioning material is customary in the packaging of liquids in receptacles, that material shall be:

.1   capable of minimizing the dangers to which the liquid may give rise;

.2   so disposed as to prevent movement and ensure that the receptacle remains surrounded; and

.3   where reasonably possible, of sufficient quantity to absorb the liquid in the event of breakage of the receptacle.

3   Receptacles containing dangerous liquids shall have an ullage at the filling temperature sufficient to allow for the highest temperature during the course of normal carriage.

4   Cylinders or receptacles for gases under pressure shall be adequately constructed, tested, maintained and correctly filled.

5   Empty uncleaned receptacles which have been used previously for the carriage of dangerous goods shall be subject to the provisions of this part

for filled receptacles, unless adequate measures have been taken to nullify any hazard.

Regulation 4

Marking, labelling and placarding

1   Packages containing dangerous goods shall be durably marked with the correct technical name; trade names alone shall not be used.

2   Packages containing dangerous goods shall be provided with distinctive labels or stencils of the labels, or placards, as appropriate, so as to make clear the dangerous properties of the goods contained therein.

3   The method of marking the correct technical name and of affixing labels or applying stencils of labels, or of affixing placards on packages containing dangerous goods, shall be such that this information will still be identifiable on packages surviving at least three months' immersion in the sea. In considering suitable marking, labelling and placarding methods, account shall be taken of the durability of the materials used and of the surface of the package.

4   Packages containing dangerous goods shall be so marked and labelled except that:

.1   packages containing dangerous goods of a low degree of hazard or packed in limited quantities;* or

.2   when special circumstances permit, packages that are stowed and handled in units that are identified by labels or placards;*

may be exempted from labelling requirements.

Regulation 5

Documents

1   In all documents relating to the carriage of dangerous goods by sea where the goods are named, the correct technical name of the goods shall be used (trade names alone shall not be used) and the correct description given in accordance with the classification set out in regulation 2.

2   The shipping documents prepared by the shipper shall include, or be accompanied by, a signed certificate or declaration that the shipment offered

---

* Reference is made to the specific exemptions provided for in the International Maritime Dangerous Goods Code (IMDG Code).

for carriage is properly packaged and marked, labelled or placarded, as appropriate, and in proper condition for carriage.

3   Each ship carrying dangerous goods shall have a special list or manifest setting forth, in accordance with the classification set out in regulation 2, the dangerous goods on board and the location thereof. A detailed stowage plan which identifies by class and sets out the location of all dangerous goods on board may be used in place of such special list or manifest.

Regulation 6

Stowage requirements

1   Dangerous goods shall be stowed safely and appropriately in accordance with the nature of the goods. Incompatible goods shall be segregated from one another.

2   Explosives (except ammunition) which present a serious risk shall be stowed in a magazine which shall be kept securely closed while at sea. Such explosives shall be segregated from detonators. Electrical apparatus and cables in any compartment in which explosives are carried shall be so designed and used as to minimize the risk of fire or explosion.

3   Dangerous goods in packaged form which give off dangerous vapours shall be stowed in a mechanically ventilated space or on deck. Dangerous goods in solid form in bulk which give off dangerous vapours shall be stowed in a well ventilated space.

4   In ships carrying flammable liquids or gases, special precautions shall be taken where necessary against fire or explosion.

5   Substances which are liable to spontaneous heating or combustion shall not be carried unless adequate precautions have been taken to minimize the likelihood of the outbreak of fire.

Regulation 7

Explosives in passenger ships

1   In passenger ships the following explosives only may be carried:

.1   safety cartridges and safety fuses;

.2   small quantities of explosives not exceeding 10 kg total net mass;

.3　distress signals for use in ships or aircraft, if the total mass of such signals does not exceed 1,000 kg;

.4　except in ships carrying unberthed passengers, fireworks which are unlikely to explode violently.

2　Notwithstanding the provisions of paragraph 1, additional quantities or types of explosives may be carried in passenger ships in which special safety measures approved by the Administration are taken.

PART B – CONSTRUCTION AND EQUIPMENT OF SHIPS CARRYING DANGEROUS LIQUID CHEMICALS IN BULK

Regulation 8

Definitions

For the purpose of this part, unless expressly provided otherwise:

1.　"International Bulk Chemical Code" means the International Code for the Construction and Equipment of Ships Carrying Dangerous Chemicals in Bulk adopted by the Maritime Safety Committee of the Organization by resolution MSC.4(48), as may be amended by the Organization, provided that such amendments are adopted, brought into force and take effect in accordance with the provisions of article VIII of the present Convention concerning the amendment procedures applicable to the Annex other than chapter I.

2　"Chemical tanker" means a cargo ship constructed or adapted and used for the carrige in bulk of any liquid product listed in chapter 17 of the International Bulk Chemical Code.

3　For the purpose of regulation 9, "ship constructed" means a ship the keel of which is laid or which is at a similar stage of construction.

4　"At a similar stage of construction" means the stage at which:

.1　construction identifiable with a specific ship begins; and

.2　assembly of that ship has commenced comprising at least 50 tonnes or 1% of the estimated mass of all structural material, whichever is less.

Regulation 9

Application to chemical tankers

1   Unless expressly provided otherwise, this part applies to chemical tankers constructed on or after 1 July 1986 including those of less than 500 tons gross tonnage. Such tankers shall comply with the requirements of this part in addition to any other applicable requirements of the present regulations.

2   Any chemical tanker, irrespective of the date of construction, which undergoes repairs, alterations, modifications and outfitting related thereto shall continue to comply with at least the requirements previously applicable to the ship. Such a ship, if constructed before 1 July 1986, shall, as a rule, comply with the requirements for a ship constructed on or after that date to at least the same extent as before undergoing such repairs, alterations, modifications or outfitting. Repairs, alterations and modifications of a major character, and outfitting related thereto, shall meet the requirements for a ship constructed on or after 1 July 1986 in so far as the Administration deems reasonable and practicable.

3   A ship, irrespective of the date of construction, which is converted to a chemical tanker shall be treated as a chemical tanker constructed on the date on which such conversion commenced.

Regulation 10

Requirements for chemical tankers

1   A chemical tanker shall comply with the requirements of the International Bulk Chemical Code and shall, in addition to the requirements of regulations I/8, I/9, and I/10, as applicable, be surveyed and certified as provided for in that Code. For the purpose of this regulation, the requirements of the Code shall be treated as mandatory.

2   A chemical tanker holding a certificate issued pursuant to the provisions of paragraph 1 shall be subject to the control established in regulation I/19. For this purpose such certificate shall be treated as a certificate issued under regulation I/12 or I/13.

PART C – CONSTRUCTION AND EQUIPMENT OF SHIPS CARRYING LIQUEFIED GASES IN BULK

Regulation 11

Definitions

For the purpose of this part, unless expressly provided otherwise:

1   "International Gas Carrier Code" means the International Code for the Construction and Equipment of Ships Carrying Liquefied Gases in Bulk as adopted by the Maritime Safety Committee of the Organization by resolution MSC.5(48), as may be amended by the Organization, provided that such amendments are adopted, brought into force and take effect in accordance with the provisions of article VIII of the present Convention concerning the amendment procedures applicable to the Annex other than chapter I.

2   "Gas carrier" means a cargo ship constructed or adapted and used for the carriage in bulk of any liquefied gas or other product listed in chapter 19 of the International Gas Carrier Code.

3   For the purpose of regulation 12, "ship constructed" means a ship the keel of which is laid or which is at a similar stage of construction.

4   "At a similar stage of construction" means the stage at which:

.1   construction identifiable with a specific ship begins; and

.2   assembly of that ship has commenced comprising at least 50 tonnes or 1% of the estimated mass of all structural material, whichever is less.

Regulation 12

Application to gas carriers

1   Unless expressly provided otherwise, this part applies to gas carriers constructed on or after 1 July 1986 including those of less than 500 tons gross tonnage. Such gas carriers shall comply with the requirements of this part in addition to any other applicable requirements of the present regulations.

2   Any gas carrier, irrespective of the date of construction, which undergoes repairs, alterations, modifications and outfitting related thereto shall continue to comply with at least the requirements previously applicable to the ship.

Such a ship if constructed before 1 July 1986 shall, as a rule, comply with the requirements for a ship constructed on or after that date to at least the same extent as before undergoing such repairs, alterations, modifications or outfitting. Repairs, alterations and modifications of a major character, and outfitting related thereto, shall meet the requirements for a ship constructed on or after 1 July 1986 in so far as the Administration deems reasonable and practicable.

3   A ship, irrespective of the date of construction, which is converted to a gas carrier shall be treated as a gas carrier constructed on the date on which such conversion commenced.

Regulation 13

Requirements for gas carriers

1   A gas carrier shall comply with the requirements of the International Gas Carrier Code and shall, in addition to the requirements of regulations I/8, I/9 and I/10, as applicable, be surveyed and certified as provided for in that Code. For the purpose of this regulation, the requirements of the Code shall be treated as mandatory.

2   A gas carrier holding a certificate issued pursuant to the provisions of paragraph 1 shall be subject to the control established in regulation I/19. For this purpose such certificate shall be treated as a certificate issued under regulation I/12 or I/13.

Chapter VIII

NUCLEAR SHIPS

		Page
1	Application	395
2	Application of other chapters	395
3	Exemptions	395
4	Approval of reactor installation	396
5	Suitability of reactor installation for service on board ship	396
6	Radiation safety	396
7	Safety assessment	396
8	Operating manual	397
9	Surveys	397
10	Certificates	397
11	Special control	398
12	Casualties	398

Regulation 1

Application

This chapter applies to all nuclear ships except ships of war.

Regulation 2

Application of other chapters

The regulations contained in the other chapters of the present Convention apply to nuclear ships except as modified by this chapter.*

Regulation 3

Exemptions

A nuclear ship shall not, in any circumstances, be exempted from compliance with any regulations of this Convention.

---

* Reference is made to the Code of Safety for Nuclear Merchant Ships (resolution A.491(XII) which supplements the requirements of this chapter.

Regulation 4

Approval of reactor installation

The design, construction and standards of inspection and assembly of the reactor installation shall be subject to the approval and satisfaction of the Administration and shall take account of the limitations which will be imposed on surveys by the presence of radiation.

Regulation 5

Suitability of reactor installation for service on board ship

The reactor installation shall be designed having regard to the special conditions of service on board ship both in normal and exceptional circumstances of navigation.

Regulation 6

Radiation safety

The Administration shall take measures to ensure that there are no unreasonable radiation or other nuclear hazards, at sea or in port, to the crew, passengers or public, or to the waterways or food or water resources.

Regulation 7

Safety assessment

(a) A safety assessment shall be prepared to permit evaluation of the nuclear power plant and safety of the ship to ensure that there are no unreasonable radiation or other hazards, at sea or in port, to the crew, passengers or public, or to the waterways or food or water resources. The Administration, when satisfied, shall approve such safety assessment which shall always be kept up to date.

(b) The safety assessment shall be made available sufficiently in advance to the Contracting Governments of the countries which a nuclear ship intends to visit so that they may evaluate the safety of the ship.

Regulation 8

Operating manual

A fully detailed operating manual shall be prepared for the information and guidance of the operating personnel in their duties on all matters relating to the operation of the nuclear power plant and having an important bearing on safety. The Administration, when satisfied, shall approve such operating manual and a copy shall be kept on board the ship. The operating manual shall always be kept up to date.

Regulation 9

Surveys

Survey of nuclear ships shall include the applicable requirements of regulation 7 of chapter I, or of regulations 8, 9 and 10 of chapter I, except in so far as surveys are limited by the presence of radiation. In addition, the surveys shall include any special requirements of the safety assessment. They shall in all cases, notwithstanding the provisions of regulations 8 and 10 of chapter I, be carried out not less frequently than once a year.

Regulation 10

Certificates

(a)   The provisions of paragraph (a) of regulation 12 of chapter I and of regulation 14 of chapter I shall not apply to nuclear ships.

(b)   A certificate, called a Nuclear Passenger Ship Safety Certificate shall be issued after inspection and survey to a nuclear passenger ship which complies with the requirements of chapters II–1, II–2, III, IV and VIII, and any other relevant requirements of the present regulations.

(c)   A certificate, called a Nuclear Cargo Ship Safety Certificate shall be issued after inspection and survey to a nuclear cargo ship which satisfies the requirements for cargo ships on survey set out in regulation 10 of chapter I, and complies with the requirements of chapters II–1, II–2, III, IV and VIII and any other relevant requirements of the present regulations.

(d)   Nuclear Passenger Ship Safety Certificates and Nuclear Cargo Ship Safety Certificates shall state: "That the ship, being a nuclear ship, complied with all requirements of chapter VIII of the Convention and conformed to the Safety Assessment approved for the ship.

(e) Nuclear Passenger Ship Safety Certificates and Nuclear Cargo Ship Safety Certificates shall be valid for a period of not more than 12 months.

(f) Nuclear Passenger Ship Safety Certificates and Nuclear Cargo Ship Safety Certificates shall be issued either by the Administration or by any person or organization duly authorized by it. In every case, that Administration assumes full responsibility for the certificate.

Regulation 11

*Special control**

In addition to the control established by regulation 19 of chapter I, nuclear ships shall be subject to special control before entering the ports and in the ports of Contracting Governments, directed towards verifying that there is on board a valid Nuclear Ship Safety Certificate and that there are no unreasonable radiation or other hazards at sea or in port, to the crew, passengers or public, or to the waterways or food or water resources.

Regulation 12

Casualties

In the event of any accident likely to lead to an environmental hazard the master of a nuclear ship shall immediately inform the Administration. The master shall also immediately inform the competent governmental authority of the country in whose waters the ship may be, or whose waters the ship approaches in a damaged condition.

---

* Reference is made to the IMO/IAEA Safety Recommendation on the Use of Ports by Nuclear Merchant Ships.

APPENDIX

Form of Safety Certificate for Passenger Ships

PASSENGER SHIP SAFETY CERTIFICATE

(*Official seal*)   (*Country*)

for $\dfrac{\text{an}}{\text{a short}}$ international voyage.

Issued under the provisions of the

INTERNATIONAL CONVENTION FOR THE SAFETY OF LIFE AT
SEA, 1974

Name of ship	Distinctive number or letters	Port of registry	Gross tonnage	Particulars of voyages, if any, sanctioned under regulation 27(c) (vii) of chapter III*	Date on which keel was laid (see NOTE below)

The	(*Name*) Government certifies
I, the undersigned	(*Name*) certify

I.   That the above-mentioned ship has been duly surveyed in accordance with the provisions of the Convention referred to above.

II.   That the survey showed that the ship complied with the requirements of the regulations annexed to the said Convention as regards:

(1)   the structure, main and auxiliary boilers and other pressure vessels and machinery;

(2)   the watertight subdivision arrangements and details;

(3)   the following subdivision load lines:

---

* Regulation III/20.1.2 of the 1983 SOLAS amendments.

Subdivision load lines assigned and marked on the ship's side at amidships (regulation 11 of chapter II-1)*	Freeboard	To apply when the spaces in which passengers are carried include the following alternative spaces
C.1	....	....
C.2	....	....
C.3	....	....

III.   That the life-saving appliances provide for a total number of .... persons and no more, viz.:

.... lifeboats (including .... motor lifeboats) capable of accommodating .... persons, and .... motor lifeboats fitted with radiotelegraph installation and searchlight (included in the total lifeboats shown above) and .... motor lifeboats fitted with searchlight only (also included in the total lifeboats shown above), requiring .... certificated lifeboatmen;

.... liferafts, for which approved launching devices are required, capable of accommodating .... persons; and

.... liferafts, for which approved launching devices are not required, capable of accommodating .... persons;

.... buoyant apparatus capable of supporting .... persons;

.... lifebuoys;

.... lifejackets.

IV.   That the lifeboats and liferafts were equipped in accordance with the provisions of the regulations.

V.   That the ship was provided with a line-throwing appliance and portable radio apparatus for survival craft in accordance with the provisions of the regulations.

VI.   That the ship complied with the requirements of the regulations as regards radiotelegraph installations, viz.:

	Requirements of regulations	Actual provision
Hours of listening by operator...	....	....
Number of operators	....	....
Whether auto alarm fitted..	....	....
Whether main installation fitted	....	....
Whether reserve installation fitted	....	....
Whether main and reserve transmitters electrically separated or combined	....	....
Whether direction-finder fitted...	....	....
Whether radio equipment for homing on the radio-telephone distress frequency fitted	....	....
Whether radar fitted..	....	....
Number of passengers for which certificated....................	....	....

---

* Regulation II-1/13 of the 1981 and 1983 SOLAS amendments.

VII. That the functioning of the radiotelegraph installations for motor life-boats and/or the portable radio apparatus for survival craft, if provided, complied with the provisions of the regulations.

VIII. That the ship complied with the requirements of the regulations as regards fire-detecting and fire-extinguishing appliances, radar, echo-sounding device and gyro-compass and was provided with navigation lights and shapes, pilot ladder, and means of making sound signals, and distress signals in accordance with the provisions of the regulations and also the International Regulations for Preventing Collisions at Sea in force.

IX. That in all other respects the ship complied with the requirements of the regulations, so far as these requirements apply thereto.

This certificate is issued under the authority of the ....
Government. It will remain in force until ....

Issued at .... the .... day of .... 19......

Here follows the seal or signature of the authority entitled to issue the certificate.

(*Seal*)

If signed, the following paragraph is to be added:

The undersigned declares that he is duly authorized by the said Government to issue this certificate.

(*Signature*)

NOTE: It will be sufficient to indicate the year in which the keel was laid or when the ship was at a similar stage of construction except for 1952, 1965, 1980, 1981, 1984 and 1986, in which cases the actual date should be given.

In the case of a ship which is converted as provided in regulation 1(b)(i) of chapter II–1* or regulation 1(a)(i) of chapter II–2** of the Convention, the date on which the work of conversion was begun should be given.

---

* Regulation II–1/1.1.3.3 of the 1981 and 1983 SOLAS amendments.

** Regulation II–2/1.1.3.3 of the 1981 and 1983 SOLAS amendments.

Form of Safety Construction Certificate for Cargo Ships including Supplement

CARGO SHIP SAFETY CONSTRUCTION CERTIFICATE

(*Official seal*)   (*Country*)

Issued under the provisions of the

INTERNATIONAL CONVENTION FOR THE SAFETY OF LIFE AT SEA, 1974

Name of ship	Distinctive number or letters	Port of registry	Gross tonnage	Date on which keel was laid (see NOTE below)

The _____   (*Name*) Government certifies

I, the undersigned   (*Name*) certify

That the above-mentioned ship has been duly surveyed in accordance with the provisions of regulation 10 of chapter I of the Convention referred to above, and that the survey showed that the condition of the hull, machinery and equipment, as defined in the above regulation, was in all respects satisfactory and that the ship complied with the applicable requirements of chapter II–1 and chapter II–2 (other than that relating to fire-extinguishing appliances and fire control plans).

This certificate is issued under the authority of the ....
Government. It will remain in force until ....

Issued at .... the................. day of .... 19..........

Here follows the seal or signature of the authority entitled to issue the certificate.

(*Seal*)

If signed, the following paragraph is to be added:

The undersigned declares that he is duly authorized by the said Government to issue this certificate.

(*Signature*)

NOTE: It will be sufficient to indicate the year in which the keel was laid or when the ship was at a similar stage of construction except for 1952, 1965, 1980, 1981, 1984 and 1986, in which cases the actual date should be given.

SUPPLEMENT TO THE CARGO SHIP SAFETY CONSTRUCTION CERTIFICATE $\boxed{\text{P}}$

(Official seal)   *(Country)*

Issued under the provisions of the

PROTOCOL OF 1978 RELATING TO THE INTERNATIONAL CONVENTION FOR THE SAFETY OF LIFE AT SEA 1974

Name of ship	Distinctive number or letters	Port of registry	Deadweight of ship (metric tons)	Year of build

Type of ship:

Tanker engaged in the trade of carrying crude oil*

Tanker engaged in the trade of carrying oil other than crude oil*

Tanker engaged in the trade of carrying crude/other oil*

Cargo ship other than a tanker engaged in the trade of carrying oil*

Date of contract for building or alteration or modification of a major character** ....

Date on which keel was laid or ship was at a similar stage of construction or on which an alteration or modification of a major character was commenced** ....

Date of delivery or completion of an alteration or modification of a major character** ....

This Supplement shall be permanently attached to the Cargo Ship Safety Construction Certificate.

---

* Delete as appropriate.

** When the date of the building contract is known, this should be recorded, a dash (—) entered in the space for the keel-laying date and the delivery date also recorded.

When the date of the building contract is not known, a dash (—) should be entered in the space for this date and the keel-laying and delivery dates recorded.

Whether a ship is "new" or "existing" would then be decided on the basis of the above dates (PSLS.2/Circ. 8).

THIS IS TO CERTIFY:

That the ship has been surveyed in accordance with regulation 10 of chapter I of the Protocol of 1978 Relating to the International Convention for the Safety of Life at Sea, 1974; and

that the survey showed that the condition of the hull, machinery and equipment as defined in the above regulation was in all respects satisfactory and that the ship complied with the requirements of that Protocol.

This certificate is valid until .... subject to intermediate survey(s) at intervals of ....

Issued at ....
(Place of issue of certificate)

................19...... ....
(Signature of duly authorized official issuing the certificate)

(Seal or stamp of the issuing authority, as appropriate)

Intermediate survey

This is to certify that at an intermediate survey required by regulation 10 of chapter I of the Protocol of 1978 Relating to the International Convention for the Safety of Life at Sea, 1974, this ship was found to comply with the relevant provisions of that Protocol.

Signed ....
(Signature of duly authorized official)

Place ....

Date ....

Next intermediate survey due ....

(Seal or stamp of the authority, as appropriate)

Signed ....
(Signature of duly authorized official)

Place ....

Date ....

Next intermediate survey due ....

(Seal or stamp of the authority, as appropriate)

Signed ....
(Signature of duly authorized official)

Place ....

Date ....

Next intermediate survey due ....

(Seal or stamp of the authority, as appropriate)

Signed ....
(Signature of duly authorized official)

Place ....

Date ....

(Seal or stamp of the authority, as appropriate)

Form of Safety Equipment Certificate for Cargo Ships including Supplement

CARGO SHIP SAFETY EQUIPMENT CERTIFICATE

(*Official seal*)   (*Country*)

Issued under the provisions of the

INTERNATIONAL CONVENTION FOR THE SAFETY OF LIFE AT SEA, 1974

Name of ship	Distinctive number or letters	Port of registry	Gross tonnage	Date on which keel was laid (see NOTE below)

The   (*Name*) Government certifies

I, the undersigned   (*Name*) certify

I.   That the above-mentioned ship has been duly inspected in accordance with the provisions of the Convention referred to above.

II.   That the inspection showed that the life-saving appliances provided for a total number of .... persons and no more viz.:

.... lifeboats on port side capable of accommodating .... persons;

.... lifeboats on starboard side capable of accommodating .... persons;

.... motor lifeboats (included in the total lifeboats shown above), including .... motor lifeboats fitted with radiotelegraph installation and searchlight, and .... motor lifeboats fitted with searchlight only;

.... liferafts, for which approved launching devices are required, capable of accommodating .... persons; and

.... liferafts, for which approved launching devices are not required, capable of accommodating .... persons;

.... lifebuoys;

.... lifejackets.

III.   That the lifeboats and liferafts were equipped in accordance with the provisions of the regulations annexed to the Convention.

IV.   That the ship was provided with a line-throwing apparatus and portable radio apparatus for survival craft in accordance with the provisions of the regulations.

V.   That the inspection showed that the ship complied with the requirements of the said Convention as regards fire-extinguishing appliances and fire control plans, echo-sounding device and gyro-compass and was provided with naviga-tion lights and shapes, pilot ladder, and means of making sound signals and distress signals, in accordance with the provisions of the regulations and the International Regulations for Preventing Collisions at Sea in force.

VI.   That in all other respects the ship complied with the requirements of the regulations so far as these requirements apply thereto.

This certificate is issued under the authority of the ....
Government. It will remain in force until ....

Issued at .... the .... day of .... 19.........

Here follows the seal or signature of the authority entitled to issue the certificate.

(*Seal*)

If signed, the following paragraph is to be added:

The undersigned declares that he is duly authorized by the said Govern-ment to issue this certificate.

(*Signature*)

NOTE: It will be sufficient to indicate the year in which the keel was laid or when the ship was at a similar stage of construction except for 1952, 1965, 1980, 1981, 1984 and 1986, in which cases the actual date should be given.

SUPPLEMENT TO THE CARGO SHIP SAFETY EQUIPMENT CERTIFICATE $\boxed{P}$

(Official seal) *(Country)*

Issued under the provisions of the

PROTOCOL OF 1978 RELATING TO THE INTERNATIONAL CONVENTION FOR THE SAFETY OF LIFE AT SEA 1974

Name of ship	Distinctive number or letters	Port of registry	Deadweight of ship (metric tons)	Year of build

Type of ship:

Tanker engaged in the trade of carrying crude oil*

Tanker engaged in the trade of carrying oil other than crude oil*

Tanker engaged in the trade of carrying crude/other oil*

Cargo ship other than a tanker engaged in the trade of carrying oil*

Date of contract for building or alteration or modification of a major character** ....

Date on which keel was laid or ship was at a similar stage of construction or on which an alteration or modification of a major character was commenced** ....

Date of delivery or completion of an alteration or modification of a major character** ....

This Supplement shall be permanently attached to the Cargo Ship Safety Equipment Certificate.

---

* Delete as appropriate.

** When the date of the building contract is known, this should be recorded, a dash (—) entered in the space for the keel-laying date and the delivery date also recorded.

When the date of the building contract is not known, a dash (—) should be entered in the space for this date and the keel-laying and delivery dates recorded.

Whether a ship is "new" or "existing" would then be decided on the basis of the above dates (PSLS.2/Circ. 8).

THIS IS TO CERTIFY:

That the ship has been surveyed in accordance with regulation 8 of chapter I of the Protocol of 1978 Relating to the International Convention for the Safety of Life at Sea, 1974; and

that the survey showed that the condition of the safety equipment as defined in the above regulation was in all respects satisfactory and that the ship complied with the requirements of that Protocol.

This certificate is valid until .... subject to intermediate survey(s) at intervals of ....

Issued at ....
(Place of issue of certificate)

.................19......   ....
(Signature of duly authorized official
issuing the certificate)

(Seal or stamp of the issuing authority, as appropriate)

Intermediate survey

This is to certify that at an intermediate survey required by regulation 8 of chapter I of the Protocol of 1978 Relating to the International Convention for the Safety of Life at Sea, 1974, this ship was found to comply with the relevant provisions of that Protocol.

Signed ....
(Signature of duly authorized official)

Place ....

Date ....

Next intermediate survey due...

(Seal or stamp of the authority, as appropriate)

Signed ....
(Signature of duly authorized official)

Place ....

Date ....

(Seal or stamp of the authority, as appropriate)

Under the provisions of regulation 14 of chapter I of the Protocol the validity of this certificate is extended until

....

Signed ....
(Signature of duly authorized official)

Place ....

Date ....

(Seal or stamp of the authority, as appropriate)

Form of Safety Radiotelegraphy Certificate for Cargo Ships

CARGO SHIP SAFETY RADIOTELEGRAPHY CERTIFICATE

(Official seal)   *(Country)*

Issued under the provisions of the
INTERNATIONAL CONVENTION FOR THE SAFETY OF LIFE AT SEA, 1974

Name of ship	Distinctive number or letters	Port of registry	Gross tonnage	Date on which keel was laid (see NOTE below)

The _____ *(Name)* Government certifies

I, the undersigned   *(Name)* certify

I.   That the above-mentioned ship complies with the provisions of the regulations annexed to the Convention referred to above as regards radiotelegraphy and radar:

	Requirements of regulations	Actual provision
Hours of listening by operator	....	....
Number of operators	....	....
Whether auto alarm fitted	....	....
Whether main installation fitted	....	....
Whether reserve installation fitted	....	....
Whether main and reserve transmitters electrically separated or combined	....	....
Whether direction-finder fitted	....	....
Whether radio equipment for homing on the radio-telephone distress frequency fitted	....	....
Whether radar fitted	....	....

II.   That the functioning of the radiotelegraphy installation for motor lifeboats and/or the portable radio apparatus for survival craft, if provided, complies with the provisions of the said regulations.

This certificate is issued under the authority of the ....
Government. It will remain in force until ....

Issued at .... the .... day of .... 19..........

Here follows the seal or signature of the authority entitled to issue this certificate:

(*Seal*)

If signed, the following paragraph is to be added:

The undersigned declares that he is duly authorized by the said Government to issue this certificate.

(*Signature*)

NOTE: It will be sufficient to indicate the year in which the keel was laid or when the ship was at a similar stage of construction except for 1952, 1965, 1980, 1981, 1984 and 1986, in which cases the actual date should be given.

Form of Safety Radiotelephony Certificate for Cargo Ships

CARGO SHIP SAFETY RADIOTELEPHONY CERTIFICATE

(Official seal)   *(Country)*

Issued under the provisions of the
INTERNATIONAL CONVENTION FOR THE SAFETY OF LIFE AT
SEA, 1974

Name of ship	Distinctive number or letters	Port of registry	Gross tonnage	Date on which keel was laid (see NOTE below)

The _____   *(Name)* Government certifies
I, the undersigned   *(Name)* certify

I.   That the above-mentioned ship complies with the provisions of the regulations annexed to the Convention referred to above as regards radiotelephony:

	Requirements of regulations	Actual provision
Hours of listening..............................	....	....
Number of operators...........................	....	....

II.   That the functioning of the portable radio apparatus for survival craft, if provided, complies with the provisions of the said regulations.

This certificate is issued under the authority of the ....
Government. It will remain in force until ....

Issued at .... the .... day of .... 19......

413

Here follows the seal or signature of the authority entitled to issue this certificate:

(*Seal*)

If signed, the following paragraph is to be added:

The undersigned declares that he is duly authorized by the said Government to issue this certificate.

(*Signature*)

NOTE: It will be sufficient to indicate the year in which the keel was laid or when the ship was at a similar stage of construction except for 1952, 1965, 1980, 1981, 1984 and 1986, in which cases the actual date should be given.

Form of Exemption Certificate

EXEMPTION CERTIFICATE

(Official seal)   *(Country)*

Issued under the provisions of the

INTERNATIONAL CONVENTION FOR THE SAFETY OF LIFE AT SEA, 1974

Name of ship	Distinctive number or letters	Port of registry	Gross tonnage

The _____   *(Name)* Government certifies

I, the undersigned   *(Name)* certify

That the above-mentioned ship is, under the authority conferred by regulation .... of chapter .... of the regulations annexed to the Convention referred to above, exempted from the requirements of † .... of the Convention

on the voyages ....

to ....

*   Insert here the conditions,   *
if any, on which the exemption
certificate is granted.

This certificate is issued under the authority of the ....
Government. It will remain in force until ....

Issued at .... the .... day of .... 19..........

Here follows the seal or signature of the authority entitled to issue this certificate:

                                 (Seal)

If signed, the following paragraph is to be added:

The undersigned declares that he is duly authorized by the said Government to issue this certificate.

                                 (Signature)

---

† Insert here references to chapters and regulations, specifying particular paragraphs.

NUCLEAR PASSENGER SHIP SAFETY CERTIFICATE

(*Official seal*)   (*Country*)

Issued under the provisions of the
INTERNATIONAL CONVENTION FOR THE SAFETY OF LIFE AT
SEA, 1974

Name of ship	Distinctive number or letters	Port of registry	Gross tonnage	Particulars of voyages, if any, sanctioned under regulation 27(c) (vii) of chapter III*	Date on which keel was laid (see NOTE below)

The _____   (*Name*) Government certifies
─────────────   ──────────────────────
I, the undersigned   (*Name*) certify

I.   That the above-mentioned ship has been duly surveyed in accordance with the provisions of the Convention referred to above.

II.   That the ship, being a nuclear ship, complied with all the requirements of chapter VIII of the Convention and conformed to the safety assessment approved for the ship.

III.   That the survey showed that the ship complied with the requirements of the regulations annexed to the said Convention as regards:

  (1)   the structure, main and auxiliary boilers and other pressure vessels and machinery;

  (2)   the watertight subdivision arrangements and details;

  (3)   the following subdivision load lines:

───────────────

* Regulation III/20.1.2 of the 1983 SOLAS amendments.

416

Subdivision load lines assigned and marked on the ship's side at amidships (regulation 11 of chapter II–1)*	Freeboard	To apply when the spaces in which passengers are carried include the following alternative spaces
C.1	....	....
C.2	....	....
C.3	....	....

IV. That the life-saving appliances provide for a total number of .... persons and no more, viz.:

.... lifeboats (including .... motor lifeboats) capable of accommodating .... persons, and .... motor lifeboats fitted with radiotelegraph installation and searchlight (included in the total lifeboats shown above) and .... motor lifeboats fitted with searchlight only (also included in the total lifeboats shown above), requiring .... certificated lifeboatmen;

.... liferafts, for which approved launching devices are required, capable of accommodating .... persons; and

.... liferafts, for which approved launching devices are not required, capable of accommodating .... persons;

.... buoyant apparatus capable of supporting .... persons;

.... lifebuoys;

.... lifejackets.

V. That the lifeboats and liferafts were equipped in accordance with the provisions of the regulations.

VI. That the ship was provided with a line-throwing appliance and portable radio apparatus for survival craft, in accordance with the provisions of the regulations.

VII. That the ship complied with the requirements of the regulations as regards radiotelegraph installations, viz.:

	Requirements of regulations	Actual provision
Hours of listening by operator...................................	....	....
Number of operators	....	....
Whether auto alarm fitted.......................................	....	....
Whether main installation fitted	....	....
Whether reserve installation fitted	....	....
Whether main and reserve transmitters electrically separated or combined	....	....
Whether direction-finder fitted..................................	....	....
Whether radio equipment for homing on the radio-telephone distress frequency fitted	....	....
Whether radar fitted..	....	....
Number of passengers for which certificated..................	....	....

---

* Regulation II–1/13 of the 1981 and 1983 SOLAS amendments.

VIII. That the functioning of the radiotelegraph installations for motor life-boats and/or the portable radio apparatus for survival craft, if provided, complied with the provisions of the regulations.

IX. That the ship complied with the requirements of the regulations as regards fire-detecting and fire-extinguishing appliances, radar, echo-sounding device and gyro-compass and was provided with navigation lights and shapes, pilot ladder, and means of making sound signals, and distress signals in accordance with the provisions of the regulations and also the International Regulations for Preventing Collisions at Sea in force.

X. That in all other respects the ship complied with the requirements of the regulations, so far as these requirements apply thereto.

This certificate is issued under the authority of the ....
Government. It will remain in force until ....

Issued at .... the .... day of .... 19.......

Here follows the seal or signature of the authority entitled to issue the certificate.

(*Seal*)

If signed, the following paragraph is to be added:

The undersigned declares that he is duly authorized by the said Government to issue this certificate.

(*Signature*)

NOTE: It will be sufficient to indicate the year in which the keel was laid or when the ship was at a similar stage of construction except for 1956, 1980, 1981, 1984 and 1986, in which cases the actual date should be given.

In the case of a ship which is converted as provided in regulation 1(b)(i) of chapter II–1* or regulation 1(a)(i) of chapter II–2,** the date on which the work of conversion was begun should be given.

---

* Regulation II–1/1.1.3.3 of the 1981 and 1983 SOLAS amendments.

** Regulation II–2/1.1.3.3 of the 1981 and 1983 SOLAS amendments.

Form of Safety Certificate for Nuclear Cargo Ships

NUCLEAR CARGO SHIP SAFETY CERTIFICATE

(Official seal) *(Country)*

Issued under the provisions of the
INTERNATIONAL CONVENTION FOR THE SAFETY OF LIFE AT
SEA, 1974

Name of ship	Distinctive number or letters	Port of registry	Gross tonnage	Date on which keel was laid (see NOTE below)

The _____ (*Name*) Government certifies

I, the undersigned (*Name*) certify

I.   That the above-mentioned ship has been duly surveyed in accordance with the provisions of the Convention referred to above.

II.   That the ship, being a nuclear ship, complied with all requirements of chapter VIII of the Convention and conformed to the safety assessment approved for the ship.

III.   That the survey showed that the ship satisfied the requirements set out in regulation 10 of chapter I of the Convention as to hull, machinery and equipment, and complied with the relevant requirements of chapter II–1 and chapter II–2.

IV.   That the life-saving appliances provide for a total number of .... persons and no more, viz.:

.... lifeboats on port side capable of accommodating .... persons;

.... lifeboats on starboard side capable of accommodating .... persons;

.... motor lifeboats (included in the total lifeboats shown above) including .... motor lifeboats fitted with radiotelegraph installation and searchlight, and .... motor lifeboats fitted with searchlight only;

419

.... liferafts, for which approved launching devices are required, capable of accommodating .... persons; and

.... liferafts for which approved launching devices are not required, capable of accommodating .... persons;

.... lifebuoys;

.... lifejackets.

V.   That the lifeboats and liferafts were equipped in accordance with the provisions of the regulations annexed to the Convention.

VI.   That the ship was provided with a line-throwing apparatus and portable radio apparatus for survival craft in accordance with the provisions of the regulations.

VII.   That the ship complied with the requirements of the regulations as regards radiotelegraph installations, viz.:

	Requirements of regulations	Actual provision
Hours of listening by operator..	....	....
Number of operators	....	....
Whether auto alarm fitted..	....	....
Whether main installation fitted	....	....
Whether reserve installation fitted	....	....
Whether main and reserve transmitters electrically separated or combined	....	....
Whether direction-finder fitted.....................................	....	....
Whether radio equipment for homing on the radio-telephone distress frequency fitted	....	....
Whether radar fitted..	....	....

VIII.   That the functioning of the radiotelegraph installations for motor lifeboats and/or the portable radio apparatus for survival craft, if provided, complied with the provisions of the regulations.

IX.   That the inspection showed that the ship complied with the requirements of the said Convention as regards fire-extinguishing appliances, radar, echo-sounding device and gyro-compass and was provided with navigation lights and shapes, pilot ladder, and means of making sound signals and distress signals in accordance with the provisions of the regulations and the International Regulations for Preventing Collisions at Sea in force.

X.   That in all other respects the ship complied with the requirements of the regulations, so far as these requirements apply thereto.

This certificate is issued under the authority of the ....
Government. It will remain in force until ....

Issued at .... the .... day of .... 19......

Here follows the seal or signature of the authority entitled to issue the certificate.

(Seal)

If signed, the following paragraph is to be added:

The undersigned declares that he is duly authorized by the said Government to issue this certificate.

(Signature)

NOTE: It will be sufficient to indicate the year in which the keel was laid or when the ship was at a similar stage of construction except for the years 1965, 1980, 1981, 1984 and 1986, in which cases the actual date should be given.

CONSTRUCTION AND EQUIPMENT REQUIREMENTS RELATING TO EXISTING SHIPS*

Ship type	Ship size	Subject of compliance	1978 SOLAS Protocol Ships built before 1 May 1981			1981 SOLAS amendments Ships built before 1 September 1984		
			Chapter	Regulation	Effective date	Chapter	Regulation	Effective date
Passenger ships	Any	Carriage of goods vehicles and their personnel	–	–	–	II-1	16	1.9.84
Passenger ships	Any	Marking, operation; inspection of watertight doors				II-1	24	1.9.84
Passenger ships	Any	Entries in log				II-1	25	1.9.84
Tankers, chemical tankers, gas carriers	>10,000 gt >40,000 gt	Steering gear requirements Steering gear single failure criterion	II-1	29(d)(i)	1.5.83	II-1 II-1	29.19 29.20	1.9.86 1.9.88
Passenger Cargo	Any >500 gt	Response to initial fire alarms Response to initial fire alarms				II-2 II-2	40 40	1.9.84 1.9.84
Crude oil tankers	>70,000 gt	Fixed deck foam system and inert gas system†	II-2	60(d)(i)	1.5.83	II-2	60.4.1	1.9.84 or delivery of ship
Crude oil tankers	20,000 to 70,000 dwt	Fixed deck foam system and inert gas system†	II-2	60(d)(ii)	1.5.85	II-2	60.4.2	1.5.84 or delivery of ship
Crude oil tankers	20,000 to 40,000 dwt‡	May be exempted	II-2	60(d)(ii)	1.5.85	II-2	60.4.2	1.5.85 or delivery of ship
Tankers other than crude oil	>70,000 dwt	Fixed deck foam system and inert gas system†	II-2	60(e)(i)	1.5.83	II-2	60.5.1	1.9.84 or delivery of ship
Tankers other than crude oil	20,000 to 70,000 dwt	Fixed deck foam system and inert gas system†	II-2	60(e)(ii)	1.5.85	II-2	60.5.2	1.5.85 or delivery of ship
Tankers other than crude oil	20,000 to 40,000 dwt‡	No requirement	II-2	60(e)		II-2	60.5	

* Requirements relating to passenger ships built before 26.5.1980. Part F – Special fire safety measures for existing passenger ships – of chapter II-2 of the 1974 SOLAS applies.
† See regulation II-2/62.20 for tankers fitted with inert gas systems before or after 1.6.81.
‡ Not fitted with tank washing machines with throughput >60 m³/h.

CONSTRUCTION AND EQUIPMENT REQUIREMENTS RELATING TO EXISTING SHIPS

Ship type	Ship size	Subject of compliance	1978 SOLAS Protocol Ships built before 1 May 1981			1981 SOLAS amendments Ships built before 1 September 1984			1983 SOLAS amendments Ships built before 1 July 1986		
			Chapt.	Reg.	Effective date	Chapt.	Reg.	Effective date	Chapt.	Reg.	Effective date
Passenger ships Cargo ships	Any ≥500 gt	Replacement of or additions to life-saving appliances							III	1.4	1.7.86 and 1.7.91
Passenger ships Cargo ships	Any ≥500 gt	Survival craft emergency position-indicating radio beacons							III	6.2.3	1.7.91
Passenger ships Cargo ships	Any ≥500 gt	Two-way radiotelephone apparatus*							III	6.2.4	1.7.91
Passenger ships	Any	Lifejacket lights							III	21.3	1.7.91
Passenger ships	Any	Immersion suits and thermal protective aids							III	21.4	1.7.91
Cargo ships	≥500 gt	Additional liferafts							III	26.3	1.7.91
Cargo ships	≥500 gt	Lifejacket lights							III	27.2	1.7.91
Cargo ships	≥500 gt	Immersion suits and thermal protective aids							III	27.3	1.7.91
Passenger ships Cargo ships	Any ≥500 gt	Retro-reflective material and life-saving appliances							III	30.2.7	1.7.91

* Apparatus need only comply with the frequency requirements of regulation IV/14-3.

CONSTRUCTION AND EQUIPMENT REQUIREMENTS RELATING TO EXISTING SHIPS

Ship type	Ship size	Subject of compliance	1978 SOLAS Protocol Ships built before 1 May 1981			1981 SOLAS amendments Ships built before 1 September 1984			1983 SOLAS amendments Ships built before 1 July 1986		
			Chapt.	Reg.	Effective date	Chapt.	Reg.	Effective date	Chapt.	Reg.	Effective date
Passenger ships Cargo ships	Any ≥300 gt	VHF radiotelephone installation				IV	4-1(a)	1.9.84			
Radiotelegraph ships	Any	Radiotelephone transmission and reception facilities				IV	10(g–2)	1.9.84			
Radiotelegraph ships	Any	Radiotelephone alarm generator*				IV	10(h) (iv)(1)	1.9.84			
Passenger ships Cargo ships	Any ≥500 gt	VHF radiotelephone installation energy source capacity				IV	17(b), (c)	1.9.84			

* For installations fitted prior to 1.9.86, fitting as determined by Administration.

Ship type	Ship size	Subject of compliance	1978 SOLAS Protocol Ships built before 1 May 1981			1981 SOLAS amendments Ships built before 1 September 1984			1983 SOLAS amendments Ships built before 1 July 1986		
			Chapt.	Reg.	Effective date	Chapt.	Reg.	Effective date	Chapt.	Reg.	Effective date
All ships	≥150 gt	Magnetic compasses				V	12(b)	1.9.84			
All ships	Any	Steering compass and means for taking bearings				V	12(c)	1.9.84			
All ships	≥1,600 gt	Gyro-compass				V	12(e)	1.9.84*			
All ships	≥10,000 gt	Second radar	V	12(a)	1.5.81	V	12(h)	1.9.84*			
Tankers	≥40,000 gt	Automatic radar plotting aid				V	12(j)(i)(2)	1.1.85*			
	10,000 to 40,000 gt	Automatic radar plotting aid				V	12(j)(i)(2)	1.1.86*			
All ships except tankers	≥40,000 gt	Automatic radar plotting aid				V	12(j)(i)(3)	1.9.86*			
	20,000 to 40,000 gt	Automatic radar plotting aid				V	12(j)(i)(3)	1.9.87*			
	15,000 to 20,000 gt	Automatic radar plotting aid				V	12(j)(i)(3)	1.9.88*			
Ships on international voyages†	≥1,600 gt	Echo-sounding device				V	12(k)	1.9.84*			
All ships	≥1,600 gt	Rudder, revolution and propeller mode indicators				V	12(m)	1.9.84*			

* If structural alterations necessary. Administrations may allow fitting not later than 1.9.89 or first dry docking (regulation 12(t)).
† New requirement if constructed before 25.5.80. NB: Composite pushing/pushed vessel unit regarded as single ship by regulation V/12(s) of 1981 amendments.

ANNEX 2

FUTURE AMENDMENTS TO THE 1974 SOLAS CONVENTION

The Maritime Safety Committee at its forty-eighth session agreed to proposed amendments to chapters II–1 and II–2 of the Convention, as set out hereunder, which could not be included in the 1983 SOLAS amendments.

By resolution A.515(13), the Assembly at its thirteenth session recommended to Contracting Governments to the Convention to implement, as an interim measure, the provisions of these proposed amendments and to accept ships flying the flag of other States, constructed and equipped in accordance with the 1974 SOLAS Convention and with these proposed amendments as complying in all respects with the provisions of that Convention, as amended.

CHAPTER II–1 OF THE 1983 SOLAS AMENDMENTS

Regulation 11 – Collision bulkheads in cargo ships

Amend the heading to read:

"Peak and machinery space bulkheads and stern tubes in cargo ships"

Add the following paragraphs:

"8   Bulkheads shall be fitted separating the machinery space from cargo and passenger spaces forward and aft and made watertight up to the freeboard deck.

9   Stern tubes shall be enclosed in a watertight space (or spaces) of moderate volume. Other measures to minimize the danger of water penetrating into the ship in case of damage to stern tube arrangements may be taken at the discretion of the Administration."

Regulation 21 – Bilge pumping arrangements

Add a new paragraph 1.6 as follows:

"1.6 Provision shall be made for the drainage of enclosed cargo spaces situated on the bulkhead deck of a passenger ship and on the freeboard deck of a cargo ship, provided that the Administration may permit the means of drainage to be dispensed with in any particular compartment of any ship or class of ship if it is satisfied that by reason of size or internal subdivision of those spaces the safety of the ship is not thereby impaired.

1.6.1 Where the freeboard to the bulkhead deck or the freeboard deck respectively is such that the deck edge is immersed when the ship heels more than 5°, the drainage shall be by means of a sufficient number of scuppers of suitable size discharging directly overboard, fitted in accordance with the requirements of regulation 17 in the case of a passenger ship and the requirements for scuppers, inlets and discharges of the International Convention on Load Lines in force in the case of a cargo ship.

1.6.2 Where the freeboard is such that the edge of the bulkhead deck or the edge of the freeboard deck, respectively, is immersed when the ship heels 5° or less, the drainage of the enclosed cargo spaces on the bulkhead deck or on the freeboard deck, respectively, shall be led to a suitable space, or spaces, of adequate capacity, having a high-water level alarm and provided with suitable arrangements for discharge overboard. In addition it shall be ensured that:

.1 the number, size and disposition of the scuppers are such as to prevent unreasonable accumulation of loose water;

.2 the pumping arrangements required by this regulation for passenger ships or cargo ships, as applicable, take account of the requirements for any fixed pressure water-spraying fire-extinguishing system;

.3 water contaminated with petrol or other dangerous substances is not drained to machinery spaces or other spaces where sources of ignition may be present; and

.4 where the enclosed cargo space is protected by a carbon dioxide fire-extinguishing system the deck scuppers are fitted with means to prevent the escape of the smothering gas."

Amend the definition of "D" in paragraph 2.9 to read:

"D is the moulded depth of the ship to the bulkhead deck (metres) provided that, in a ship having an enclosed cargo space on the bulkhead deck which is internally drained in accordance with the requirements of paragraph 1.6.2 and which extends for the full length of the ship, D shall be measured to the next deck above the bulkhead deck. Where the enclosed cargo spaces cover a lesser length, D shall be taken as the moulded depth to the bulkhead deck plus lh/L where l and h are the aggregate length and height respectively of the enclosed cargo spaces (metres)."

Include a new regulation 23–1 to read:

"Regulation 23–1 – Damage control in dry cargo ships

1   There shall be permanently exhibited, for the guidance of the officer in charge of the ship, a plan showing clearly for each deck and hold the boundaries of the watertight compartments, the openings therein with the means of closure and position of any controls thereof, and the arrangements for the correction of any list due to flooding. In addition, booklets containing the aforementioned information shall be made available to the officers of the ship.

2   Indicators shall be provided for all sliding doors and for hinged doors in watertight bulkheads. Indication showing whether the doors are open or closed shall be given in the vicinity of the aforementioned plan. In addition, shell doors and other openings which, in the opinion of the Administration, could lead to major flooding if left open or not properly secured, shall be provided with such indicators.

3.1   General precautions shall consist of a listing of equipment, conditions and operational procedures, considered by the Administration to be necessary to maintain watertight integrity under normal ship operations.

3.2   Specific precautions shall consist of a listing of elements (i.e. closures, security of cargo, sounding of alarms, etc.) considered by the Administration to be vital to the survival of the ship and its crew."

Regulation 42 – Emergency source of electrical power in passenger ships

Replace subparagraph 2.2 with:

"For a period of 36 hours:

.1   the navigation lights and other lights required by the International Regulations for Preventing Collisions at Sea in force;*

.2   the main transmitter and main receiver of the radiotelegraph installation specified in regulation IV/10(a)(ii)."

---

* This subparagraph is identical to the corresponding subparagraph in the 1981 SOLAS amendments.

Regulation 43 – Emergency source of power in cargo ships

Replace subparagraph 2.3 with:

"For a period of 18 hours:

.1   the navigation lights and other lights required by the International Regulations for Preventing Collisions at Sea in force;*

.2   the main transmitter and main receiver of the radiotelegraph installation specified in regulation IV/10(a)(ii);

.3   the transmitter and receiver of radiotelephone installations specified in regulation IV/16(a)."

CHAPTER II–2 OF THE 1983 SOLAS AMENDMENTS

Include a new regulation to read:

"Regulation 13–1 – Sample extraction smoke detection systems

1   *General requirements*

1.1   Wherever in the text of this regulation the word 'system' appears, it shall mean 'sample extraction smoke detection system'.

1.2   Any required system shall be capable of continuous operation at all times except that systems operating on a sequential scanning principle may be accepted, provided that the interval between scanning the same position twice gives an overall response time to the satisfaction of the Administration.

1.3   Power supplies necessary for the operation of the system shall be monitored for loss of power. Occurrence of loss of power shall initiate a visual and audible signal at the control panel and the navigating bridge which shall be distinct from a signal indicating smoke detection.

1.4   An alternative power supply for the electrical equipment used in the operation of the system shall be provided.

1.5   The control panel shall be located on the navigating bridge or in the main fire control station.

1.6   The detection of smoke or other products of combustion shall initiate a visual and audible signal at the control panel and the navigating bridge.

1.7   Clear information shall be displayed on or adjacent to the control panel designating the spaces covered.

1.8   The sampling pipe arrangements shall be such that the location of the fire can be readily identified.

1.9   Suitable instructions and component spares shall be provided for the testing and maintenance of the system.

1.10   The functioning of the system shall be periodically tested to the satisfaction of the Administration. The system shall be of a type that can be tested for correct operation and restored to normal surveillance without the renewal of any component.

1.11   The system shall be so designed, constructed and installed as to prevent the leakage of any toxic or flammable substances or fire-extinguishing media into any accommodation and service space, control station or machinery space.

2   Installation requirements

2.1   At least one smoke accumulator shall be located in every enclosed space for which smoke detection is required. However, where a space is designed to carry oil or refrigerated cargo alternatively with cargoes for which a smoke sampling system is required, means may be provided to isolate the smoke accumulators in such compartments for the system. Such means shall be to the satisfaction of the Administration.

2.2   Smoke accumulators shall be located for optimum performance and shall be spaced so that no part of the overhead deck area is more than 12 m measured horizontally from an accumulator. Where systems are used in spaces which may be mechanically ventilated, the position of the smoke accumulators shall be considered having regard to the effects of ventilation.

2.3   Smoke accumulators shall be positioned where impact or physical damage is unlikely to occur.

2.4   Not more than four accumulators shall be connected to each sampling point.

2.5   Smoke accumulators from more than one enclosed space shall not be connected to the same sampling point.

2.6   Sampling pipes shall be self-draining and suitably protected from impact or damage from cargo working.

3   Design requirements

3.1   The system and equipment shall be suitably designed to withstand supply voltage variations and transients, ambient temperature changes, vibration, humidity, shock, impact and corrosion normally encountered in ships and to avoid the possibility of ignition of flammable gas air mixture.

3.2   The sensing unit shall be certified to operate before the smoke density within the sensing chamber exceeds 6.65% obscuration per metre.

3.3   Duplicate sample extraction fans shall be provided. The fans shall be of sufficient capacity to operate with the normal conditions of ventilation in the protected area and shall give an overall response time to the satisfaction of the Administration.

3.4   The control panel shall permit observation of smoke in the individual sampling pipe.

3.5   Means shall be provided to monitor the airflow through the sampling pipes and to ensure that as far as practicable equal quantities are extracted from each interconnected accumulator.

3.6 Sampling pipes shall be a minimum of 12 mm internal diameter except when used in conjunction with fixed gas fire-extinguishing systems when the minimum size of pipe should be sufficient to permit the fire-extinguishing gas to be discharged within the appropriate time.

3.7 Sampling pipes shall be provided with an arrangement for periodically purging with compressed air."

Regulation 15 – Arrangements for oil fuel, lubricating oil and other flammable oils

Replace paragraph 2.6 by:

".6 Safe and efficient means of ascertaining the amount of oil fuel contained in any oil fuel tank shall be provided.

.6.1 Where sounding pipes are used they shall not terminate in any space where the risk of ignition of spillage from the sounding pipe might arise. In particular, they shall not terminate in passenger or crew spaces. As a general rule they shall not terminate in machinery spaces. However, where the Administration considers that these latter requirements are impracticable, it may permit termination of sounding pipes in machinery spaces on condition that all the following requirements are met:

.6.1.1 in addition, an oil-level gauge is provided meeting the requirements of paragraph .6.2;

.6.1.2 the sounding pipes terminate in locations remote from ignition hazards unless precautions are taken such as the fitting of effective screens to prevent the oil fuel in the case of spillage through the terminations of the sounding pipes from coming into contact with a source of ignition;

.6.1.3 the termination of sounding pipes are fitted with self-closing blanking devices and with a small-diameter self-closing control cock located below the blanking device for the purposes of ascertaining before the blanking device is opened that oil fuel is not present. Provision must be made so as to ensure that any spillage of oil fuel through the control cock involves no ignition hazard.

.6.2 Other oil-level gauges may be used in place of sounding pipes. Such means, like the means provided in paragraph .6.1.1, are subject to the following conditions:

.6.2.1 in passenger ships, such means shall not require penetration below the top of the tank and their failure or overfilling of the tanks will not permit release of fuel;

.6.2.2 in cargo ships, the failure of such means or overfilling of the tank shall not permit release of fuel. The use of cylindrical gauge glasses is prohibited. The Administration may permit the use

433

of oil-level gauges with flat glasses and self-closing valves between the gauges and fuel tanks.

Such other means shall be acceptable to the Administration and shall be maintained in the proper condition to ensure their continued accurate functioning in service."

Replace paragraph 3 by the following:

"The arrangements for the storage, distribution and utilization of oil used in pressure lubrication systems shall be such as to ensure the safety of the ship and persons on board. The arrangements made in machinery spaces of category A and whenever practicable in other machinery spaces shall at least comply with the provisions of paragraphs 2.1, 2.4, 2.5, 2.6, 2.7 and 2.8, except that:

.1 this does not preclude the use of sight-flow glasses in lubricating systems provided that they are shown by test to have a suitable degree of fire resistance;

.2 sounding pipes may be authorized in machinery spaces; the requirements of paragraphs 2.6.1.1 and 2.6.1.3 need not be applied on condition that the sounding pipes are fitted with appropriate means of closure."

Regulation 38 – Protection of cargo spaces, other than special category spaces, intended for the carriage of motor vehicles with fuel in their tanks for their own propulsion

Replace paragraph 1 by the following:

"1   *Fixed fire detection*

There shall be provided a fixed fire detection and fire alarm system complying with the requirements of regulation 13 or a sample extraction smoke detection system complying with the requirements of regulation 13–1. The design and arrangements of this system shall be considered in conjunction with the ventilation requirements referred to in paragraph 3."

Regulation 40 – Fire patrols, detection, alarms and public address systems

Replace paragraph 2 by the following:

"2   A fixed fire detection and fire alarm system complying with the requirements of regulation 13 or a sample extraction smoke detection system complying with the requirements of regulation 13–1 shall be provided in any cargo space which, in the opinion of the Administration, is not accessible, except where it is shown to the satisfaction of the Administration that the ship is engaged on voyages of such short duration that it would be unreasonable to apply this requirement."

Regulation 53 – Fire protection arrangements in cargo spaces

Replace subparagraph 2.1 by the following:

"2.1 There shall be provided a fixed fire detection and fire alarm system complying with the requirements of regulation 13. The fixed fire detection system shall be capable of rapidly detecting the onset of fire. The type of detectors and their spacing and location shall be to the satisfaction of the Administration taking into account the effects of ventilation and other relevant factors. After being installed the system shall be tested under normal ventilation conditions and shall give an overall response time to the satisfaction of the Administration."

Replace paragraph 3 by the following:

"3   *Cargo spaces, other than ro-ro cargo spaces, intended for the carriage of motor vehicles with fuel in their tanks for their own propulsion*

Cargo spaces, other than ro-ro spaces intended for the carriage of motor vehicles with fuel in their tanks for their own propulsion, shall comply with the requirements of paragraph 2 except that in lieu of the requirements of paragraph 2.1 a sample extraction smoke detection system complying with the requirements of regulation 13–1 may be permitted and paragraph 2.2.4 need not be complied with."

Regulation 54 – Special requirements for ships carrying dangerous goods

Replace subparagraph 2.3 by the following:

"2.3 Ro-ro cargo spaces shall be fitted with a fixed fire detection and fire alarm system complying with the requirements of regulation 13. All other types of cargo spaces shall be fitted with either a fixed fire detection and fire alarm system complying with the requirements of regulation 13 or a sample extraction smoke detection system complying with the requirements of regulation 13–1. If a sample extraction smoke detection system is fitted, particular attention shall be made to regulation 13–1.1.11 in order to prevent the leakage of toxic fumes into occupied areas."

FORMS OF ATTACHMENTS TO THE CARGO SHIP SAFETY CONSTRUCTION CERTIFICATE AND CARGO SHIP SAFETY EQUIPMENT CERTIFICATE

The Assembly at its eleventh session adopted the Guidelines on Mandatory Annual Surveys, Unscheduled Inspections of All Cargo Ships as well as Intermediate Surveys on Tankers of Ten Years of Age and Over, under the Protocol of 1978 relating to the International Convention for the Safety of Life at Sea, 1974 (resolution A.413(XI) which was amended at its twelfth session by resolution A.465(XII) to include, *inter alia*, forms of attachments to the Cargo Ship Safety Construction Certificate and the Cargo Ship Safety Equipment Certificate).

In accordance with the Guidelines, attachments to the Cargo Ship Safety Construction Certificate and to the Cargo Ship Safety Equipment Certificate as shown hereunder should be issued to cargo ships by contracting States to the 1978 SOLAS Protocol to confirm that the surveys under the 1978 SOLAS Protocol have been instituted and carried out as appropriate.

Form of Attachment to the Cargo Ship Safety
Construction Certificate

(Official seal)   *(Country)*

Issued under the requirements of the
PROTOCOL OF 1978 RELATING TO THE INTERNATIONAL
CONVENTION FOR THE SAFETY OF LIFE AT SEA, 1974[1]

Name of ship	Distinctive number or letters	Gross tonnage	Year of build

In implementation of regulation 6(b) of chapter 1 of the Protocol of 1978 relating to the International Convention for the Safety of Life at Sea, 1974 (SOLAS Protocol), the Government of .... has instituted:

– Mandatory annual surveys[2,3]

– Unscheduled inspections[2]

This is to certify that the ship has been surveyed in accordance with regulation 6(b) of chapter 1 of the SOLAS Protocol and the appropriate provisions of the Annex to resolution A.413(XI), as amended by resolution A.465(XII).

1st mandatory annual survey[2,3]

1st unscheduled inspection[2]

Signed ....

Place ....

Date ....
(Seal or stamp of the authority, as appropriate)

2nd mandatory annual survey[2,3]

2nd unscheduled inspection[2]

Signed ....

Place ....

Date ....
(Seal or stamp of the authority, as appropriate)

3rd mandatory annual survey[2,3]

3rd unscheduled inspection[2]

Signed ....

Place ....

Date ....
(Seal or stamp of the authority, as appropriate)

4th mandatory annual survey[2,3]

4th unscheduled inspection[2]

Signed ....

Place ....

Date ....
(Seal or stamp of the authority, as appropriate)

Issued at ....
(Place of issue of attachment)

.... 19 ....

....
(Signature of duly authorized official issuing the attachment)

---

[1] This attachment shall be attached to a SOLAS 1974 Certificate or a current SOLAS 1960 Certificate and shall expire on the same day as the Certificate to which it is attached.

[2] Delete as appropriate.

[3] An intermediate survey, but not an unscheduled inspection, may take the place of a mandatory annual survey.

Form of Attachment to the Cargo Ship Safety Equipment Certificate

(Country)

Issued under the requirements of the
PROTOCOL OF 1978 RELATING TO THE INTERNATIONAL
CONVENTION FOR THE SAFETY OF LIFE AT SEA, 1974[1]

Name of ship	Distinctive number or letters	Gross tonnage	Year of build

In implementation of regulation 6(b) of chapter 1 of the Protocol of 1978 relating to the International Convention for the Safety of Life at Sea, 1974 (SOLAS Protocol), the Government of .... has instituted:

– Mandatory annual surveys[2,3]

– Unscheduled inspections[2]

This is to certify that the ship has been surveyed in accordance with regulation 6(b) of chapter 1 of the SOLAS Protocol and the appropriate provisions of the Annex to resolution A.413(XI), as amended by resolution A.465(XII).

Mandatory annual survey[2,3]

Unscheduled inspection[2]

Signed ....

Place ....

Date ....
(Seal or stamp of the authority, as appropriate)

Issued at ....
(Place of issue of attachment)

.... 19 ....

....
(Signature of duly authorized official issuing the attachment)

---

[1] This attachment shall be attached to a SOLAS 1974 Certificate or a current SOLAS 1960 Certificate and shall expire on the same day as the Certificate to which it is attached.

[2] Delete as appropriate.

[3] An intermediate survey, but not an unscheduled inspection, may take the place of a mandatory annual survey.